DILIP KUM

With love.

[signature]

DILIP KUMAR
The Substance and the Shadow
an autobiography

as narrated to
Udayatara Nayar

Capt K. Mohan
London 2021.

HAY HOUSE INDIA

Australia • Canada • Hong Kong • India
South Africa • United Kingdom • United States

Hay House Publishers (India) Pvt. Ltd.
Muskaan Complex, Plot No.3, B-2 Vasant Kunj, New Delhi-110 070, India
Hay House Inc., PO Box 5100, Carlsbad, CA 92018-5100, USA
Hay House UK, Ltd., Astley House, 33 Notting Hill Gate, London W11 3JQ, UK
Hay House Australia Pty Ltd., 18/36 Ralph St., Alexandria NSW 2015, Australia
Hay House SA (Pty) Ltd., PO Box 990, Witkoppen 2068, South Africa
Hay House Publishing, Ltd., 17/F, One Hysan Ave., Causeway Bay, Hong Kong
Raincoast, 9050 Shaughnessy St., Vancouver, BC V6P 6E5, Canada

Email: contact@hayhouse.co.in
www.hayhouse.co.in

ISBN 978-93-84544-95-9

Designed and typeset at Hay House India

Printed and bound at
Rajkamal Electric Press, Sonipat, Haryana (India)

To
Amma and Aghaji

Sukoon-e-dil ke liye kuch to ehtemaam karoon
Zara nazar jo miley phir unhein salaam karoon
Mujhe to hosh nahin aap mashwara dijiyey
Kahan se chedoon fasana kahan tamaam karoon

CONTENTS

Reminiscences

FOREWORD

---•⊙ ⦂⊙⦂ ⊙•⦁---

*J*T IS WITH FEELINGS OF EXCITEMENT AND JOY THAT I PEN THIS foreword to my husband's autobiography, narrated by him, after years of persuasion by me, to my close friend Udayatara Nayar. It has always been an arduous task to prevail upon him to talk about himself, his life and his achievements. I understand it is neither proper nor right for me to extol the virtues of the book you are holding in your hands although I am tempted to do so, the primary reason being my widely known admiration for my husband and the ardent pride with which I have always hung on to every word he has uttered to me or to anyone in my presence over the decades we have spent together as a couple. Such is the magic of his command over words and language, be it English or Urdu, and I have no doubt I am not alone when I say this.

When a shy 22-year-old son of a Pathan fruit merchant was selected by the diva of Indian cinema, Devika Rani, to star in her Bombay Talkies' production *Jwar Bhata* (released in 1944), it led to a small change of name for the young man. Yousuf Khan became Dilip Kumar.

It was the beginning of the arrival of a new legend in Indian cinema and Hindi cinema's first definitive actor was born. Dilip Kumar almost single-handedly redefined histrionics in one screen portrayal after another – from *Shaheed* (1948), *Andaz* (1949), *Devdas* (1955), *Naya Daur* (1957), *Gunga Jumna* (1961) to *Azaad* (1955), *Kohinoor* (1960) and *Mughal-e-Azam* (1960) – and from *Ram Aur*

Shyam (1967), *Gopi* (1970), *Kranti* (1981) to *Shakti* (1982), *Mashaal* (1984) and *Saudagar* (1991). Dilip Sahab has, in his illustrious career, refined acting to an art form of exalted brilliance. Down the decades every actor of calibre has held him in high respect as the reference point in acting. He went to no school of acting but created his own method of emoting long before 'method acting' came to be known in India or abroad.

From the wolf-whistling frontbencher to the most serious critic of cinema, Dilip Sahab's varied range of histrionics has aroused spontaneous admiration while he has been considered the epitome of fine acting for generations of actors who looked up to him for inspiration. His understated elegance and, Mashallah, voice modulation have become role models for all of us actors over the years.

Few among his countless followers know that Dilip Sahab has always been a voracious reader. Whether it is novels, plays or

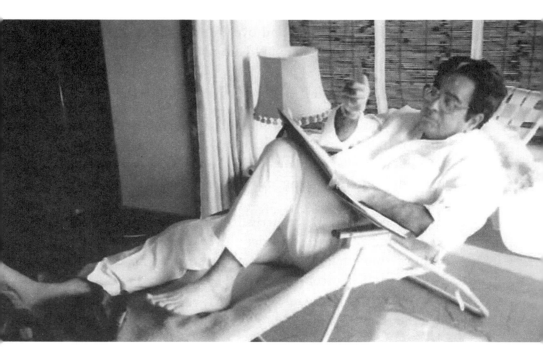

Reading a script.

biographies, his love of classic literature has been foremost. The classics of Urdu, Persian and English literature adorn the bookshelves of our home. When he's done with the library bookshelves, we have to be ready to offer him a pick of the thousands of books tucked away carefully in our huge store rooms. Down the years and all through the lifetime I have spent with him, the reading lamp that burns bright by his armchair has shone through the dark hours of the night to the wee hours of the early morning. Be it at home in Mumbai,* or a remote daak bungalow in Dachigam in Jammu and Kashmir, where it would be no surprise to find a hairy bear from the wilderness snoozing on our verandah, or in Kulu-Manali (in Himachal Pradesh), in Switzerland or in any part of the world, when he reads, he is like a child engrossed in his favourite game, unwilling to put it away until time and again I plead with him to rest. If not the biographies or classics or master plot plays by great writers such as Eugene O'Neill, Joseph Conrad, Fyodor Dostoyevsky and Tennessee Williams, he is sure to be engrossed in the writing of a script or a scene that waits to be picturized the next day morning.

He took up one film at a time and that was his absolute commitment and focus. I remember once he was writing and discussing scenes with producer-director Subhash Ghai in the freezing cold weather of Kulu till very late into the night during the outdoor shooting of *Saudagar* and, after he sent Subhash away to rest in his room, he continued to examine the scene passionately. At about 4:30 a.m. Dilip Sahab had a bright idea and he did not hesitate to wake up Subhash from his slumber to exchange this new brainwave! Then both of them were like busy bees working on the scenes until they were happy with what they finalized and, mind you, they diligently started the morning outdoor schedule bang on time!

With the completion of his autobiography my happiness is as though a dream has come true. The first section of this volume, set

*In this book, we have used Mumbai and Bombay interchangeably as also Madras/Chennai, Calcutta/Kolkata and Poona/Pune.

against varying backdrops, will make you part of his journey from the rugged mountain-hemmed North West Frontier Province in British India to hilly Deolali in Nasik district of Maharashtra to glamorous Bombay to traditional Madras to sophisticated London. The poignant as well the mirthful experiences he narrates will give you an insight into the making of the legend called Dilip Kumar who, as the title symbolizes, is the shadow while the substance is a simple, child-like, trusting and genial man called Yousuf Khan.

Indeed, what I can and would love to share in this unconventional foreword are the unseen and unknown facets of the man and actor I have been lucky enough to know and love deeply from the age of twelve when I first set eyes on him.

I want the world that is full of his admirers to be acquainted, through incidents and episodes in the book, with Dilip Sahab's innate simplicity, straightforwardness and immeasurable goodness of heart.

I started my life as an admiring fan, and fortunate am I to marry him and see the different aspects and qualities of this great human being who was not like any of the people I had met and spoken to during my extensive travelling almost all over the world with my mother Naseem Banuji from the age of seven onwards. Such a man as Dilip Kumar Sahab, I would say, walks rarely on this earth.

We are all aware of his brilliance as an actor and an intellectual but, his persona transcends everything – lands, religions and castes. His is the unspoilt, innocent, untainted smile of a babe in arms – his eyes have the purity and honesty of crystal-clear running water in a brook. His stern refusal to see the negative side (flip side) of anyone, or any situation, has always worried me as also his preference to turn a blind eye to the flaws in people he chooses to like and trust. He would rather focus on the positive qualities and plus points in people and tide over the negative side because he is convinced that he has yet to see a faultless, infallible and perfect human being. From my very first meeting with him as a shy girl, I knew he was different and superior to other men. He had that aura of greatness and class, which made him stand out in a gathering anywhere, be it at home in a family get-together or a grand celebrity-filled film event or amidst royalty and people of high lineage in a royal palace.

His secular beliefs spring straight from his heart and from his respect for all religions, castes, communities and creeds.

For instance, a group of amazing Jain community children who fast sometimes for thirty days (known as Maaskhaman) or sometimes for eight days (known as Atthai) once wanted him to be amidst them and taste the drops of sugarcane juice with which they broke their holy fasts (in 1980 when he was the sheriff of Bombay) to mark the close of their magnificent abstinence from food. He gladly obliged. His knowledge of the contents of the Holy Quran and his recitation of the verses retained indelibly in memory from childhood are no less brilliant than his knowledge and recitation of the Sanskrit verses in the Bhagvad Gita. Many have been the times when he has amazed Udayatara with quotations from the Bhagvad Gita and drawn parallels with the words of wisdom in the Holy Quran and the Bible during their informal conversations while recording his narration of the story of his life. He enjoys celebrating Deepawali with firecrackers and rows of lamps lit at our home by Narmada Gawde, our Maharashtrian cook of forty-odd years, as much as he enjoys the celebration of Eid with his family and close friends at our house. His *azaan* (call to prayer) is the most captivating, welcoming lilt to bow down to the Almighty as we all scramble to our prayer mats happily to pray together at the command of Allah.

When he 'sings' a bhajan (as in the 1970 film *Gopi*: *Sukh ke sabh saathi, dukh mein na koi, mere Ram, tera naam* ...),* no Hindu can believe that Dilip Kumar is a Muslim or that it is Yousuf Khan who is 'singing' this bhajan with such *shraddha* (reverence) and *bhakti*

---

*Actually sung by Mohammed Rafi, composed by Kalyanji Anandji and written by Rajinder Krishan.

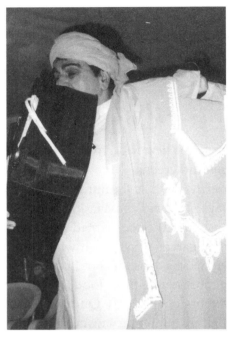

Imitating Saira.

(devotion). For instance, there is a famous paanwala in Lucknow whose shop is covered and adorned with Dilip Sahab's photographs. He is not prepared to believe that Dilip Sahab is not a Hindu.

Among my husband's closest friends are Parsis and it is a treat to hear him speak Parsi Gujarati the way only Parsis can speak. Needless to say, he has ever so many Sardar (Sikh) friends, some of them having close friendships with him from his Khalsa College days. To say that he is a citizen of the world is certainly no tall claim.

I want people also to know that Dilip Sahab is a man full of joie de vivre (the joy of living). He is as mischievous as a child prankster. When I stopped my work in films and took over the management of the house, sometime after marriage, my new avatar was replicated hilariously by Dilip Sahab a few times having me and my mother in splits. He would perch a pair of spectacles on his head, a telephone diary pressed under his arms, and carry a dress outfit precariously for showing to the tailor in one hand while keeping one half of his pyjama drawn high on his leg (much like me) and he would romp around absentmindedly in the house impersonating me. It was a sight.

Another hilarious and perfect copy was his grand depiction of the dancing queen Helenji's* famous cabaret item. It had to be seen to be believed! His imitation of the *Monica, O my darling*** number was

---

*Born as Helen Richardson, she has appeared in more than 500 films.
**From the 1971 film *Caravan*, sung by Asha Bhosle and Rahul Dev Burman, written by Majrooh Sultanpuri and composed by Rahul Dev Burman.

mind-boggling! I was amazed! What a superb duplication he did of Helenji! He seductively projected his leg out of the slit of a towel and with the batting of his thick eyelashes to give that come-hither look, he paid his own tribute to Hindi cinema's most adorable seductress! I wish I had filmed it quietly to show all of you what a good mimic he is.

Great prankster.

Similarly, he once did a fantastic copy of famous Kathak dancer star Gopi Krishna from V. Shantaramji's *Jhanak Jhanak Payal Baaje* (1955), depicting Gopiji's famous but difficult steps. To add conviction to the dance performance Dilip Sahab would recite the necessary tabla '*bols*' (words) exquisitely, chanting and doing *chakkers* (rounds) like a professional dancer, his tousled mop of hair bouncing in a frenzy all over his forehead and you could not miss his mischevious eyes darting to and fro. We rolled over on the ground with laughter. Once Gopiji himself was a sporting witness to one such spectacle, when he visited us with the renowned danseuse Sitara Devi.

For me to introduce his admirers to the countless 'qualities' of Dilip Sahab, I will have to write my own book, narrating my life experiences with him over the (Mashallah) wonderful four decades and more I have been blessed by God to spend with him.

Dilip Kumar, whom the world hails as the greatest actor of all time and is also a brilliant orator and intellectual, does not just play brainy chess or bridge, but also plays like a child with the family. He is superb at the game of dumb charade, the adept actor in him leading us through a labyrinth of expressions to give us clues to hit upon unlikely names of films of yore like *Pataal Ke Neeche*, *Shin Shinaki Boobla Boo*, *Hatim Tai* and *Shaque*.

He has always wanted to live life to the fullest, never wanting to miss out on enjoying any of the splendours of nature's beauty. He hates to miss a sunset. Earlier, he used to love to stop at the local bakery where we got freshly hot roasted bread then got a slab of 'lite-butter', which we slapped onto the bread and drove merrily, munching along Mumbai's Bandstand, straight into the great crimson sunset, watching the awesome but humbling sight. Once, when I was working a lot and did not have enough time to myself as I went from my make-up room when it was daytime to the stage floor for my shot and then emerged out of the set when it was dark outside, Dilip Sahab stopped me in my tracks in my mad rush to report from one studio to another and he asked me: 'Saira, tell me, when did you last see a sunset?'

He loves his simple white cotton attire, but the suave and sophisticated Dilip Kumar loves his beautiful collection of shoes, suits and ties too. I have learnt from him the finest way of maintaining these items. Down the years, I have loved to master the art of going through the various steps to achieve a good polish for the exquisite Dilip Kumar footwear, which are then lodged in shoe trees and wrapped in covers to keep off any moisture. His clothes are lined up and kept colour-wise: 'White is white and off-white is off-white' he has driven into our heads. All this looking after of Dilip Sahab was inculcated into me by my mother and you will read in the book that he has Pyarelal, his special *dhobi*, who launders better than any international cleaner and whom Sahab has known since the time they were both young men.

Humility is what I have learnt from Dilip Sahab. If ever I was in a mild disagreement with my much loved mother, Dilip Sahab would gently reproach me and induce me to go across to her immediately and profusely apologize. He would say: 'You can never fulfil the debt of your Maa who has given birth to you and brought you up in this big world with so much love and sacrifice.'

In our homes at Pali Hill in Mumbai we have always slept inside old-fashioned net curtains around our beds to ward off the onslaught of so many mosquitoes breeding amidst the lush greenery of our garden. Once we had tucked ourselves into our bed, I always mischievously requested him to help me get a glass of water placed on the other side of the bed. In my *laad* (affection or endearment), I loved to see him deftly scramble out of the netting and give me that precious sip of water. Never once did he have a grudge or make a face; he always gracefully and lovingly sat by my side until he had the empty glass back in his hand. I have always blessed him for his gesture of love with a peck on his great forehead and it has been a regular ritual between us for all these years.

On one occasion, a new refrigerator arrived in the house and, on opening it excitedly, I found one of the racks inside the door broken. I was in tears that the new fridge had a broken rack. Dilip Sahab calmed me down and within no time he had shaped a metal clothes hanger into a rack and fitted it beautifully. That's how he is – ever the chivalrous, helpful husband who hates to see his wife in tears over anything. I wonder how many star husbands or for that matter how many husbands would try to do something like that to cheer up a tearful wife! Truly, Dilip Sahab's greatness can be best seen in his unaffected simplicity and the complete absence of ego.

Early in the evenings, he loved to fly kites with the whole family in tow holding the *charkhi* (reel of thread). We maintained a treasure of kites and *manja* (special thread for kites) from all over India in a large trunk. The kites and *manjha* are carefully wrapped up in paper to preserve them and protect them from moisture. From surrounding buildings, friends like actor Tabrez Barmavar (Farida Jalal, my close friend's husband) and others would try and cut Dilip Sahab's kite. It was like a festival, with family, friends and visitors all participating in the hubbub, while the expert cooks Narmada and Kavita churned out delicious snacks! I remember producer-director-actor Manoj Kumar also coming up to fly kites with Dilip Sahab when he wanted to present the proposal of his film *Kranti* (released in 1981). He also gave us the recipe for whipping up a special *aachar* (pickle) omelette, which Dilip Sahab enjoyed very much.

Dilip Sahab had suffered terrible migraine headaches for years when we had to press his head for hours with the curtains drawn to provide darkness in the room so that he could get some relief. Surprisingly, watching the colourful kites soaring in the sky gave him much relief from his headaches. In the terrace kitchen, we would whip up hot *bhajias* (savouries) and omelettes for visitors to relish during the kite sessions.

Since time immemorial, my own family has loved good poetry, classical music and dance and I am so fortunate that Dilip Sahab has been like-minded in his love of the arts. Our home has resounded with the music of the great maestros of classical dimension such as Bade Ghulam Ali Khan Sahab, who was a colleague of my own grandmother, Begum Shamshad Abdul Waheed Khan (Ammaji), the renowned classical vocalist, who used to sing live over All India Radio, Delhi, and had recorded for Columbia Records. Sitar maestro Vilayat Khan Sahab, noted musicians and singers like Ghulam Ali Sahab, Ustad Mehdi Hasan Sahab, the Sabri Brothers (the famous *qawwals*), and Reshma, Kathak queens Sitara Devi and my guru, Padmashri Roshan Kumari, who has most lovingly taught me all that I know of classical dance, and many more illustrious performers have performed at our house.

One day while Ammaji was at *riyaz* (practice of her classical singing) on the first floor of our residence, the *durbaan* (doorman) came to her and announced that a '*qawwal*' *fakir* had defied the

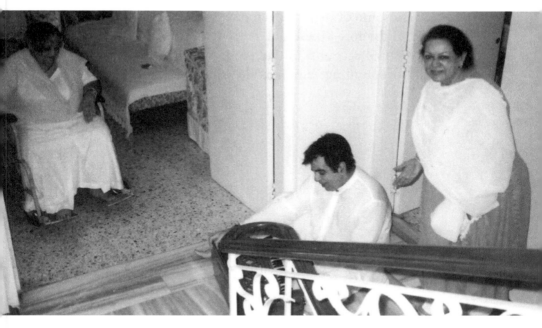

Singing *Naseeb dar pe tere aazmane aaya hoon ...*

security at the gate and wanted to have a *darshan* of Ammaji and take her *aashirwaad* (blessing). He had come with his *paytee baaja* (harmonium), the *durbaan* added. Soon enough what do we see? Wearing a simple cotton apparel and *gamcha* (a kind of scarf) tied tight across his forehead, Dilip Sahab slowly climbed the stairs with his *paytee baaja* and started to sing, regaling Ammaji who was in splits of laughter until tears of happiness rolled down her cheeks! Such is my wonderful Dilip Sahab! My priceless gem! My Kohinoor.

I leave you now to read the story of the life of this wonderful and uncomplicated man who is described as an enigma by those who know him not as well as some of his close friends and colleagues do. In the section of this book where his co-stars and admirers have drawn their own portraits of Dilip Sahab in their narrations to Udayatara, some unknown facets and some of his contributions to society as also some of the achievements he has never talked about are brought to the fore. Therefore, there is much to learn from the insightful personal accounts in that section, too, which, if I may say so at the risk of sounding vain, is as electrifying as the first part.

– Saira Banu

Introduction:
A Dream Come True

———●◉ ⦂◉⦂ ◉●———

I have consciously never oversold or overexposed myself to the audience. When I look back I feel it was quite risky to be starring in one film when other actors were busy with two or three films on the floors simultaneously. I determinedly decided to work in only one film at a time. It was simply my confidence in the subjects I chose and the hard work I was ready to put into them.

*I*T WAS A SULTRY AFTERNOON IN MUMBAI'S MIDSUMMER. THE year was 2004.

I was helping Saira Banu rearrange the books on the bookshelf in her bedroom when Dilip Sahab picked up a book written by an author who claimed to have known him as no one else did. 'This is supposed to be my biography and it is full of distortions and misinformation,' he told Saira. 'Why don't you write the story of your life yourself?' Saira queried, gladly seizing the opportunity to pursue her continuous effort to pin him down to write his autobiography.

Saira has always maintained that the inspiring journey of a simple youth named Yousuf Khan, son of a well-to-do fruit merchant and the story of his flight to hitherto unparalleled heights of fame and success as Dilip Kumar, who became India's first ever superstar and

23

one of the world's greatest actors, had to be recounted. The real story, she was sure, would enthuse and motivate all young aspirants in any walk of life who have chased dreams of making it big in their chosen professions.

After a moment's silence, Dilip Sahab spoke, turning to both of us as we waited to hear his reply.

'All right, I will narrate my story. It has to be compiled by someone who is enlightened and ready to put in the hard work that goes into anything I do and it should be someone who knows us really well,' he said.

I was listening and continuing to arrange the large collection of fiction and poetry works in English and Urdu, which had been read by Dilip Sahab seriously and meticulously, with pencil lines under sentences that piqued him and notes jotted in green ink in the margins in his elegant handwriting.

'She is right here', Saira pointed out, looking at me.

Dilip Sahab too looked at me and laughed gently, seeing the disbelief on my face.

'When do we start?' he asked me and I could hear my heart thumping away with mixed feelings of happiness and fright. Can this be reality or is it a dream, I asked myself since I was not in the fray of renowned writers who were pursuing Dilip Sahab to tell the story of his life to them.

Being an extremely private person, he was not always comfortable talking about himself and his unequalled achievements. He had understandably not encouraged anyone to explore his personal life for a book. As a result, some of the books that were written by people who claimed to know him and by writers who culled excerpts from published interviews and gathered dubious information from 'close friends' of Dilip Sahab and Saira did not tell the real story.

Saira was gleefully hugging Dilip Sahab and exhorting him: 'Let us start today, now, after lunch Jaan,* before you change your mind.'

'Don't neglect your job's demands for this. I have chosen you because you are capable of painstaking work and you can follow my

*Saira Banu called Dilip Sahab 'Jaan', which means 'life'.

With Udayatara Nayar and Saira.

thoughts and expressions accurately. Also, I am assured you will not misquote me. We will do it at my pace and don't hesitate to tell me if it gets boring,' Dilip Sahab joked.

Saira, the perfectionist that she is, arranged for high-class tape recorders and writing pads to take notes if the recorders failed. She suggested to Dilip Sahab that it would be a good idea to sit on the lawns in her garden and talk to me, knowing him and his impatience in case his work was interrupted or disturbed. Anywhere else in the house, she knew the phones would ring incessantly. More importantly, Saira knew her husband's love for nature and open spaces. She knew how he disliked talking about himself and how disinclined he was to do an autobiography because that meant, in his words, the profuse use of capital I, which he abhorred. And now that he had agreed, she wanted to make sure he did not lose interest on any account.

It was not the easiest assignment of my life for sure. The mood had to be created every day and that was something only Saira could do. The gentle prodding to get him to talk about the leading ladies was again something only Saira could do. Even the untold story of how he decided to marry Saira in late 1966, who was the country's most sought after and highest paid actress at that time, and the charming sequence of the dignified Dilip Kumar style courtship that preceded his proposal to Saira to be his wife had to be gently coaxed out of him. Needless to say, his account of the love story is one of the best chapters in this book.

Week after week I sat with him, sometimes in the shade of the large mango tree in the garden, sometimes in the drawing room, sometimes at the Otters Club (a sports institution in Bandra, Bombay) on the lawn facing the sea from where he loved to watch the sun go down, leaving behind a trail of gold and vermillion in the sky. The tape recorder accompanied us wherever we went and, quite often with his permission, a video camera, too, followed us unobtrusively.

As the recordings continued, the real picture began to emerge. I began to see the unfolding of his saga like the scenes in a movie. While he narrated his story in his soft voice, I noticed how much he enjoyed the recapitulation of his childhood years in Peshawar and Deolali. I could equally feel the pain in his heart when he talked about his elder brother Ayub Khan's brilliance and his chronic ill health, which cut short a promising life.

His was simply not just the amazing story of the young graduate Yousuf Khan, who excelled in school and college sports, seriously searching for a job in British-ruled India and hesitatingly accepting the job of an actor from the premier film studio of Bombay, Bombay Talkies. It was also not just about Yousuf Khan's unrelenting hard work, which propelled his rise to superstardom as Dilip Kumar and his occupying the pedestal as the icon of acting in Indian cinema for more than seven decades. I also learnt, more interestingly, how he set an example by the management skills he evolved by instinct and native intelligence to manage his career and create his USP.

In the early 1940s, when Dilip Sahab started his career, the concept of management had not arrived in India as far as actors were concerned. Actors, as professionals in their own right, had no need to acquire management skills or even understand the concept of management.

The majority of actors believed that an actor's business was to act as instructed by the director, take a fee for the time and effort put into their work and take no responsibility for the quality and success of the movie. Among the few actors who thought differently and worked differently was Dilip Kumar.

As the young actor progressed from *Jwar Bhata* (1944), his first film, to *Jugnu* (1947), his first hit at the box office, he began to grasp the essential secret of making a successful film. By his own study and observation of the process of film making and marketing of the end product, he arrived at the conclusion that an actor's responsibility did not end with his work as an actor. The actor had as much of a stake in the quality and finesse of a film, which ensured its commercial success. It meant an efficient and dedicated management of the infrastructure and resources of the production as well as a creative management, which started with the writing of the script and the screenplay.

He was just twenty-two when *Jwar Bhata* was made and released and he had quickly understood that enterprise and courage to think differently would pay handsomely as it did during his stint at the British Army club in Poona. Instead of just doing the jobs allotted to him by the club manager, he had ventured to seek permission to set up a small sandwich and fruit stall. It not only helped him earn extra money and establish a rapport with the British officers but it also attracted more visitors to the club; its revenue showed a marked increase.

The rising star who had no one to show him the way asked himself: 'Why not think differently and take the initiative to get involved with the creative management of the different departments of a film to ensure that a quality product was delivered?'

In the course of one of our conversations Dilip Sahab explained to me how he learnt the art of managing the creative processes of film making, which was as important as the financial processes. He paused to reflect and said: 'S. Mukherjee Sahab [more about him later in the book] used to give a lot of thought to the production and mould the project and never called himself a director. I decided to take after him.'

The 1930s and 1940s were the decades when Hollywood set trends in the management of studios. Talking about the Western influence, Dilip Sahab observed: 'Abroad, at the great management tables, when the financial prophets selected themes, they measured the potential of success since they were businessmen and did not want their money to sink. They set a world trend and we too began to emulate them.'

Dilip Kumar selected his story material with utmost care. It is not difficult to see that he chose ideas and concepts for scripts that had the potential to enthral and delight viewers and went on to become blockbusters. At the same time, he also used his wisdom to choose subjects that would remain fresh and appealing decades thereafter. Take any of his superhits and you cannot miss the contemporary relevance.

Not surprisingly, the producers and directors of his films understood that whatever he was suggesting in the choice of subject or actors or music composition or cinematography or art direction was in the interest of the overall quality of the product. 'Nobody taught me this but I came to the conclusion that I should consider a film in its entirety as a product. It was only much later when I was reading a book on management that I read that the basic principle of good management was to take care of and ensure the quality of the final product,' Dilip Sahab confided to me.

Nimmi (his co-star in several films) has pointed out, in her remembrances in this book, a case in point. She has revealed that it was Dilip Kumar who suggested to Mehboob Khan to cast Premnath in the negative role in *Aan* (1952). It turned out a casting sensation; the media helped in whipping up curiosity about the film from the day of the *mahurat* itself. There was enough publicity already about the casting of Dilip Kumar in the film as the swashbuckling, sword-wielding Jai Tilak, a villager who could tame a horse within minutes and vanquish anyone in a fencing contest. The talking point was all about Dilip Kumar's ability to make an impact in a totally different role after the mass acceptance he had gained as a tragic hero.

'People said, "*yeh kya ho raha hai*, Dilip Kumar *ke haath mein talwar de di*"?'* Nimmi reveals. This was something unthinkable at

'What is happening, a sword has been placed in Dilip Kumar's hands?'

that stage. The result is history. *Aan*, India's first Technicolor film, was the biggest grosser of 1952 and the first Hindi film to net Rs 75 lakh in a year, then an astronomical amount.

With no professional marketing agencies to create any kind of hype for films those days, it was left to Dilip Kumar to strategize the promotion of films and he did it with imagination and style in his own dignified manner without resorting to cheap publicity gimmicks.

'You know, I have consciously never oversold or overexposed myself to the audience. When I look back I feel it was quite risky to be starring in one film when other actors were busy with two or three films on the floors simultaneously. I determinedly decided to work in only one film at a time. It was simply my confidence in the subjects I chose and the hard work I was ready to put into them. Overselling is not good business practice. I agree advertising and publicity are necessary but only to the extent that you promise to the audience a product in which you have invested hours and days and months of relentless hard work and given your best. I therefore never appointed a publicist to promote me or my work,' Dilip Sahab disclosed.

Long before management gurus began to include human resources as a vital component of successful business ventures, Dilip Kumar put his finger on the need to mobilize and motivate human resources in a film production unit to deliver quick and satisfying results.

As famous actor Dharmendra has summed up in his piece on Dilip Sahab in this volume: 'From the most exalted admirer, Pandit Jawaharlal Nehru, to the lowest paid studio worker, who waited to say [*sic*] salaams to him, his warm extension of his hands in greeting was the same. He never faked anything be it his appreciation for another actor's good work or his concern for a colleague who was in distress.'

To a question I put to Dilip Sahab regarding his mingling with the production workers, he answered:

All over the world the principles of management are the same. Only the applications differ. You have to apply the principles in a manner that anyone can understand. To make a lightman understand what you want from him in a scene you cannot do it by ordering him. If you order him he will do it but if you are good to him and you speak to him in his language he will go out of his way to give you the result that exceeds his usual performance.

I do not know how I came to be known as a method actor. Marlon Brando [an acclaimed Hollywood actor] was called a method actor . . . . The epithet was used to describe me much before it was used for Brando. The truth is that I am an actor who evolved a method, which stood me in good stead. I learned the importance of studying the script and characters deeply and building upon my own gut observations and sensations about my own and other characters. It was always meaningful for me to study even those characters who would be close to me or opposed to me. I was lucky to have worked with directors who trusted me and allowed me to work without restraint. They believed as much as I did in the necessity for team work. Unlike other arts and crafts, the art of film making draws its sustenance from team work.

Yet another lesson to be learned from Dilip Sahab is his unflinching awareness of his social responsibility as a star and a role model. He has plainly revealed in the chapters related to the formative years of his career that he chose a film in terms of its totality. He tried even at that early stage to look for stories that had a certain social relevance and a meaningful message. He also made sure his love scenes with heroines did not embarrass family audiences.

In one of his enlightening interviews, he confessed:

I have sincerely tried to be a good role model. I strongly subscribe to the belief that an actor should be aware and conscious of his social responsibilities and contribute as much as he can to build the character of the admirer who looks up to him and derives inspiration from his work and personality.

The Dilip Kumar I know is a simple man with simple but fine tastes. At times Dilip Kumar is a bit bewildered and wonders how he accomplished all that he is credited with when he did not have any teacher or role model to guide him. Yes, Dilip Kumar had a robust, earthy upbringing from parents who told him that he should be faithful to his occupation whatever that may be and sincerely earn his wages. So, the hard work and dedication were never lacking. Also a strong sense of integrity, commitment and compassion came naturally from the Pathan genes.

Hence, it was not surprising at all that it was Dilip Kumar who set the example for his contemporaries to take the initiative to use their stardom and popularity to support good causes and raise funds for the government's relief work during times of national distress and deprivation.

He led the first troupe that visited the Himalayan border areas to boost the morale of the Border Security Force personnel stationed there after India's humiliating defeat in the 1962 Indo–China war. He has distinct memories of one such arduous trip when his friend Mohammed Rafi (the renowned singer) developed a throat irritation in the freezing cold and felt awful that his voice had gone for a toss. 'We consoled him and kept giving him hot water and honey at hourly intervals till he got back his splendid voice. Rafi was a teetotaller and would not touch any of the strong liquids the other members

With Mohammed Rafi.

of the troupe drank to beat the cold. Needless to say he was the star attraction with the jawans [soldiers who are not officers] and the young newly commissioned officers,' Dilip Sahab remembers.

In his recollections, veteran actor Chandrashekhar speaks about all the star processions in trucks on the streets of Bombay, about the many benefit cricket matches and about the live entertainment shows he had witnessed with Dilip Sahab at the helm and how Dilip Sahab was never on the dais when the spotlight was turned on. The funds raised under Dilip Sahab's capable and tireless management, upon his insistence, had to be handed over to the chief minister or the prime minister.

Ages before the concept of corporate social responsibility made its entry into management mantras, Dilip Kumar took the responsibility of serving the National Association of the Blind as its chairman. In her heartfelt appreciation of the work Dilip Sahab did for NAB, esteemed social worker Veera Rao, who worked enthusiastically with him in the fund-raising efforts for the association to become a self-sufficient body, describes the joy with which Dilip Sahab lent his support to every occasion to raise the money needed to motivate, educate and train the visually handicapped to lead their lives purposefully.

Readers are bound to ask what made us add the section to this autobiography where actors, directors and eminent friends of Dilip Kumar, apart from relatives and others, have contributed their personal and professional experiences and provided insights into the man and his working style. There is a good reason for adding that section, which is rather unusual. The reason is that Dilip Sahab did not speak to me about his achievements and social service as his wont. Basking in self-praise was, and still is, not something he enjoys. When coaxed, he gave meagre information about, for instance, his efforts to get a huge land allotment for the industry from the Maharashtra State Government for a film city. Nor did he wax eloquent about his behind-the-scenes spadework to prepare a solid proposal along with Rajni Patel (a Congressman and a lawyer by profession) to give Bombay a first-class cultural centre with an adjoining science centre, which was eventually named Nehru Centre (after India's first prime minister: Jawaharlal Nehru). In his very readable biography of Dilip

Sahab,* Lord Meghnad Desai (an Indian-born British economist and politician) has beautifully described Dilip Kumar as Nehru's hero. It is perhaps not too well known that Nehru was Dilip Kumar's hero and idol as well.

In conclusion I must say that if it weren't for the persistence with which Saira Banu prevailed upon him to open up and recount the story of his life perhaps this book would not have come into existence. Also, if it weren't for the long association – almost half a century – I have had with my idols Dilip Kumar and Saira Banu, I would not have been chosen to put the narrative together. I can never ever forget the encouraging words Dilip Sahab spoke to the former editor of *Screen*, S. S. Pillai, after I wrote a long analytical article on Dilip Sahab in one of the issues, when I was new in the world of cinema journalism. He told Pillai Sahab: 'Groom her, make her work hard and she will go places. She has the potential to become a biographer someday.' The words were prophetic and it is an unbelievable twist of Destiny that I was unhesitatingly chosen to put Dilip Sahab's erudite words on paper for generations of aspirants in the entertainment industry to read and absorb.

Thank you Dilip Sahab.

– Udayatara Nayar

Nehru's Hero: Dilip Kumar in the Life of India, Roli Books, New Delhi, 2004.

1

BIRTH

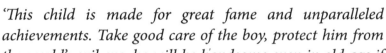

'This child is made for great fame and unparalleled achievements. Take good care of the boy, protect him from the world's evil eye, he will be handsome even in old age if you protect him and keep him untouched by the evil eye. Disfigure him with black soot if you must because if you don't you may lose him prematurely. The Noor *[light] of Allah will light up his face always.'*

HISTORY HAS RECORDED MANY NAMES THAT WERE GIVEN TO Peshawar, the main city in the North West Frontier Province, where I was born. It was known as the City of Flowers, the City of Grain and even Lotus Land. For me the Peshawar I took birth in was a part of India and, like many of my friends belonging to different walks of life and different communities, who were also born in Peshawar in undivided India, I am proud of my nativity in the then Indian city so strategically situated in the region between Central Asia and South Asia that it came to be known aptly as the Gateway to India.

I remember the vivid colours, the smells and the seasons of my homeland. The arrival of autumn was visible in the orchards where the apricot trees would turn bright red and orange. In the evenings,

A latter-day view of Kissa Khwani Bazaar.

as dusk approached, the towering mountains would somehow seem taller and intimidating to me and I can still recall my little feet aching with the momentum of the speed with which I scurried home. There were men who knew my parents walking home slowly, ruggedly handsome men with bushy beards, wearing caps with the sides rolled up or the typical skull cap or the turban, and they would stare at me wondering why I was running like that.

Our house was in the heart of the city, in the Kissa Khwani Bazaar, so named because wandering traders stopped there either to tell their own stories or listen to stories told by the local inhabitants. The images of the Mahabat Khan Masjid (mosque), the Cantonment, the bazaar where I wandered with the ladies of the house and the street where roses of varying shades of pink and red were sold to British gentlemen who, perhaps, took them home gallantly to their women, often appear before my eyes like a motion picture when I am in a thoughtful mood.

Winter in the North West Frontier region of Peshawar was unbearable for its inhabitants, however strong and accustomed they were to its harshness and inclemency. During winter, the days invariably dawned without a hint of sunshine and there was no knowing whether it was night or day if one did not ascertain what the time was. The mountains and the hills that rose majestically in the landscape came to sight only when a good part of the morning had gone by.

In the winter months those who had risen early for Fajr prayers (the first of the five daily prayers offered by practising Muslims) had to go through the ordeal of breaking sheets of ice that had formed on the water stored in the tanks kept for *wuzoo* (ablution) near the masjid. The ice-cold water and the tingle of pain it caused when it touched the peeling skin of the body are still fresh in my memory. Whether it was due to the harshness of winter or due to the distress caused by the blinding dust storms that frequently swept the plains in the scorching heat of the summer months, life was not easy for those who toiled outside in the orchards and fields.

I have a vivid memory of Chacha Ummer, my paternal uncle who lived close by, but spent most of his waking hours in our house and went out with Aghaji, as we addressed our father, to take stock of the fruits ripening in our orchards. He complained when it was winter and he complained when it was summer. He would have very much liked to stay indoors but it did not fall to his lot to do so. He was literally the man who withstood all the seasons and my parents and grandparents turned to him when they wanted something or someone to be fetched at any odd time or in any complicated situation. He was Aghaji's cousin and I think he quietly enjoyed the position he had acquired in the family as the indispensable man for all purposes.

Chacha Ummer never stopped talking about the Goldsmiths' Lane, where the goldsmiths had their shops and workshops, and about the fire that engulfed it on the night I was born. The street was one of the more busy parts of the Kissa Khwani Bazaar where our house was situated. As it housed the prosperous goldsmiths' residences and their workplaces, there was always the bustle of business and personal interactions throughout the day and well into the night when the rest of the bazaar had pulled down the shutters. The fire had started in one of the workshops from the embers that got fanned by

The house where I was born.

a gale that unexpectedly swept the locality as the shopkeepers began closing their business for the day. The blaze spread uncontrollably in no time and there was fear and panic as the men began to gather in knots to hurl buckets of water at the raging fire. The operation was tough no doubt as the water in the upper parts of most of the water storage tanks had turned to ice and it took several strong Pathan fists to shatter the ice and draw the water in buckets from the lower levels of the tanks.

Since the men in the house had rushed to the lane to help in the fire-fighting operations and Chacha Ummer had been asked to stay behind, as the women were alone in the house, it was he who had to go in search of a midwife when my mother (whom I called Amma) threatened to bring me into this world. He had to bring the midwife safely and then rush to inform Aghaji about the exciting development at home. 'You know', he related to me once when he was in a recall mood, 'I was angry and cursing myself that night because it was so cold and the wind was blowing with a menacing strength. It was like a punishment to be out alone and entrusted with the responsibility of saving a life. But the minute the midwife completed her job and we got to see you, all ruddy and cherubic and glowing with health, I felt strangely rewarded and extremely happy.'

Chacha Ummer always took great delight in describing my cries and the exchange of *mubaraks* (congratulations) as the family welcomed the grand arrival of the fourth child of Mohammad Sarwar

Khan and Ayesha Bibi in the midst of all the chaos and scramble in the neighbouring street.

The winter months' only delight for me as a child was that I could sit unnoticed among the elders in front of the fireplace and listen to their conversations. They seldom made small talk. They either narrated bizarre stories they had heard or recalled spine-chilling events they had witnessed. I was all ears, especially when they spoke in low voices and exchanged recollections of nightmares. On one such occasion, I heard my paternal grandmother (Dadi) utter Amma's name, Ayesha, in a low whisper, not knowing I was present. I held my breath and listened. She was talking in Pushtu and her, whisper was hoarse but audible and her beady eyes had widened as wide as they could.

Translated into English, she was saying something frightening like this: 'Poor Ayesha, she could have died that freezing night. The men of the house opened and shut the door so many times while poor Ayesha bit her lips and suffered the acute pain. The blizzard was raging outside and, what was worse, the Goldsmiths' Lane was in flames, blocking normal transport.'

She was talking in a low voice to her curious audience. A chill ran down my spine. What a strange occurrence! A blizzard and a fire! And my sweet Amma, why was she in pain?

Then, the iron lady, as Dadi was known, broke into tears, looked up at the ceiling and praised Allah profusely. The midwife was brought safely in the nick of time, she informed her eager listeners, who then relaxed and heaved a sigh of relief. *'Aur Ayesha ka sona beta Yousuf tashreef laaya,'** she announced now in her normal, sturdy voice startling everyone in the gathering. My small jaw dropped. She was yet one more person talking about my birth!

Not just Dadi, but also every member of the family of Mohammad Sarwar Khan and Ayesha Begum tirelessly narrated the story of

*Can be roughly translated as 'and Ayesha's handsome son Yousuf arrived'.

As a small boy in Peshawar.

my grand arrival at every opportunity as if it was an uncommon event. The date was 11 December 1922. I suspect the date is mentioned somewhere in some chronicle of Peshawar's history not because I was born on that dramatic day but because fire had gutted the goldsmiths' workshops. Never before and never after that dismally cold day had any such disaster shaken up the Kissa Khwani Bazaar as the fire in the Goldsmiths' Lane had.

In Dadi's opinion, my arrival in the midst of the blizzard and the fire meant something significant. Her belief was not taken seriously by my parents till one ordinary day, when I was playing in the front room of our house, a fakir came to the door seeking food and some money. It was common practice in the house to give good food and a little money whenever fakirs and wandering minstrels singing ballads in their own tongue came to the door. Amma hurried inside to pack the food while my Dadi sat lazily in her armchair.

I stopped playing as I could feel the man's gaze riveted on me. In a loud voice, which made Dadi sit up and listen, he asked her to bring me in front of him. She hesitated for a moment but the man was all excitement and was quivering with some emotion building up within him. I was now standing before him, fright and curiosity alternating in my five-year-old head. He announced that I was not an ordinary child. I shut my eyes and pretended I had not heard him. First the dramatic fire and blizzard at my birth and now this remark that I was not ordinary! I was wondering what he was going to say next.

He fixed his stare on my face and told Dadi: 'This child is made for great fame and unparalleled achievements. Take good care of the boy, protect him from the world's evil eye, he will be handsome even in old age if you protect him and keep him untouched by the evil eye. Disfigure him with black soot if you must because if you don't you may lose him prematurely. The *Noor* [light] of Allah will light up his face always.'

I opened my eyes, relieved that he did not say anything untoward. I was now looking at him and he was smiling a soft benevolent smile. Dadi gathered me in her arms instinctively as if she would lose me if she did not hold me close to her. The man took the food and money Amma brought and he left.

After he left, I ran out of the house to join my cousins who were playing and were unaware of what had occurred. Little did I anticipate then what was to begin from the next day. Dadi took it upon herself to protect me from the evil eye of the world. She had my head shaven and every day, when I started for school, she made a streak on my forehead with soot to make me look ugly. Amma tried hard to convince her not to make her child so ugly that other children would poke fun and give him a complex. Aghaji tried to reason with his stubborn mother about the consequences of what she was doing to me. But Dadi wouldn't budge. Her love and protectiveness towards me were too overwhelming for her to accept their pleadings.

Needless to say, I was a spectacle when I arrived in the school every morning. The murmurs and sniggers that greeted me on the first day amplified in my subconscious and made me find reasons not to go to school the next day. I gave vent to my unhappiness and narrated the derision I faced from my classmates and older boys of the school who were always ready to seize occasions to have fun at the expense of any junior who was easy prey to their pranks and jokes. Amma, who rarely argued with her mother-in-law, appeared extremely pained when she pulled me close to her and told Dadi: 'You cannot do this to my child. See how miserable he is.'

Dadi was aghast. *'Maine aisa kya kiya, Ayesha? Aap ne bhi suna woh fakir kya keh raha tha. Us ne sirf Yousuf ko chunke baat ki thi. Hamare ghar ke bachche sab the uske saamne,'** she was almost shouting. It was plain that she believed she was right. She tried to draw me close to her to soothe me and comfort me and explain to me why she was disfiguring me. I was so angry and hurt that I pushed her away and buried my head in Amma's lap trying hard not to let my sobs be heard lest my cousins get a chance to make fun of me for that too. Pathan boys are told from early childhood that it is not manly to weep. Even when we hurt our knees and elbows while playing and stinging mixtures were applied on the wounds, we were told to bear the pain like men and not wail like women at the drop of a hat. Tears rolling down the cheeks were fine but not audible crying. Though the dark streak on my forehead was less pronounced the next day, the routine did not stop. I became a loner at school and played very little. I chose to stay quiet and play with the colouring books that were available in the small library of the school. A couple of kind teachers urged me to go out and play but I was loath to listen to them. Instead I found myself getting lost in the make-believe world of the pictorial books with increasing interest. I was not more than five years old then.

My *phoopis*, *chachis* and *chachas*** doted on me for two reasons. First, I was a healthy robust baby and, second, I gave little trouble to my Amma because of my friendly nature and my willingness to be passed on from one aunt to the other while Amma went about her chores. As I grew up and began to comprehend the conversations that I heard, my little mind often weighed with concern for my Amma who used to be summoned by my despotic Dadi and given tasks to do while her own daughters relaxed and did not do anything. I remember Aghaji asking Amma one morning why she was toiling

---

*What have I done wrong Ayesha? You too heard what the fakir said. He singled out Yousuf to talk to while the other children of the house were also in front of him.

**Paternal aunts, paternal uncles' wives and paternal uncles, respectively.

single-handedly in the kitchen when there were other women in the house who could share her chores.

I can still hear the echo of my mother's soft, gentle voice as she hushed my father and explained to him that she was assigned the kitchen chores because that was her forte and she was happy that she was given charge of making endless pots of tea and all the delicacies that went well with it because no other lady of the house could equal her in that activity. Phoopi Babjan (Aghaji's sister) would turn red in the face whenever she heard this explanation and she would take my mother aside to chide her for the camouflage.

2

The Matriarch and Her Brood

… there was a divine purpose in the episode of Dadi blindly believing the fakir and giving me the ugly appearance that made me the butt of unpleasant remarks in school. It was the pain I endured as the alienated child in school that surfaced from my subconscious when I was playing the early tragic roles in my career and I had to express the deep mental agony of those characters.

I⟨t⟩ WAS NOT FOR NOTHING THAT DADI WAS REFERRED TO AS THE 'iron lady'. She had a commanding air about her, which my eldest sister Sakina Aapa inherited genetically. Dadi shared all her thoughts with Aghaji and often listened to his accounts of what was going on in the country with her brows knit and her gaze fixed on her son's handsome face. It was a daily routine when he returned home from the market, often after Maghrib (the evening prayer). He always went straight to Dadi, who would be waiting for him in her room, rocking majestically in the wooden armchair that was exclusively reserved for her use. Her lips would be moving and we knew she was mutely saying her Tasbeeh (the repetition of short sentences glorifying Allah).

She was tall and broad shouldered and she appeared to completely fill the armchair when she sat in it. She wore loose Pathan salwars and long, flowing kameezes, which made her look more masculine than feminine. Her head was always covered with a dupatta (a long piece of cloth usually used to cover head and the bosom). For some reason, she always wrapped around herself a large shawl, which was almost the size of a single bedsheet. When I chose to hide from Aghaji or Amma after getting into some mischief, I invariably found refuge in the folds of her shawl, which she would open for me like a magic tent to engulf me and hide me from whoever was indignantly searching for me. I enjoyed the mystery and the suspense the whole exercise triggered in the household when little Yousuf went missing. Few in the large household could guess that I was concealed within Dadi's shawl with my head buried cosily in the cleavage of her enormous, heaving bosom. The delightful part of the escapade was that Dadi was such a sport that she simply sat with her eyes shut while Amma and Phoopi Babjan searched the room several times muttering where on earth Yousuf was.

Dadi loved me for more reasons than one. The fakir's prediction was one reason but the more important reason was that I was very different from Noor Bhai, my eldest brother. He was an eternal bundle of trouble as he got into scuffles with our cousins and the boys in the neighbourhood. Though they were not serious brawls, still complaints reached Dadi from parents in the locality. However, Noor Bhai, with his light eyes and charming ways, had the support of the ladies in the house when he feigned innocence and artfully cast the blame on the boys who came with the complaints. Dadi was no fool to fall for his pretence but it must be said to her credit that she never rebuked Noor Miyan in front of the boys or the parents. She took him to task when they were out of earshot and his wails were only for our ears.

Sakina Aapa stayed out of Dadi's way and the matriarch chose not to intervene in the arguments between Sakina Aapa and others in the house. In her heart of hearts, I think she knew where Sakina Aapa's obstinacy and quarrelsomeness came from.

Ayub, who was elder to me by a year and a half, was a quiet fellow and his presence in the house was felt only when he and I played together and chased each other up the stairway or played noisily in the *aangan* (courtyard). He was the one who was privy to a secret I kept for a long, long time even after we moved out of Peshawar. I was once told by my paternal grandfather (Dada) that I could keep coins that I wished to save inside a crevice where a tile had partially come off beneath the staircase. Dada had made up the story that the crevice had the magic power to double the coins and create a fortune for the one who kept it a secret and placed the tile back over the crevice with a wish to let them grow.

I had listened to Dada's story with a sense of awe and thrill and so had Ayub. Together we had pulled off the tile when no one was around and I had buried a couple of coins in the crevice reverentially. Dada had told us that we should let the coins be for as long as we could to let them multiply. 'If you keep opening it the magic will cease,' he had told us ominously, without batting an eyelid, in a hoarse whisper, his face taut with a serious expression.

Indeed, I forgot all about the crevice and the coins after we shifted to Bombay (now Mumbai) till Ayub reminded me of them during one of our visits to Peshawar during school holidays. The sizzling story still had its credibility even though by then Dada was no more and a mound of dust and heaps of unwanted things had covered the area under the staircase. Ayub and I had tiptoed in the dark one night and unearthed the hidden coins only to realize that it was Dada's fable to entertain us and nothing more. We felt awful not because the coins had not doubled but with the realization that Dada was not there to laugh with us and stroke his flowing beard and tell us with his sparkling, beady eyes how he had fooled us.

Phoopi Babjan was the only friend Amma had in the family and she was genuinely fond of her brother's loving wife. She lived in the rear side of our house, which was skirted by a canal full with flowing water, beyond the large courtyard and the expanse of vacant land stretching up to the walls of other similar houses on that side. Phoopi Bajban lived in one of those houses, while Chacha Ummer too lived in a house near the canal, which had the appearance of a lake when seen from a distance. Though they had their own residences, they were almost always with us in our house, which was a large two-storeyed, well-constructed dwelling put together by men whose sole concern was to provide security to the occupants from the harsh variations of the climate and from petty thieves.

The truth was that my Dadi was known and feared for her authoritarian ways and she ensured that the heavier responsibilities of the household were not shared by her daughters. My Dadi knew about Phoopi Babjan's fondness for Amma and there was no dearth of occasions when this bold, outspoken daughter gave her mother a verbal bashing in the presence of shocked, but delighted, family members.

I must confess that the isolation I suffered at school did not affect my activities at home. My eldest sister, Sakina Aapa, went to a school for girls. She being the eldest, was Amma's aide and I found her mostly with Amma or my paternal aunts. She exercised her authority as the eldest sibling and I could see my elder brothers Noor and Ayub plotting innocent mischief behind her back. They tried in vain to frighten her with spiders and insects that scare most girls. Sakina Aapa was made of sterner stuff even as a twelve-year-old and she never spared an opportunity to catch them and our cousins when they were up to mischief and report the matter to Dadi, who was the acknowledged ruler of the household. Sakina Aapa left me alone because she was wise enough to know that I was my grandparents' favourite child and was not party to the conspiracies against her as my interests were different.

As for me, I derived great pleasure in trailing behind Amma, seizing her flowing dupatta with which she covered her head at all times. She would walk briskly from one room to the other in the sprawling house we lived in. She never tired of answering Dadi's calls from wherever she was and she would flurry to find out that Dadi wanted her to listen to some gory gossip she had heard. I would be hiding just behind her and she rarely noticed my presence when they would converse about happenings in the neighborhood that were sometimes spooky and sometimes silly.

One morning Dadi called Amma urgently and, as usual, I was running behind her unnoticed. Dadi was unusually serious and she was not in a mood to whisper. I could see that she was sad and disturbed. 'Go immediately,' she was loudly telling Amma. 'The bodies may not be there for long. It is a case the police have begun to investigate, you know. Poor parents. May Allah give them strength. Come back soon.'

The houses in Peshawar were constructed in a manner that the terraces were inter-connected. If the ladies wished to visit neighbours, they just had to cross a terrace or two. The buildings were so designed as to give the ladies who observed purdah those days the mobility they needed without coming out of their houses on the streets to walk to the house they wished to visit.

In an instant, Amma was hurrying across the connecting passage from our house to another house some distance away. She was unaware that I was following her noiselessly. She reached a house where there was gloom and an ominous silence. She stood beside a plump woman who was wailing inconsolably and tried in vain to comfort her with gentle words of solace. Then, she walked into a room where three dead bodies lay in a row covered in white cloth and there was blood oozing out from the sides, staining the cloth and flowing out to the floor like a red ribbon. The stench was unbearable. Amma was covering her nose with her hand. She was in purdah but I could see her eyes brimming with tears.

Amma had no clue that I had followed her to the house and to the room where the bodies lay still and cold. The investigating officers walked in and out talking in Pushtu to each other and one of them had a writing board and he was taking notes of what the seniormost among them was asking him to record. It was apparent that they were so absorbed in the business of jotting down their observations that they did not notice Amma. Suddenly, an English officer pushed both the doors wide open and walked in making a lot of noise with his boots and with his loud conversation with the local police officers.

I was completely engrossed in the movements of the uniformed men, especially the way they walked, talked and grimaced at the sight of the dead bodies. I did not notice Amma's absence or realize when she had slipped out of the room. The Englishman walked out with the local policemen following him and suddenly the door slammed shut and I found myself alone in the room crouching behind a table not far from the bodies.

Terror and panic gripped me as thoughts began to whir in my mind about the possibility of spending the night in the room if no one came to know that I was trapped inside. I reasoned with myself that even if no one else missed me, surely my Dada and Dadi would notice my not being in the living room when the family gathered at home in the evening for tea.

The high tea every day in the living room was an elaborate affair and, as the evening passed, I did not miss my chance ever to take a ride on Dada's back while he moved on all fours pretending to be a horse. It was his way of entertaining the grandchildren and, since I was his favourite, I got a longer ride and he did not mind my holding on to his beard with both my hands.

It was a comforting thought (my being missed) but then who knows I thought to myself. It may just happen that Dada may not be at home for the tea gathering and Dadi too may not be in the room for some reason of her own. Who will miss me then? Surely not Amma, because she would be too preoccupied with the preparation of the snacks and the tea in the kitchen.

The more my mind worked, the more frightened I became and, though the room was not cold, I found myself shivering slightly. The window of the room was open and the wind unexpectedly blew the white cloth away from the face of one of the victims. He was a youth I had often seen in the market place and it was chilling to see his ashen face. I felt for a moment that his eyelids moved and I would have screamed if my throat had not run dry and my voice had not been stifled by the dryness.

The only thing I could do was pray and pray as hard as I could. Just then the door opened with some force and the same English officer barged in. His eyes fell on me now. He stared at me and then shouted: 'Who is this boy? What is he doing here?'

I was now shaking with fear. Two policemen came up to me and physically lifted me and took me out. It was still bright outside and I felt relieved. There were men standing in the corridor who recognized me as the son of Sarwar Khan. The officer asked me: 'How did you get in there my boy?'

Now that I was outside and breathing the air freely I found my voice and I told the policemen how I had followed Amma and had got shut inside accidentally. There were some more civilians who recognized me and the English officer was convinced by my explanation to let me go. I took off as fast as I could.

At home the table was being set for the tea gathering of the family. My Dadi saw me first and she guessed from my facial expression and from the fact that I had neither bathed nor changed for teatime that I must have been out for a fairly long time. She was curious to know what I was doing all afternoon. I avoided telling her the truth but Dadi was not one to buy any concoction from me or anyone for that matter. She possessed an uncanny ability to get to the bottom of any unusual happening in the house. When she heard what I had experienced she called out to Amma and began scolding her for not being in the know of my movements and doings. Fortunately, Aghaji arrived and he diffused the situation.

At tea, the talk was all about the brothers who had got into a physical encounter with men of a family that had a score to settle with the elders of the boys' family. Blood spilling was not unusual between warring and feuding families in the locality but seldom did it end with the finality of death. A normal Pathan family comprised at least a dozen children and it was not such a big loss when one or two sons died in such encounters. Quite practically, the parents consoled themselves that they still had sons who could be counted upon as sons. As a matter of fact, the quick arrival of offspring one after the other at intervals of two years was a must in a Pathan Muslim family for this very reason.

On most days when the family gathered for tea, it was a pleasant occasion with the ladies sitting together and making meaningless conversation and the men indulging in serious discussion. Dadi presided and she quite enjoyed her queenly position and the fact that her daughters, barring Phoopi Babjan, and her sons did not dare to question her or oppose her when she spoke on domestic issues or anything that concerned the family. It pained me to see Amma not at the table but in the kitchen making pots of tea on clay *choolas* (stoves) emitting fire and smoke that made her feel uncomfortable and breathless at times. There was unstinted praise always for the delicacies she prepared for meals and at tea time but there was no offer of help from her sisters-in-law and mother-in-law. The only help that she got occasionally was from Phoopi Babjan.

What I remember most about Amma in my childhood years was her ungrudging slogging in the house. It wasn't as if there were no servants to help her but Amma preferred to do the work assigned to her in her own fastidious way. She always told those who asked her why she was not leaving the task to the servants that she liked doing whatever she was doing and Dadi had given her the responsibility because it was her forte. She stayed calm and unruffled all the time and it made life easy for Aghaji as he never had to hear complaints about his young wife or intervene in squabbles that usually abound in joint families with innumerable members. Amma hailed from an aristocratic family. Her parents and sisters who came visiting were always well dressed and they came in horse-drawn carriages with an attendant or two carrying bags of silk cloth or sweets or whatever they brought as a gesture of goodwill. They knew there was no dearth of fruits and dry fruits in our house, so they brought freshly made sweets and *namkeens* (savouries). Amma found time to sit and chat with them, especially her sisters who were beautiful and delicate unlike Aghaji's sisters who were broad shouldered and sturdy.

When Amma took a break (perhaps just once) from the drudgery of our household chores to spend time with her parents, it was for the marriage of one of her sisters. Since I was only five or six years old then, she took me along. I did not know about my going with her to her *maika* (mother's house) till I returned from school and I heard Dadi telling Aghaji that he and Amma should take extra care of me and not let me go out with other children. She reminded them of the fakir's words. I was no doubt delighted at the opportunity I was getting to undertake a short journey with Amma and Aghaji but I shuddered at the thought that I would stand out in the crowd with my forehead covered with soot. It was Phoopi Babjan who came to my rescue and quietly advised Amma to spare me the humiliation at least for the time I was in her own parental domain.

I had such a wonderful time being an unobtrusive little observer of all the gaiety in that quarter of the sprawling house exclusively occupied by the women who had come to attend the wedding as well as the daughters and daughters-in-law of the house. It was a sharp contrast to the dictatorship I was familiar with in the house I had come from. My Nani and Nana (maternal grandmother and grandfather) were anything but severe and, for the first time, I was seeing Amma being attended to and given the rightful position at the table during meal times. It gave me great happiness to see Amma laughing and being very much a part of the merriment that was going on continuously till it was time to hit the beds covered with silk quilts.

How I wished Amma could get the same carefree life back at the house she returned to as soon as the festivities of the wedding were over. I returned with all the black streaks on my forehead much to Dadi's pleasure and triumph that her orders had been obeyed. Without a murmur or even the slightest sign of resentment, Amma resumed her chores in the kitchen.

I went back to school and neither Aghaji nor Amma noticed that I was becoming an introvert. I was filled with a deep sense of unworthiness and loneliness. I waited to get back home where I took refuge in the security of Amma's gentle, comforting presence. In retrospect, I feel there was a divine purpose in the episode of Dadi blindly believing the fakir and giving me the ugly appearance that made me the butt of unpleasant remarks in school. It was the pain I endured as the alienated child in school that surfaced from my subconscious when I was playing the early tragic roles in my career and I had to express the deep mental agony of those characters.

The human mind, I have come to understand, has the fascinating capacity to store experiences and fertilize the imagination with those stored experiences when an occasion demands it. As I attained manhood, I learned to voluntarily keep my mind open to thoughts and experiences that I thought should be kept in the inner recesses of the mind for recollection at a later day. I also learned to pull down the shutters when I did not want to add thoughts or experiences that would only augment the burden of the mind and serve no purpose whatsoever. It is a feat that can be achieved only when one's mind has matured with education and learning from the school of life. But, as a child, however, I could not do anything about experiences, good and bad, finding their way into my subconscious and staying there.

3

ESCAPADES AND ADVENTURES

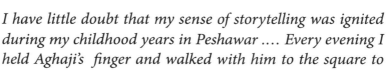

I have little doubt that my sense of storytelling was ignited during my childhood years in Peshawar .... Every evening I held Aghaji's finger and walked with him to the square to listen to the unfolding of a narrative by one of the maulanas ... I enjoyed the narrative and my fertile imagination conjured up the characters and situations in my mind so graphically that I went home and tried enacting the characters with the lines spoken by the maulana ... who could have foreseen that several years later I would be participating in storytelling exercises for a medium called cinema!

$\mathscr{I}$ WAS NOT AN EXCEPTIONALLY STUDIOUS CHILD BUT I WAS A curious and observant one. Being an introvert, I liked being alone, left to my own devices. I left my cousins and other children alone, not wanting to get into senseless arguments with them. I remember I used to ask Dada why the brook near the house flowed ceaselessly and where all the water came from and where it all went. He used to laugh and hoist me on his broad shoulders and walk to the brook and stand and stare at the water. I waited for an answer but it never came. I realized he had no answer for me. I once overheard him tell Aghaji that I asked him questions that were difficult for him to answer and that he wished he had some answers. He also jovially mentioned to Aghaji that I was not like the other boys in the family who never wondered or asked difficult questions.

I took keen pleasure in roaming around the open spaces in the afternoons on hot summer days when Dadi, after a sumptuous meal, rested in her room. There were no electric fans those days. There were only manually operated *pankhas* made from thick canvas with feather-lined cloth wrapped over them, which the servants of the house knew how to loosen from the clasps on the walls. When they tugged the strings, the *pankhas* moved to and fro to create the movement of air. It was a strenuous exercise but the men who were given the task were quite fit to do it. All of us children of the family were made to sleep in the afternoons as it was not advisable to go out and wander in the lonely streets. I always pretended to sleep and, at times, when I saw the *pankhawalas* and the others in the room sleeping soundly, I stepped out stealthily into the streets.

The streets were narrow and some of them were cobbled. I used to make my way through them into the open spaces where there were trees with berries that no one ate. We were always told that the berries were no good and they should be left for the birds and insects to feed upon. Being the curious one, I once climbed one of the trees and began to pluck the berries. I had just begun to shove the berries I had plucked into the pocket of my kurta, when I heard the voices of men and one of them was chasing the other. I recognized the one who was chasing while I held my breath and sat quietly on the branch I was perched on. The man I recognized was Ghani who was the caretaker of the orchards my family owned. He was a man of incredible physical strength and height. From the way they were arguing, it seemed that Ghani had caught the man snooping around one of the godowns where the dry fruits were stored.

I was scared that if Ghani looked up at the tree and saw me, he would report my escapade to Aghaji. Fortunately, the two parted amicably after the man apologized to Ghani profusely. I heaved a sigh of relief and scampered home, happy that I had had a lucky escape.

My cousins and I were frightened of Ghani. Most times when

I met him in the orchard, he was friendly and he liked lifting me and keeping me on one shoulder while a huge basket of freshly plucked *badams* (almonds) and grapes occupied the other shoulder. The grapes were sent by Dadi in baskets to the Kissa Khwani Bazaar market square to be given away to the poor and needy who came asking for food. There was an interesting way the grapes were given as food to the poor. The men who rolled out rotis and naans (Indian bread) used to make pouches within the large naans by slitting them neatly with a sharp knife and they stuffed handfuls of grapes inside and slammed the slits deftly to close them. Each such naan made a substantial and nutritious meal for a poor, hungry man.

Ghani used to stride towards our house with ease and unload me and the basket gleefully at the door. Dadi was kind to him and she always gave him money and offered him food. The frightening thing about him was not his demonic appearance but the mental condition he suffered from. He was in the habit of going into a trance and howling like a wolf on full moon nights while dutifully keeping vigil at the orchard. He could not be quietened by anyone and had to be chained and locked in a room all night. Some nights when he could not be quietened by anybody and had to be chained and locked in a room all night, someone else kept vigil at the orchard. Sometimes, he became all right by the morning and went about his work as if nothing had happened and, sometimes, the seizure lasted for a couple of days. Since he could get violent on such occasions, no one went near him.

Ghani had everybody's sympathy and there were all kinds of interpretations about his condition. Some said he had a spirit visiting him on full moon nights and the spirit could be chased away by someone who practised exorcism. Others said he was mad and needed treatment. Whatever it was, nobody did anything to rid him of his strange behaviour on full moon nights and it went on unabated till he became very ill and died suddenly on the bed he was chained to.

After he died, people living around the orchard said they saw him moving like a shadow in the night, especially on full moon nights. It was frightening even though absurd. The stories did not scare me because my surreptitious outings were in the afternoons and now that Ghani was not going to catch me, I felt free to continue with my exploration of the plains.

One afternoon I set out and my first halt was at the godown from where I grabbed handfuls of *badams* and pistachios and filled my pockets with them. Hardly had I taken my hand out of the pockets, when I saw a gun carriage approaching the godown. I immediately pulled the shutter down and crouched on the ground watching the carriage from a slit in the shutter. I was inside and the action was right outside, so close to the godown, that I began to get nervous. There were volleys being fired from the carriage and I saw some tribals falling prey to the bullets.

The men in the gun carriage were English soldiers and they were yelling and challenging other tribals, who were hiding near the godown, to come out. Their guns were pointed in the direction of the godown and there I was hopelessly caught in yet another perilous situation. After some time, the men got tired of waiting for the tribals of the hills to come out and they turned the carriage to go back. Now my fear was how to face the tribals if they were really hiding there and if they saw me. I was sensible enough to know that the hill tribes were a dangerous lot and they were outlaws who came to loot and plunder.

The daylight outside was waning and I had to return home soon. The spirit in me even at that tender age egged me on to take a risk. I briskly raised the shutter and ran out, sprinting at a speed that surprised me when I reached the doorstep of our house. Breathless and exhausted, I just ran into Amma's arms. She and Dadi had been praying and a search party had been sent to find me. Amma held me close and I could hear her murmur prayers of gratitude to Allah for having brought her son home without a scratch. The news of the firing near the godown had reached the house and its neighbourhood when Amma realized that I was not inside.

I told them what I had seen from the crack in the shutter. There was anger at first when Aghaji and Dada heard what I had narrated, but the fact that I was safe diluted the anger.

Aghaji was tall, broad shouldered and handsome. He had an impressive moustache. He and Dada were both hairy and that explains my hairiness. Aghaji walked erect and he wore his Pathan pyjamas and kurtas well. They were made of good cotton and stitched by expert tailors. He preferred pastel shades and was fond of white.

He loved Amma very much but he seldom demonstrated his affection in front of the family members. When he bought something for Amma, he gave it to her quietly in the room they occupied in the upper floor. Since I was always hovering round Amma, I used to see him take out a dupatta or an English talcum powder and give it to her quietly. She would take it matter-of-factly from him, put it away in the almirah and steal out of the room quickly, lest she be seen alone with her *miyan* by Dadi.

Amma was frail, fair and petite. By the time I was two, my younger brother Nasir had arrived and, by the time I was four, she was expecting my sister Taj. I was awestruck each time a sister or brother joined the line-up and it irked me somewhat to see Amma all wrapped up with each new arrival, almost forgetting the elder ones who became passé, so to say, for everybody in the family. I did not quit following her under any circumstance and it remained my prerogative to find space by her side when we slept at night. At times, in the summer months on moon-lit nights we slept on *chattais* (mats) on the terrace and I would be stunned by the serene beauty of my Amma's face as the light of the moon fell on her. She would be sound asleep, tired after all the toil during the day. My unmarried *phoopis* (father's sisters) would also be sleeping there as also the healthy Persian cats, which were kept as pets largely because they were needed to warm the beds on winter nights.

Winter nights assured great fun for the children of the house. The family members frequently gathered on the large terrace with a bonfire lit inside a large *sigdi* (brazier) placed in the centre. All of us would sit around the *sigdi*, which provided sufficient warmth to keep the night young and spirited. Quilts were brought along by each member to cover the body from the legs right up to the waist. It was customary for every member to tell a story or to sing a song. If it was a story it had to be one with a moral and not anything with adult content because the children were listening.

Dadi was indeed the first censor I came across in my life. She could abruptly curtail a story if she felt it was not good enough to be told in the presence of the women and children. One of my *khalas* (maternal aunts) was married to a man who had a penchant for telling stories that could have made Dada Khondke* feel awkward. When he tried unleashing one of his stories, he was instantly told by Dadi to go and sleep in his own room and not come up again on the terrace. It was a ban for a lifetime.

Dadi welcomed the narration of stories of valour and nobility and did not mind a wee bit of romance thrown in. If it was an evening of songs, the melodies had to be of clean folk verses or ghazals of eminent Persian poets. It was like the *antakshari*** of today except that the continuity depended on content. If the theme for the evening was love, then it had to be love all through the night or if it was a spiritual theme it had to continue to be so all night. I was not one to sit quietly on one lap all night. If it was an interesting story, I listened with rapt attention, if not, I moved from one lap to another till I fell asleep quite unknowingly as children do. I would wake up the next morning on my warm soft bed and rub my eyes and wonder who got me there. While the singing and storytelling went on, the Persian cats would be made to sleep on the beds to keep the beds warm for the occupants. That was something peculiar to Peshawar.

I have little doubt that my sense of storytelling was ignited during my childhood years in Peshawar. It was not just the winter nights on the terrace that stimulated my imagination. The main market square in Kissa Khwani Bazaar was known those days for the gathering of traders and shop keepers after the Maghrib prayers in the quadrangle of the square for some austere entertainment. Every evening I held Aghaji's finger and walked with him to the square to listen to the

---

*Dada Khondke (real name Krishna Kondke) was an actor and film producer. His films were famous for their double entendres.
**Antakshari* is a game in which each participant begins with the consonant on which the previous participant's song has ended.

unfolding of a narrative by one of the maulanas, men known for their piety and religious knowledge. The stories were interesting and were told with appropriate pauses and voice modulations by the narrators. The voice would rise to a high pitch when the story took a dramatic turn and it would fall to an audible low note when the narrative moved on to something tender and tearful. I enjoyed the narrative and my fertile imagination conjured up the characters and situations in my mind so graphically that I went home and tried enacting the characters with the lines spoken by the maulana. I would be alone by myself in some corner of the house where no one would come looking for me. I feel amused now when I reflect on those wonderful evenings when I sat with open-mouthed wonder by Aghaji's or Dadi's side in the bazaar absorbing the twists and turns in the stories. Who could have foreseen that several years later I would be participating in storytelling exercises for a medium called cinema!

Yet another pastime I indulged in solitude was imitating the ladies and men who came visiting my parents. Amma caught me at it one day and chided me gently, saying it was not good to make fun of elders. I was mimicking Khala Mariam when she came in unexpectedly and saw what I was up to. I did not tell Amma that I was not making fun of Khala Mariam but I was trying to be Khala Mariam for a few moments because she was such an intriguing character. May be unconsciously I was preparing for what was in store for me in the years to come.

Khala Mariam was the nightingale of the family. She had a good voice for singing and all of us grew up from infancy listening to the lullabies she sang to put us to sleep. She was married to a man who was a dandy and dressed up flamboyantly and colourfully. He was the man Dadi had banned from her terrace when he began telling a story that had a naughty slant. He was very different from the other men in the family in that he had scant regard for the decorum and etiquette the other members observed and he brought cigars from somewhere and smoked them while all the other men smoked hookas. He argued with Dada that it made no difference what you smoked. Khala Mariam was quite good looking and she too smoked cigarettes held in a holder. She and her husband had many differences between them and they spoke to each other only to get into a squabble. He had a chest of drawers in the room, which was his prized possession and he protected it zealously. She often mocked him saying: 'You sit on that chest of money and treasures like a cobra with its hood unfurled ... take it with you to your grave.' He laughed a wicked laugh whenever she said that.

It was nothing but entertainment for me at that age when they locked horns. The real drama occurred when Khala Mariam was confined to an isolated room on certain days because she would get possessed by a spirit. I hid myself in the room one day and I heard her voice change into that of a man as she raved about something I could make nothing of. She stood up and tore her hair and looked completely different from what she was otherwise. I remember Amma coming rushing into the room to take me away when she realized I was up to my usual exploration of the unknown and was in the room. Khala Mariam suddenly turned soft and gentle and said: 'Don't hurt the child, let him be.' Amma muttered something and quickly whisked me away.

By the next day, she was normal and behaved as if nothing happened. She was close to Amma and confided in her about her husband's wanton ways.

On Fridays the ladies went out to the market and I remember Amma always waiting for Khala Mariam who took longer to dress up. Amma wore simple salwars and kameezes that were long and loose. Her head was always covered and when she stepped outside she was so completely in purdah that I would have had difficulty in identifying her if it weren't for her small build and her petite stature that made her stand out among the sturdy, almost masculine Pathan women who swarmed the shops selling women's garments and burkhas. There was something she kept chewing, an elaichi (cardamom) perhaps.

I was always following her to the market place and she kept a watch on my movements knowing my propensity to get lost in the crowd. Khala Mariam and Phoopi Babjan were not very cordial with each other, though both were very fond of Amma. They dressed up in silks while Amma preferred cottons with small prints. I seldom saw her buy things for herself. She was always buying things for the house. The market was crowded on Fridays because the men too made their purchases after the Juma prayers in the main mosque. When Amma wanted me to get her favourite bath soap, she would call out to me, saying: 'Yousuf *mera* Pears soap *saboon laana.*' That was how she referred to the soap she used.

One side of the market was lined with eateries that served chapli kebabs with *anardana* (pomegranate seeds) and rotis besides rice preparations and light snacks. There was always a crowd at the eateries because the tempting aroma of gravies and kebabs wafted to the nostrils of passersby so strongly that it was difficult for the susceptible to resist a bite.

There were shops that sold beautiful silks and cottons, laces of all colours, dupattas and *parandhas* (braid tassels). We were living in undivided India at that time and there was a sizable Hindu population and the menfolk as well as the women mingled freely with Muslims in the market square wishing each other and exchanging pleasantries ever so cheerfully. Aghaji had many Hindu friends and one of them was Basheshwarnathji, who held an important job in the civil services. His elder son came to our house with him a few times and he stunned the ladies with his handsome appearance. That was Raj Kapoor's father Prithviraj Kapoor.

Basheshwarnathji was very friendly with Aghaji and I often heard them discuss an impending war (the Second World War) and what was in store for the inhabitants of Peshawar. I listened to their talk intently but I could not fathom what they were talking about. They were talking about a city called Bombay where business opportunities were many. Then one day I heard Aghaji tell Dada that he was going to Bombay to explore such opportunities and he intended to go alone first. The war was inevitable and it was bound to impact the fruit business as transportation of marketable produce from the orchards in Peshawar to markets elsewhere would become difficult. Before I knew it he was off to Bombay one morning.

When Aghaji was away something silly occurred. As always I was the centre of the excitement that mounted one afternoon in the house. I vividly recall that afternoon when a cousin, who was somewhat older than I, was injured in the eye by something that had hit him while he was out in the orchards. He was brought home by the servants and all my aunts rushed to inspect his injury. It was found to be minor but my aunts decided to treat it with their own prescription. I was playing quietly in one of the rooms in the house and was startled by an aunt coming into the room to drag me out. 'You can play later,' she ordered me as I reluctantly walked by her side, her hand holding my arm in a tight grip. She took me to the terrace, made me stand next to an earthenware pot and commanded me to pull down my pyjamas and underwear and told me to urinate into the pot. I was so terrified that it was all out in a jiffy straight into the pot with my aunt watching over me with satisfaction. She then took the pot to the other aunts who were waiting to wash my cousin's wounded eye with the precious excretion. I was overwhelmed by a strange feeling of fear, shame and disgust and, for days together, avoided my aunts and the cousin who had benefited from me.

As mentioned earlier, the eldest of my parents' offspring was my sister Sakina Begum. She was most unlike Amma in her nature and demeanour. When we were in Peshawar, she was quite young. She was attractive in her own way, though not blessed with the serene beauty of Amma. She was stubborn and difficult by nature. I can recall now that she disagreed with Amma often and there was a mild but ceaseless conflict brewing between them all the time. Aghaji took little interest in their altercations and I think he feigned ignorance only because he felt that women had their own way of solving the internal riddles in their family life without external help.

My elder brothers were Noor and Ayub. Noor Sahab (as I was supposed to call him) was a good five years senior and Ayub Sahab was just a year and a half older. Noor Sahab was a colourful character right from his juvenile years and he dazzled me and my cousins with his escapades, which came to light from time to time and provoked Aghaji to use a cane on him.

Evidently, Aghaji didn't believe in sparing the rod and spoiling his son, but, from whatever I can remember of those years in Peshawar, all the blows showered on Noor Sahab had only a transient effect on his unbridled energy and enthusiasm to explore forbidden territories. After each episode, Noor Sahab would be quiet for a while. He'd wait for Aghaji to go out on his business and back he would go on his promises to him. As the eldest son, Noor Sahab had a rightful sense of seniority, which, rather unrightfully, gave him the feeling that he could boss over all of us who were younger than he.

Thanks to the age difference, I was seldom in his company. He summoned me occasionally to run an odd errand for him in the market place and I docilely obeyed him, knowing him to be quite a bully. Without doubt, he irritated Amma who tried relentlessly to curb his mischief.

I was close to Ayub. Since he was just a little older I kept calling him Ayub and I was rebuked often for that. I had to address him as Ayub Sahab in the presence of my parents. He didn't go to school like the rest of us. I could never fathom why he was tutored at home in Urdu and he never received formal school education. I guessed I was not healthy like me and Noor Sahab. There was some intrinsic problem I was not fully aware of and, quite understandably, not made aware of. The divine compensation was that Ayub Sahab was blessed with an amazing intellect and sensibilities that were far from ordinary. He was very specially gifted and my parents were very proud of him.

Aghaji's absence was hardly felt in the house. I knew he had gone to Bombay but I did not know why. I remember asking Amma and she simply told me he had to go there for an important reason and he would be back soon. She was as usual busy and attending to something Dadi had asked her to do. I was never one to trouble Amma with questions that she had no time to answer, so I heard her reply without pausing to think too much about it.

4

Off to Bombay:
A New Chapter Begins

In Bombay I was enrolled at the Anjuman Islam High School and there was no more shaving of my pate. I now wore my skull cap over a thick growth of black hair, which elicited compliments from all the ladies who visited Amma. They would ruffle my hair and say something to her and she would wait for their departure to perform the ritual of shooing away the evil eye cast on me as instructed by Dadi.

As mentioned earlier, Aghaji had gone to Bombay to explore the business potential there in the wake of the news about the impending world war. He knew that the transportation of marketable produce from the orchards in Peshawar to traditional markets outside would become difficult once the war started.

Travel was easy those days by the Frontier Mail. Tickets were purchased at the railway station on the day of the journey itself and not booked in advance. During his stay in Bombay, he often took a stroll along the Apollo Bunder (on the seafront) to while away time in the evenings. One evening, he saw a child in a pram with a healthy appearance and rosy cheeks and he was instantly reminded of me. As I mentioned earlier, I was regarded as a handsome child and Aghaji was quite proud of my appealing, cherubic looks. He picked up the child in the pram spontaneously and the parents of the child panicked and ran towards him. It was a natural reaction on seeing a strong, sturdy Pathan impulsively picking up a happy, gurgling child without introducing himself formally to the child's parents.

Aghaji often recalled this incident at family gatherings amidst much laughter. He apologized to the child's parents and told them about his family in Peshawar and little Yousuf who was as good-looking as their son.

I would like to believe quite justly that I was responsible in a large measure for the family's moving to Bombay. Had it not been for the incident at Apollo Bunder, Aghaji wouldn't have returned to Peshawar to take Amma and the seven children to Bombay. Back home in Peshawar, it was Dada who sensed Aghaji's loneliness in Bombay, especially when he heard about the amusing encounter with the baby at Apollo Bunder.

Though Dadi didn't quite agree with her son's move to shift the family to Bombay, for once Dada stood firm on his decision to give his daughter-in-law the right to live with her husband.

We travelled by the Frontier Mail to Bombay. I can't recall when exactly since I was quite young then, but I think it was some time in the mid-1930s. If I remember correctly, the terminal those days was in Colaba. It was our first train journey and was very exciting for all of us. At some of the stations on the way, friends of my parents came to meet us with refreshments that we could consume on the way. Some of them were Hindus. I recall now the boxes they brought for us contained vegetarian items like puris and stuffed brinjals. The train sped past green pastures and valleys and, at times, dark mountains. The visuals are still vivid in my mind, especially the grandeur of the mountains. When the train stopped at stations, there were men carrying casks of tea and water in pots calling out: 'Hindu chai, Hindu paani, Muslim chai, Muslim paani.' My parents, I remember, took little notice of the difference. They drank water and tea without discrimination and so did many others in the compartment. The train had a dining car, which was meant only for the English officers and their wives.

In Bombay we alighted at Colaba. It was in the morning hours and my younger siblings were sleepy. Aghaji had arranged for a tonga (a horse-drawn carriage) to take us to the house he had rented out. It was the beginning of a new chapter in our lives as we stepped into an altogether new environment filled with excitement and wonder.

The apartment rented out by Aghaji was in a four-storeyed structure called Abdullah Building on Nagdevi Street, near the bustling Crawford Market, where he had set up his fruit business on a wholesale basis at first. Our apartment was on the top floor and though we missed the spaciousness of our home in Peshawar, all of us settled down quite well in the fairly large space we got over the entire floor with individual rooms for us children and a separate room for Aghaji and Amma besides a guest room. There was a terrace, which was a luxury, because the other houses in the neighbourhood did not have one. All of them had flat roofs.

Amma initially faced only one problem – she couldn't speak Hindi. But it was amazing how she made friends in the neighbourhood. In fact, soon after our arrival in the locality, we were being discussed as the nice Pathan family that had occupied the fourth floor of the Abdullah Building. Amma with her chiselled features, flawless rosy complexion, slight build and gentle smile radiated instant warmth. Aghaji, strong, well-built and virile like most of his clan, was already known as a gentleman and a pious Pathan.

Amma had two friends on Nagdevi Street, who were close to her. How they communicated with her was always a mystery to Aghaji because she didn't speak Hindi. One of them had a son with whom my eldest brother Noor Sahab struck a rapport. Noor Sahab, with his adventurous nature, had become popular on Nagdevi Street in a short span. He had begun experimenting with cigarettes as did other boys of his age group. It was all done covertly with that spirit of discovery and bravado commonly felt in adolescence among boys who are in a hurry to attain manhood.

One afternoon, there was bad news for Amma. Her friend's son had been stifled to death with a pillow in his room and the mother of the lad was naturally inconsolable.

I was confronted once again by the dread of seeing a dead body and the coming and going of policemen. Being somewhat older now, I was less terrified. But Amma was shocked beyond belief.

We grew up quite happily in the large apartment on Nagdevi Street. Aghaji seemed satisfied with his fruit business, which was prospering. He didn't have to go to the fruit stall at Crawford Market every day as he had employed men to receive the consignments and deliver them at the market besides managing the daily sales. He only paid a visit once a day to see if all was well. As such, he had time to spend with us and with his friends who enjoyed his company and visited him regularly.

We had a family doctor who was tall and well built and I can vividly recall his visits to our house and our visits to his clinic in the evening when he would examine patients and prescribe medicines. Aghaji often gifted him fruit baskets. Something funny happened one evening when Aghaji took me along to his clinic to get a medicine for Ayub Sahab. I was carrying a rubber ball, which I played with, bouncing it on the floor and testing my ability to catch it without a miss. At the clinic after Aghaji had had a good ten-minute conversation with the doctor, he came out to get the mixtures from the compounder. I was playing with the ball in the corridor outside and, on seeing Aghaji come out of the doctor's chamber, I missed the ball, which fell on the floor and rolled into the doctor's cabin. While Aghaji was exchanging pleasantries with the compounder, I hurriedly ventured into the doctor's chamber to find the ball. I was on all fours looking for the ball, so the doctor did not hear or see my entry. I found the ball and I also witnessed a sight I described to Ayub Miyan when I returned home to his great amusement. The doctor's nurse, a fair, plump woman with light eyes and dark brown hair tied up high in a knot stylishly, was seated on the doctor's lap and they were talking and laughing about something. I quickly crawled out before they went on to something that could have been outrageously bold, considering that the door was not locked and anybody could have walked in.

I grew up in an atmosphere of warmth and affection. I was extremely shy but not unhappy. There was no pressure on my parents. Amma's work load decreased considerably in Bombay where she only had to care for her children and her husband. She looked healthier and happier though she often spoke nostalgically about Peshawar. She worked quietly and happily. I was enrolled at the Anjuman Islam High School in the fifth standard in 1937 and there was no more shaving of my pate. I now wore my skull cap over a thick growth of black hair, which elicited compliments from all the ladies who visited Amma. They would ruffle my hair and say something to her and she would wait for their departure to perform the ritual of shooing away the evil eye cast on me as instructed by Dadi.

Today, in my ninety-second year, my wife Saira performs the same ritual every time a visitor says something about my looks or my good health or when we go to a gala event and dozens of people come to take my signature in their autograph books and praise my work.

Noor Sahab had his own set of friends in the locality. Diametrically opposite our apartment was the residence of a Bohra Muslim businessman. His daughter became Noor Sahab's heartthrob and I became a participant in their juvenile affair and, sadly enough, the climactic separation between the lovers was also precipitated by me. I must narrate the love story because it is a chapter in my childhood that I have retained in my memory more for its bathos than for its romance and humour.

Noor Sahab had a way of ordering me to run errands for him. He was an assertive young man and he spent a lot of time with his friends who stayed in the neighbourhood. When the friends visited him, he took them up to the terrace where neither Amma nor Sakina Aapa came. His friends often brought cigarettes with them and Noor Sahab did not like to accept the cigarettes they offered him. He would summon me and send me out to get cigarettes for himself and his friends – his favourite brand was Cavender – and he would tell me to go as quickly as I could to get the cigarettes. At other times, he sent me to fetch bananas for him when he was alone and then he sweetly told me to take my own time to bring the bananas. I obliged without a murmur.

By and by, I found out what he was up to. At a specific time in the evening when Noor Sahab was alone on the terrace, his heartthrob in the opposite apartment would take a position at a window facing our terrace. I was not old enough to know what was happening but I never failed to notice the glances exchanged from our terrace when the charming neighbour took her place at the window to do her sewing. That was the time when the banana errand was ordered by Noor Sahab to keep me out of the way. He used to thrust a little note written on a page torn out of an exercise notebook and ask me to give it to her on the way back. I was immensely pleased with her because she rewarded me each time I sprinted across the street to her house with a poetic outburst from Noor Sahab. She would quietly thrust peppermints, lemon toffees or chocolates wrapped in gleaming silver paper into my hands and affectionately run her fingers through my hair but never spoke a word. My little mind was certainly aware that Noor Sahab, who was handsome and had light eyes that twinkled with sprightliness, was conveying something secret to her and vice versa. A few times, I mischievously chose to surprise him by doubling the speed of my sprint and completing the errand in record time and taking the stairs two steps at a time to reach the terrace huffing and panting only to spoil his flirtation through glances with the girl. He had turned to me with annoyance on those occasions with a look that said: 'Ok, you think you can outsmart me, I will show you!'

The next errand would be to get chana (chickpeas) from a vendor who had his stall some distance away. Not one to be vanquished, I used all the stamina I had to run and get the chana in record time! On each such occasion, I could see the girl chuckling and giving

Noor Sahab a naughty glance. This silent love story enacted through glances and looks as well as the notes I carried was destined to end very soon.

One afternoon I was on the terrace silently enjoying a toffee she had given me when Amma came searching for me and found my mouth full. She wanted to know at once where I had got the sweet from. I told her the truth.

Needless to say, there was utter commotion as the lid flew open and Noor Sahab's secret dalliance came to light. The girl disappeared the next day and Noor Sahab was a picture of desolation. He was not annoyed with me because he knew I had not spoiled his romance intentionally. It was an innocent child's confession and, as days went by, he resigned himself to the realization that real-life love stories don't always end happily.

She was bundled off to Surat (now in Gujarat) where she married and settled down. Her parents continued to meet Aghaji and Amma cordially. And Noor Sahab left the past behind to everybody's relief and began to look for new sources of excitement.

5

THE GROWING UP YEARS

I have gone into all this detailing [given later in this chapter] for a specific purpose. It is meant to inform those readers, who may have been misled into imagining that Raj Kapoor and I only professed friendship while a deep professional rivalry brewed between us, that ours was not merely a friendship of two individuals in the same profession but a bonding that grew from well-placed trust and respect.

As Ayub Sahab grew up, he developed a respiratory disorder, which necessitated our moving to Deolali (a hill station in Maharashtra, located about 180 km from Bombay). The fresh air in Deolali and the availability of medical care there made it the ideal location for his treatment and recovery.

Being an army station, Deolali had good educational institutions, and one of them was Barnes School where I was admitted. There were soldiers who didn't seem to be of Indian origin at the army centres. I learned later that they were Turkish, who were captives of war.

Deolali is of significance in my life in more than one respect. First, it was at Deolali that I learned the English language and became quite proficient in it. Secondly, it was during our stay in Deolali that I began to take keen interest in soccer.

Aghaji visited us once a week from Mumbai. He loved my brother Ayub and was very concerned about his progress. He found me reading and writing English and that was also something that gladdened his heart. There was an English poem that I learned in school, which I recited before Aghaji one day and he was so happy that he made me recite it before all his distinguished English-speaking friends. The poem ran as follows:

I have two eyes.
And I can see the door
The ceiling, the wall
And the big blue sky
Bent over all.

During school vacations when we went to Peshawar to spend time with our Dada and Dadi, there used to be social gatherings to mark our visits. At each gathering I was made to stand on a platform and vigorously egged on to recite the poem. It gave Aghaji great pride to tell the world that his son was conversant with English and all his Pathan friends were equally joyous about the achievement. If there happened to be an English officer of some rank in the local administration in the gathering, it made the scenario even more thrilling. Each time I completed the recitation there would be encores. There would be cries of 'shabash [well done] Yousuf. Each time I had to start all over again.

The encores came again and I would straighten myself, take a deep breath and begin reciting the same poem once again.

The recitation went on endlessly till I was tired and just could not continue. For me, it was something I always tried to wriggle out of. As a shy, reticent youngster, public attention was the last thing I wanted. But I think Destiny had already begun to chart out the life I had to lead. I had to obey Aghaji's orders on such occasions and, though it was difficult to recite the poem in the open air – no door, no wall, no ceiling – I think I was stimulated to perform by the applause and encores I received. It was as if I could see a door, a wall and a ceiling when I recited. I had my first brush with the make-believe world into which I was to make my fateful entry years later.

At Deolali, Ayub Sahab had no option but to spend his waking hours reading whatever Urdu literature he could lay his hands on. He always liked to read the latest novels and he devoured newspaper articles and short stories with great delight. To make him happy, as I grew up and progressed in my study of English, I read the short stories (in translation) of the nineteenth-century French writer, Guy de Maupassant, and narrated them to him. That was my first introduction to published literature from abroad and I was fascinated by the plot structure and storytelling ability of the author. In a latent sort of way, I was developing a keen narrative skill by reading the works of English and other European authors that I found in the library of Barnes School.

I can't recall when exactly but Ayub Sahab suffered a spinal injury after he fell from a horse in Kashmir where Aghaji had taken him and Noor Sahab on one of his business trips. Fruits that were of typical Kashmir origin had interested Aghaji and he made quite a few trips in a year to negotiate and make arrangements for their transport to Bombay. As a result of the injury, Ayub Sahab had to stay in bed or just sit in a wheelchair for almost a year. Orthopaedic treatment was not as advanced as it is today and such injuries took time to be healed.

I remember how Aghaji used to sit by Ayub Sahab's side and look at him with moist eyes that betrayed his pain within. Here was a son gifted with unusual intelligence and creative energy and he just couldn't move from his chair. Relatives of my parents who visited us at Deolali were not many. Among them, I remember an uncle, Ghulam Mohammad, who seemed well acquainted with Urdu poetry and spent time with Ayub Sahab appreciating the Urdu verse that Ayub Sahab penned.

I had a classmate who was the school bully. He was twice my size and he made it a point to threaten me and my small circle of friends.

On the way to school, there was a plateau where we played. I had a cycle, which I rode to school sometimes and, at other times, I just ran to school, taking off on my feet swiftly with the breeze as if one was being airlifted from the ground. It was an experience I really enjoyed.

To get back to the school bully, he was the local baker's son. The bakery owned by his father was well known. One day while I was returning from school, he sprang on me and began punching me. I was alone and I took the beating without attempting to retaliate.

Days later, my friends and I cornered him and really gave it to him. It became a major talking point amongst the boys. What he did to me only I knew but what we – my friends and I – did to him became known to all.

His father was away at that time. So we knew that the news hadn't reached the principal.

The same weekend, Aghaji was expected and I was sent by Amma to fetch him from the railway station. At the station my opponent, the bully, was waiting for his dad who was travelling by the same train.

When Aghaji alighted, the baker also stepped down. I walked silently behind Aghaji, a strapping six-footer with broad, heavy shoulders while the bully walked sheepishly behind his small-built father. The next morning, when I encountered him on my way to school, he seemed to be in a hurry to go out of my sight. He quickened his pace and started to run. He was behaving as if he was afraid of me. My friends who were walking with me noticed the change in him. That afternoon, as we made our way home, my friends and I found a place to hide at the foot of a hill. We waited for him. He had stayed back in the class pretending that he had something to do. After a few minutes of waiting we saw him coming. He was alone. As he came closer I could feel my heartbeat quickening. The next instant we surrounded him. There was the kind of fisticuffs that children have with their opponents at that age.

I returned home feeling triumphant but unusually silent. I heard Aghaji asking Amma what was wrong with me. 'Why is he so quiet? Just feel his brow and see if he's alright,' I heard him saying after he passed my room and entered his room where Amma was frantically searching for something she had misplaced.

Amma, of course, knew better. 'I hope you've not done something you want to hide from me,' she said in her usual gentle voice. I simply shook my head, keeping my gaze on the floor till she left. As always, she had some work in the kitchen or the garden or the backyard to attend to.

I imagined what would transpire in school the next day. The principal would get a complaint and I would be summoned along with my friends. I sincerely wished I hadn't behaved as I did. My peace-loving conscience was in a turmoil. Moreover, the Pathan in me was rather uncomfortable about the way we caught him alone, unawares, and retaliated.

I reached school somewhat early the next day. I saw the baker and his son in the principal's room. After an exchange of words, they came out and the boy was asked to go to his class. In a little while I saw Aghaji walking, straight and erect, rather briskly towards the principal's office. He too exchanged a few words and came out. I waited breathlessly, wondering what had brought Aghaji to my school. To my surprise, the principal, too, came out and they were all talking and shaking hands. The boy's father was all respect as he stood before Aghaji, listening to whatever Aghaji was saying. In the end, Aghaji patted the baker on his shoulder and they walked out of the school together.

I went to my classroom and took my seat in the first row. I looked at my friends and they seemed to be happy. I then looked at the boy and, to my surprise, he smiled at me. When school broke, he walked home with us, laughing and talking as if nothing had happened.

As a boy I was extremely happy in the green surroundings in Deolali. Having spent a free, spirited childhood in Peshawar, wandering gleefully in open spaces, breathing fresh air, stopping by the brooks and streams in the valleys, it was sheer delight to be in Deolali. When we had arrived there, I had this strange feeling that I may just relive my happy childhood in Peshawar. The earth, brown and red in parts, smelt as good as the earth back home and the hills, craggy and verdant in the monsoons, filled my boyish heart with nostalgia. The climate was perfect and we had flowers and fruits in the trees in our garden, which was tended to by a jovial *maali* and his wife who spoke a UP (then known as United Provinces and later called Uttar Pradesh) dialect, which fascinated me. Many years later, when I began to work on the dialogues of the film *Gunga Jumna* (released in 1961), it was this dialect that came to my mind and ears repeatedly.

Amma often sent me to the *maali's* house to either summon him urgently or to deliver a portion of the goodies Aghaji would bring from Bombay for us. Amma was always generous towards those who served us. She always spoke gently and kindly. Even when she got annoyed and reprimanded them, she did so without hurting their self-esteem.

Deolali, as a picturesque place, figured prominently in my imagination when we got down to detailing locations in the screenplay of *Gunga Jumna*. The hills, the plains and the thick groves made up of all varieties of woodland trees lining the banks of the winding streams, sprang up before my eyes when I pictured the locations for *Gunga Jumna* in my mind. In retrospect, I feel Deolali provided as much impetus to my creative thoughts as the lands and forts, mountains and valleys of Peshawar when I sketched the rugged setting of *Gunga Jumna's* core conflicts and dramatic scenes. I am inclined to subscribe to the belief that childhood images cling to the subconscious surreptitiously and they can emerge before your eyes quite unexpectedly like an unexpected visitor who sneaks in through the back door to give you a lovely surprise.

During our search for the outdoor locales of *Gunga Jumna*, I visited some of my childhood haunts and, though a great deal had changed in the environs, I felt extremely happy taking deep breaths of the familiar air.

The cantonment was unchanged. I instantly recalled how I used to gaze at the officers in their smart uniforms and sometimes wondered how they mounted the horses so quickly and rode them with such poise and confidence. I was fascinated by the houses of the English officers with their well-kept lawns, trimmed hedges, mango trees, wild raspberry and blackberry bushes. There were English flowering plants and the Indian hibiscus as also roses of various hues and sizes. Our own house was large and we had a flower garden in front and a kitchen garden in the rear. Like the English ladies who sat in the verandah of their houses with their knitting, Amma and the aunts who came visiting from Peshawar, too, sat in the verandah of our house enjoying the warmth of the afternoon sun in the winter months doing embroidery or crisscrossing fine needles and producing beautiful lace.

Deolali and Poona (now Pune; located about 150 km from Bombay) are of special significance in my life. If Deolali restored the abandon of my early childhood in Peshawar with its plains and hills and valleys, Poona gave me a sense of self-assurance and the initial opportunity to develop my character.

When the doctors felt Ayub Sahab was doing better, Aghaji shifted us back to Bombay and we were back in our house near Crawford Market. Amma was once again cleaning up the big apartment though she had servants now to help her. There were additions to the family also. My younger brother Nasir was followed by Mumtaz. One by one my siblings arrived with gaps of a year or a year and a half. Amma was suffering from asthma and she had frightening bouts of breathlessness off and on.

It was not just for my education that Aghaji had to find resources. All my younger brothers and sisters had to be educated as well. The recession was setting in as I began attending high school and then Khalsa College at Matunga (a locality in central Bombay). It was easy to walk to Anjuman Islam from home but the only way to reach Khalsa College was by taking a tram ride. I do not remember now as to where I boarded the electric tram every day, perhaps it was at Crawford Market, but I have lovely memories of the tram journeys terminating at Dadar (another locality in central Bombay). I think it was operated by the BEST (Bombay Electric Supply and Transport), which also ran the bus services on the

With my brothers. (*L to R*): Aslam, Noor Sahab and Ahsan.

roads. I enjoyed a tram ride more than a bus ride for the leisurely way it meandered through its route and made a lot of noise when it picked up speed. I had friends in college who travelled by tram every day and somehow evaded the conductor who gave the tickets for the journey. They were very triumphant about it. The tram conductors, unlike the bus conductors, were usually laid back and conscientious commuters like me had to go to the conductor who could be dozing in his seat, wake him up, get an angry stare and buy a ticket to the destination. I therefore did not blame my friends who commuted ticketless. There were days when I ran on the road keeping pace with the tram, the wind beating against my face, for the mere fun and joy of it.

When the decision to do away with the tram service in Bombay appeared in the newspapers, I was among the thousands of citizens who felt a pang in the heart. A large number of people reportedly lined the streets between Parel and Dadar (both localities in central Bombay) to bid farewell to the last tram on the fateful day (31 March 1964) it made its last journey. Had I not ceased to be the young Yousuf Khan, who travelled in the electric trams of Bombay, and become the star Dilip Kumar, I would have been one of the spectators of the tram service's swan song.

For some reason Aghaji had great dreams for me. He wanted me to pursue my education and acquire impressive degrees. His ultimate desire was to see OBE (Order of the British Empire) attached to my name. (India was then ruled by the British.)

'He is capable of much more than you think,' I overheard him chiding my Amma once. 'He should not be selling fruits. He should be studying law. He must go abroad and study there. He has the potential to become somebody.'

I was happy to know from Amma what Aghaji thought of me but it scared me, too. Will I be able to measure up to his expectations? I was industrious and diligent by nature. I was sure I could be a successful soccer player if given the encouragement and support to become one ... but the OBE? How would I get that?

I was an avid reader. I enjoyed reading English and Urdu authors. I was shy and reserved by nature but I made friends easily with select college mates. At the Khalsa College I met Raj Kapoor after years. Raj's grandfather, Dewan Basheshwarnath Kapoor, used to visit us in Peshawar, as noted earlier, and the two families met in Bombay as well with the lingering warmth and gusto that Pathans are famous for. The joy of speaking the same language, Pushtu, was itself something special for the two families. Aghaji had a flair for picking up languages, a forte I have inherited and honed. He could speak Pushtu and the Punjabi spoken by the Punjabi residents of Lahore as also Persian and Urdu besides sufficient English to be understood by his anglophone friends. When we moved to Bombay, he became conversant with Hindustani and Gujarati which his Memon and Bohra friends spoke. (Memons and Bohras are ethnic Muslim communities in western India.)

With Amma.

Our residence in Bombay was like an open house for Aghaji's and Amma's friends. Close to the building where we lived on Nagdevi Street, there were the two-storeyed houses occupied by Memon and Bohra families. The ladies from those families were very friendly with Amma and my eldest sister Sakina. There was one Memon lady, Baisabi, who regularly visited us in the afternoons and carried on long, endless conversations with Amma, punctuated by interludes of hearty laughter. She was very fond of Amma and she embarrassed me frequently by complimenting me about my looks.

The fact is I could never get over my shyness even after I entered my twenties. I envied Raj who had by then become a friend as the families had once again become close, carrying forward the friendship of the Peshawar days. Raj was always at ease with the girls in the college and his extrovert nature and natural charm earned him considerable popularity. If there was anything impressive about me at that stage, it was my performance in sports and my acquaintance with English and Urdu literature.

On the field, while playing football or hockey, I was completely at ease and focused to the point of forgetting everything else. It was soccer that I loved and wanted to play seriously and professionally. I saved every rupee of my pocket money to buy expensive and comfortable sports shoes from a shop near Metro Cinema (in south Bombay). I used to walk to the grounds behind Metro where we played and also had our practice sessions. Aghaji did not mind if I went after college to watch a football game at the Cooperage grounds (also in south Bombay) or wherever there was a match being played and if I asked for extra money. He was happy with the thought that this son on whom he had pinned hopes of high education and the OBE was spending as much time in libraries and seldom missed lectures in college. He had made friends with lawyers, doctors and professors who visited his fruit shop and he felt proud when they came home and, when they spoke to me, I conversed freely and articulately with them. He would send me to their residences with choice fruits and their wives would drop in with home-made sweets, biriyani and other preparations. I never failed to notice the respect they had for Aghaji who was, indeed, more than a fruit merchant to them and to all those who came in his contact. Though he never had access to formal education, which was absent during his boyhood and youth in Peshawar, he was a man of native wisdom and culture. In poise, demeanour, refinement and prudence in speech and thought, he was equal to them. Though he was not a native of Bombay and, as such, was an outsider, hailing from a social milieu that had little in common with the urban sophistication and mores of that city, Aghaji was always confident and assured in the company of his friends from different walks of life. He stood out among them with his impressive appearance. He had a bodily presence and a gait with his head held high that commanded deference. He was also full of the Pathan robustness and charm that made him stand out among the local Muslims when we gathered at the Juma Masjid (near Crawford Market) for our Friday afternoon prayers. Since the building we stayed in had four floors, we could see the terraces of the two-storeyed buildings nearby as also the Juma Masjid, which was close by.

Ours was a predominantly Muslim locality but Aghaji had Hindu and Christian friends who had their offices and shops in nearby places such as Bhendi Bazaar, Mohammad Ali Road, Masjid Bunder and Pydhonie market.

There was one good Parsi friend of Aghaji who had a shop in the vicinity of Crawford Market from where he purchased crockery for the house as well as for our relatives in Peshawar. He was a genial, good-humoured man who enjoyed Aghaji's company and was a frequent visitor at our house on days when the market was closed.

There was also another kind friend who had a shop where kites of all sizes and colours were sold. He gave the boys in the locality the liberty to bargain and pick up kites at throwaway prices. He had other shops and other businesses and was quite prosperous.

January was the month in which the new kites arrived in his shop and we never wasted time in forming our kite-flying groups. It was a sport I enjoyed very much. The terraces would be full of enthusiastic kite-fliers in the evenings and it was always great fun to be a participant in the aerial combats of kites. There was a tingling sense of achievement when my kite sailed past that of an adversary and, after a stiff test of manoeuvring skills, succeeded in sending the competitor's kite to the ground. Each time I was hailed for my victory, I felt buoyant and ecstatic.

My love for kites and kite-flying continued even after I had become busy as an actor and the family moved to a house in Bandra (a locality in west Bombay). Among the many big trunks in the basement of our house is one that contains the exquisite kites I had purchased from small towns in Gujarat, Rajasthan, Tamil Nadu and Andhra Pradesh.

At Khalsa College, I had very few friends. Raj Kapoor became a close pal and he used to take me to his house in Matunga where his father Prithvirajji and his demure wife kept the doors of the house open all the time as the sons as well as Prithvirajji's brothers and her brothers kept coming and going constantly. Prithvirajji's imposing personality and his warm, agreeable nature made him a popular resident of the locality. In fact, I felt completely relaxed with Raj's family. The liberal and infectiously friendly Kapoors had no hesitation whatsoever in sharing their heartiness with whoever was willing to absorb it. I would find myself voluntarily participating in the feasting and merriment among the young uncles and nephews without a trace of my shyness. As in all good Indian families, the respect Prithvirajji commanded as the head of the family was never lessened by the freedom he gave to his sons and brothers to be their own selves. He did not want them to pretend to be what he wished them to be. He obviously believed in letting his sons grow up as individuals with their individual personality intact.

I have gone into all this detailing for a specific purpose. It is meant to inform those readers, who may have been misled into imagining that Raj Kapoor and I only professed friendship while a deep professional rivalry brewed between us, that ours was not merely a friendship of two individuals in the same profession but a bonding that grew from well-placed trust and respect.

Raj's younger brothers, Shammi and Shashi, were in school then. Raj had only that much interest in soccer as most others in the college. The majority of my college friends were interested in cricket and Raj, too, was more a keen cricket player than a soccer player. But he played soccer too, and was very encouraging when he noticed my dedication and enthusiasm. With his handsome appearance and the twinkle in his blue eyes, he had made friends with many girls and he played with unusual élan when the girls cheered him. He was a born extrovert and charmer.

When he introduced me to the girls from the college and from his class, I spoke less and preferred to let them talk. I always admired the ease with which Raj conducted himself in their company while I hesitated to be in their midst for too long.

I remember an occasion when Raj tested my guts by telling me that a beautiful girl studying in the college wanted to be introduced to me and he pointed to one standing some distance away. He

With Raj Kapoor – lifetime friends.

urged me to go and speak to her. There were quite a few boys and girls around us and Raj kept on urging me to walk up to her. I was extremely embarrassed and I told him I could not do that with so many eyes staring at me. He then said: 'Okay, let us go to the canteen.' He signalled to the girl to come to the canteen and, to my dismay, she was right there at the table that Raj was leading me to. I had to speak to her and I think she realized she would be wasting her time if she chose me to be her friend. She just got up and left after a few minutes.

Raj was determined to rid me of my shyness. One evening he came over to my house and insisted on going to Colaba for a walk on the promenade opposite the Taj Mahal Hotel. I readily agreed. When we alighted from the bus near the Gateway of India, he said: 'Let us take a tonga ride.' I agreed. We boarded a tonga and just when the tongawala was about to prod the horse to get going, Raj stopped him. He noticed two Parsi girls standing on the footpath. They were wearing short frocks and giggling about something. Raj craned his neck and addressed them in the Gujarati that the Parsis speak. The girls turned to him. Very chivalrously and politely he asked them if he could drop them somewhere. They must have thought he was a Parsi, his fair complexion and good looks being such. They said they would appreciate a lift to the nearby Radio Club. He asked them to hop in. I was holding my breath in suspense not knowing what he was up to.

The two girls got in and one of them sat next to Raj while the other sat next to me in the opposite seat. I made ample space for the girl to sit comfortably while Raj did nothing of the sort. He had the girl sitting very close to him and, after a minute, they were talking like long-lost friends. Raj had his hand around the girl's shoulder and she was not in the least bothered. While I began to squirm with embarrassment, Raj was chatting away merrily.

They alighted at the Radio Club and I heaved a sigh of relief. It was Raj's way of getting me to feel relaxed in the company of women. He was a natural charmer and he was anything but shy. Yet he was not disrespectful or uncouth. He was plain mischievous.

As Prithvirajji's son he had an aura around him and was popular in the college campus. He knew he was heading for a profession in which there was no room for reticence or shyness. I did not have a clue about what was in store for me. All I wanted then was to become the country's best soccer player.

Playing cricket with Mohammad Umar Mukri as the wicketkeeper.

I was indeed very serious about preparing for a sports career. Every evening after college, it became a routine for me to go to the grounds behind Metro Cinema (where the Home Guards Division now has its headquarters) and play football with others who were also equally serious about pursuing a career in the sport. There was a shop near Metro from where I purchased my sports shoes and my first cricket bat. Although soccer was my first love, I played cricket too with passion. The athletic side of me was also strong when I participated in school and college athletics. I emerged victorious in every 200 metres race.

Aghaji was proud of my interest in sports and he patted me on my back whenever I brought home a trophy or a certificate for my achievements in that field. He was fine with all that but his dream was to see me in a profession like law or in the civil services.

I personally felt it was premature for me to disclose to Aghaji that I had a desire to become either a soccer champion or a cricketer. I was aware of his dreams for me. I thought maybe I could try my hand at business. In a small way I always tried to help Aghaji in keeping records of the inflow and outflow of revenues. It was not known to me then, as it is with all mortals, that a destiny was being carved for me by the Almighty.

6

THE POONA INTERLUDE

As I sat alone in my room that night, I kept hearing the jailor's words in my subconscious and a sense of pride built up within me that I had spent a night in jail with Gandhiji's followers and, even if it was for a few fleeting moments, I was unafraid of expressing my pride about my country and my compatriots.

I DON'T REMEMBER WHEN EXACTLY BUT I WAS IN MY TEENS WHEN I impulsively set out for Poona (now Pune) from Bombay after a mild disagreement with Aghaji. We did not exchange harsh words or any such thing. He lost his temper over some trivial matter and I still do not know what got into me at that moment. None of us dared to look into his eyes when he was angry and, on that fateful day, I decided to leave home quietly with more hurt and humiliation in my heart than anger or spite.

The Second World War was raging and the family was going through a crisis caused by diminishing income from the fruit business, which was becoming difficult to maintain as the supply from the North West Frontier had dwindled due to strict wartime curbs on trade and transport of non-essential commodities. This was because the train bogies were being used for carrying ammunition and soldiers. All our orchards were in Peshawar and we had no land here that we could call our own. I could sense the insecurity Aghaji was feeling about the future. We were a large family comprising a large brood of daughters and sons. My sweet and kind-hearted Amma was ailing already with symptoms of asthma and my brother Ayub Sahab was being treated for the bone dislocation he had suffered when he fell off a horse while looking around for fresh supplies of apples in Kashmir and had been bedridden ever since. Also, two aunts from Aghaji's side had become permanent fixtures in our home in Bombay as well. They continued to wallow in comfort here, too, as they did in Peshawar while Amma slogged in the kitchen.

I wished to be of some help to Aghaji by generating substantial income but I had no idea how I could do so. My elder sister, Sakina Aapa, was of marriageable age and it was a constant worry to Amma that she lacked the feminine softness that made young women attractive to prospective parents looking for brides for their sons. Sakina Aapa was literally the ruler of the house and had perhaps inherited the despotic ways of my Dadi (paternal grandmother). She argued endlessly with Amma over silly matters, only to have her way and emerge triumphant.

I could see that Aghaji was carrying the burden of an uncertain future in his mind and I should have not behaved the way I did on that morning. I left home with just forty rupees in my pocket, boarding a train to Poona from Bori Bunder station. I found myself seated amidst all sorts of men and women in a crowded third-class compartment. I had never before travelled third class and I hoped no one known to Aghaji had seen me at the railway terminal boarding that compartment because he was always one to give his sons the best in everything and all of us had first-class passes for our local travel. I chose to travel by third class that morning because I had to conserve the limited money I had with me till I found myself gainful employment.

When I alighted at the Poona railway station, I was still hurting inside and was at a loss to figure out why Aghaji had got angry with me the way he did. Had the hurt lessened during the journey, may be I would have bought myself another ticket and returned to the comfort of my home and to my dear Amma who I knew would go crazy with worry over my disappearance.

As Destiny would have it, I was determined to prove to Aghaji that I could survive away from the security of our home and the easy life he had provided us with. Strangely, my elder brother, Noor Sahab, never felt the way I did. He took it for granted that Aghaji would be there always to give him money. It did not bother him at all how hard it was for Aghaji to make the kind of money that was needed to keep us all in comfort. He was of the opinion that the girls in the family did not have to go to school and college. He tried to convince me that I was wrong when I endorsed Aghaji's decision to send our sisters to school and later college to study the subjects they were interested in.

In retrospect, I think I was really adventurous to leave home and head for a city where I knew no one and had no idea of the employment opportunities there. In Poona, I went first to an Iranian café, where I ordered tea and crisp *khari* (salty) biscuits. I was feeling happy that I had chosen a city far away from home where I would be anonymous and could seek any kind of employment. In Bombay, I could not have done that as people would have known me as Sarwar Khan Sahab's son and it would have hurt Aghaji's pride if I had taken up a job not befitting our social status.

I spoke to the Iranian owner of the café in Persian, which made him very happy. I gingerly asked him if he knew anybody who wanted a shop assistant or something. He told me to go to a restaurant that was not far from his café and meet the owners, an Anglo-Indian couple.

It was a beautiful winter morning and the sun was shining through the clouds that seemed to move with haste as if they had to get somewhere urgently. I paused outside the Iranian café to take in the beauty of the day, warming up to the city's bustle, which was of course nothing compared to what we see now in the happening second metropolis of Maharashtra.

It was my habit to walk briskly, so I reached the restaurant in no time. It was a quaint restaurant with its doors open for people who came there regularly, I guessed, for a good English breakfast. The tables were not too close to each other and were covered with clean cloth. There was only one waiter who bustled from one table to another, carrying omelettes and slices of bread. Being an ardent omelette lover even at that young age, the aroma was inviting but I decided to pursue my objective first. I spotted the couple having an animated conversation at the cash counter. I walked up to them but for a few minutes they did not notice me. They were talking about a regular customer who hadn't shown up for some days and I could guess they were talking about a soldier of the British Army.

When they noticed me, I quickly introduced myself without revealing much. I referred to the Iranian café owner who had directed me to them. The lady was plump and matronly. She smiled hesitatingly through the dimples in her freckled cheeks and nudged her tall sturdy husband saying: 'The boy speaks good English. Send him to the canteen contractor.'

Mr Welsely, as I understood his name was, looked at me carefully, paying scant attention to his wife's recommendation, and asked me if I hailed from the North West Frontier Province. When I murmured in the affirmative, he told me that he knew the army canteen contractor who was a native of Peshawar and had settled down in Poona and was a much respected person. This was something I was dreading. Anyone from Peshawar would know Aghaji and that would lead to trouble for me as the news would reach him about my job hunting in Poona. Brushing aside all the wild thoughts crowding my mind, I told Mr Welsely I would be grateful if he could put in a word for me. He agreed and the next thing on my agenda was to find a place to stay, a room may be in a hotel that could give me decent comforts like a clean bed and a bathroom with hot water. I asked Mr Welsely if he could suggest such a hotel. He sent me to one that had the amenities I had mentioned.

Alone in my room that night, I felt the first pang of separation from my parents, especially from Amma. I could imagine her simmering grief and her helplessness. I knew she felt Aghaji shouldn't have got so furious with me but it was not in her nature to question him or oppose him. I never ever saw them exchanging endearments or sitting close to each other. Theirs was a relationship that had layers of implicit understanding, trust, respect and love. Much of what they wished to tell each other about immediate concerns – be it about the financial needs for running the kitchen of a home, which had its doors open all day for visitors who enjoyed Aghaji's company and his hospitality or the social interactions of Noor Sahab – remained unspoken.

I could not sleep for a long time because I was feeling sorry for Amma and missing the soft lullaby she sang for me when I could not fall asleep easily. However, my determination to stand on my feet and earn a good income was foremost in my mind and that sense of purpose helped to dispel all my sadness. Before long I fell asleep.

The next morning, I walked to the office of the canteen contractor with a prayer that he should not recognize me. Lo and behold! I found myself standing in front of the younger brother of Aghaji's friend from Peshawar. He was polite and he asked me to be seated. The gentleman in front of me was Taj Mohammad Khan and his elder brother was Fateh Mohammad Khan OBE (Order of the British Empire). There was no sign of recognition when I introduced myself rather vaguely as a job seeker from Bombay. I was fully aware of his background since Aghaji had often mentioned his name in conversations with friends who came from Poona to visit him.

Taj Mohammad Khan had the usual awe-inspiring bearing of a Pathan and he did not ask me any questions. He gave me a sheet of paper and a pen and dictated a letter to the canteen manager requesting him to employ me as his assistant. I took the dictation obediently and corrected the English, which betrayed his not having much familiarity with the language. He was impressed but he did not want to show it to a rank outsider, I surmised.

The manager was indeed in search of an assistant who could take charge of some of the more irksome burdens he was shouldering in the daily management of the canteen. He was extremely happy that I could converse fluently in English. He showed me my room and confirmed my appointment by shaking my hand vigorously. There was no talk of wages but I presumed it would be decent and sufficient to sustain myself.

My immediate need of getting employment was fulfilled and it gave me a great sense of achievement. Here I was in a city, where I was a stranger, and I had not only found a job but decent accommodation as well. The alienation I felt the previous day was lessening already. There was much to look forward to and I thought I could prove to Aghaji that I wasn't as worthless as he had made me feel with his ranting on the day he lost his temper.

My job entailed several responsibilities bundled together under the head: general management. I had to check the stock of fruits, grocery, vegetables, eggs, milk, cheese and butter every day and get fresh stock from the market, taking care not to buy old stock that shopkeepers tried to palm off as new. I had to ensure that the kitchen and its environment were clean and hygienic. The poolside and the cleanliness of the water in the pool also had to be attended to. The bar that Army Club members frequented in the summer afternoons had to be well stocked with barrels of beer and other alcoholic beverages for the men and fruit punches for the ladies. Finally, I had to maintain registers and account books for cash inflows and outflows. By the time the canteen manager showed me around and listed my responsibilities, I had half a mind to ask him what was left for him to do as manager if I was being entrusted with all the tasks he had enumerated. Better wisdom prevailed and I followed him meekly while he talked in a jumble of English and Urdu, which was exasperating for me as a listener.

I started off with great confidence since I could judge the quality of the fruits, vegetables, cheese, butter, eggs and so on with ease. There was something fishy going on between the vendors and the manager about which I came to know by and by when I rejected some of the stuff that was of lesser quality but was being purchased at a higher price. The beer in the barrels was being mixed with buckets of ice and cold water to augment the quantity and I brought the matter to the manager's attention dutifully. He advised me to overlook it and, without stopping to explain why, he went about doing whatever he was pretending to do.

It did not take long for me to realize that I should keep my distance from whatever the manager was doing, legitimately or illegitimately. I think he appreciated my feigned ignorance of his doings and, in return, he was extremely nice to me. He did not mind the attention I got from the colonels, brigadiers, majors and captains who frequented the club and ordered snacks during the day and reappeared in the evenings for drinks. A part of the club was open only to the officers and another part in the rear was open to the Tommies (British soldiers who were not officers). The ladies who accompanied the officers sometimes changed to swimwear and plunged into the swimming pool. Initially I did not know what to do – whether I should be around or not when the ladies in their swimsuits splashed around in the pool. I came from a conservative background, from a family where the ladies were virtually covered from head to toe and showed only their beautiful faces and hands. I realized that the ladies did not mind my presence at all and the officers were unaware of my embarrassment. They were all very fond of me and called me Chico – a name my wife Saira still uses when she wants to flirt with me in her own refined manner. I learned that Chico in Spanish meant a youngster or a lad.

There were officers who called me by my name, Yousuf Khan, pronounced with a strong British accent. They were at first very curious to know how I could speak English the way the language should be spoken. They liked the way I dressed immaculately in clean, ironed trousers and full-sleeved shirts. From the time I can remember I had a fetish for wearing well-stitched trousers and full-sleeved shirts of good quality material. The friendliness of the officers gave me solace and a wonderful feeling of belonging.

I mingled freely with the officers and the Tommies. I observed that the Tommies would get drunk and they did not even know that the beer was diluted. There were bathrooms at the club where the

Tommies used to bathe and it was such a shock for poor me to see them undress in front of one another without the slightest hesitation. They would often stand stark naked under the shower with the doors open. They would often tell me to come along and join them. One hot summer day, one of the Tommies got sozzled and he dragged me to the bathroom and forced me to take off my clothes and take a shower.

It was a bit of a shock and a huge embarrassment because I was extremely conscious of my hairy body, especially the hair on my hands, which would fall limp on one side when water fell over them and so would all the hair on the rest of my body. Hence, I never liked the idea of exposing my body. It is for this very reason that I have had a preference for long-sleeved shirts.

My hairiness was also the despair of mosquitoes, which got entangled in the thick clusters on my hands and legs. I would see the helpless creatures trying to escape from what could be like an African jungle to them and I always felt sorry for the poor insects and helped them fly out. So in all fairness to the unsuspecting mosquitoes and the aesthetic senses of whoever might set eyes on my ape-like appearance in a swimming pool, I had sensibly decided not to ever descend into one.

There was a lot of camaraderie in the rank and file of the British Army while the officers were reserved and extremely gentlemanly. An idea occurred to me one day when the regular chef was absent and the manager asked me if I could come up with something as a major general was having a few important guests for tea. I told him I could make sandwiches with reasonable success. He asked me to go ahead, but warned me to be careful to use fresh bread and butter and other ingredients. I assured him that I would make sure everything was fresh even as I wondered how I could ensure that with all the conniving going on between him and the vendors.

Fortunately, the sandwiches were a hit. The guests of the major general praised the manager, who received the compliments smiling broadly. That was when the idea occurred to me to request him to get sanction from the contractor and the club's office bearers to let me set up a sandwich counter at the club in the evenings. Since he was very pleased with me and he knew I had knowledge of what was going on between him and several suppliers, he sent my request to the concerned authorities with his recommendation and permission was granted.

My sandwich business opened very successfully. All the sandwiches were sold out in no time and the latecomers were disappointed when they found out that the sandwiches were very tasty and they had missed the chance to enjoy them. On the second day, I brought out a large table and covered it with white, starched cloth and laid out fresh fruits that I had selected carefully from the market along with sandwiches and chilled lemonade. The second day was a bigger success and, in less than a week's time, I was counting the rewards with a sense of joy that comes when one's hard work yields unexpected results.

The officers were now friendlier and they would ask me about my family and it astonished them that Amma could deliver so many children and still be alive. When I began making money from the sandwich business, I found the courage to send a telegram to my brother Ayub Sahab informing him that I was in Poona and he may please tell Amma that 'I am well and working in the British Army canteen'. My telegram must have given Amma much relief. The following week, Ayub Sahab arrived without prior intimation and he brought dry fruits and *sooji* (semolina) halwa prepared by Amma for me. He had also brought some money, which Amma had saved from her household allowances. I was so happy to see Ayub Sahab, who couldn't hide the tears glistening in his eyes when he and the attendant who came with him met me at the reception counter of the club.

I told Ayub Sahab that I was comfortable and doing well and I did not need the money Amma had sent through him. He could see for himself how everybody knew me and I was well fed, hale and hearty. If there was anything I did not have, it was the warmth of my family. I was always very comfortable talking to Ayub Miyan. He and I shared a brotherly bond that was strong and deep. I poured out my heart to him, talking to him while sitting on a bench in a park nearby as the sun went down inch by inch on the horizon in a blaze of orange and gold, while the birds flew hurriedly into the branches of trees creating a cacophony of twitters and screeches, perhaps signalling to one another that one more day was done. I recounted to Ayub Sahab how I had set out impulsively and how I felt remorseful about not confiding in him or Amma. I told him how much I wanted to be of support to Aghaji, given the difficult situation he was in. Ayub Sahab understood and, sensitive as he was, he just listened and spoke little.

He returned to Bombay the next morning and I went back to work after seeing him off at the railway station, somewhat less burdened and more relaxed. At the club a surprise was awaiting me. Corporal Marlowe, who was known to me at Deolali, had arrived on duty in Poona. As I set eyes on him in the club, standing at the bar with his drink in hand, looking as severe as he always did, a torrent of gruesome memories flashed before my mind. At Deolali he was known as 'the dog man'. My school friends and I took to our heels when we ran into him because we imagined he was some kind of an ogre and not a human being. His stocky figure, even in the distance as we returned from school in the late afternoons, frightened us. The reason was that he had the regular habit of aiming his revolver at any stray dog he saw and shooting the poor, unprepared animal dead in one shot. After the dog stopped breathing, he would take a knife out of a bag he kept in the rear of his jeep and tiptoe up to the dead animal, cut its tail and put it into the bag.

I was too young to be convinced about his action when Chacha Ummer explained to me that he was doing so because stray dogs were not allowed to wander in the cantonment premises and in the vicinity and that he was cutting the tails to keep a count of the dogs he had shot and to account for the bullets he had used. It was an eerie memory that I had successfully erased from my mind as I grew up and we moved back to Bombay.

When the bar tender called out to me to introduce the corporal, I felt the same tingle in my spine that I used to whenever I bolted to hide and watch him drive past in his jeep on Deolali's rugged roads. He greeted me without a smile and walked away.

Initially, the corporal had no intention of being friendly. However, he began to show signs of thawing as the days passed and, before long, we were on very friendly terms as he realized that all the officers liked me and treated me well. His obsession with killing of stray dogs continued in Poona, too, but it was not as regular as it was in Deolali since stray dogs could rarely be sighted near the cantonment. He stayed nearby and I noticed he had a pretty daughter who came with him to the club often. The girl had something going with a junior officer who gave her enough encouragement to be seen with him alone at late hours outside the club. I knew what was going on and kept a discreet distance from them.

My room within the club premises was nice and comfortable, though small. It had a glass window, which provided a clear view of the hall where the officers gathered in the evenings when there was a party hosted by one of the seniors. There would be music and I could see the officers and their wives dancing to it. The officers would be wearing elegant suits with smart Indian silk ties that were bought at exclusive shops. I wondered if I would ever possess one such suit. Little did I know then that one day I would possess the finest suits a man of good taste could buy and own! I sometimes reflect, when I see the array of garments in my wardrobe, perhaps my preference for suits as formal wear has something to do with the longing I had during the Army Club days.

One day, after I closed my sandwich stall, I decided to go to my room for a nap. I walked towards my room lazily and, to my surprise, I found the door of my room half open. A couple of days earlier there had been a burglary, which created a commotion and the police had to be called to investigate. I feared the same burglar had broken into my room perhaps and made away with my hard-earned savings. I quickened my pace and walked to my room. The sight before me was unbelievable. The corporal's daughter was sprawled on my bed completely naked!

I stood frozen at the door and she saw me from the inviting position she had taken knowingly. I turned and almost ran to the manager's cabin, my heart almost bursting with anger, disgust and fear. I informed him about what I had seen and he immediately accompanied me to my room, giving vent to his suppressed suspicions about the girl, her clandestine affair and her weird mental state. Fortunately for me, he knew me well by then and was certain that I was telling the truth. By the time we reached my room, the girl was gone. The manager looked at me, his eyebrow raised questioningly. I held him by his elbow and made him turn around and walk back with me. I had this lurking feeling that she had headed for the poolside. We reached the pool and there she was, standing on the raised board above the pool sans her clothes and was swaying as if she was on a dance floor. The wind was blowing her hair over her face and the sight frightened the manager as much as it scared me because she could have fallen headlong into the pool and created a panic situation where the whole club would have unnecessarily come into the spotlight. For a teenager, I think I had quite some maturity as I remained cool and nudged the manager to act fast and get her down from the springboard where she was standing almost on the edge. Brought up strictly by God-fearing Pathan parents and grandparents, the only women I knew were my Dadi, Amma, my sisters (including cousins) and my aunts, who were always covered from head to toe in the typical attire that the Muslim women of the North West Frontier wore virtually throughout the day. Here I was staring at a nude girl in the flush of youth as one could see. It wasn't as if I was not libidinous as most young chaps are at that age. It was just that the whole episode evoked embarrassment and shock more than all the normal responses of youth and approaching manhood in a robust teenager.

The manager had the presence of mind to send two women staff members (who were in the premises doing the cleaning) to bring her down with a blanket wrapped around her. She was completely unaware of what was happening and submitted herself to be taken away by the cleaning women. I don't know where they took her and what happened to her after that incident. The manager did not tell me anything and I did not ask him any questions because I thought it best to close the chapter and forget about it.

As mentioned earlier, it was wartime and there used to be discussions among the senior officers about India's neutral stand in the war. One evening an officer asked me to give my opinion on this topic and as to why we were fighting for independence from British rule so relentlessly while we chose to stay unaligned in the war. I gave him what I thought was a good reply and he asked me if I would make a speech before the club members the next evening when the attendance would be full. I agreed and spent the night preparing my speech. I had studied the British Constitution as a student at Anjuman Islam School and put that knowledge to good use in preparing a speech that outlined our superiority as a nation of hard-working, truthful and non-violent people.

While making my speech in the club, I emphasized that our struggle for freedom was a legitimate one and it was they, the British administrators, who were consciously misrepresenting the civil laws of their Constitution and creating the consequences.

My speech evoked genuine applause and I felt elated but the enjoyment of my success was short-lived. To my surprise, a bunch of police officers arrived on the scene and handcuffed me, saying I had to be arrested for my anti-British views. I was taken away to the Yerawada Jail and locked up in a cell with some very decent-looking men, who I was told, were satyagrahis (followers of Mahatma Gandhi who offered passive resistance). On my arrival, the jailor referred to me as a 'Gandhiwala'; I could not figure out why he was using this term for me till I heard the policemen refer to all the inmates of the cell as Gandhiwalas. It was their way of herding us together as followers of Gandhiji.

I exchanged pleasantries with my fellow inmates and they told me that Sardar Vallabhbhai Patel (one of the prominent leaders of the freedom movement) was in one of the cells and they were all on a hunger strike along with him. I don't know why, but I too felt I should fast with them. So I refused the food that was brought for me in an unclean plate. The night was long and pangs of hunger kept me awake till dawn. In the morning, I heard the sound of boots approaching my cell and soon the jailor was standing before me accompanied by an army major. 'Here is your Gandhiwala,' he said sarcastically. The major had come to release me and take me back. He was a good chap with whom I had played badminton when I could find time for the sport on an occasional Sunday.

As soon as I reached the club, I asked for food and it amused everybody around me when I told them I had fasted all night. It might have sounded funny to them but for me it meant being a Gandhiwala at least for one night. As I sat alone in my room that night, I kept hearing the jailor's words in my subconscious and a sense of pride built up within me that I had spent a night in jail with Gandhiji's followers and, even if it was for a few fleeting moments, I was unafraid of expressing my pride about my country and my compatriots.

7

THE RETURN OF THE PRODIGAL

He was happy that one of his sons had the acumen to carry on the fruit trade. However, something inside me was giving me the feeling that it was all very well to take over the mantle from Mohammad Sarwar Khan, the successful fruit merchant, and carry on the family trade, but this was not what I was made for.

AS THE WAR SITUATION WORSENED, SOME INEVITABLE CHANGES occurred. The office bearers of the club changed and the contractor, Taj Mohammad Khan, was replaced by someone whom the new executive committee chose. The manager too did not wish to continue and he advised me to move on. By that time, I had earned a bundle of currency notes, which I counted for the first time. I had a good five thousand rupees, which was a great deal of money those days. The month of Ramzaan (when Muslims are supposed to keep a *roza* or fast from sunrise to sunset) was coming to a close as I found out from the maulvi sahab (religious scholar) and others I kept in touch with at the local mosque. I thought it was time to return to Bombay and seek a job that Aghaji would approve of or assist him in the running of the fruit business. I was now a far more confident and free-spirited young man than I was earlier and I wondered how I would explain

102

my going away to Aghaji. I was certain that he would be unforgiving till Amma pacified him in her own gentle way. In fact, had I not gone away in a huff over the trivial incident and Aghaji's rage over it, the whole situation would have returned to normal the next day itself, with Amma's winsome persuasive abilities coming to the fore in blowing the crisis over. It was sheer Destiny that I did not give her or myself a chance to normalize the situation.

I was now happy that I had ventured out on my own and gained some valuable experience but, as I had tasted a little bit of 'freedom', I was unsure whether I would be able to continue to submit to Aghaji's will and do everything as he wished.

I returned to Bombay a few days before Eid-ul Fitr, which is celebrated with gaiety and bonhomie after a month of *roza* on the sighting of the crescent moon. My elder brother Ayub Sahab knew the date of my arrival but he kept it a secret to give a surprise to Amma. My younger brother Nasir and my sisters were also aware that the prodigal was coming home but they too remained tight-lipped. My youngest sister was still a child and knew nothing more than to cry for her feeds when she was hungry. When I climbed the stairs to our house on the fourth floor, I could hear my heartbeats loud and clear. The familiar sounds of the street, the nosy neighbours staring as they always did and the screeching horns of the few cars that plied on the street and begged cool, indifferent pedestrians to move out of the way were all so welcoming and lovely for once. I realized how much I had missed all these sights and sounds while I was away in a city where I imagined I was revelling in my anonymity, whereas, in reality, I was subconsciously pining for the warm, indescribable security of my family and familiar surroundings.

When I entered the house, my younger sisters first saw me and they ran to give Amma the news. She came out hurriedly and I stood transfixed where I was, unable to take a step forward because I was trembling with relief and happiness. In the next instant, while I embraced Amma, who was talking inaudibly in the din my sisters and brothers were making, I heard footsteps near the door, which I feared were Aghaji's. It turned out to be Chacha Ummer who had heard from the men on the first floor about my reappearance and had come up to verify. To put it briefly, the reunion was of the nature one saw in the good family films we used to make at one time except that nobody knew who was saying what to whom and why somebody was laughing and somebody was clamouring to be heard. Amma's sobs turned to gentle laughter and then her habitual concern surfaced as she asked me if I was on *roza*. I was not, I told her. There was no way I could observe the fast in the club where the discipline and abstinence expected of one during the holy month of Ramzaan were hard to observe, thanks to the irregular hours of work.

I soon found myself sitting with Amma in her room after all the months of separation from her. It took me some moments to believe that I was actually back home and sitting by Amma's side on her nice, big bed. She was looking pale and tired, her lace-bordered dupatta covering her jet-black hair combed back neatly. I remembered that it was the same dupatta that was covering her head on the day that I had set out for Poona. I had got her the lace from a place close to Crawford Market from where English and Parsi ladies bought borders and laces to add elegance to their attire. Amma was least bothered about the glamour of her dress but my aunts were extremely choosy and they always picked on me to go to the cloth stores and get them yards and yards of silk and cotton for their attire. They liked my selections but they always complained that I brought the best colours for Amma and not for them. The fact was that I always chose colours that suited Amma's complexion and, despite her indifference to what she wore, she always looked elegant and beautiful.

As I sat by her side, I thought it was the right time to take out the money I had earned and give her a surprise. I opened my bag and took out the neat packet containing all the money I had earned and I placed it in her soft hands while she looked at me curiously. I waited anxiously for her to express her happiness as she untied the packet carefully. She looked at the bundle of currency notes and looked up at me with worry and fear writ large on her face.

'What is this? Where did you get it from?' she asked, her low voice betraying her anxiety. I was hardly prepared for this reaction. I told her it was the money I had earned by dint of hard work and enterprise. She stared hard at me and, without saying a word, she went up to the mantelshelf where the Holy Quran was kept and beckoned to me. She asked me to swear on the Quran that it was money earned honourably by me. Smarting inside and trying hard not to let my hurt show, I put my hand on the holy book and took a solemn oath. I could see that she was satisfied.

Aghaji came home as usual in the evening, in time to break the Ramzaan fast with the family. I was in my room by then, bathed and wearing my crisp white trousers and shirt, ready for the repast my mother had prepared. I could hear her telling Aghaji that I was back and I heard him say he knew about it. It was typical of Aghaji to pretend to be unemotional and detached. His warmth and concern surfaced only once when Amma had a serious attack of asthma and she was choking and gasping for breath. He began yelling for someone to rush and fetch the doctor who lived across the street. His face was then a picture of helpless alarm and I still can recall the tall strapping figure bending to hold my frail Amma in his arms.

If you can recall the famous scene in *Mashaal*,* I must tell you that, while going through my rehearsals, I drew my emotions for the rendering of the scene, shot over four nights in a row, from the memory of that episode and the agony of Aghaji in his urgency to get instant medical help.

Aghaji and I met cordially as if nothing had changed. It was a relief to me, to say the least. In less than a week after Eid, which we celebrated with the usual camaraderie by inviting our friends from

*Film maker Yash Chopra's *Mashaal* (1984). The scene depicts me on a rainy night desperately seeking help to take my seriously ill wife (played by Waheeda Rehman) to hospital by trying to stop any vehicle that comes along, but in vain.

other communities to share a festive meal with us, Aghaji was talking to me about an apple orchard in Nainital* that was on sale. He wanted me to go there and see if I could negotiate and close the deal for a certain figure. It was a welcome situation for me because this was the first time my father was talking business with me. Though he and I never exchanged a word about the Poona episode, it was obvious from the way he engaged me in the conversation about finding newer avenues for procuring fruits for the business that he now felt I had a yen for business. He also discussed an idea he had for canning peaches and exporting them.

Indeed, I was personally convinced, after my success with the sandwich stall, that I could do business and earn handsome profits. As I listened to my father's idea of buying an orchard in Nainital that was apparently going for a song, I was also toying with the idea of taking up a completely new line of business: feather pillows. I had made contact with a man who was ready to make me a partner and give me a substantial commission for selling such pillows to the gentry. I accepted his offer and deposited the earnest money.

After losing some money, I found out soon enough that the business of selling pillows wasn't up my alley and thought it was a better idea to go to Nainital and do as my father wanted me to. I went there and met the owner of the orchard, a kind man who respected Aghaji and was keen to sell his land and trees to us. I could see that more than half the orchard had been destroyed by locusts and what remained was hardly worth buying. I told him we would have to negotiate the price. He said: 'Of course, I understand.' I had no idea what price to quote and sensing my inexperience in the business, he told me: 'Son, I will take a rupee from you as token and we will close the deal. After you go back Khan Sahab can offer me whatever he deems good for the property.'

I returned home with the rupee and told Aghaji about the property. He was very pleased. He was now getting the feeling that I was a good businessman and asked me to keep the accounts and maintain

---

*A hill station then in United Provinces and now in the state of Uttarakhand.

registers and do all that he thought I was capable of doing. He was happy that one of his sons had the acumen to carry on the fruit trade. However, something inside me was giving me the feeling that it was all very well to take over the mantle from Mohammad Sarwar Khan, the successful fruit merchant, and carry on the family trade, but this was not what I was made for.

8

THE TURNING POINT

His dark hair was combed back and he smiled through his eyes at me. Devika Rani introduced me, saying I had just joined as an actor. He held my hand in a warm handshake that marked the beginning of a friendship that was to last an entire lifetime between us. He was Ashok Kumar, who soon became Ashok Bhaiyya (brother) to me.

ONE MORNING, I WAS WAITING AT THE CHURCHGATE STATION from where I was to take a local train to Dadar (in central Bombay) to meet somebody who had a business offer to make to me. It had something to do with wooden cots to be supplied to army cantonments. There, I spotted Dr Masani, a psychologist who had once come to Wilson College, where I had been a student for a year. Dr Masani had then given a lecture on vocational choices for arts students. At Churchgate, I went up to him and introduced myself. He knew me well since he was one of Aghaji's acquaintances. 'What are you doing here Yousuf?' he asked me. I told him I was in search of a job but since there was none in sight, I was trying to do some business. He said he was going to Malad (in the western suburbs) to meet the owners of Bombay Talkies (a movie studio) and it would not be a bad idea if I went with him and met them. 'They may have a job for you,' he mentioned casually. I pondered for an instant and then I joined him, giving up the idea of going to Dadar.

I had a railway first-class season ticket only up to Bandra. (Malad is about 18 km beyond Bandra.) Dr Masani knew the ticket checker, who gave me an extension chit up to Malad. Though Bombay Talkies was not very far from the Malad station, he, nevertheless, took a cab to the studio since it was almost lunchtime and he was afraid that Mrs Devika Rani, the boss of Bombay Talkies, may go home for lunch.

I had never ever seen a film studio in my life, not even in photographs. I had heard of Bombay Talkies from Raj Kapoor who spoke about it as the studio where films starring his father Prithvirajji were shot. Bombay Talkies was a complete surprise. It was spread over several acres and there was a garden with a fountain in it. The office building looked more like a lovely bungalow and less like a typical office structure. When Dr Masani entered, there was warm recognition from Devika Rani who offered him a seat and looked at me wonderingly while I waited to be introduced. She was a picture of elegance, and, when Dr Masani introduced me, she greeted me with a namaste and asked me to pull up a chair and be seated, her gaze fixed on me as if she had a thought running in her mind about me. She introduced us to Amiya Chakraborthy (a famous director, as I later came to know), who was seated on a sofa. She asked me if I had sufficient knowledge of Urdu. I replied in the affirmative and Dr Masani intervened to give her my background, going back to my antecedents in Peshawar and told her about Aghaji and the business we were in. She listened with interest and I observed her face, which had a natural glow and the flush of good health. I wondered what sort of a job she was going to give me since she was so keen to know about my proficiency in the Urdu language.

She turned to me and, with a beautiful smile, asked me the question that was to change the course of my life completely and unexpectedly. She asked me whether I would become an actor and

Devika Rani.

accept employment by the studio for a monthly salary of Rs 1250. For a moment I did not know what to say. I looked at Dr Masani, who was equally surprised but was not showing it. He merely shrugged and I knew it was a silent hint for me to take a call and give her a reply. I was never one to lose time in futile thinking. So I returned her charming smile and told her that it was indeed kind of her to consider me for the job of an actor but I had no experience and knew nothing about the art. What's more, I had seen only one film, which was a war documentary screened for the army personnel in Deolali. She was quick with her reasoning. She asked: 'How experienced are you in the fruit trade of your family?' I told her that as I was learning, I could not claim much experience. She then said: 'There you are. If you can take pains to learn about fruits and fruit cultivation you can surely take pains to learn the craft of film making and acting. I need a young, good-looking, educated actor and I can see that you possess the qualifications to become a good actor.'

It was soon lunchtime and she asked us graciously if we would care to join her. Dr Masani declined politely and we took leave of her. On the way back, Dr Masani did not talk much. The rattling sound of the speeding train and the conjecture that I needed to contemplate over the offer that was least expected by both of us must have silenced him. It no longer worried me that I did not know anything about cinema and acting. As the train rocked me to a state of relaxation, I was actually feeling good and thankful that a job with a handsome remuneration was waiting for my acceptance.

On reaching home I told Ayub Sahab about the offer. He found it hard to believe that Devika Rani had offered me Rs 1250 per month. He said it must be the amount she would pay annually. He said he knew that Raj Kapoor was getting a monthly salary of Rs 170. I felt Ayub was right. How could she give me such a whopping amount every month? And, if it was for a year, I felt it was not worth accepting as it would not ease Aghaji's burden. It was of utmost urgency for me to earn enough to augment Aghaji's income from the fruit trade.

Apart from Ayub Sahab, nobody in the house knew about the episode. Noor Sahab (my eldest brother) was least concerned and lived in a world of his own. He was seen in the house only at meal times. I thought it would be decent on my part to tell Dr Masani about my decision, so I went to his house at Churchgate and told him that Rs 1250 annually was rather meagre for all the travelling I had to do every day to Malad by the electric train and for all the pains I had to take to initiate myself into a challenging profession. Dr Masani was certain that the salary offered was on a *monthly* basis. He volunteered to ascertain the figure from Devika Rani and made a phone call to her and, from the nods and smiles he was giving as he held the receiver to his ear, I could understand that she was telling him something that pleased him immensely. When he put the receiver down, he told me she had made the offer of Rs 1250 per month and not annually because she thought I held great promise and she should make an offer that I would accept gladly.

The next day I met Dr Masani at the Churchgate station after lunch. The year was 1942 and the day was a Friday (I cannot recall the date). I left home quietly after prayers and a good lunch. Nobody knew where I was heading.

The gates of Bombay Talkies somehow looked more inviting and welcoming that afternoon as the watchman opened them for our taxi to enter. In her office, Devika Rani was alone, seated at the desk, which was always clean and uncluttered. The conversation was brief because she knew I had come to accept the offer. She said the employment formalities and the paper work would be done by one Mr Iyer, her assistant. She was emphatic that I should join at the earliest and get into the stride of the job. She said it would be nice if I could come to the studio the next day and meet some of the people I would be working with. My hesitation to talk about money prevented me from reconfirming the salary, though the prospect of earning the four-digit figure, which was a big achievement those days, had drawn me to a profession I knew my father had little respect for. On more than one occasion I had heard him tell Raj Kapoor's grandfather, Dewan Basheshwarnath Kapoor, jokingly that it was a pity his son and grandsons couldn't find anything other than *nautanki** as their profession.

Tea arrived for us in a tray covered with a starched white cloth bordered with English lace. The tea cups were handed to us by a neatly dressed office boy whose good training had taught him to pour the brew and the milk with a steady hand without spilling a drop anywhere. It was wonderful to see an Indian boy handle the service with the finesse that English butlers and valets thought they alone could manage.

When I returned home late in the evening, I told Amma I had found myself a job that would get me a pay packet of Rs 1250 every month, which would take care of her kitchen expenses as well as the education of my younger brothers and sisters. There were a lot of miscellaneous expenses and some money could be set aside for that, too. She wanted to know what job it was that was so paying. I assured her it was a respectable job and I had got it because of my strong proficiency in the Urdu language. She seemed happy with that reply since it sounded like a job of some consequence if it required proficiency in Urdu especially during the turbulent times we were living in, when the Second World War was raging and our freedom struggle had gathered great momentum.

The next day dawned like any other. I got dressed and left home quietly. I reached the studio on time at 9 a.m. Devika Rani welcomed me and took me personally to the floor where preparation for a

---

Nautanki is a drama form from Uttar Pradesh. It also means acting.

With Ashok Kumar – lifelong friends.

shooting was going on. She led me up to a man who was very well dressed and looked distinguished. He looked familiar and I recalled having seen the handsome countenance on posters and hoardings near Crawford Market. His dark hair was combed back and he smiled through his eyes at me. Devika Rani introduced me, saying I had just joined as an actor. He held my hand in a warm handshake that marked the beginning of a friendship that was to last an entire lifetime between us. He was Ashok Kumar, who soon became Ashok Bhaiyya (brother) to me. (He passed away on 10 December 2001.)

Ashok Kumar came out of the floor and called out to one of the boys to open his make-up room. As the boy ran to fetch the door keys, I recognized another young man walking towards us. That was Raj Kapoor, who was justly shocked to see me there. He was his wonderful jovial self as he gathered from me that I had joined the studio as an actor. 'Does your father know?' he asked me mischievously. I did not reply because both Ashok Bhaiyya and Devika Rani were standing by our side and they were pleasantly surprised to learn that Raj and

I knew each other. Raj gave a short account of our football days at
Khalsa College, which made Devika Rani observe: 'That's indeed
nice. It's a game I wished I could play like the boys at school.'

Devika Rani left us to chat with one another and walked briskly
back to her office. There was an informality in the way Ashok Kumar
and Raj interacted, which I liked. It was not like an office where you
addressed somebody senior as 'sir' and spoke only when spoken
to. Here Raj was talking continuously, describing our escapades at
Khalsa College and I thought he would give away the secret that I
had joined the studio without Aghaji's knowledge. It was something
I did not want the people in the studio to know just then because
it would have created an impression of my doing things secretly.
Fortunately, he did not bring up the subject and I was relieved. There
was no doubt that Raj was happy to see me and welcome me into the
profession. He knew how painfully shy I used to be in college and he
must have wondered how I would fit into a profession that was not
for shy, reserved people.

At the studio the next day, I was introduced to one Shah Nawaz
Khan. He came across as a crude, rough man to me. He asked me if I
was a Pathan and when I replied in the affirmative, he bellowed and
laughed as if I had told him something incredibly funny. He said he
knew about my being a Pathan from the colour of my cheeks and my
aloofness. So, if he knew it, what was so funny that he had to laugh
like a neighing horse, I wanted to ask him. He next asked me how
many brothers I had. I told him I had five. He went into a fit again
and I was sure I was wasting time with a crazy man. He said: '*Tum
agar chhe bhai hote to mera kya bigaad lete?*' (This can be roughly
translated as: 'Even if you are six brothers, what can you do to me?')
Now it was getting too much and too personal, so I just got up and
went to see Devika Rani and told her how stupidly the man had
spoken to me. She did not say anything; she simply patted me on the
back and sent me home.

After my departure, she must have given him a piece of her mind because, the next day, he was apologetic and said he wasn't meaning to offend me. Such jibes were common at Bombay Talkies, he added. I wondered if he was telling me the truth because the people I had met like Ashok Bhaiyya and David Abraham (a noted character actor) were ever so civilized and soft-spoken. I realized that David knew what Shah Nawaz had told me. We were a few days away from Bakhri Eid. 'Do you exchange greeting cards on Eid?' David asked us when he saw me avoiding Shah Nawaz.

On the day of Eid, I received a greeting card from Shah Nawaz. It was accompanied by a small yellow packet with a tiny note: this is for your pubic hair. I was speechless with horror. At first, I wanted to go and show the note to Devika Rani. Then I thought it would be very stupid of me to do so. I did not show any trace of anger and I just left for home. When I arrived at the studio the next day, I went up to David and I left the small yellow packet with my pubic hair on his table along with the card and the note. When David saw the materials on his table, he called Shah Nawaz and showed him the mess. They laughed and laughed for quite a while. After that, Shah Nawaz told me: 'Now you are one of us. We thought you needed some ragging to make you overcome your reticence.' He spontaneously embraced me and assured me that there wouldn't be any more ragging.

9

LIGHTS, CAMERA, ACTION!

I ... became aware that an actor needed to strengthen his instincts because the duality between the real and unreal cannot be sorted out by the mind, which is more concerned with truth and logic in any normal situation. The mind will always tell you this is nonsense .... It is only instinct that will help you to absorb what you have to absorb from the script and drive you to render a performance coated with realism and conviction despite the knowledge of it all being fiction and drama.

$\mathscr{B}$OMBAY TALKIES WAS THE BEST THING THAT HAPPENED TO ME at that juncture in my life. I couldn't have found a better job than the one offered to me by Devika Rani. Sure, I had no clue what acting in front of a camera was. It was something to be studied and learned and practised. What was delightful was the ambience of the studio, which was a mix of what one would seek and find in a university or any educational institution and what one would expect to find in a fantasy world straight out of one's fertile imagination of houses, façades, artefacts, streets, gardens and so on, which I got to know were the permanent sets created for the shootings. It interested me to know how all that I was seeing would be used in shooting a film. So, for the first two months, Devika Rani made sure that I was present at all the shootings. I arrived at the studio every day in the morning and went straight to those sets where shooting was going on.

Ashok Bhaiyya was shooting for the final portions of *Kismet* (released in 1943) those days and there was a lot of activity going on as Gyan Mukherjee, the director, and his assistants moved the equipment on the sets according to the lighting pattern. Ashok Bhaiyya was a very successful star as I came to know from the assistants. His 1941 film *Jhoola*, opposite Leela Chitnis, had become a huge success and the same director was making *Kismet*. So, the excitement was palpable and it was all so new to me because I had no idea how a film became a huge success and earned money for the studio and the producer.

I realized I was in the presence of a very well-known star when Ashok Bhaiyya came on the set and began talking cheerfully to the director, Gyan Mukherjee, and the producer, Shashadhar Mukherjee (popularly known as S. Mukherjee), with whom he appeared to be at ease. When he saw me, he came up to me and began talking informally as if we had known each other for years. He said he knew why I was there. 'It is all very simple,' he continued, as he walked with me to the door and stepped into the open area outside the studio floor. He called for chairs and the studio hands came hurriedly to attend to him. He went on: 'You are a handsome man and I can see that you are eager to learn. It's very simple. You just do what you would do in the situation if you were really in it. If you act it will be acting and it will look very silly.'

He noticed the confusion on my face and began to laugh. There was genuine warmth in his laughter and his words gradually began to make sense to me. In the scene that I had observed the previous day, sitting unobtrusively with the assistants of the cameraman behind the camera, he had laughed exactly the way he had just done.

He reacted to a response very naturally as he just did to my puzzled look.

Ashok Bhaiyya soon introduced me to Shashadhar Mukherjee Sahab, who was his brother-in-law. (Ashok Bhaiyya's sister Sati Devi was married to Mukherjee Sahab and that explained the informality between them.) Ashok Bhaiyya's nature was such that he did not resist friendship with strangers and went all out to make things easy and comfortable for everybody in the studio from the canteen boy to the technicians and actors who worked with him. I met him every day and he treated me like a younger brother who had to be led and protected. My shyness and reticence began to recede in his company and his friendliness and affection for me were a fillip for me to be on the sets while the shooting of *Kismet* was going on.

I quite liked what I was watching and I thought it was more interesting and absorbing than office drudgery or the work Aghaji would have given me to do in the fruit business.

Ashok Bhaiyya lived nearby and so did S. Mukherjee Sahab. It was a period of transition for Bombay Talkies as Devika Rani, who had been managing the studio after the death of her husband and co-founder of the studio, Himanshu Rai (on 16 May 1940), was planning to marry the famous Soviet painter Svetoslav Roerich and leave the management of the studio in the hands of S. Mukherjee Sahab and Amiya Chakraborthy.

She used to visit the sets during shootings and give pertinent suggestions. She had substantial knowledge of everything related to film making, having worked as a trainee at the Universum Film Aktiengesselschaft (UFA) in Germany. She was not only trained in acting but was also well versed with the art of make-up, set design and costume design. Always elegantly attired, she radiated a dignified charm when she interacted with all of us. She was happy I was bonding very well with Ashok Bhaiyya and S. Mukherjee Sahab. Most of the personnel kept quiet when she made her entry during the breaks in filming and the German cameramen, who were handling the cinematography, talked to her in their mother tongue and it was delightful to hear her reply in the same language.

Ashok Bhaiyya was learning French those days as a pastime to add to the growing list of foreign languages he could converse in. He used to join in the conversation between Devika Rani and the German cinematographers while S. Mukherjee Sahab and I would stand by silently.

By now I had established a reasonable rapport with S. Mukherjee Sahab who was a refined and polished gentleman. He asked me one afternoon if I could recite Urdu poetry well. I replied that I could recite Persian verses too with ease since I had grown up in an environment where my educated aunts and uncles enjoyed poetic exchanges in Persian and Urdu when they got together in our house in Peshawar. He nodded and said: 'Today, when we meet for tea after pack-up I am going to egg you on to recite some Persian and Urdu verses. You oblige me casually. I want to see how he reacts.' I knew S. Mukherjee Sahab was referring to Ashok Bhaiyya and the purpose of it all was pure fun since he sometimes overdid his linguistic showing off. That evening as the sun began to slip inch by inch behind the large trees that lined the studio's compound boundaries, Ashok Bhaiyya, S. Mukherjee Sahab and I sat down on cane chairs outside the stage as we always did. S. Mukherjee Sahab then asked me to recite some Urdu verses. 'It's such a beautiful evening. Yousuf, let us hear some Urdu poetry from you,' he said casually. I was naturally ready and I recited the lines that I often used to when my brother Ayub Sahab was confined to bed after his accidental fall from a horse in Kashmir. Ashok Bhaiyya listened attentively and, surprisingly, it was S. Mukherjee Sahab who was more engrossed and lost in my recitation.

After I had finished, Ashok Bhaiyya rose from his chair to give me a standing ovation and, to my surprise, S. Mukherjee Sahab also stood up to applaud me. As expected Ashok Bhaiyya was clamouring for lessons in Urdu from me. He said he was prepared for a deal. He would teach me whatever French and German he knew and, in return, I should teach him Urdu. We agreed mutually, but the surprise element was the reaction of S. Mukherjee Sahab. He said he wanted me to meet all the writers, especially those from Bengal.

'I want you to be there at all our story meetings and be a part of our writing teams. You have the grasp of the language that is wanting in our Bengali writers,' he pointed out.

I thought it would be awkward for me to be participating in the discussions pertaining to the dialogues for the stories written by such eminent directors as Amiya Chakraborthy and Gyan Mukherjee. However, it wasn't so. At least S. Mukherjee Sahab had made it both easy and friendly for them and me in his own genial way. It was something I had least expected. Here, I was, a rank newcomer who hadn't even faced the camera for a trial shot, and I was sitting with experienced writers as an equal. They were brilliant in their mother tongue, Bengali, and they were gracious in their admission that due to their lack of proficiency in Urdu they needed the fine-tuning that I could offer to the dialogues with my knowledge of that language.

Everybody in the studio respected S. Mukherjee Sahab. He was held in high esteem for his superior academic qualifications and for the facility with which he communicated in English. He had been brought to the studio by Himanshu Rai, the founder of Bombay Talkies, who had met him accidentally in Bombay where S. Mukherjee Sahab (a brilliant professor of physics at the Allahabad University) had come to meet an academician who had the required information and contacts to get him admission in the faculty of his choice in a foreign university. Himanshu Rai was then on the lookout for a qualified person to set up the sound department at Bombay Talkies and he felt S. Mukherjee Sahab was the man he was looking for. He convinced the scholarly Bengali professor to abandon the idea of going abroad for higher studies in physics and become a part of his dream to set up a professionally managed film studio in India on the lines of the UFA Studios in Germany where he had worked as a producer and was the only Asian to be in charge of an entire production unit with directors like Fritz Lang and Josef von Sternberg.

S. Mukherjee Sahab always drew parallels between our individual destinies that brought us to a profession that was not in our wildest imagination. He was a product of Western education having studied in the English medium from his school days in Jhansi (now in Uttar Pradesh) and so was I with my schooling at the Barnes School at Deolali, which was very, very English in its curriculum. He conversed mostly in English except when we were with the Bengalis, of whom there were quite a few in the studio. My regular witnessing of shootings and my interactions with Ashok Bhaiyya were preparing me for my debut. I had begun to observe Ashok Bhaiyya closely when he would be rehearsing or facing the camera. I noticed that he had made calculated movements before the camera, which he had worked out all by himself. For example, he would hold a cigarette between his lips without lighting it and he would look around searchingly. He would then take the cigarette off from his lips, walk two steps, then put the cigarette back between his lips and light it and speak the given dialogue looking into the camera. It was all very fascinating for me and I could figure out what he meant when he told me that the secret of a good rendering of a scene was *not to act* before the camera. Ashok Bhaiyya had hit upon the secret of 'non-acting' but he had a definite calculation in his mind when he performed and the arithmetic of that calculation was entirely his. I began to understand that I would have to arrive at my own approach to the whole business of simulating feelings and emotions.

When I got a chance to speak to S. Mukherjee Sahab alone, I mentioned my observation to him and he suggested that I go and view as many feature films as I could so that I could observe how different actors attained their levels of competence before the camera in rendering long-winded and difficult scenes. I thought there was a point in what he was saying but it was difficult to go straight from the studio to a cinema theatre and watch a film and go home late in the night. Besides, if someone saw me going to a theatre and reported it to Aghaji, it would raise questions in his mind because he knew I had no interest in the amusement offered by films. In his eyes, I was an athlete and a passionate soccer player who derived pleasure and thrill from a good game of soccer or cricket in any open ground in the city.

I would leave for home every evening at about six, taking a local train to Churchgate from Malad. I had a second-class season ticket, which gave me the comfort of travelling without being elbowed by passengers getting in and out. From Churchgate, I boarded a bus, and alighted at Crawford Market and walked to our residence at Nagdevi Street. On the way, every day, I met friends who asked me casual questions about the job I was doing and I always told them it was a company that was doing well and had around 1500 employees and I was learning the ropes. I never waited to prolong the conversation and pretended to be in a hurry to get home.

At home, Amma would be bustling around to give the family or the visiting relatives whatever they desired. I don't remember seeing her ever taking a nap or sitting pretty, making frivolous conversation. She asked me a couple of times about the work I was doing and I gave her the impression that it was a good, honourable job and I was quite happy. She was so preoccupied with the responsibilities of running the large household that she did not question me any more. My elder sister, Sakina Aapa, was the curious one. She was nosy enough to get deep into everything that everybody did, be it in our home or in the neighbour's home. She seldom extended help to Amma in the kitchen and Amma never complained for fear of provoking a senseless argument with Sakina Aapa. Every time Sakina Aapa tried to probe, I told her different things and successfully confused her about my employment. She was happy when she heard about the salary I was going to bring home and generally remained content with that knowledge.

My brother Ayub Sahab was well aware of what I was doing because I had confided in him. Ayub Sahab was very close to me and we shared a bond that was inseverable. As noted earlier, he was an extremely intelligent and sensitive person whose voluminous reading of Urdu and English literature had made him a kind of scholar and littérateur. He was excited about my job but he also feared whether I would be successful in my vocation being the shy, reserved person I was. More than anything else, he wondered what would be Aghaji's reaction when he would learn about my job. I assuaged his fears by telling him what I tell anybody who worries about the outcome of something he or she is about to do. I told him I would not think too much about what could happen because that could distract me from my efforts to do my job to the best of my ability.

I was not the least nervous or anxious. One morning, as I entered the studio I was given the message that Devika Rani wanted to see me in her office. I wondered what it could be. I was certain it couldn't be for expressing any displeasure because she was always courteous and pleasant whenever she met me and enquired how I was doing. So what could it be?

When I walked into her office, she was seated at her desk looking stunning and dignified as always. She smiled warmly and asked me to take a seat. I sat down and looked curiously at her. She began with the usual courtesies of asking me whether I would care for some tea made specially for her from leaves she had purchased from the English store in the city. I was wondering what she had in mind when she came to the point, speaking in English, the language she was most fluent in. She said, quite matter-of-factly: 'Yousuf, I was thinking about your launch soon as an actor and I felt it would not be a bad idea if you adopted a screen name. You know, a name you would be known by and which will be very appropriate for your audience to relate to and one that will be in tune with the romantic image you are bound to acquire through your screen presence. I thought Dilip Kumar was a nice name. It just popped up in my mind when I was thinking about a suitable name for you. How does it sound to you?'

I was speechless for a moment, being totally unprepared for the new identity she was proposing to me. I said it sounded nice but asked her whether it was really necessary. She gave her sweet smile and told me that it would be prudent to do so. She added that it was after considerable thought that she came to the conclusion of giving me a screen name. With her customary authority, she went on to tell me that she foresaw a long and successful career for me in films and it made good sense to have a screen identity that would stand up by itself and have a secular appeal. I was quick to appreciate her concern

but I told her I needed to think about it a bit. She responded: 'Fine …
come back to me with your thoughts.'

'We are now ready to begin preparations for your debut. So we
must hurry up,' she said breezily as I rose from my seat to leave.

I spent the rest of the day as per my routine but with the name
Dilip Kumar ringing in my mind's inner recesses. S. Mukherjee
Sahab noticed that I was rather contemplative that afternoon as we
ordered lunch from the canteen and shared some fried fish that came
from Ashok Bhaiyya's house. After lunch, when work started on the
shooting stage, he asked me if there was something disturbing me and
if I could share with him. It was plain to all of us that S. Mukherjee
Sahab was the Number 2 man in the studio's management hierarchy
and the general feeling was that he would take over the reins of
management soon. I had developed a rapport with him because I
found him to be a man of considerable worth not only in terms of
the technical knowledge he had painstakingly acquired by regular
interactions with the foreign technicians and consistent reading of
relevant literature but also in a personal sense as a friend one could
trust and rely upon.

I told S. Mukherjee Sahab about the suggestion that had come
from Devika Rani. He reflected for a second and, looking me straight
in the eye, said: 'I think she has a point. It will be in your interest
to take the name she has suggested for the screen. It is a very nice
name, though I will always know you by the name Yousuf like all
your brothers and sisters and your parents.' (I later came to know that
Ashok Kumar was the screen name of Kumudlal Kunjilal Ganguly.)

I was touched and it was a validation that cleared my thoughts
then and there. I decided not to speak about the new name to anyone,
not even to Ayub Sahab. The days that followed were pretty hectic at
the studio because *Kismet* had released to a great opening response
in 1943 and was on its way to creating box-office records. Ashok
Bhaiyya was a superstar now but he remained completely unaffected
and behaved as if nothing had changed in his life. He began to take a
keen interest in the management alongside S. Mukherjee Sahab and
he was delighted that I was going to be launched with a film titled
Jwar Bhata to be directed by Amiya Chakraborthy.

I had been earlier interacting with Amiya Chakraborthy but now we were spending time more as director and actor as he prepared for starting the shooting of *Jwar Bhata*. A strange truth was that I was not even slightly nervous or excited about the fact that I was going to face the camera for the first time when the D-day arrived for my first shot. I was given a simple pant and shirt to wear and Devika Rani came on the sets and looked at me and found me as unruffled as ever. She was a great expert in make-up and knew what exactly suited the lighting of the set and the nature of the scene to be shot. She checked the light strokes of make-up given to me and asked where the camera would be placed. She was quite satisfied with everything except my bushy eyebrows. She asked me to sit down on a chair and she called for tweezers from the make-up man and very deftly pulled off some unruly growth of straggling hair from my eyebrows to give them a proper shape while I held my breath and endured the pain it was causing. She smiled when she saw the tears brimming in my eyes as a result of the tweezing and very jovially suggested that I take a look at my face while the make-up man quickly applied some cream to ease the painful sensations on my poor eyebrows. She left after wishing me luck.

My first shot was explained to me by Amiya Chakraborthy. He made a mark on the ground and told me: 'You will take your position here and you will run when I say "ACTION". I will first say "START CAMERA" but that is not for you. "ACTION" is for you to start running and you will stop running when I say "CUT".' I asked him very politely if I may know why I was running. He replied I was running to save the life of the heroine who was going to commit suicide. Satisfied with the explanation, I told him I was ready. It was an outdoor scene and the camera was somewhere in the distance. It was a brand new gadget imported from Germany and it was being used for the first time. I stood where I was shown to take my stand. I had been an athlete at college consistently winning 200-metre races, so it did not perturb me at all when I was asked to run up to the call for 'CUT'. I was mighty pleased that it was something so easy and simple!

The shot was ready and the minute I heard 'ACTION', I took off like lightning and I heard the director scream: 'CUT, CUT, CUT.' I saw him gesticulating and trying to tell me something I couldn't figure out. I stood rooted to the spot I had reached in a flash and Amiya Chakraborthy ambled over, looking highly displeased. He told me that I ran so fast that it was a blur that the camera had captured. I clarified that I had no idea of the speed I was supposed to maintain. He then said: 'Never mind; we will do it again but keep the pace slower.' It was a bit perplexing for me when he told me at first to slow my pace because I thought it was important for me to run as fast as I could and save the girl who was going to end her life. However, when Amiya Chakraborthy explained the action as something that should register on the film in the camera, which would move at a particular pace, I understood in no uncertain terms that I faced a big challenge and the business of acting was anything but simple. The shot was okayed after three or four calls for 'CUT'.

I am often asked what I thought of my first performance and my first film, which was released in 1944. Honestly, the whole experience passed by without much impact on me. I did what I was told to do and it was not easy at times, or most times rather, to come to terms with the fact that it was all unreal and unrelated to one's real self and real existence. To express love to someone completely unknown and unattached to one in reality was, at that age and time, a tough demand. I think Amiya Chakraborthy understood my predicament but he was persuasive enough to get a reasonably good output from me in the romantic scenes. When I saw myself on the screen, I asked myself: 'Is this how I am going to perform in the films that may follow if the studio wishes to continue my services?!' My response was: 'No.' I realized that this was a difficult job and, if I had to continue, I would have to find my own way of doing it. And the critical question was: HOW?

I think I was really lucky to have started working at an early age in the stimulating environment of Bombay Talkies. The writers – who left New Theatres in Calcutta (now Kolkata) to join Bombay Talkies, which enjoyed the prestige of being the studio that produced highly successful films, most of them having Ashok Bhaiyya in the lead – were very creatively gifted but they would turn to me for Urdu vocabulary on S. Mukherjee Sahab's advice. I benefited from my interactions with them and it became obvious to me that the screenplay was the backbone of a film. I also became aware that an actor needed to strengthen his instincts because the duality between the real and unreal cannot be sorted out by the mind, which is more concerned with truth and logic in any normal situation. The mind will always tell you this is nonsense: this woman you are addressing as 'maa' is not your mother or that you are not in love with the girl who is fluttering her eyelashes and looking at you soulfully. You know that your own mother is a lovely woman and does not have teeth stained by paan chewing and you don't even know who the girl is. It is only instinct that will help you to absorb what you have to absorb from the script and drive you to render a performance coated with realism and conviction despite the knowledge of it all being fiction and drama.

10

NEW ASPIRATIONS, NEW EXPERIENCES

The silence was broken by Aghaji when he came home one evening after a visit to a family friend's house where he had heard praises about me and my emergence as the star of Jugnu *[1947]. He saw me coming in and he called me as he always did and began talking to me with ease. I was relieved and happy, considering that he was always upfront in giving expression to his thoughts and sentiments. He said quite matter-of-factly that he had come to terms with the reality that I had chosen a profession he had least expected me to enter.*

I BEGAN TO VIEW MOVIES REGULARLY, BRAVING THE POSSIBILITY of being caught by someone known to my family. I must confess that the new identity as Dilip Kumar had a liberating impact on me. I told myself Yousuf had no need to see or study films but Dilip surely needed to accumulate observations of how actors reproduced the emotions, speech and behaviour of fictitious characters in front of a camera. So I started seeing films, one film a day, at two successive shows. It was necessary to view the same film at the 3.30 p.m. and

With Meera Mishra in *Milan* (1946).

6.30 p.m. shows because in the first viewing something that caught my attention could be reviewed closely in the second viewing. Hence, I had to leave the studio early for a few days.

I started getting the hang of it as I watched Hollywood actors and actresses like James Stewart, Paul Muni, Ingrid Bergman and Clark Gable but it did not take long for me to realize the essence, which was that an actor should not imitate or copy another actor if he can help it because the actor who impresses you has consciously and even painstakingly moulded an overt personality and laid down his own ground rules to bring that personality effectively on the screen. I understood very early on, while I was at Bombay Talkies itself, following such films as *Milan* (1946), that I had to be my own inspiration and teacher and it was imperative to evolve with the passage of time.

S. Mukherjee Sahab was a great help when I discussed with him such topics as the evolution of an actor or the elusive phenomenon of stardom that actors aspire to attain. Ashok Bhaiyya was a phenomenally successful star at that time but he was so unaffected by his stardom. I remember an evening when he decided to travel with me and P. Jairajji (a senior actor and director) to Churchgate by the local train. We had purchased tickets for a film and he was insistent on going to the cinema hall by train. At the Malad station, when people saw him and recognized him, there was a wave of adulatory attention but he seemed unmindful of the gasps of admiration as he talked to us. When the train arrived a crowd got into the compartment that we boarded and people started talking to him about *Kangan* (1939) and *Jhoola* and *Kismet* and he responded warmly and wittily. I was witnessing the phenomenon of stardom, which was quite baffling for me then.

I narrated the whole incident to S. Mukherjee Sahab the next day in the presence of Ashok Bhaiyya. Ashok Bhaiyya listened to my narration and, looking seriously at me, said: 'It is a preview of what you are going to experience on a much bigger scale in the future. A handsome man like you will have trouble keeping the women away.' He saw my expression and laughed heartily because it was well known by then at Bombay Talkies how shy and formal I was in the presence of women.

S. Mukherjee Sahab, who was in agreement with Ashok Bhaiyya, was laughing, too. I thought it was the right time to talk to both of them about stardom and what it entailed as well as the impact it could have on an actor's mind and personality, especially if he had a dual image – his real self with his real name and personal and social background juxtaposed with his screen image with another name and personality, which changed from one fictitious character to another and from one film to another.

Ashok Bhaiyya noted that he would give stardom and success little importance because for him they were not the be-all and end-all of his existence. 'It [stardom] should never be more important for you than your self-respect and your will to do what you want to do in the manner you want to do', he emphasized. I knew what he was meaning to say and his attitude was obvious in the train when he jostled with the common folk who were his ardent fans. He was interacting with them as the real Ashok Kumar, completely divorced from his screen image and his stardom.

It was S. Mukherjee Sahab who gave me an answer that has lingered in my mind since then. He pointed out to me that the distinction was easy to achieve if one understood that 'the actor is more important than the star. The star is a creation of marketing and stardom is the result of the hard work of the actor when it finds mass acceptance and adulation. When fans will come to you some day, remember they are coming to see you and feel you because they have liked your acting and are touched by it. You should know that it is Dilip Kumar they are clamouring to meet.'

It was S. Mukherjee Sahab's wont to talk seriously and analytically when a topic aroused his intellectual interest. The professor in him surfaced at such times. He was in many ways my guru and a source of inspiration. He could explain to me in the simplest of terms the grammar of cinema. He took pains to take me behind the camera and show me how the camera sees the actor in front of it. He would make me view the way he would simulate the gait of a woman in front of the camera. It would be a funny sight but seeing the act through the camera lens gave me the much-needed help in understanding the relation between the camera and the actor facing it or turning his back to it under the light that is falling on him. He always liked to show his actors by performing what he wanted them to portray. He was very sharp in noticing not only technical flaws but also flaws in dialogue delivery and facial expressions. Above all, he had great respect for writers and believed that cinema's prime objective was to engage the viewer with imaginative storytelling.

My formative years at Bombay Talkies were memorable for the lovely time I spent with Ashok Bhaiyya and S. Mukherjee Sahab. They lived close to the studio those days and I was always welcome in their homes to have hot *bhajias* (a savoury fried dish) prepared by Ashok Bhaiyya's wife, Shobha Bhabhi. It was also wonderful to be in the company of Raj Kapoor again after our Khalsa College days. Raj was happy to know I had seriously entered the profession of film acting. 'I told you, didn't I?' he said, hugging me like a little, excited boy when I was ready for my debut. When we were at Khalsa he used to tell me in Punjabi: '*Tusi* actor *banjao. Tusi ho bade* handsome.' (You should become an actor. You are very handsome.) I thought then it was not my cup of tea. It was fine for him because his Papaji (Prithvirajji) was a great actor and one of the most handsome and virile men I had seen on the screen. Naturally, Raj and his younger brothers, Shammi and Shashi, were all genetically gifted with talent and exceptional good looks. It did not seem a good proposition for me with the background I came from.

At Bombay Talkies, Raj was regarded with respect and a measure of awe because he was Prithvirajji's son. There was no actor or, for that matter, anyone who had anything to do with the performing arts who did not admire Prithvirajji whose commanding presence in the plays staged by Prithvi Theatres inspired awe. Raj neither showed off nor leveraged his father's eminence to get special treatment at the studio. He and I often slipped off to Ashok Bhaiyya's house for a game of badminton in which Bhabhiji also joined us, playing the game by her own rules and filling the air with her chatter and giggles. She enjoyed the game and the relief she got from the boredom of being alone in a large house. After the game, she would ask me and Raj to stay on for tea and *bhajias*. Ashok Bhaiyya sometimes arrived while we were munching the *bhajias* and we would think it was time for us to leave because he was home after a long day's work. However, Ashok Bhaiyya would have none of it. He would chide us and say jokingly: 'You both should be ashamed of yourselves. You come here and flirt with my wife, eat such nice *bhajias* without me to give you company and you want to leave without giving me a chance to play a game with you guys.' We would then sheepishly stay back while Bhabhiji promised more hot *bhajias* and hot tea. After such a frontal attack, we had no option but to acquiesce.

Ashok Bhaiyya was an agile badminton player. Raj was a splendid referee when we had played soccer on the grounds off Khalsa College and he looked so robust when he stood on the field, whistle in hand, and refused to budge from his decisions. He got easily tired when we played badminton because he was least interested in the game. He was there more for the delicious *bhajias*. Both Ashok Bhaiyya and

Raj found my stamina incredible. I could only attribute it to the dry fruits I grew up on and the indomitable will power I inherited from Aghaji. There were days when S. Mukherjee Sahab joined us. He and Ashok Bhaiyya carried on a continuous powwow in Bangla, which is a typical Bengali habit. When two Bengalis get together they make no bones about bringing their personal lives into the ambit of their conversation in their mother tongue while others who are in their company wonder what they are so engrossed about that they are talking and chuckling nonstop.

One person who was a steady friend at Bombay Talkies was Jairajji. He was very different from the other people like Shah Nawaz Khan and he took a keen interest in my work and gave me useful advice in his quiet manner. Jairajji and David Abraham were good friends and they exchanged naughty jokes, some of which they let me into and others they told me were not for my ears yet. The notable fact was that all the wonderful people I got to know and share great times with were older than I except Raj Kapoor. I was barely 21 when I faced the camera for my first shot and it was indeed my good fortune that senior professionals in the acting department and writers like Pandit Narendra Sharma and Bhagwaticharan Verma were there. Jairajji was very protective and, even though we made very little conversation while travelling from Churchgate to Malad by train, we were very close as professionals.

Bombay Talkies was in the process of changing hands at that juncture as Devika Rani was sure she did not want to continue with the management of the studio after her marriage to Svetoslav Roerich. By the time I had made my debut in 1944 she was contemplating voluntary retirement. She had appointed S. Mukherjee Sahab and Amiya Chakraborthy to take care of all the productions. She would, nevertheless, take her rounds of the studio and talk to everybody warmly. She was so stunning in her appearance that everyone in the studio stopped to look at her when she moved around. She made it a point to ask about me if I was not around and, if I ran into her, she asked me how I was doing and about my progress as a learner. Ashok Bhaiyya was the only one who joked with her and S. Mukherjee Sahab was the one she consulted about every step she took in the running of the studio.

She introduced me once to Svetoslav Roerich, the famous Soviet painter she was going to marry. She told me how much Svetoslav loved the Kulu Valley (now in Himachal Pradesh) and she told him about my family's fruit business and how we got fruits from the valley: apples, cherries and juicy pears. I looked at Roerich, who had a stately gait and a twinkle in his eyes exactly like Aghaji. I thought she would be very happy with him the way Amma was with Aghaji.

As 1945 rolled by, the Second World War was coming to an end and the freedom movement was gaining momentum in the country. At the studio every day, Ashok Bhaiyya and S. Mukherjee Sahab would engage in discussions about what they had heard or read. They would seriously discuss Muhammad Ali Jinnah's speeches and ask me for my opinion. Having had a 'memorable' experience when I spoke my mind at the Wellington Soldiers Club in Poona, I thought it best to maintain a discreet silence. At home, Ayub Sahab used to be extremely well acquainted with the developments on the freedom movement front and he would hold forth before awed listeners who were friends of Aghaji and Chacha Ummer. Aghaji would feel very proud of Ayub Sahab's accomplishment and his fluency in Urdu, both spoken and written. Personally, I was equally awed by Ayub Sahab's ability to speak and write well in English and Urdu despite not having had formal school education. As mentioned earlier, he had been taught at home due to ill health as a boy and he was studious and painstaking as a home-bound student.

By the time I finished my work in *Jugnu*, our country was heading for its emancipation from British rule. I remember the day – 15 August 1947 – vividly when independence was won for us by the great men and women who fought for it tenaciously and relentlessly for decades. I was walking on the pavement near the Churchgate station, quite unnoticed despite having acted in three films – *Jwar*

With Noor Jehan in *Jugnu* (1947).

Bhata (1944), *Pratima* (1945) and *Milan* (1946) – when I noticed people were rushing homewards with joyous expressions on their faces. It was only when I reached home and I saw the whole family together for a change with every face shining with happiness that I realized it was independence day. I wasted no time in being a part of the celebration of the independence of India.

Jugnu was released in late 1947. The film became a hit and the hoardings were put up in many places, including a site near Crawford Market. One morning while Aghaji was supervising the unloading of a consignment of apples at his wholesale shop in the market, Raj's grandfather, Basheshwarnathji, walked in and the two greeted each other warmly as always. They had been friends for years and Aghaji used to tell him jokingly that it was no use twirling his impressive moustache because his son and grandson were in the acting business. Aghaji felt the Kapoor boys were worthy of being in government service, which was the aspiration of most fathers for their sons those days. He knew Raj and I were studying in the same college and those days getting a college education and acquiring a graduation certificate at a convocation held by the Bombay University was a big event. He was mighty displeased therefore that Raj had chosen to be an actor and not an important government official like Basheshwarnathji who had held a high position as a commissioner in Peshawar. Basheshwarnathji, however, was not at all unhappy that his son Prithvirajji had chosen to become an actor and was very famous already and his grandson Raj had begun to follow in the footsteps of Prithvirajji.

It was Aghaji's ambition that I, too, would find a respectable government job and I would attain such an important position that I would have OBE as a suffix to my name. Aghaji had seen that suffix somewhere and it fascinated him as a mark of esteem and honour. When I started going to college, he felt proud and he confided to me that his big dream was that I should write my name as Yousuf Khan OBE.

That morning Basheshwarnathji had a naughty smile playing beneath his moustache. He twirled his moustache and told Aghaji he had something to show him: something that would take his breath away. Aghaji must have wondered what it could be. Basheshwarnathji took him out of the market and showed him the large hoarding of *Jugnu* right across the road. He then said: 'That's your son Yousuf.'

Aghaji told me later on that he could not believe his eyes for a moment but there was no mistaking me for someone else because the face he knew so well was printed large and the blurb on the hoarding was hailing the arrival of a bright new star on the silver screen. The name was not Yousuf. It was Dilip Kumar.

Basheshwarnathji, who was standing next to him, was gleefully observing his expression and telling him that there was no need to be dismayed because I had adopted another name to keep the family honour intact and, what was more important, I was on my way to big stardom. All those words were not music to Aghaji's ears. He described to me much later, after he accepted my choice of career, the awful feeling of disappointment that overwhelmed him at that moment. He was naturally very angry. Aghaji did not reveal his anger and hurt pride through harsh words or any other form of resentment. He was very quiet for some days and did not speak to me. Even at other times, when we spoke to each other in monosyllables, I did not dare to look him in the eye. Soon, the situation became awkward and I did not know what to do.

The thick layer of ice had to be broken somehow. I confided in Raj and he said he knew this was going to happen and the best person to mediate was Prithvirajji. And he was right. Prithvirajji paid a casual visit to our home one day. Amma told me when I got home in the evening that the powwow with Prithvirajji had done considerable good and she noticed that Aghaji was a lot more relaxed and cheerful. I still did not have the courage to go up to him and start a conversation.

The silence was broken by Aghaji when he came home one evening after a visit to a family friend's house where he had heard praises about me and my emergence as the star of *Jugnu*. He saw me coming in and he called me as he always did and began talking to me with ease. I was relieved and happy, considering that he was always upfront in giving expression to his thoughts and sentiments. He said quite matter-of-factly that he had come to terms with the reality that I had chosen a profession he had least expected me to enter. He always spoke to me in Pushtu and his speech was clear and precise and never wanting in good taste. He was never loud and I don't have even a faint recollection of any argument between my parents in front of us. If they had to sort out anything between them, they did it without our knowledge. He spoke to me that evening without anger or unhappiness. He was enjoying the hookah, which he usually shared with his friends who visited him. The very gesture of asking me to sit down before him while he asked for the flavoured tobacco to be brought and filled into the hookah by the lad who attended on him indicated to me that he was not in a bad mood and it was sufficient for me to know that he had forgiven me for keeping it all under wraps. I could sense from the easy manner in which he conversed with me that evening, as he took puffs of the hookah, that he no longer disapproved even if he did not feel good about the development.

11

BETWEEN THE PERSONAL AND
THE PROFESSIONAL

What Devika Rani had told me was also a lesson I have borne in mind and applied to my work sometimes to the surprise of my directors. She had pointed out that a director may be satisfied with the shot an actor had given but it is for the actor to discern for himself whether he had really given his best. The actor, she told me, was within his rights to request for another take if he felt he could do better.

$\mathcal{M}$Y HAPPINESS WAS, HOWEVER, SHORT-LIVED. AYUB SAHAB SOON took ill seriously with a lung ailment. The best doctors were unable to prolong his life with the medicines I managed to get from abroad. He knew he was not going to be with us for long, so he often requested me to take him to Marine Drive, where we could sit and watch the sun go down inch by inch into the sea. He used to tell me that he never ceased to wonder how the sun took away all the brilliance it spread in the sky when it went down, making way for the night to fall.

One day I came home earlier than usual and noticed that Ayub Sahab was looking pale and was having difficulty in taking even small breaths. I sent Chacha Ummer to bring Aghaji from the market and also fetch a doctor. I took my brother in my arms and he was calm and smiling at me as I looked him in the eye fearing the worst. Chacha Ummer brought Aghaji and hurried off to fetch the doctor. Aghaji sat close to Ayub Sahab and I could see his hand tremble while he took his son's hand in his. Ayub Sahab was smiling and, though he was struggling to breathe, there was an unusual radiance and calm on his handsome face. Before we knew it, like the radiant evening sun he loved to watch, he went in a few moments, even before the doctor could arrive, taking away all the brilliance with him.

My contract with Bombay Talkies was coming to an end and there were changes taking place in the studio management. Ashok Bhaiyya had moved out and so had S. Mukherjee Sahab to form Filmistan. As we were no longer fettered by foreign rule, there was a surge of creative activity and spirited unravelling of the communicative powers of the medium. Movies were being made with a sense of introspection, patriotism and social purpose by many talented and dedicated film makers. V. Shantaram had already made *Duniya Na Mane* (1937), *Admi* (1939), *Padosi* (1941), *Shakuntala* (1943) and *Dr Kotnis Ki Amar Kahani* (1946), which were well received and appreciated for the focus on social issues. Baburao Painter had made *Ram Joshi* (1947). Sohrab Modi was making films with historical stories and his Minerva Movietone was in the news already as the film *Sikandar* (1941, with Prithviraj Kapoor in the title role) had stirred a controversy* and *Pukar* (1939) had become a huge hit. Mehboob Khan had made National Studios famous with his association. There was no dearth of job opportunities for me and others who had been nurtured by Bombay Talkies.

The stamp of quality and prestige that was inherent in the name, Bombay Talkies, made it easy for most employees of the studio to find

*The film was released when the political atmosphere was in turmoil, in the wake of Mahatma Gandhi's call for civil disobedience. *Sikandar* stirred up patriotic feelings and nationalist sentiments. The screening of the movie was forbidden in some British Indian Army cantonments.

worthy openings in productions going on the floors in other studios. I did not hesitate to accept S. Mukherjee Sahab's invitation to work in the pictures to be made at Filmistan. The beneficial aspect was that he did not talk about a contract or agreement restricting me to work only in his pictures. As it was, the studio employment system was inevitably being replaced by managements seeking services of actors and technicians on a freelance basis with varying remunerations commensurate with experience, expertise and track record.

My preference for Filmistan, however, was not driven by the monetary increment it offered. The pay packet I was receiving every month at Bombay Talkies was sufficient to take care of some of the more critical expenses that Amma had to manage every month in the house with its growing population of visiting family members from Peshawar and all twelve of her children besides Chacha Ummer and two of Aghaji's sisters and a never-ending stream of visitors. A substantial increase in the earnings was no doubt welcome, but I was firm in my resolve that my choice of work and my career moves would not be determined or dictated by monetary gains and the trappings of transient success. It was a hard decision to take for a young man on the threshold of a successful career. I consider it a blessing that I was able to harness the equilibrium acquired from years of upright breeding to remain level headed and not be swept away by the illusionary glory and grandeur that surround an actor when he acquires the label of a star. There were many producers who had noticed me then and had called me over to talk about the films they were proposing to make with me in the male lead. S. Mukherjee Sahab was aware of this development and he respected my decision to work in his venture at Filmistan. The film was *Shaheed* (released in 1948). The subject fired my imagination and I felt it was a wise decision to make a patriotic film at that juncture when we had all gone through the experience of witnessing the struggle for freedom from British rule and the sacrifices made by freedom fighters who belonged to different religions, castes, age groups and social strata. I was completely in synch with the character in *Shaheed* because of the social and political climate prevailing at that time and my own patriotic sentiments were seeking an outlet, which was there for the

With Kamini Kaushal in *Shaheed* (1948).

asking in the well-written scenes and dialogues. Though the film was directed by Ramesh Saigal, it was the inspiration we got from S. Mukherjee Sahab that fleshed out the performances and added momentum to the movement of the narrative.

I had an understanding and facile co-actor in Kamini Kaushal who was very attentive to the demands of the director and had the intelligence to grasp the intrinsic sensitivity of some of the more poignant situations in the script. She was an artiste who could perform with the required authority when needed. She was not new to the profession, having acted in Chetan Anand's *Neecha Nagar* (1946) earlier. Moreover, she was an educated person with whom one could have an interesting conversation. She had a noticeable fluency in speaking English, which was unusual those days for an actress and that delighted S. Mukherjee Sahab who generally preferred to talk in that language. In fact, after a day's intense work on scenes that called for serious emoting, we formed a small circle for some nice light-hearted conversation, in which occasionally Ashok Bhaiyya also joined. Ramesh Saigal was a good conversationalist and he was the first one to address Kamini Kaushal by her real name Uma (Kashyap) and all of us followed suit.

Shaheed met with deserving success at the box office. My pairing with Kamini Kaushal in that film got an encore from the audiences and Filmistan had us teaming up in *Nadiya Ke Paar* (released later in 1948) and *Shabnam* (1949), which became even bigger successes. As far back as the 1940s, the gimmick of pleasing the mass audience by bringing together artistes who were believed to share an attraction for each other in the life they lived outside their work environment was as common as it is today. The difference was that we conducted ourselves with dignity and we did not make headlines in newspapers and magazines or let our private lives become the target of public debate and derision. There were snoopy journalists even then, although television was yet to make its appearance. If we were emotionally involved, there was no public exhibition of it and the decorum at work was consciously maintained.

I was in my twenties when I acted in *Shaheed, Nadiya Ke Paar* and *Shabnam*. I was no super human being. Cinema then did not attract educated ladies and being in cinema wasn't a distinction for a girl or a woman. Coming as I did from a family that had a literary bent of mind and, having grown up in a house that had such distinguished visitors as Maulana Abul Kalam Azad (a scholar and close associate of Mahatma Gandhi and Jawaharlal Nehru), Sadat Hasan Manto (an acclaimed writer) and Mirza Ghulam Ahmed (another noted writer), who talked freely with Aghaji and, at times, with me and Ayub Sahab, I preferred the company of colleagues who were educated and well informed. Stardom bothered me more than it pleased me and I guess I was drawn more intellectually than emotionally to Uma, with whom I could talk about matters and topics that interested me outside the purview of our working relationship. If that was love, may be it was. I don't know and I don't think it matters any more.

Yes, circumstances called for us to discontinue working together and it was just as well because, after a few films together, star pairings generally tend to pall on viewers, which is bad for business.

A question I have often been asked is the somewhat intrusive one whether it makes a difference to the potency of the emotions drawn from within oneself in an intimate love scene if the actors are emotionally involved in their real lives. My honest answer is both yes and no. In the love scenes, especially the scenes involving emotional warmth and physical proximity, a certain temperature is expected to be created by the director from both the actors and that temperature need not necessarily be generated by the familiarity between the artistes outside the work environment because, as actors, we get used to performing such scenes with the full knowledge that we are feigning the emotion for the camera and there is no truth or reality in it. On the other hand, it is quite possible that the familiarity between the artistes due to their emotional involvement with each other in real life may give an edge to the emotional intensity and raise the temperature of the act to that electrifying level that is not contained in the script per se.

I have been asked this question specifically with reference to the scenes I had to do as Prince Salim in *Mughal-e-Azam* (released in 1960) with Madhubala* as Salim's beloved Anarkali and to that I will reply as honestly as decency permits in one of the chapters to come.

To continue with my story, it became imperative now for us to shift our residence to a suburb that was closer to Goregaon (in western Bombay), where many film studios were (and are) situated. Aghaji now visited the fruit market only once a week since my income was quite adequate to support the family. He would not stop going to the market for two reasons. First, he would not hear of letting me be the sole bread winner and wanted to contribute whatever he could get from the dwindling business to the running of the household and, secondly, he had friends whose warm greetings and conversations he missed when he stayed away from the bustle of the market for

*Madhubala was born as Mumtaz Jehan Begum Dehlavi on 14 February 1933.

too long. With some earnest convincing, Aghaji agreed to shift to Bandra (also in western Bombay). We took a bungalow at Pali Mala in the midst of a cluster of dwellings owned by Goan Christian settlers.

Amma's asthmatic condition needed regular medical attention and the physician treating her was accessible at a stone's throw from our new residence at Pali Mala. Amma never got over the passing of Ayub. She did not weep in front of Aghaji or us but I knew she spent many nights crying softly into her pillow. The grief was gnawing at her from within and it began to tell on her health, which was declining steadily despite the best treatment we were providing for her at home now that we were in Bandra. She fought against the debilitating condition and put on a brave front before my younger sisters and brothers, who needed her and turned to her for even the smallest requirements in their lives. It was only when I was alone with her that she spoke softly about the inevitability of death and she would notice the pain on my face and swiftly change the subject. Aghaji was aware of Amma's trust in me and the fact that she shared her thoughts and dreams with me in her own quiet way. One day he emerged from their room and saw me getting ready to go out. He beckoned to me and told me to go and sit by Amma's bedside. 'Be with her,' he said and left the house to bring the doctor from his home across the road.

From the corner of my eye I could see him controlling his surging emotions. I hurried in, taking quick strides. Amma was relaxed but the extreme pallor on her face indicated that she needed immediate medical attention. I took my seat at the bedstead, raising her head to my chest as I always did. I held her soft hand and raised it to my lips in a silent gesture of love. I had a lump in my throat and tears were welling up in my eyes. The premonition was unmistakable and, at that point, all that I prayed for was the strength to give her the sense of assurance and security she was seeking from me. As always, she understood my feelings and, when Aghaji returned with the doctor, she was composed and bravely trying to look well. Somehow, Aghaji knew that we were going to lose her soon. He made arrangements to move her to our house in Deolali so that she could feel better in the unpolluted environment of the hill station. At Deolali, he looked gaunt and bleary eyed and he seldom went out of the house. Though he was not expressing it in words, it was obvious that his inner voice was disturbing him with anxious thoughts and the dread of losing the quiet companion from whom he had derived solace and strength for years.

In a few days, on 27 August 1948, she was gone from our midst, passing peacefully from the turmoil of life to eternal tranquillity. I did not let my pain show, concealing it from Aghaji and my siblings the way I did when Ayub Sahab had passed away. All those who knew her and Aghaji came to offer condolences when we returned to Bombay. The real mourners were the poor who lived in the neighbourhood. She never let anyone who came to our door go away empty-handed.

A regular visitor was our *dhobi*'s (washerman's) wife who came with her young son Pyarelal and left the house with goodies packed for him. Pyarelal learned the art of laundering from his parents and became my personal launderer after his parents died. He is now in his seventies and he is serving in our house as the master *dhobi*, taking care of my white trousers and shirts as only he can besides the beautiful clothes Saira wears. To this day, Pyarelal remembers the halwas and other goodies Amma used to pack for him to take home and share with his younger brothers. All this was in addition to the sumptuous meal she would serve to him and his mother in the kitchen.

It took me all my strength and will power to suppress the pain and deep sense of loss I felt and stand up manfully before my brothers and sisters and give them the implicit understanding of being both mother and father to them since Aghaji spoke very little and kept more and more to himself now. One day when we were alone he expressed a wish: he said it was his wish to be laid to rest at Deolali, close to where Amma rested.

I bought a Fiat car (sometime in the late 1940s) not so much because I needed it but more because my sisters required a vehicle to go out. My first drive was to the Brabourne Stadium. A cricket match was going on and it must have been the second day. I no longer stood in a queue to get an admission ticket to watch a match as I was now somewhat recognized in public. I had got to know the ace cricketer Vijay Merchant, who had been introduced to me by Dr Masani, who was himself a great cricket enthusiast. I asked my driver to take me to Churchgate, from where I picked up Dr Masani and we reached the stadium in time to be ushered to the enclosure meant for special invitees, which I used to eye longingly whenever I took my seat in the stands at a lofty height from where one could see the players by craning one's neck and inviting a crick if one was not prudent. I found myself seated beside an impressive looking man wearing an unbuttoned jacket over his shirt. He was talking to a lean man seated on his right, tilting his broad frame to hear what the lean man was trying to tell him on seeing me. I took my seat and since both of them smiled at me I thought it fit to greet them. They were obviously my co-religionists because they were in the Muslims' enclosure, so I said 'Salaam Alaikum' (peace be upon you), and they returned my greeting warmly.

After the match started and progressed, the impressive looking man felt he should speak to me. He introduced himself as Mehboob Khan and introduced his friend as Naushad Miyan. It was the beginning of two enduring friendships and professional relationships in my life and career. Naushad Miyan (basically a music composer) had written the story of what became the film *Mela* and he invited me to meet him and the director, S. U. Sunny, the following week. Both Naushad Miyan and Mehboob Khan had seen *Shaheed*.

My meeting with Naushad Miyan took place in Sunny's small office where he narrated to me briefly the story of *Mela*. He also told me that they had recorded the title song with which they would like to start the shooting. It was a bit awkward for me to ask questions about the details of the story but I thought it would be a risk if I did not know enough to be in a position to accept the film.

I must mention here that my work choices from the very beginning were not governed by the remuneration I was offered. This was something I learned from Nitin Bose and Devika Rani who were my first and most influential teachers. While working with Nitin Bose during the making of *Milan* (1946), I understood how vital it is for an actor to get so close to the character that the thin line between the actor's own personality and the imagined personality of the character gets ruthlessly rubbed off for the time when you are involved in the shooting. To get that close to the character it is very important to know everything about the character and his mind and emotions.

While I was deeply involved with *Milan*, one day Nitinda asked me whether I had seriously read the novel *Nauka Dubi* (written in Bengali by the Nobel Laureate Rabindranath Tagore). I told him that I had read the translation given to me and, of course, the script, which was very detailed. We were preparing to shoot the scene in which the character named Ramesh has travelled all night by train and has reached Varanasi (now in Uttar Pradesh), where he has to immerse the mortal remains of his mother in the Ganga. He performs his duty with a heavy heart, tired and weather-beaten as he is bound to be after the overnight journey. Nitinda asked me if I had given sufficient thought to the state of Ramesh's mind and his feelings during the journey by train sitting up all night holding the urn securely so that the last remains from it did not spill out. Nitinda also asked me to think over the scene, imagining the disturbed state of Ramesh's mind as he sat looking at the urn and remembering his mother who used to talk to him affectionately and serve him food and wake him up in the mornings with a cup of hot tea. He finally asked me: 'Don't you think Ramesh would have thought to himself, this is my mother who has been reduced to ashes, my mother who had such soft hands and such gentle eyes?' I told Nitinda frankly that I had not thought so deeply because such depth was not in the script. Nitinda of course understood but he gave me a valuable lesson that has stood me in good stead. He made me write four to five pages expressing my feelings as Ramesh during the journey. I sat up half the night and wrote and rewrote until I was overcome by sleep. The next day the scene was to be shot at a location in Ghodbunder in Bombay. When the camera started to roll I was into the scene emotionally and the experience was satisfying for me and Nitinda.

That was how Nitinda groomed me. He explained that a good script always helped an actor to perform effectively but there were areas beyond what was given to him in the script that were waiting to be explored by one who wished to rise above the given areas in his performance. When Rabindranath Tagore wrote *Nauka Dubi*, he would never have thought that the fine literary work would become the base of a feature film. So it was entirely up to the script writer to take the work to another level as a visual experience with the characters coming alive and living through all the experiences narrated in the book. 'There is no stopping you if you as an actor felt emboldened to discover niches in the character's emotional make-up that you would like to bring to the fore even if they are not there in the script,' he advised me.

He agreed that it was not easy for an actor to rise above the script, but it was not impossible either if the collaboration among the writer, actor and director worked well.

What Devika Rani had told me was also a lesson I have borne in mind and applied to my work sometimes to the surprise of my directors. She had pointed out that a director may be satisfied with the shot an actor had given but it is for the actor to discern for himself whether he had really given his best. The actor, she told me, was within his rights to request for another take if he felt he could do better.

I have not only borne all this in mind where my own work is concerned but also respected my co-actors' wishes if they wanted another take when it seemed fine for the director to can the shot. Devika Rani had advised me and all the actors she employed at Bombay Talkies that it was important to rehearse till a level of competence to perform was achieved. In the early years, it was a necessity for me to rehearse, but, even in the later years, her advice stayed with me when I had to match a benchmark I had mentally set for myself. In fact, I am aware that I am known for the number of rehearsals I do for even what seems to be a simple scene.

With Nargis and Ashok Kumar in *Deedar* (1951).

Let me give an example. There was a situation in Nitin Bose's *Deedar* (1951), in which Ashok Bhaiyya and I had lines to deliver and the cue for his lines had to be taken from my lines. In our rehearsals we had mutually decided that the word '*mulayam*' (meaning soft) in my dialogue would be his cue to speak and turn his face towards me. Being a Bombay Talkies man, Ashok Bhaiyya had as much of a fetish for rehearsals as I had and so we had already had almost eight to ten rehearsals. The director told us to be ready for the take and he called for action. When I spoke my dialogue, quite inadvertently, I replaced the word '*mulayam*' with '*narm*' (also meaning soft) and Ashok Bhaiyya was thrown off track. I don't know what went wrong with me that day. The director called: 'CUT'; and I need not tell you what followed. Though not one to lose his temper, Ashok Bhaiyya gave me a piece of his mind and said gruffly: 'OK, now we will stick to "*narm*".'

12

REEL LIFE VERSUS REAL LIFE

⸺⸺◦⊙⸳⊙⸳⊙◦⸺⸺

K. Asif was seriously trying to mend the situation for her [Madhubala] when matters began to sour between us, thanks to her father's attempt to make the proposed marriage a business venture. The outcome was that half way through the production of Mughal-e-Azam, *we were not even talking to each other. The classic scene with the feather coming between our lips, which set a million imaginations on fire, was shot when we had completely stopped even greeting each other.*

$\mathcal{G}$ETTING BACK TO *MELA* (RELEASED IN 1948), I REMEMBER driving to Filmistan Studios with S. U. Sunny, discussing the story on the way. When we reached the studio and walked on to the stage, the title song was being played. The description I got from the director of the proposed picturization was absolutely flat. I suggested changes in the situation and the picturization, which were appreciated by the director and Naushad Miyan, the music composer.

The storyline of *Mela* was a sketchy one and, having had the good fortune of getting involved in stimulating discussions with such thought-provoking writers as Bhagwaticharan Verma, Narendra

In *Mela* (1948).

Sharma, Gyan Mukherjee and Nabendu Ghosh, I was able to sense
the absence of meat in it for the actors and I felt it had to be brought to
the director's attention at the very outset. He agreed with me, which
was very good not only for me but for the other artistes as well. We
had some healthy brainstorming sessions, which helped us to add
depth and intensity to the story besides logic. We also managed to
give the characters more emotional sensitivity and depth.

Mela still evokes some wonderful memories of the past that I must
share. First of all, it was the first film Aghaji watched in a cinema
house because Naushad Miyan persuaded him to view it. He must
have gone for a matinee show with Chacha Ummer and one of his
friends. He was seated in the front room of our new house in Pali Mala
when I returned a little early that day because I had to get some new
medicines the doctor had prescribed for my mother and somehow get
her to gulp down the mixture she disliked. I greeted him as I always
did and he asked me to sit next to him. Chacha Ummer was already
seated near him and he had a mischievous smile playing round his
lips. So I wondered what was going on. Then, Chacha Ummer came

out with it. He disclosed they had gone to a cinema house and watched *Mela* and it was a revelation that so many people had actually bought admission tickets and had filled the hall. He elaborated that it was a very enjoyable experience and it was incredible that I was right there on the screen behaving and talking very differently and wondered whatever had happened to all the shyness and the reluctance I had shown generally when it came to making free conversation with the opposite sex. He now waited for Aghaji to take up the conversation. Aghaji looked at me and his expressive eyes showed his concern for something that was going on in his mind. He then said: 'Look if you really want to marry that girl, I can talk to her parents. Just tell me who she is. You don't have to be so unhappy.'

For a moment, I failed to fathom what was being spoken by both of them. Then it dawned on me that they were speaking about Nargis,* the heroine in *Mela*, carried away as they were by the story and the performances. I could clearly see their inability, as first-time viewers of a feature film, to accept and enjoy it all as make-believe. I could not help laughing to myself but I knew it was an impression I had to correct immediately lest Aghaji and Chacha Ummer take steps to find Nargis and put me in an embarrassing situation.

Secondly, the picture was memorable for the enduring friendship that began between me and Naushad Miyan and between me and Nargis. With Nargis it was a no-holds-barred friendship. It was as though we were of the same gender because she was not at all hesitant to join the menfolk in their talks and was not one to be shocked if a bawdy remark was made in front of her. Her mother, Jaddan Bai, had become friendly with Amma and my elder sister due to her frequent visits to our home and later Aghaji came to know Nargis was an actress who feigned emotions while acting with me and there was nothing but a healthy friendship between us.

Nargis was no doubt a very capable actress who was getting better with every film. I could see that she had improved vastly when we were cast in Mehboob Khan's *Andaz* (1949). It was a delightful experience doing *Andaz* because Raj Kapoor was there in the film

*Nargis was born as Fatima Rashid on 1 June 1929.

With Nargis and Raj Kapoor in *Andaz* (1949).

and it was like the times we spent at Khalsa College when we played soccer. He used to stand red faced in the blazing sunlight, shouting and yelling in Punjabi when I scored a goal for my team.

Raj and Nargis shared a chemistry that made a good equation for their scenes together. With Nargis, in front of the camera, I shared a different equation, and I felt all through the making of *Andaz* that she was there and yet not there when we emoted scenes that had to have a certain temperature – to use my own coinage to describe the intensity that holds an emotional scene between two artistes.

For instance, Ashok Bhaiyya and Nalini Jaywant were able to build that temperature possibly due to their knowing each other well. Nargis and Raj could bring up the feelings demanded of them and, consequently, they did their scenes with ease. I was able to attain that ease with Madhubala in *Tarana* (1951), which has remained, for many reasons, one of the films I would count among the memorable ones I have done in the early years of my career. She was a vivacious artiste and was so instantaneous in her responses that the scenes became riveting even when they were being filmed. The scenes would move at a brisk speed when we rehearsed a few times and when we went for the final take. And that was because she was an artiste who could keep pace and meet the level of involvement demanded by the script.

I felt instantaneously comfortable with Mehboob Sahab. There are some people with whom one starts feeling relaxed and secure as though one has known them for ages. With Mehboob Sahab it was that kind of comfort from day one. He gave me the freedom to talk to him about the way I wanted to perform a scene and he let me show him how I intended to do it before he told me how he had visualized it. He liked healthy debates and believed that it was the end result that mattered and the trivial question of whose idea it was had no relevance in team work.

We held our meetings in Mehboob Sahab's house or at Naushad Miyan's residence and it was in one such meeting (I think in the early 1950s) that I disclosed my intention of switching over to comedy since I had been clinically advised to do so by one Dr W. D. Nichols who had been introduced to me by Dame Margret Rutherford and Dame Sybil Thorndike with whom I had long discussions when I had met them through a drama coach in London.

With Madhubala in *Tarana* (1951).

Dr Nichols was kind enough to spend a good one hour with me when I called on him. I shared my fears with the eminent psychiatrist and he assuaged me saying it was not a cause for worry since many of his celebrity patients from the acting profession had come to him with the same fears and he had told them what he was going to tell me. He suggested a quick change of the genre of films I was doing. He explained to me that most actors who repeatedly worked in the same genre of films found it difficult to overcome the dichotomy that confronted them between the two lives they were leading. The unreal sometimes, or rather most times, became so overpowering that the real called for protection from caving in and getting submerged. I had been playing characters who were ill-fated and a morbid outlook had seized me as a result of my extreme involvement and my living the character beyond the working hours.

Dr Nichols said he was certain that I took my work home in my subconscious and turned the spoken lines and the scenes over and over in my mind in my bid to review the work I had done during the day. I was naturally appalled by his accuracy in diagnosing my condition. He added with utmost seriousness: 'My dear young man, you are not alone in this crisis. It is a similar condition that a student who gears himself for excellence and top ranking goes through. The only way out is to go for variety in your work. Spend more time in leisure that you enjoy or with friends you feel happy to be with.'

I understood what he meant. Indeed, I had got so involved in the work I was doing that I had unintentionally distanced myself from my brothers and sisters, seeing them only for a short time on returning home every night and I had almost stopped playing football and cricket with my friends.

It is not as if I did not realize that whatever I was doing in the films was unreal and diametrically opposite to my real life and my real self. But the situation was such that people came and talked about some of the tragic scenes I had done convincingly or about a film that had attracted them to view it repeatedly because a death scene in it was beautifully performed and that made me think about it even if I didn't want to. It was good to hear the compliments, especially at a stage when one was in the process of evolving as an actor but the impact was overwhelming to say the least. I was barely in my twenties and I was doing tragedy. Renowned tragedians in Western cinema like Sir John Gielgud, for example, had never done tragedy at such an early impressionable age. They were in their thirties when they played tragic roles.

I spoke at length and I remember both Mehboob Sahab and Naushad Sahab just stared at me. They were unable to grasp my dilemma and my need to get a comforting approval from them. They thought I was crazy to go and seek advice from psychiatrists and drama coaches in England. They named other actors who were sticking to the same genre and had no problems whatsoever. I went home somewhat distraught.

The next day I went over to meet S. Mukherjee Sahab and I told him I had seen a Tamil film,* which a producer from Madras (now Chennai) had arranged for me to see. The producer Sriramulu Naidu wanted to make it in Hindi and it meant a complete change of screen image if I chose to do it. K. Asif (the director of the 1960 *Mughal-e-Azam*) also happened to be present when I was talking to Mukherjee Sahab and, smiling provocatively, he said: '*Karke dikhaiye.*' (Let's see you do it.) Asif's look was like a gauntlet thrown down for me. Mukherjee Sahab had no second thoughts about the decision I was waiting to take. He said: 'Go ahead and do it. An actor's business is acting and it should not matter to him whether he is doing tragedy or comedy. What counts is the actor's ability and enterprise.'

I returned home with a feeling of confidence. I knew that comedy required a broad base and an exceptional sense of timing, which was a carefully honed skill more than a gift or flair. Initially, my fear was whether I possessed that skill. Now it was a challenge, a necessity that cried out for some daring on my part.

Azaad (released in 1955), in many ways, was the first film that gave me the much-needed confidence to forge ahead with a feeling of

*The film was *Malaikallan* (1954), featuring M. G. Ramachandran (MGR) as the hero.

In *Azaad* (1955).

emancipation and sense of achievement. I was in Mahabaleshwar (a hill station in Maharashtra) on the opening day, deliberately staying away from home and friends in Bombay.

I was woken up by V. V. Purie Sahab* at midnight and he was calling from Delhi to tell me the great news that the film was a hit. We kept congratulating each other till we hung up out of a sheer need to get some sound sleep.

The delirious caller to wake me up early next morning was Sriramulu Naidu and I felt ever so happy for him because he had such confidence in me that he gave me absolute freedom to incorporate whatever ideas occurred to me to make the script and screenplay entertaining. It was also a pleasant experience working with Meena Kumari,** for whom the film offered a welcome switchover to light-hearted acting from the serious acting she came to be known for with *Baiju Bawra* (1952) and *Parineeta* (1953). She was a sprightly person who got along very well with every member of the unit and enjoyed taking lessons in Tamil from Naidu who was forever on a Tamil instruction spree during the indoor shooting we did in Coimbatore and Madras.

*V. V. Purie, then a film financier, was the father of Aroon Purie of *India Today* fame.
**Meena Kumari was born as Mahjabeen Bano on 1 August 1932.

Naidu and I hit it off quite unexpectedly from the very first day of shooting. He was so happy about the start of the production that he insisted on hosting a lunch at a house in Madras, which belonged to a wealthy Chettiar (a business community), to introduce me to all the famous people he knew well in the southern film industry. The lunch was laid out for all the invitees on banana leaves as is customary in the South on festive occasions. It was the first time I was being treated to a typical South Indian meal served in four courses with three different desserts coming one after the other as the climax. After a whole series of vegetables were served on the leaf in an order that seemed fixed and unchangeable, a mound of rice was served in the middle of the leaf and *sambhar* (a kind of broth) was added to it. I was seated next to a gentleman who had a beatific smile on his face and took it upon himself to tell me in detail what each of the vegetable dishes was called in Tamil and how I should proceed from one dish to the other to get the right combinations. I did exactly as he instructed, not wanting to disappoint him and the host, Naidu, who was seated opposite me and engaged in an animated conversation with someone he seemed to know well.

All was well till the *rasam*, which resembles a watery soup, came in a ladle and the man who was serving stood anxiously by my side, directing a curious smile at me. I was at a loss and completely taken by surprise. I had seen my friend seated next to me take the *rasam* in his cupped palm ever so casually and slurp it down with relish. I was certain I couldn't manage that!

As the man stood waiting for me to cup my palm and take a ladle full of the tempting liquid, an idea crossed my mind. I made a small well in the rice mound, made a dam around it for safety and to arrest its flow, and asked him to pour it there. He obliged with a knowing smile, which I returned. I was pleased with myself for having artfully got out of a tricky situation and hastened to finish the meal. The real test, however, was yet to come.

After the hearty meal, we retired to a drawing room where large sofas waited for the invitees to be seated as relaxingly as decency permits. There was a lot of chatter in Tamil and Telugu and I could gather that they were all thinking aloud about Naidu's madness to make the film in Hindi and court failure. Naidu had a sole ally in L. V. Prasad (a well-known producer-director from the South) who kept on speaking encouragingly and shaking his hand. All the invitees were polite and nice to me, though.

The climax of the afternoon came when a large silver bowl arrived on a plate with a semi-thick liquid in it. The valet who brought the bowl into the drawing room went from one invitee to the other and I watched each of them take a scoop and rub it all over the belly, lifting up their shirts and then cover the smeared paste with the shirt back in its place as if there was nothing on the belly. I could distinctly get the fragrance of sandalwood, so I knew it was nothing but sandalwood paste.

I did not ask any questions when the bowl came to me. I took a scoop and smeared it on my hairy belly and decided to forget about it. But sure enough, it wasn't easy for me to forget about it. The paste began to dry up and the hair on my belly was beginning to get taut and it was becoming painful for me. I could feel a hundred pinpricks on my belly and the discomfort was distracting. What does one do in such a perilous situation? I excused myself and headed straight for the washroom. I bolted the door and removed my shirt and *banian* (vest). I soaked the *banian* in running water from the wash basin and wiped out the dried paste with it. The feel of cold water gave me a great relief. I saw an open window at the rear end of the large washroom overlooking a garden. I flung the *banian* out, wore my shirt and returned triumphantly to the drawing room. No one there apparently noticed my absence and no one came to know about the Chaplinesque episode. The gardener certainly would have wondered the next day about the bundled *banian* he would have found beneath one of the bushes and he would have dismissed it as someone's mischief.

I did not feel the need to tell Naidu about the episode. I tried to avoid formal lunches and dinners after that and Naidu imagined it was the language problem perhaps that deterred me from participating in such social activities. In truth, it was quite the contrary. I discovered a latent flair in me to assimilate both Tamil and Telugu as speedily as I had learned Bengali from Ashok Bhaiyya and S. Mukherjee Sahab. Besides, all the wonderful people I came to know in southern cinema capital were capable of speaking English with adequate fluency. We will go into that topic when I take you through my southern experiences.

If I presented myself with my first car after the success of *Shabnam* (1949), *Azaad*'s success, which gave me a true sense of achievement, made me think about having my own residence in the city, which was carving a very special place in my heart as my homeland, even transcending my sentimental attachment to my birth place, Peshawar, in the North West Frontier.

It had been my earnest desire to give Amma the security and comfort of being in a house that she could call her own when she was alive. Her health had been failing and she had to willy-nilly let go of the management of the household, which Sakina Aapa took over happily. As already mentioned, in temperament and attitude Sakina Aapa was more like my Dadi (paternal grandmother) whose Hitlerian authority pervaded the house administration in Peshawar. I had no doubt that my elder sister's high-handedness was what psychologists call 'learned behaviour'. But then the logical question was: Why did she not learn from Amma's gentle and kind behaviour? I guess some questions are best left unanswered.

Memories are hard to erase from the mind. Often, when I was alone in my room I recalled how on most evenings, I returned to my house after a day's exacting work to find Amma struggling with her asthmatic cough and feigning to be well. She had been extremely concerned about Ayub Sahab's deteriorating health condition. Ayub Sahab, she knew, was the closest to me among my brothers. So she had never failed to ask me curious questions about Ayub Sahab's lung functioning, which had been impaired since he fell from a horse. I was aware how much she missed him when he passed away.

I could not forget how Amma used to look up at me when I would

Clockwise: During the early days • The unit of Mehboob Khan (seated to my right) during the shooting of *Aan* (1952) • With the winners of the 1958 *Filmfare* awards (*L to R:* Composer O. P. Nayyar and actresses Nargis and Shyama) • With Bimal Roy, one of India's most talented film makers • Playing badminton with the nimble-footed Vyjayantimala as my partner • Fun times with Raj Kapoor and Dev Anand.

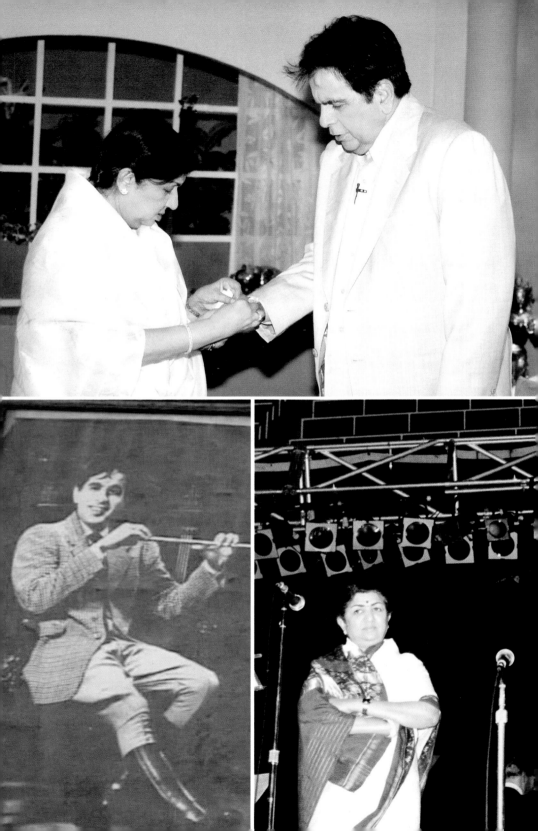

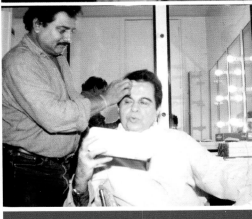

Clockwise: 'Younger sister' Lata Mangeshkar tying a Raakhee on my wrist • With my debonair colleague Dev Anand • Mingling with the public at a function • Getting the camera angle right • My make-up man giving the final touches before a shoot • Introducing Lata Mangeshkar at a stage show • A framed photograph of mine kept in my Peshawar house

Meeting my life partner Saira
• Got married on 11 October 1966
• Being received at the Madras airport by producer Nagi Reddy with Baby Farida on my right
• Celebrating with flowers

With Saira and her grandmother Shamshad Begum Abdul Waheed Khan (Ammaji) • Happy times with Saira • Saira with her brother Sultan and his wife Rahat Beg • With Saira and her mother Naseem Banu at a function

In a jovial mood with Saira • Giving the 'clap' during the shooting of one of Saira's films in the presence of poet Sahir Ludhianvi, composer Naushad and actors Murad, Kanwaljeet, Raaj Kumar and Rajendra Kumar, among others • With Saira at an outdoor location • Discussing a musical point with Naushad • With Indira Gandhi and Raj Kapoor at a function

tiptoe to her room after I had bathed and changed. She would beckon to me with her beautiful eyes and I would take my usual place at the bedstead so that she could rest her head on my chest while I talked soothingly to her. When she would be fatigued with the effort of breathing, I helped her to breathe effortlessly by giving support to her ribs, pressing with hand support then letting go. Sometimes, when she wanted to get up and sit on a chair in the room, I just carried her in my arms, amidst protests and gentle laughter from her, and placed her in the chair. Aghaji, in jest and to make light the atmosphere would say: '*Itna shauq hai meri biwi ko utha kar ghoomaney ka, to apni biwi lao!*' (If you are so fond of lifting my wife and going around with her, then find your own wife!)

My eldest brother, Noor Sahab, was forever in the company of his friends. My younger brothers were busy with their studies and so were my younger sisters. They had Sakina Aapa's watchful eye over them and they had been so disciplined by her that if they wanted something they dared not approach me directly as it annoyed Aapa who had made herself the sole authority in the house. My aunts too feared her and made uncomplimentary remarks behind her back. The one person who did not treat her with awe was Chacha Ummer. He made all sorts of harmless and jolly remarks about the heroines I worked with, much to Aapa's irritation. Every time he mischievously suggested matrimony for me with one of the ladies I teamed with, she either politely asked him to go and find himself something to do or she stormed out of the room indignantly. I sensed that she disapproved of most of the actresses I was working with, though she was very civil and cordial when they visited our home. I felt that she got along well with Nargis whose mother, Jaddan Bai, was very fond of me and affectionately addressed me as Prince. It amused me when Aapa asked me one evening whether I knew what was going on between Raj and Nargis. I told her that she should ask Raj who used to drop in unexpectedly and make his presence felt in our quiet house by talking to everyone and demanding the aromatic milkless tea that Aapa made specially for him.

It was not in my nature to intrude into anyone's personal life. I remember having lunch with Askok Bhaiyya and Nalini Jaywant one afternoon in Filmistan Studio where they were also shooting on another floor. After we finished eating, Ashok Bhaiyya headed for the washroom to wash his hands and Naliniji followed him. Quite unsuspectingly, I followed too because I had to quickly get back to work after washing my hands. In a moment, I realized how foolish I was to have followed them like that. I should have known better or at least have tried to make some sound to alert them. However, I never took the liberty to make any reference to that embarrassment in any of our conversations though I knew Ashok Bhaiyya, being the carefree man he was, would not have taken it amiss and he would probably have laughed it off.

The gossip press, even in those years, was quick to smell any emotional involvement between actors and the leading ladies they worked with and splash exaggerated and imaginary news in the columns of their publications. The spotlight then, as it is now, was always on the successful actors who had a following and whose private lives interested their readers. Initially, I was annoyed by this invasion, which was very unbecoming at times. I felt it was not fair to the ladies and it would cause them needless worry about their public image getting tarnished.

I spent time with some of the leading writers of gossip to impress upon them the role they should play as cinema journalists. I tried to explain to them that actors were like any other professionals who did a job from nine to five or two to ten or whatever the schedule was. The only difference was that we entered an unreal world as unreal people every day when we got down to work unlike other working men and women who remained themselves and expressed real emotions in their interactions with their colleagues. In our world of mimic laughter and tears, as actors emoting intense feelings for each other in close physical proximity, we sometimes lost consciousness of the slender line separating the real and unreal.

Did it happen with me? Was I in love with Madhubala as the newspapers and magazines reported at that time? As an answer to this oft-repeated question straight from the horse's mouth, I must admit that I was attracted to her both as a fine co-star and as a person who had some of the attributes I hoped to find in a woman

With Madhubala in
Mughal-e-Azam (1960).

at that age and time. We had viewers admiring our pairing in *Tarana* and our working relationship was warm and cordial. She, as I said earlier, was very sprightly and vivacious and, as such, she could draw me out of my shyness and reticence effortlessly. She filled a void that was crying out to be filled – not by an intellectually sharp woman but a spirited woman whose liveliness and charm were the ideal panacea for the wound that was taking its own time to heal.

The announcement of our pairing in *Mughal-e-Azam* made sensational news in the early 1950s because of the rumours about our emotional involvement. In fact, K. Asif (the film's director) was ecstatic with the wide publicity and trade enquiries he got from the announcement. It was not anticipated or planned that it would be in production for such a long period as it was and Asif was aware of Madhu's feelings for me because she had confided in him during one of their intimate talks. And, he was equally aware of my nature *as a man who made no haste* in taking critical personal or professional decisions. As was his wont, he took it upon himself to act as the catalyst and went to the extent of encouraging her in vain to pin me down somehow. He went on to advise her that the best way to draw a commitment from an honourable and principled Pathan, brought up on old-world values, was to draw him into physical intimacy.

In retrospect, I feel he did what any selfish director would have done for his own gain of creating riveting screen chemistry between actors who are known to be emotionally involved. Also, I sensed Asif was seriously trying to mend the situation for her when matters began to sour between us, thanks to her father's attempt to make the proposed marriage a business venture. The outcome was that half way through the production of *Mughal-e-Azam*, we were not even talking to each other. The classic scene with the feather coming between our lips, which set a million imaginations on fire, was shot when we had completely stopped even greeting each other. It should, in all fairness, go down in the annals of film history as a tribute to the artistry of two professionally committed actors who kept aside personal differences and fulfilled the director's vision of a sensitive, arresting and sensuous screen moment to perfection.

Asif and I were temperamentally and intellectually poles apart. Though as friends we shared an informality in our interactions, he knew he was not welcome to share my thoughts unless I invited him. Frankly, I had more concerns occupying my thoughts than the love scenes in the film. I had very little textual reference to study the personal characteristics of Prince Salim. It was imperative for me to establish a mental bond with the character and I knew from the moment I agreed to play the role that it was going to be a lone journey of research and discovery from whatever material was available.

Interestingly, Asif had wanted me to play Prince Salim in a project he had started way back when I was working in *Nadiya Ke Paar* (1948). He had invited me over to his house and introduced me to his wife, the Kathak danseuse Sitara Devi, with whom an instant rapport developed as we talked about classical Hindustani music and dance forms. As our conversation progressed and she had served us tea and snacks, Sitara Bhabhi hesitatingly asked me if she could call me Bhaijaan (brother) as she felt a sisterly affection for me and she had only one brother and had room in her heart for one more.

Asif remained quiet and observant while Sitara Bhabhi talked seamlessly about dance, music, films, weather, food, servants and what have you. Finally, Asif got a chance to get in a word. He said he liked everything about me but he felt I was rather too young to play Prince Salim at that juncture. He remarked: 'You have the royal bearing of a prince but I want an older look.' I told him he was right. Rather prophetically, he then declared that in the future he would make a film relating the love story of Salim and Anarkali on a scale that would inspire awe and he would cast me as the romantic prince. I was somewhat amused by his overweening sense of supreme confidence but I had enough sense not to reveal my amusement. He announced the film shortly with Sapruji (D. K. Sapru. who later became a character actor) in the lead but due to financial curbs he could not go beyond a few reels.

So when he approached me years later with the proposal of *Mughal-e-Azam*, it was like a dream come true for him. I had by then moved up the echelons of stardom and our friendship and my fraternal ties with Sitara Devi had continued uninterrupted despite there being no talk of work between us. Then, one day, he came to meet me with a twinkle in his eyes and, after the usual pleasantries, he began to recall our first meeting and he reminded me of the promise he had made to himself to film the story of Anarkali and Prince Salim on a scale of grandeur and opulence that would inspire awe and I would play the prince. I remembered the episode vividly and couldn't help marvelling at the ways of Destiny.

I worked on Salim's personality by fine-tuning my instincts appropriately to create a screen persona who closely matched the descriptions I read in some fine books I got hold of in the Anjuman Islam school library. I could always depend on my friend Mohammad Umar Mukri (a short-statured character actor) to help me out on such occasions. He rummaged through bookshops and got me whatever he could lay his hands on. To cut the story short, I think I more or less succeeded in approximating my get-up and screen persona of Prince Salim to the picture I had formed in my mind. I knew at the very start of the project that I was not going to get much help from Asif. He had numerous concerns to deal with as the director and in his typical manner he laughed away my worries saying: 'Just be yourself. You are Prince Yousuf.'

13

MADHUBALA

I did feel sorry for Madhu and wished she had the will to protect her interests at least on the professional front without thoughtlessly bowing to her father's wishes all the time. Such submission had an adverse impact not only on her professional reputation but also on her health needlessly.

MADHUBALA WAS NO DOUBT THE RIGHT CHOICE FOR THE ROLE of Anarkali. She grasped the essence of the character in no time with her agile intelligence. Yes, there was talk of our marriage while the shooting of *Mughal-e-Azam* was in progress in the 1950s. Contrary to popular notions, her father, Ataullah Khan, was not opposed to her marrying me. He had his own production company and he was only too glad to have two stars under the same roof. Had I not seen the whole business from my own point of view, it would have been just what he wanted, that is, Dilip Kumar and Madhubala holding hands and singing duets in his productions till the end of our careers. When I learned about his plans from Madhu, I explained to both of them that I had my own way of functioning and selecting projects and I would not show any laxity even if it were my own production house. It must have tilted the apple cart for him and he successfully convinced Madhu that I was being rude and presumptuous. I told her in all sincerity and honesty that I did not mean any offence and it was

With Madhubala in a romantic scene from
Mughal-e-Azam (1960).

in her interest and mine as artistes to keep our professional options away from any personal considerations. She was naturally inclined to agree with her father and she persisted in trying to convince me that it would all be sorted out once we married. My instincts, however, predicted a situation in which I would be trapped and all the hard work and dedication I had invested in my career would be blown away by a hapless surrender to someone else's dictates and strategies. I had many upfront discussions with her father and she, not surprisingly, remained neutral and unmoved by my dilemma. The scenario was not very pleasant and it was heading inevitably to a dead end. In the circumstances, therefore, it seemed best that we did not decide to marry or even give each other a chance to rethink because my resolve by then had become strongly against a union that would not be good for either of us.

I was truly relieved when we parted because I had also begun to get an inkling that it was all very well to be working together as artistes but in marriage it is important for a woman to be ready to give more than receive. I had grown up seeing Amma's steadfast devotion to the family and her flawless character as a woman. I was

now increasingly seized with the feeling that I was letting myself
into a relationship more on the rebound than out of a genuine need
for a permanent companion. What's more, I did not want to share
a lifetime with someone whose priorities were different from mine.
Besides, she certainly would have been drawn to other colleagues in
the profession, as I found out, and they to her but that wasn't an issue
because I was myself surfacing from an emotional upheaval at that
point of time.

The parting of ways did not affect me as was concocted by writers in
the media. Journalists were not as rash as they are now but they were
just as unmindful of factual accuracy when they wrote about actors.
Some of them wrote 'authoritatively' in their gossip magazines and
attributed my choosing to remain a bachelor all my life to the assumed
heartbreak of not marrying Madhubala. The story had sentimental
appeal for readers. Nobody bothered to check out the facts and, at
that point of time, I was far too absorbed in my work and my family
responsibilities to give clarifications. Let me state categorically that I
chose to remain a bachelor because I had young sisters to be married
off and for me the taking care of, and ensuring the happiness of, my
brothers and sisters were paramount.

The absolute truth is that I had mentally stayed all thoughts
of sharing my space with a spouse because I had taken on the
responsibility of settling my sisters and brothers. As mentioned earlier,
Amma was ailing with an acute respiratory disorder and Aghaji was
trying hard to hide the debilitating impact of advancing age from all
of us. He was not one to ask for a helping hand to rise from a chair or
descend a steep staircase. He was dressed and ready every morning
to visit his fruit shop. The premature death of Ayub Sahab had dealt
an emotional blow, from which my parents could only pretend to
recover. Another widespread canard was that the break-up between
Madhu and me caused the heart condition that finally claimed her
life. The heart condition that was diagnosed was congenital in her.
It was unfortunate that she began to succumb to the condition and

had to discontinue the commitments she had made to producers. Unfortunately, medical facilities then were not as advanced as they are now in the area of cardiology.

I had become a star by the early 1950s and Aghaji was reconciled to the truth that whatever he had wished for me in all his prayers had been granted by Allah. The initial unhappiness and hurt pride that he experienced when he came to know that the son on whom he had pinned hopes of achievements as a high-ranking bureaucrat or statesman had become an entertainer had given way to grateful and humble acceptance of the will of Allah.

Among my brothers and sisters, I knew I was the one whom both Aghaji and Amma trusted implicitly for shouldering, in ever so many unspoken and unanticipated ways, the responsibility of educating and settling the daughters and sons who were younger than I. Noor Sahab had married and moved out with his wife. My eldest sister, Sakina Aapa, remained unmarried and, as Amma often felt, it was providential that she was single as her unyielding character was not suited for a successful marriage. As she grew older, she mellowed and became softer in her relationship with Amma but wilful she still was. It was always worrying for Amma how her eldest daughter would live her life alone in the world and whenever she spoke of it, her moist eyes would search for an assuring whisper from me.

I loved Amma deeply. She was the fountainhead of all the merits and virtues we – her children – possessed. She dealt with all the exigencies of life with a quiet poise and calmness of mind. I took pleasure even as a child in observing her when she prayed. As I grew up I began to feel that the time she took off from her chores for namaaz was her time in her own space to meditate and attain control over her mind and thoughts and achieve that nearness to the Supreme Being, which is a rare achievement. She appeared frail and delicate but she was strong and invincible inside. Aghaji and I knew it.

Let me get back to the main narrative. Madhubala's father, in a bid to show me his authority, got her entangled in a lawsuit with producer-director B. R. Chopra by suddenly making a fuss about the long outdoor work scheduled for *Naya Daur* (eventually released in 1957) giving her heart condition as a reason for her withdrawal from the film. He came up with an excuse about his daughter's inability to work at the outdoor locations in Bhopal and Poona for the film after some reels were canned. Chopra Sahab was upset and very angry because it was made clear at the very outset, when the script narration was given to the artistes, that it was an outdoor film. There were all sorts of conclusions drawn by people who did not know the sequence of events and the true background when Chopra Sahab, who held a bachelor's degree in law before he took to journalism in Lahore in the pre-independence period, took legal steps to challenge the whimsicality on Madhu's part. As a fellow artiste, I could do little but fall in line with the producer's decision to replace Madhu with Vyjayantimala, when all sincere and genuine efforts on my part to negotiate an easy compromise without making the issue public became futile. I did feel sorry for Madhu and wished she had the will to protect her interests at least on the professional front without thoughtlessly bowing to her father's wishes all the time. Such submission had an adverse impact not only on her professional reputation but also on her health needlessly.

All through my career I respected the producer's right as an employer to discipline the cast and crew and demand cooperation from them once the contract was signed. Vyjayantimala and I had worked with a fair measure of respect and understanding in Bimal Roy's *Devdas* (1955) and Chopra Sahab had liked her work. (She had played the role of Chandramukhi, a tender-hearted dancing girl.) He had heard from his own sources that she was hard working and malleable as an artiste. Chopra Sahab went ahead with the replacement of Madhubala by Vyjayantimala without wasting time once he accepted the situation that all the shooting done with Madhubala would have to go into cold storage and the loss of time and substantial funds would have to be reconciled with. The announcement of the renewal of the project and the start of fresh shooting for *Naya Daur* created a stir in the media. Much of what appeared in the media was misreporting by gossip writers who twisted and twirled facts to make them palatable to readers. Like Chopra Sahab, I took it all in my stride, though it caused anger and pain at times when I was made to appear as if I had got Madhu out of the film while the truth was that her father pulled her out of the project to demonstrate his authority.

14

DEVDAS, NAYA DAUR AND BEYOND

It was during the making of Naya Daur *that I noticed Vyjayanti's ability to feign a rustic character's mannerisms with conviction. When I was scripting* Gunga Jumna, *I felt she would fit the role of Dhanno if she took pains to render the Bhojpuri dialect (used in the film) with the right accent and inflexions .... It was during the production of* Naya Daur *that I began to form the story idea of* Gunga Jumna *in my mind. I decided too that if I went ahead and made* Gunga Jumna, *I would cast Vyjayanti in the lead.*

BEFORE I MOVE ON TO *NAYA DAUR* AND VYJAYANTIMALA, I MUST dwell on *Devdas*, the first of the seven films with her as my leading lady.

When Bimal Roy (popularly called Bimalda) approached me sometime in 1954 with the idea of playing the title role in the film *Devdas*, neither had I seen the earlier 1936 K. L. Saigal starrer nor had I read Sharat Chandra Chattopadhyay's famous novel of the same name. In fact, Bimalda did not tell me at once, when he visited me, that his intention was to discuss the film he was so keen to make. After some pleasant talk he let our mutual friend Hiten Choudhury (basically a producer), who accompanied him, bring up the subject.

It was something I had not anticipated, so I asked for a few days to think it over. He nodded and smiled. Then, as he was leaving, he said very quietly, 'read the novel, I will send you a fine translation.'

Bimalda was a man of few words. He left and I received the translation the next day. I won't go into details but it troubled me initially to experiment with the rendering of a character who carried a heavy measure of pain and despondency under the skin and could mislead the more vulnerable youth to believe that alcoholism offered the best escape from the pain of losing in love. As I reflected over the subject, which had already been filmed very successfully with K. L. Saigal in the title role, I felt that it could become a memorable film and find itself a place among the iconic films of all time if I played the part with appropriate discretion.

Today's cinema and its audience, sadly, don't have the kind of emotional give and take that the cinema of the 1950s had. The basic reason was that cinema was the main source of entertainment those days and, more often than not, its content was taken seriously by most viewers. I am emphasizing this aspect to give credit to the directors

With Motilal in *Devdas* (1955).

who shouldered serious moral responsibility in our times when they chose to make films that had deep social relevance and implications for the audience.

I think Bimalda knew from his own sources that I was a stickler for making the writing base of a film strong. So he made it comfortable for me to participate in the writing work along with his formidable team comprising Nabendu Ghosh and Rajinder Singh Bedi, among others. The lines from *Devdas*, I must mention here, are some of the most responsible and sensitive ever written for a Hindi film hero.

In fact, the dialogues of *Devdas* are replete with a haunting sensitivity, spontaneity and meaning. They came from the pen of Rajinder Singh Bedi, one of those rare writers whose syntax was so perfect that the simple lines he wrote inspired actors to build up deep emotions in their rendering. Being myself not given to superfluous speech, I appreciated the precision and brevity of the lines he wrote for *Devdas*. They were lines of profound meaning at times, but they were so simply and sensitively worded that generations of viewers have found pleasure in repeating them lovingly.

Vyjayanti and I carried forward the professional understanding and bonhomie we had developed during *Devdas* to the six films we worked in thereafter. She emerged as a capable artiste and a quick learner. After *Devdas*, when we came together for *Madhumati* (released in 1958), she had made considerable progress in her rendering of scenes and dialogue. She was diligent and took pains to grasp the pace and complexity of the situations, especially when the surrealistic and metaphysical scenes and situations were given to her for study before we went before the cameras to film *Madhumati*.

It was not easy for me or, for that matter, for Pran and Johnny Walker,* my co-artistes in *Madhumati*, to know whether or not Bimalda liked the shots he had taken when we were shooting

*Pran Krishan Sikand, the ace villain and character actor, and Johnny Walker (born as Badruddin Qazi), a comedian par excellence.

With Johnny Walker and David Abraham among others.

outdoors and indoors for that film. He was one director who never expressed his delight or approval vocally or through facial expression. If he liked the shot, he just moved on to the next shot, implicitly conveying to us that he had got what he had visualized. We, Pran and I, never gave up trying to get an exclamation of satisfaction from him when we gave a brilliant take but Bimalda just wouldn't succumb. He would simply say: 'Let us move the cameras for the next shot.' Then, he would amble over to cinematographer Dilip Gupta to get the next shot going.

The wonderful trait in Bimalda was his serenity and his refusal to get excited about anything. Which was very unusual for a Bengali. His exemplary virtue was his willingness to help his artistes if they failed to understand his vision. He once told me in his own gentle manner that the pain he had endured in his personal life when he was thrown to the wolves as a youth and he had to fend for himself and his mother had been an experience that taught him not to ever inflict pain on anybody.

Bimalda had a silhouette of *Madhumati* in his mind when we were concluding our work on *Devdas* and he had vaguely mentioned it to me. Later, when he gave me his first narration along with Ritwik

With Hrishikesh Mukherjee.

Ghatak, a talented film maker and script writer, I could sense his unflinching confidence in the subject. There were some people who told him it would be a risk to make a film that had metaphysical layers, which may not be easy for the viewer to absorb. There were others like Hrishikesh Mukherjee (or Hrishida),* I think, who encouraged and supported his belief in himself and egged him on to try a genre that offered splendid cinematic possibilities.

Bimalda and Dilip Gupta spent hours in conversation, often with paper and pencil, to sketch and visualize the atmosphere that had to be created for some of the scenes. Bimalda gave a patient hearing to anyone who had a suggestion.

All the three films, *Devdas*, *Madhumati* and *Yahudi* (1958) that I did under Bimalda's direction gave me the pleasure of knowing a man who believed in perfection and hard work as much as I did. He appreciated my style of working and the pains I took to endow life to the characters. Personally, I felt *Madhumati* was a clever and ingenious

*Hrishikesh Mukherjee, director, script writer and editor, who went on to make a string of superb films. In fact, I acted in his first directorial venture: *Musafir* (1957).

script. In the very first draft itself, I could see the possibilities the script offered. After *Devdas* I thought this picture would give us the much-needed relief especially since we would be shooting a sizable part of the film outdoors.

It was never the role that was of paramount importance when I agreed to do a film; there were other factors. Every role I played had its distinct merits and provocations. In *Madhumati* the incentive was the construction of the narrative and the layers of unpredictability in it. It appeared rather tricky for me to be the pivot of a suspenseful narrative that alternated between the past and present and threw up gripping situations for the audience. None of my previous characters had to get connected to a life that was lived in a previous birth. That was tricky for me and more so since my character was the pivot of the film's evolution and dramatic appeal.

I have always enjoyed outdoor work. In *Madhumati* the outdoor work was to become the core of the film and that alone filled me with the excitement of a child who is promised a long vacation at

With Vyjayantimala in *Madhumati* (1958).

a destination of his choice. To us – Pran, Johnny Walker, Bimalda, Hrishida and me – the time after 'pack-up' was very interesting. We got over the pressure of the day's work by spending the evenings in cheerful conversation and poetic exchanges while the cooks in the unit readied our dinner. Pran and I got along famously talking in Punjabi while Bimalda and Hrishida tried to outdo us in Bengali with their conversation. It used to be a little awkward the following day when Pran had to brim with hostility as the negative character in the script. I must say he was amazingly true to the character of Ugranarayan.

I have never considered any particular film crucial to the progress of my career. Each film gave me the valuable experience of discovering my own potential and adding to my understanding of the advancing medium. As I have often said, we, who worked during the formative years of Hindi cinema, had to tread a difficult terrain. In the case of *Madhumati*, there was the latent fear that the audience may just not identify with a reincarnation concept. So we worked with a common purpose of taking the picture to the goal of box-office success. And we were suitably rewarded as the film turned out to be a success.

The songs – penned by Shailendra and composed by Salil Chaudhury – and their picturization were a great success. Wherever one went those days, one heard the songs on radios and public speakers at community gatherings. It was an exhilarating experience for Bimalda I felt, though he remained as quiet and as unaffected as ever.

People who tried to find fodder for gossip mills were actively seeking a liaison between me and Vyjayanti when I selected her to play Dhanno in *Gunga Jumna* (released in 1961) after working together in four well-received films prior to it. (The fourth film was S. S. Vasan's *Paigham*, 1959.) The reality was that I had been observing her painstaking efforts to raise the scale and temperature of the emotions demanded by the challenging scenes she had to do with me for *Devdas*. She never complained about, or tired of, the umpteen rehearsals I asked for before we went for a take. I would particularly mention the scenes in which Devdas is deeply troubled and mortified by the irresistible attraction he feels for her and she, knowing it all with her feminine sixth sense, makes no bones about boldly unravelling her bruised feelings as the woman he needs but does not want to love. The complex ebb and flow of the responses we had to give each other, the modulation and timing of the pithy dialogue we were given to speak while keeping in mind the briefs given by Kamal Bose, the brilliant cameraman who used his expertise in lighting to heighten the temperature of such sensitive scenes, needed committed rehearsals. I noticed that she had the patience and the passion to achieve perfection. A virtue she had evidently acquired as a keen student of Bharata Natyam (a classical dance form that originated in South India) under fastidious teachers.

As a co-star, she was very well mannered and spoke respectfully to the senior actors and unit members. She came to the sets with her grandmother (Yadugiri Devi) who doted on her and made sure she got star treatment from her producers. Following her grandmother's instructions, no doubt, to assert her star status, she hardly lingered on the sets after the shooting and preferred to remain undisturbed in the make-up room and enjoy the vegetarian cuisine she brought along.

Her aloofness suited me and other unit members. We were unable to fathom, though, how she used the litres and litres of milk her grandmother ordered each day first thing on her arrival at the shooting venue. Did she wallow and bathe in it like Cleopatra? We wondered. My brother Nasir, who liked to play pranks, once brought a milk-laden buffalo, while we were shooting outdoors for *Gunga Jumna*, and he wanted to tie it to a pole outside the special makeshift make-up room we had put up for Vyjayanti. I got to know of it in good time and I rebuked and stopped him, averting a perilous situation.

By herself, Vyjayanti was not unsporting or unnecessarily orthodox. Nor was she given to believing or imagining that she was a bigger star than I was. She knew the facts but she simply agreed with her grandmother on all matters and, for practical reasons, never

With Vyjayantimala in *Paigham* (1959).

questioned her authority. Whenever we shot outdoors, she joined me and other members of the unit for a game of badminton while her grandmother watched her proudly. She was a fine player and she often gave us, the menfolk, tough competition with her nimble defences and serves.

On one occasion, when we were filming *Paigham*, at Gemini Studios in Madras, Vyjayanti and her grandmother found it appropriate to join us at a table that was laid out for tiffin, which usually consisted of South Indian snacks like *medu vadas* (fried, disc-shaped savouries), *upma* (a semi-solid dish made from semolina) and *chundal*. The lastmentioned item always interested me. It was boiled chick peas garnished with finely chopped onions, curry leaves and mustard seeds that had crackled in the hot oil that was used. For Vyjayanti there was always seasonal fruits and of course milk. Her grandmother sat by her side on such occasions and urged her to eat the oranges she would peel for her while she talked about Madras and the great culture of the city. Vyjayanti spoke only when she managed to get a word in.

One evening, seeing the flutter around the table arising from the news that Pandit Jawaharlal Nehru, the prime minister of India, was going to visit the sets of *Paigham* a day or two later, before driving off to the airport after an engagement in the neighbourhood, Madam Yadugiri Devi chose to recall an event in Delhi where Panditji was the chief guest and Vyjayanti was centre-stage as the performer of the evening at a cultural gathering. That evening and the next evening all we heard was about Panditji and Papa (Papa, meaning baby in Tamil, was Vyjayanti's pet name) and all the unit members listened to the Panditji–Papa story with curiosity.

The big day arrived and S. S. Vasan Sahab, the founder of Gemini Studios, got us all together and told us how Panditji would be received and ushered to his office. He wanted me to head the reception line-up but I told him that Panditji knew Vyjayanti and admired her, so I suggested that she should take my place. I was supported by all those who had heard the Panditji–Papa story and Vasan Sahab agreed. I took my position at the tail end of the line.

Panditji arrived on schedule and, as is customary in Madras, he was welcomed with a rose garland and sprayed with fragrant water from a silver jar with a spout. He acknowledged it all with his wonderful simplicity. Vasan Sahab stood by his side and I think he was waiting for Panditji to greet Vyjayanti who was right there in front of his eyes. Suddenly, Panditji's searching eyes caught a glimpse of me at the far end of the line. He walked briskly towards me, saying: 'Yousuf, I heard you were here and I decided to drop in.' Vasan Sahab hurried behind him and, in a second, Panditji had reached where I was standing, stretching his arm over my shoulder affectionately. I was least prepared for the recognition and it took an instant for me to realize that I was walking with the country's most loved and admired leader.

Panditji spent a quarter of an hour in the studio, talking mostly about the potential of the medium to awaken social introspection and the desire to change stagnant customs and conventions in society. He had little time to watch new films but he came to know a lot from people he met and interacted with in his personal circle. After that, we never heard the Panditji–Papa story from Vyjayanti's grandmother.

S. S. Vasan Sahab was a genial, unassuming gentleman. We liked each other and became friends in no time. He was the boss of the sprawling studio and was a respected figure in the South Indian film industry. He liked chatting with me and telling me tales that may or may not have had anything to do with his own life. He narrated to me the story of a little boy who spent his days on a railway platform with his mother who sold magazines and newspapers to passengers who alighted at the station to purchase them. He related to me how the boy carried magazines and newspapers and ran from one end of the platform to the other screaming out their names to sell them to passengers seated in the compartments. By the time the train belched out of the station – I think he said Chingelpat (now known as Chengalpattu, located in north-eastern Tamil Nadu) – the boy would have sold most of the material he had with him and the mother would have sold most of the rest. Between the arrival of the trains there used to be ample time for the boy to rest his agile feet and sometimes or most times his mother took a nap, resting her head on the bag she carried every day. The boy could never sleep, so he read the newspapers and magazines, often with difficulty because he did not possess a great Tamil vocabulary. He, nevertheless, absorbed enough to enhance his general knowledge. By the evening the mother and son would return the couple of unsold magazines to the agent, collect their commission, go to a vegetarian food stall and have a snack, which never quite filled the boy's stomach.

I do not know why the story was narrated to me in great detail. I remember listening to him in rapt attention because he was a great storyteller. If you ask me the most successful film makers in India or anywhere else in the world are men and women who know how to tell stories without letting the listener's mind stray even for a split second. Vasan Sahab had great knowledge about everything and an imagination that came to the fore when we discussed scenes for *Paigham*.

He took me with him everywhere he went and it was a great pleasure to be in his company because he had so much knowledge about Madras Presidency and the history of the temples we passed by when we drove around in the early hours of the day or in the evenings when the streets would be filled with working people returning home with their purchases for their households like vegetables, groceries and so on. Some of the streets were lined with flower stalls from where women purchased the flowers that adorned their hair. Vasan Sahab enjoyed talking and I enjoyed listening to him. We often spoke about the next day's work and he used to ask me my opinion about a scene he had conceived and he would ask for my inputs unreservedly.

I remember I was travelling with him by train to Madurai (about 460 km south of Madras, famous for its Meenakshi temple) where he was to inspect a printing press he wanted to buy. In the train he told me he was unsure of the development of the scene we were to shoot the next day for *Paigham* as it was a tricky one where the heroine would muster up all her feminine guile to find out the hero's feelings for her. He said he had been applying his mind to create a humorous situation but it was just not happening.

The train was speeding past fields where women in bright coloured saris were toiling to earn their day's wages unmindful of the heat of the afternoon sun. We were in a nice first-class coupé and Vasan Sahab was looking at me expectantly while he poured out hot aromatic coffee into cups from a flask the train attendant had brought in a minute ago.

I told him I had seen a foreign film in which the hero and heroine meet on the terrace of a building where they hope to share some quiet moments. The heroine asks the hero if he had dated any girls or desired anyone before he met and befriended her. He tells her he will not reveal all that because it will upset her. She tells him don't be silly, we are grown-ups and there is no question of my getting upset. Her hair keeps falling over her face and he leans forward and moves the hair back to see her face clearly. Then he begins to tell her about a girl .... He sees the colour recede on her face and her eyes betray her anxiety. Finally he tells her: 'See, I told you ....' She is almost in tears. He then tells her that the girl he was describing and talking about was none other than the girl sitting in front of him.

I suggested to Vasan Sahab we could do the scene a bit differently. The hero would do all the talking and the heroine would respond with expressions. He would go on telling her about the woman he is in love with and arouse her envy and curiosity. She would try hard to hide her reactions but the audience can see that she is getting edgy and jealous from the expressions that flit across her face involuntarily. 'You think it can be managed?' Vasan Sahab asked me. I assured him that we could do it.

He was very excited when he described the scene to Vyjayanti the next day in the studio and I could see Vyjayanti's helpless gaze turn to me because the lines were not written and she did not know what I was going to say. How was she to prepare her expressions if she did not know what I was going to speak?

I then told Vasan Sahab: 'Let's do some rehearsals'. He was surprised that I had my lines ready. I told him that I had the lines in my mind in the train itself when we had discussed the scene and finalized it. I think Vasan Sahab couldn't contain his happiness and excitement about the way the scene turned out. That day and for many days after that he was bursting with delight and, sure enough, the scene turned out to be one of the highlights in the film.

Vasan Sahab had immense respect for writers and good writing. He was a writer himself and wrote short stories and novels. He was the chief editor of a Tamil magazine (*Ananda Vikatan*), which had a huge readership. It was thanks to him that I took a liking to Madras, where I desired to move and settle down in later years.

It was during the making of *Naya Daur* that I noticed Vyjayanti's ability to feign a rustic character's mannerisms with conviction. When I was scripting *Gunga Jumna*, I felt she would fit the role of Dhanno if she took pains to render the Bhojpuri dialect (used in the film) with the right accent and inflexions.

The making of *Naya Daur* is a small story by itself. When B. R. Chopra completed the story on paper, he took it to Mehboob Sahab to get an opinion. Those were the post-independence years and screen writers were brimming with national pride and were in the flush of a movement to give Indian cinema a platform at international film competitions by exploring plots that had universal relevance. Mehboob Sahab read the story and found no meat in it

With Daisy Irani and Vyjayantimala in *Naya Daur* (1957).

for entertainment. He told Chopra Sahab it could be made into a fine documentary on the doomsday awaiting the labour force in the country once machines replaced them but, as a feature film, it was not a great idea.

Chopra Sahab listened to the senior film maker's opinion respectfully, but he had made up his mind that he would make the film if I agreed to act in it. He told me this emphatically after he gave me the idea in a nutshell. I liked the idea except for the climax in which originally the bus was to be beaten by the tonga (a horse-drawn carriage) by some kind of manipulation. It did not seem logical to me. However, I kept the thought to myself since there was no chance of my accepting the film.

Initially, it seemed as if Chopra Sahab and I were not destined to come together. When Chopra Sahab came to me with the *Naya*

Daur script, I was committed to a film Gyan Mukherjee had specially written with me in mind. So I told Chopra Sahab that his project would have to wait till Gyan Mukherjee's film went on the floors and he completed the shooting. I liked the basic premise of the *Naya Daur* story and the intent, but it was not possible for me to work on two scripts simultaneously because that would lead to overlapping of thoughts and ideas, which could affect the content of both the films adversely.

I explained to him that it was for this very reason that I had not welcomed the idea of doing *Pyaasa* (when offered to me by producer-director Guru Dutt) because I was then involved in *Devdas* and, though the subject of *Pyaasa* was very inviting for a serious actor like me, I felt there was a similarity in the shades of the character of Devdas and the hero of *Pyaasa*. The logic was quite simple: if I had accepted *Pyaasa* unthinkingly it would have been released close on the heels of *Devdas* and one of them would have overshadowed the other. It made bad business sense to me. (Guru Dutt eventually played the hero in *Pyaasa*, which was released in 1957.)

Chopra Sahab was visibly troubled but he agreed to wait. As Destiny would have it, Gyan Mukherjee's film did not take off due to some financial hassles and I was ready to consider *Naya Daur*.

The wonderful memory I have of the outdoor shooting of *Naya Daur* is the friendship that developed between me and the Chopras. Baldev Raj, the elder Chopra, and Yash and Dharam, the younger brothers, had one common love: Food! It delighted me immensely to know this. Dharam was constantly busy with the camera assistants and the lightmen as it is always quite unpredictable how the natural lights on a location would turn out as the day begins and progresses towards sundown.

Yash was assigned by his elder brother to be with me and take care of my needs. He discovered soon enough that he and I had the same needs: a man's breakfast, a man's lunch and a man's dinner. So it was agreed between us that we would get our own breakfast ready because we both loved omelettes and we knew the cook was a faint-hearted local chap who might just faint if he counted the number of eggs we consumed. So, on most days, we got the eggs from the market and, between me and Yash, we chopped the onions finely and slit and chopped the less pungent green chillies we had carefully selected from the market. We beat at least ten eggs and folded the onions and chillies into the frothy mixture and made our omelettes and *burjis* (another dish made of fried eggs) in the makeshift kitchen. The aroma would spread to the tables laid outside and we would have other egg lovers peeping in and joining the feast.

I loved outdoor work because of the emancipation it offered to my spirit. I guess it had something to do with the playful days spent in open spaces in Peshawar and Deolali as a boy. It was Chopra Sahab's idea to shoot in Bhopal and he had identified the exact locations along with Dharam. I remember all of us stayed in a large government building with an open ground near it where Yash as well as my co-artistes Ajit, Jeevan* and Johnny Walker and I played football. Sometimes, we packed up early and sometimes the man bringing the raw stock by train was delayed and this caused a lull in the shooting schedule.

It was during the production of *Naya Daur* that I began to form the story idea of *Gunga Jumna* in my mind. I decided too that if I went ahead and made *Gunga Jumna*, I would cast Vyjayanti in the lead.

Naya Daur turned out to be a huge success and Chopra Sahab invited Mehboob Sahab as the chief guest on the hundredth day of its run at the main cinema in Bombay. It was magnanimous of Mehboob Sahab to accept the invitation and tell the audience how wrong he was and how right Chopra Sahab was in judging the potential of the subject. He complimented Chopra Sahab and the two film makers stood triumphantly on the stage while coins flew from all directions. As I mentioned earlier, the audiences we had in our times were very receptive to good cinema. They showed their happiness and appreciation in overt displays like showering coins on the screen and dancing while the popular song sequences were being shown.

*Ajit, whose real name was Hamid Ali Khan, started as a hero but later went on to play villainous roles. Jeevan, born as Omkar Nath Dhar, appeared in many mythological films before going on to play negative characters.

15

ON THE DOMESTIC FRONT

———•◦◌᠁◌◦•———

*As I look back at those years when I was rising in
the profession and setting my priorities, I feel a sense
of achievement that I was able to live up to Aghaji's
expectations and give him the assurance that I could take
over the mantle of family responsibilities from him as a
parent-brother when the weariness of age began to catch
up with him.*

I FELT AMMA'S ABSENCE WHENEVER I HAD TIME TO SPEND IN
the house. More than any of us, it was Aghaji who was missing her
quiet presence and the care with which she kept his clothes in the
wardrobe and placed his personal belongings in places he liked them
to be. Sakina Aapa, my eldest sister, could not measure up to his
expectations in running the house, which led to frequent altercations
between them. He did not approve of her high-handedness on many
occasions when she unceremoniously dismissed those from the
lower strata of society like the *dhobi*, the local baker and some of the
women who came to the house to sell lace and hand-embroidered
household linen. My mother had been very kind to them and she
never let them go unfed or empty-handed. I remember getting into

an argument with Sakina Aapa once when she spoke rudely to the barber who had come home to give me a 'nice' haircut.

The poor man always had a problem with my hair, which grew at jet speed, demanding fortnightly trimming. He was constantly crestfallen by my hair's refusal to be combed back and kept in place the way he wanted. He was at a loss to explain to his regular patrons that my hair was naturally tousled and was not styled by him that way. He got a fillip to his business when my films, especially *Naya Daur* (1957), became superhits and the song, *Uden jab jab zulfen teri...** topped the popularity charts. He had young men coming to him throughout the week asking for the Dilip Kumar hair cut, which, in reality, was nothing but my unmanageably thick hair falling disobediently on my forehead. I had reason to think that the growth was in vengeance at all the humiliation my poor head had to endure when, as ordered by my grandmother, a barber had come home and shaved off all the hair to make me the ugly child in the school I attended in Peshawar.

The barber came home one afternoon and I had instructed him to wait if I did not reach the house on time. He took the liberty of sitting in the drawing room and my eldest sister took it as impudence on his part and gave him a dressing down, which was in progress when I made my entry. I apologized to him and I found him more bewildered than angry. Later, I took up the matter with Sakina Aapa and we had an unpleasant spat.

Much as I wanted to I could not spend quality time with Aghaji. The robustness of his constitution was giving way to invasions of muscular pains and, more than anything else, I felt he had lost the zest for living after Amma's demise. He, however, seldom missed his weekly visits to the Crawford Market. As the days passed, he needed help to get in and out of the car. Not that he couldn't walk or any

---

*Composed by O. P. Nayyar, written by Sahir Ludhianvi and sung by Asha Bhosle and Mohammed Rafi.

such handicap; it was a persistent knee cramp that made him halt in his steps sometimes when he walked. The ramrod-like uprightness of his walk, the broad shoulders and the twinkle in his eyes when he smiled remained intact and Naushad Miyan, who became one of his close friends, never ceased to admire his good looks and his natural noble bearing. Naushad Miyan was one of the few regular visitors he truly got along with and what made the bonding easy for Aghaji was Naushad Miyan's ability to regale him with impromptu recitations of good, meaningful Urdu ghazals and poetry.

Around our house at Pali Mala, there were a number people from the eastern part of India, who had built quaint cottages and followed their own distinct lifestyle. My eldest brother, Noor Sahab, had found his lady love but Nasir, my younger brother, who was handsome and articulate, had young ladies vying for his attention wherever he went. I did not fail to notice his interest in a particular girl who gave me a knowing smile whenever I passed by in my car. I used to see him talk to her and, when I indicated to him that I knew what was going on, he became wary and, like Noor Sahab's romance at our earlier residence (described in an earlier chapter), Nasir's infatuation also met a premature end.

When Aghaji's visits to Crawford Market became rare due to his losing interest in the business as most of his friends in the fruit trade had retired and handed over the management to their sons, I thought it was right that Noor Sahab, who was the eldest sibling, should run the show and keep the family's reputation in the market alive. Like me, Nasir too was in films. Neither he nor I had any time to devote to the business. It became a matter of concern for me as Chacha Ummer, too, took ill and was no longer keen to keep the business going.

Going from Bandra to Crawford Market did not take much time those days. It was a pleasure to drive to town when I had to meet anybody because the very roads that are now jam-packed with vehicles used to stretch invitingly for the motorist to step on the accelerator and drive fearlessly over them. There was unlimited parking space near the market and outside the market's main entrance.

I liked being at the wheel if I was not tired or thinking too much about my work. I used to drive to Hughes Road (in South Bombay) and find myself a table that would not attract much notice and order a plate of chicken or mutton biryani as the mood dictated at George's Restaurant. The dish used to be served with *shorba* (broth or soup) and a plate of green salad. All the waiters knew me from my college days at Wilson, when I used to take the boys who were in my team there after every victorious soccer match we played against St Xavier's. They knew I was an actor now but, that made little difference to the way in which they greeted me and attentively served the dishes I had ordered. I always tried not to make myself conspicuous wherever I went but one afternoon, when I took Aghaji there, a crowd gathered outside. The manager came to our table and told me that there were fans waiting to see me and talk to me. Aghaji asked me what was going on and I told him about the fans. Surprisingly, he looked pleased and told me to go and meet them without delay.

I was thrilled not because people who liked my work had come to meet me quite unexpectedly but because I saw the glint of pride in Aghaji's eyes that day. On our way back, he was as quiet as he always was. On reaching home, I heard him describe the whole episode to Chacha Ummer with the excitement of a child and the joy of a proud father.

Aghaji did not meet any of the producers who came to see me at home. However, whenever Raj Kapoor came over, he was happy to see him and he made fond enquiries about Prithvirajji. He knew Mehboob Sahab vaguely. He was content just knowing that his son may not have fulfilled his dream of securing an OBE as a suffix to his name but he was certainly an achiever. At times, Chacha Ummer used to come to me elatedly and whisper how Aghaji had carefully folded a newspaper carrying my photograph and kept it near his bed after gazing at it for some time. Surprisingly, he never asked me why I had adopted a screen name. Being a man of the world and having abundant native wisdom, he must have understood the reasons.

He was very happy that I was insisting that my younger sisters be educated at the best institutions. He never said so, but he lived with the thought that had Sakina Aapa received the grooming my younger sisters got at the more sophisticated English medium schools, she might have not been riding roughshod and unintentionally rubbing people the wrong way. He knew it was a priority for me to give my younger brothers and sisters the best education at well-known schools and colleges to equip them to meet the challenges of an advancing world they were growing up in.

As I look back at those years when I was rising in the profession and setting my priorities, I feel a sense of achievement that I was able to live up to Aghaji's expectations and give him the assurance that I could take over the mantle of family responsibilities from him as a parent-brother when the weariness of age began to catch up with him. I don't think my elder brother Noor Sahab and my younger brothers really knew what it entailed for me to keep my professional values from slipping in the face of the challenge of generating a substantial income to meet the growing demands for household expenses, fees, clothes, pocket money, books, daily travel and so on.

I remember a producer coming to me in the late 1940s with a briefcase full of money and the script for a film he intended to make. I had not seen him before or heard of him. He narrated the story to me and I listened till he came to a point where the hero starts moving around the village astride a buffalo. I stopped him there and asked: 'Why a buffalo?' He replied it was his idea of blending comedy into the hero's character. When I asked if I could make necessary changes in the script, he said that I could but the buffalo had to be retained.

I stealthily looked at the rickety briefcase on the table, which had the hard cash I needed so much at that point of time. It was shaking a little due to the breeze coming from the window and seemed to be leering at me silently.

I then politely refused to spend more time listening to the story and he couldn't believe that I was turning down such an impressive story and such a good amount of money. It was a learning experience for me because there were many more such film makers who wanted to cash in on the popularity I was enjoying. The spontaneity with which I refused the briefcase enhanced my self-esteem and firmed up my resolve to work according to my terms.

I could instinctively feel Aghaji's loneliness and pain after Amma left us all. He seemed to be living in a vacuum and he had lost the will to live. He passed away peacefully on 5 March 1950, leaving all of us in a void. I did not inform everybody I knew in the industry because I did not want synthetic sympathy and condolences from busy and materialistic people who did not know him and what he meant to me. Raj Kapoor, Naushad Miyan, Mehboob Sahab, Ashok Bhaiyya, Bimalda, Nitinda, S. Mukherjee Sahab, the family doctors, close relatives and some of Aghaji's friends were there to console me as I quietly fought the loss of yet another precious anchor of my life. As desired and wished by Aghaji, his body was laid to rest near my mother's *qabr* (grave) in Deolali.

16

THE TRAVAILS OF FILM MAKING:
GUNGA JUMNA AND AFTER

———◦◦ ⧉⦿⧉ ◦◦———

Film making, unlike some other art forms like painting or writing poetry, for instance, has a great deal to do with communication. I mean the communication between the actor and the director, between the director and the cameraman and the art director, between the director and the editor, between the artiste and the cameraman and so on. If the coordination is well orchestrated, it shows in the final product. If not, it shows equally in the frayed look of the product.

*L*IFE HAD TO GO ON AND THE STORY OF *GUNGA JUMNA* WAS developing in my subconscious. It was necessary for me to relaunch my brother Nasir – he was facing a slump in his career after having acted in a few films – and also to have my own production house. The subject was such that it needed sound financing to depict it on celluloid in the manner I had visualized. There was no dearth of money in the market but I knew that I would have to tread carefully and avoid the Shylocks.

I knew Shapoorji Mistry and Pallonji Mistry quite well. I had met them informally at their homes and the manner in which the ladies had placed some Persian delicacies on the table when we sat down for tea reminded me of the goodies that always appeared on the table in our house at Peshawar when we had our family get-togethers on holidays. They were good, hospitable people and I had got to know them when they began financially backing K. Asif as he set out to make *Mughal-e-Azam*. Shapoorji heard the story of *Gunga Jumna* from me and he had no doubts about its viability but my brother Nasir felt it was not a good idea for me to play an outlaw. He insisted that the public would not accept me joining the dacoits and taking refuge in their lawlessness to get back at the wicked zamindar who steals his own sister's jewellery and frames theft charges on Gunga's poor and honest mother. (I was planning to play the role of Gunga and cast Nasir as Jumna, a policeman.) Nasir had strong views on this subject and advised me to think about it.

I thought about it and concluded that I would go ahead with the venture since Shapoorji was confident about the movie's success. The more I worked on the basic conflict in the script between the brother who has to uphold the law of the country and the brother who flees from the law, which favours the rich and the powerful and unjustly incriminates the poor and the defenceless, the more I felt it was time for me to make a picture that raised some critical issues about the people of rural India who had gained little from the country's independence from foreign rule. The oppressed farmers and tillers of the soil were leading a life of slavery and were being exploited and swindled by the mercenary landlords. The situation has not changed much today, more than half a century after both Mehboob Khan's *Mother India* (1957) and *Gunga Jumna* (1961) exposed the exploitation of farmers, for whom the soil they till and plough is sacred.

Mehboob Sahab had made *Mother India* with a similar mission and the film became a classic study for the Western world of the ruthless manipulations that were prevalent in the long-existing money-lending system in the rural economy of India. When Mehboob Sahab discussed *Mother India* with me in the early 1950s, I thought it was a brilliant and timely concept and it had to be made at any cost. The role he could offer me was of one of the sons of the heroine Nargis and I pointed out that it would be an incongruous casting after all the romancing she and I had done in earlier films, such as *Mela* (1948) and *Babul* (1950). I felt that it was a great opportunity for Nargis to play the title role and there was no doubt that she was the apt choice. It was crucial to give her unchallenged positioning in the star cast as the most important character and the pivot of the story. Besides, I was in no mood to dip into intense tragedy again.

Mehboob Sahab was known for the offbeat casting in his films. He had cast me in a swashbuckling villager's role in *Aan* (1952), in total contrast to my public image at that time of a tragedian. He took great pleasure in doing the impossible and revelling in the applause he received when his experiments succeeded. *Aan* was a worldwide hit and he felt triumphant that he had made India's first film in Technicolor. All said and done, I did not agree with him when he wanted to cast me as Nargis's son in *Mother India*.

Coming back to *Gunga Jumna*, I told Shapoorji about my intention to tour the interior parts of North India, especially in Uttar Pradesh and Madhya Pradesh first and then travel all over interior Maharashtra. I had decided to have the dialogue in the dialect I had heard and stored away in my subconscious as a boy squatting in the *mali*'s kitchen at Deolali (as mentioned in an earlier chapter). I did not know if it was a UP or a Bihari dialect at that age. It sounded fascinating and there was a vivid expressiveness about it while conveying raw emotions. The way in which Bihari, the *mali*, and his wife, Phoolwa, conversed and quarrelled was as amusing as it was dramatic. I needed to hear and feel the dialect again with the express purpose of using it in the film. The scenic canvas of rural regions in the states of India – be it in the North or the South – has its own variations and singular attractiveness with vivid reliefs brought about by geographical features and climate changes. I was keen to witness it first-hand.

I wanted to breathe the air that the characters Gunga and Jumna grew up on and also take stock of the pangs of suffering the men

A poster of *Gunga Jumna* (1961).

who swore by the soil they tilled went through at the hands of the heartless landlords. It is one thing to know it for knowledge's sake and quite another to get a feel of it as a writer. I was in charge not only as a producer and actor but also as the writer of the screenplay and I was experiencing a stimulating challenge. In a way, I was very conscious of the fact that I was going to be judged at several levels and the thought inspired me more than it hassled me.

The most wonderful thing about playing Gunga was that it was not difficult at all for me to understand the emotional current of the story, especially the feeling of adoration and protection for the smart younger brother. It took me back to my relationship with my brother Ayub Sahab who was intellectually ahead of all of us and I always felt he could have become somebody important in the administration had he not been physically debilitated. I had nourished great aspirations for all the younger siblings, too, and never hesitated to put their needs above mine in everything so that they could be educated and fulfil their ambitions. So Gunga wasn't unfamiliar to me as a character unlike in most other films where I felt as if my own self was on one side and the other personality, the character, was on the other side and it was imperative for me to bring them together.

Recently, while we were chatting casually, Amitabh Bachchan mentioned to me that he had repeatedly viewed *Gunga Jumna* as a student in Allahabad to understand how a Pathan was effortlessly playing a rustic character of UP and speaking the dialect with such ease. I think he has a point. It had to be difficult for any Pathan to feel at home with the personality and speech of Gunga. Yet, this Pathan, whose story you are reading, did it by instinct, careful study, untiring rehearsals and a temperament to succeed even in those ventures that were new for him.

I knew that my script of *Gunga Jumna* had merits for me as an actor. Since the character was on the wrong side of the law, it was important for me to acquaint the viewer with the reasons for his taking to a lawless way of life and I had to make him pay the penalty for taking to that life, however right he may have been under the circumstances he was caught in. Gunga, I decided, should get no reprieve from the law when he tries to explain that he was the victim of a trap set by the zamindar and that he could fight the powerful feudal system only by becoming an outlaw.

When I was writing the story and the screenplay of *Gunga Jumna*, my brother Nasir, for whose comeback the picture was being made, told me I was making a mistake. As mentioned earlier, he felt that people would not like to see me as a bandit and a law breaker. I thought about the matter seriously and I decided to go ahead without making any of the changes that friends and well-wishers suggested. The film eventually opened to a splendid response and admiring notices.

When we were at Pinewood Studios in the UK, sometime in the summer of 1960, for the Technicolor processing, the technicians in the lab were very impressed and they suggested that we enter the film for the Oscars because it reflected the tyranny of the feudal lords or zamindars in independent India and the intrinsic honesty of the downtrodden farmers despite the poverty and oppression. They were full of praise for the performances, the colourful song sequences and the rugged, rural setting.

When *Gunga Jumna* was screened at Karlovy Vary in Czechoslovakia, Boston and Cairo, I was besieged by film critics, who appreciated the movie and were intrigued by my acting. They were curious to know how much research had gone into it because a film like *Gunga Jumna* would have been made after much study and deliberation in their countries. I told them how much I had worked on the script, the characters, the Bhojpuri dialect, the logical conclusion of the story and so on. Another highlight of the film was the impressive musical score by Naushad Miyan, whose folk tunes in the film are popular to this day.

Gunga Jumna's enduring achievement is the inspiration it provided to writers to give the hero a flaw or what you call a negative shade. I had done 'anti-hero' roles earlier too. For instance, the character I had played in Mehboob Khan's *Amar* (1954) did commit an outrage. Therefore this character was flawed and was not the conventional blemish-free hero. The character I played in Zia Sarhadi's *Footpath* (1953) was a black marketeer and so he was also a tarnished hero. However, those films were not as successful as *Gunga Jumna*. In the case of *Gunga Jumna*, the hero was on the wrong side of the law but he had the audience sympathy with him and the conflict in the story is not so much between the brothers as it is between the law of the country and the moral freedom of a human being to fight injustice and corruption and take the world forward.

It took months of reflection and self-questioning to arrive at the climax but it was well worth the pains taken because I still hear praises from discerning film enthusiasts for Gunga's death scene. This scene was filmed on the sets at a studio at dusk. I took the cameraman, V. Babasaheb, into confidence and told him to keep everything ready as there would not be a rehearsal or a second take. I stressed the point that the synchronization between the action and the running camera would have to be perfect. He understood and was absolutely ready. The other unit members had no clue what I was going to do. What I did was my own idea. I took several rounds of the studio's premises, jogging at first and then running. When I felt breathless and I thought that I would just collapse, I entered the sets where Babasaheb was ready with the camera running to perfection. The scene of Gunga's collapse in his house at the feet of the deity whom his mother worshipped so trustingly and devoutly could not have been achieved in any other way. It was a victory for the law when Gunga succumbs to his bullet wounds but I wanted to tell the audience that it was Gunga who has achieved a bigger triumph – the moral victory God has given him by fulfilling his objective of establishing his poor mother's innocence and restoring her reputation in the village.

The search for the ideal locations for *Gunga Jumna* was a new responsibility for me. I am told the task is left nowadays to 'production designers' who create the look of the film on paper. Which must be the reason why the films appear so hybrid and amalgamous today. In our times, the director, cameraman and art director took pains to scout for locations, and for *Gunga Jumna* it was entirely up to me to find the appropriate backdrop for the unfolding of the story. As per the sketches I had made, some of the scenes had to be shot indoors on sets that I had pictured in my mind and had to be built at Kardar Studios and Mehboob Studios, both located in Bombay.

It took a month of searching for me to pick a location close to Igatpuri in Maharashtra, about 120 km north-east of Bombay. I visited the place quite by chance while on an outing with Baddruddin Qazi (whom you all know as Johnny Walker). It caught my attention at once for its virgin beauty and its unexplored natural ruggedness. I later took along to the location Babasaheb, the cameraman, and director Nitin Bose, and they were all for it. Little did I know then that I was discovering a locale that would be repeated in several films after *Gunga Jumna* was released. The nature of the subject was such that it demanded a location of craggy hills and a valley besides a flowing river that would be skirted by a sloping land covered with tall trees and bushes. Babasaheb had seen the sketches I had made of the location that I desired and it surprised him pleasantly that there was indeed a place like the one I had drawn for him. For some minutes he stood silently with Nitinda on the hill from where Gunga slides down to seize the villain (played by Anwar Husain) and save Dhanno

With Vyjayantimala in *Gunga Jumna* (1961).

(played by Vyjayantimala). After gazing the locale for quite some time with his cameraman's eye, he clapped his hands spontaneously in delight and stamped his approval on the spot. It was understood that the valley would provide the backdrop for the villagers' houses and the zamindar's *haveli* (mansion), which we would have to build. (The zamindar was the villain in the movie.)

Making *Gunga Jumna* was a mammoth exercise at that time. Though Nitinda was there as the director, *Gunga Jumna* was essentially my baby. When shooting began for *Gunga Jumna* on location, K. Asif was reshooting some of the desert sequences of *Mughal-e-Azam* in Rajasthan. I had to endure the scorching heat of the desert with all the heavy armour that I was given to wear for the scenes that Asif had reworked, fly back to Bombay and travel by car to the *Gunga Jumna* location. The make-up material available those days was limited and it was quite a test for my personal make-up artist to camouflage the suntan and the reddish patches I used to develop due to the metal armour covering my body in the war scenes shot on desert locations.

Shapoorji, who was the co-producer of *Mughal-e-Azam*, used to call his sons and his office staff and tell them to imbibe the virtue of ceaseless hard work from me. He used to arrange for me to travel in as much comfort as possible and the concerned expression I could see on his face reminded me of the pain that would flit across Amma's face when she would see the afternoon sun's impact on my fair skin when I got home after rigorous football practice on the grounds near Metro Cinema during my college days.

I enjoyed my long chats with Shapoorji who loved me perhaps no less than his sons. We discussed everything under the sun. While it fascinated me to hear him talk to his sons about the construction business and the money matters they were dealing with ever so facilely, Shapoorji often wondered how I was able to cope with the complex and unusual demands of the acting profession. Shapoorji was a towering giant in the construction business and he commanded instant respect from the authorities because of his untainted reputation. He was a man of small build and of medium height, his intrinsic goodness being reflected in the radiance on his gentle face. He visited the location whenever he found time and, at other times, he dropped in at my new house I had bought on Pali Hill.

Those were the days when Pali Hill, Bandra, meant an address to reckon with. There were open spaces and bungalows and the bungalow I selected was at an elevation strategically commanding a good view from the upper floor. I gave my sisters and brothers a surprise by driving them to the house and opening the main entrance door with a key from my pocket. In one voice, they started asking me whose house was it and how come I had the key. I told them then that it was my house from now onwards. The house was big and had enough room for the girls to have the privacy they needed.

Life's surprises never cease, really. I was hoping to find my own exclusive space in the house where I could rest when I wanted to or just stay in the room and read. It was important for me to be left alone at times. I was used to being alone from a very early age because I had my own thoughts and fancies, which I did not wish to share. As a child, I enjoyed going out of the house alone and it often caused panic and got me into trouble (as noted in earlier chapters). Here, in the large house I had lovingly bought, I found myself often unwillingly dragged into senseless arguments and bickering. I felt completely out of synch with my brothers and sisters who were becoming increasingly concerned only with their comforts and luxuries, which they did not hesitate to ask me to provide.

Consequently, I spent more time in the outhouse and there I felt a sense of relief because it gave me the much-needed freedom to pursue my interest in reading and spending quality time with people whose company I truly enjoyed.

In the film industry there was a call from producers' bodies to place a ceiling on actors' assignments (sometime in the mid-1960s, if I remember rightly). I knew it would not affect me since I did not work in more than one film at a time but I felt it was an encroachment on an individual's personal and professional freedom.

My decision to move to Madras came at this juncture partly because I wanted to be away from the perennial cacophony in my house and partly because I could not agree with the Bombay producers' move to restrict the work of actors. There were two very cordial producers in Madras wanting me to star in the Hindi remakes of their Tamil and Telugu hits and I liked them and the stories they narrated to me. One promised ample scope for humour and comedy and the other offered me an opportunity to delve into the troubled and suspicious mind of an unfortunate, lonely man. The films were B. Nagi Reddy's *Ram Aur Shyam* (released in 1967 and directed by Tapi Chanakya) and P. S. Veerappa's *Aadmi* (released in 1968 and directed by A. Bhim Singh). Both were to be made in the city that had captured my heart when I had worked in *Paigham* (1959).

Ram Aur Shyam started with a bit of turbulence. Vyjayantimala, who was signed to play the lead, upset Nagi Reddy, the producer, with a tantrum that was uncalled for. When she stuck to her stand about something very trivial like a sari or a pair of earrings she had selected and was given to another artiste unknowingly by the director's

In *Dil Diya Dard Liya* (1966).

assistant, Reddy politely informed her she was out of the film. In a week's time, I was informed that Waheeda Rehman – whose oeuvre included films such as *Pyaasa* (1957), *Kaghaz Ke Phool* (1959), *Kala Bazar* (1960) and *Guide* (1965) – would be replacing Vyjayanti. The whole episode was misconstrued by Vyjayanti who, after working with me in six films, imagined that I had brought in Waheeda because she was my heroine in *Dil Diya Dard Liya* (1966) and *Aadmi*!

Although shooting for *Aadmi* began long before *Ram Aur Shyam* mounted the sets, its pace slowed down halfway through the production because the cash flow came in dribs and drabs. While I was shooting some hilarious scenes for *Ram Aur Shyam*, I had to agree to dub for poignant scenes with Waheeda for *Aadmi* because Veerappa would send word that some funds had come in and they were in a position to hire a dubbing studio and pay the technicians. Likewise, the editor of *Aadmi* used to invite me to take a look at the edited reels and I spent many evenings (after pack-up at Nagi Reddy's *Ram Aur Shyam*) in the suites where *Aadmi* was being edited.

Aadmi was essentially a psychological drama and I tried to give it the edge and slickness it deserved on the editing table. Those days, the French new-wave directors, especially Jean-Luc Godard, had created an interest in our editors to employ the jumpcut unnecessarily.

Although I was not formally trained in the job of editing, I had a fair idea of the contribution an editor could make to engage the viewer in the storytelling process. The subject of *Aadmi* was such that it needed imaginative editing.

As an actor I was struck by the promise that the character I played in *Aadmi* held. I had to bring out the protagonist's cerebral struggle to leave his past behind and move on. The basic conflict in the story, which had the external appearance of a common love triangle, was unusual in the sense that it was not so much a conflict between two men over one woman as is common in film stories. The friction was in the minds of the characters.

The character I played was to be explored from a psychological angle and that intrigued me. From my experience and understanding, I concluded that the film had to have a mood and an ambience that would go with the vicissitudes in the protagonist's life and the Freudian thought processes he gets into. So I got involved in two vital aspects of its making, besides the writing. I took a keen interest in the camera movements and lighting and also in the selection of shots on the editing table.

Film making, unlike some other art forms like painting or writing poetry, for instance, has a great deal to do with communication. I mean the communication between the actor and the director, between the director and the cameraman and the art director, between the director and the editor, between the artiste and the cameraman and so on. If the coordination is well orchestrated, it shows in the final product. If not, it shows equally in the frayed look of the product.

It was my practice to take an active interest in the making of a film. In *Ram Aur Shyam* too, my involvement was one hundred per cent. However, before I go into the details, I must say that *Ram Aur Shyam* was very special for me (as explained in the next chapter).

17

THE WOMAN IN MY LIFE

———◦⊙ ⦂⊙⦂ ⊙◦———

*As she quietly gazed out at the sea, we listened to the gentle
sound of waves that spread a serene calm that descended on
us and I looked at her and said: 'Saira, you are not the kind.
of girl I want to drive around with, or be seen around with
… I would like to marry you … will you be my wife?'*

RAM AUR SHYAM WAS VERY SPECIAL FOR ME IN A PERSONAL
way because I married Saira when the production of the film was
nearing completion and I would like to digress here and narrate the
true story of our marriage as there are quite a few fanciful accounts
circulating since the day the news made headlines in all publications
in the country in 1966. Until then I was reluctant to even work with
her for some reasons, which I must explain.

First of all, I knew that she was the daughter of Mohammed Ehsan
Sahab and Naseem Banuji,* a great lady whom I much respected and
admired for her dignity and self-reliance and for the way she most
gracefully conducted herself in the film industry. Naseem Aapa had

---

*Naseem Banuji's most famous film is *Pukar* (1939), in which she played
Noor Jehan, the wife of the Mughal Emperor Jehangir.

Ammaji (Shamshad Abdul Waheed Khan) performing
at a small gathering.

worked in a film made by Ayub Sahab, my brother, and there were
always small get-togethers at our residence at 48 Pali Hill. I recall
wonderful musical evenings when there was a sitar recital by Ustad
Vilayat Khan Sahab or a singing soirée with the great Bade Ghulam
Ali Khan Sahab, as I have been very fond of classical music, be it vocal
or instrumental. Naseem Aapa would always be invited by Akhtar,
my sister, who had great admiration and regard for her.

I don't recall when but at one such evening, Saira, who was on a
visit to India during her school holidays, accompanied her mother
to our house. Since I used to meet Naseem Aapa at many formal and
informal occasions, I had understood from her that Saira was growing
up in London, where she and her brother Sultan Ahmed were studying
in school and they were under the guardianship of Naseem Aapa's
mother Shamshad Abdul Waheed Khan, the renowned classical

singer. Apparently, Saira had seen my film *Aan* at Scala Theatre in London and I got to know from different sources such as Mrs Akhtar Mehboob Khan, whom I called Bhabiji, Mrs Bahaar Kardar and S. Mukherjee Sahab that this little girl was brewing up quite a storm in her mind about a liking for me, wanting to know through her letters from London to her own mother, my likes and dislikes, my way of life and even the fact that I loved poetry and the Persian language.

Later, I got to know that as soon as she finished school in London and returned to India, she convinced Naseem Aapa to get her a tutor, a Maulvi Sahab, who was a part of the Hyderabad Nizam Mir Osman Ali Khan's royal entourage, to coach her in fine, pristine Urdu and Persian at the sprawling Hyderabad Estate on Nepean Sea Road in Bombay! This was her plan to impress me! At best, I was pleasantly amused and delighted at this wonderful effort by this youngster. Naturally, I never gave this 'crush', directed at me, any importance, since for me it was difficult to reconcile myself to the fact that there was anything serious in her mind about me!

Next, I got to know that this young lady was precariously perched to take off on a film career, which, all said and done, in those times, was considered taboo for girls from conservative Muslim families and I knew that this was why Naseem Aapa had wanted to send her to school in London, far away from the atmosphere of films.

Of course, when this subject was broached by S. Mukherjee Sahab, who was a close confidant and well-wisher of the family, I myself voiced an emphatic '*NO*' to this idea and told him that Saira should be restrained from embarking on a film career.

In the early 1960s, we were about to begin the casting for A. R. Kardar's *Dil Diya Dard Liya* (eventually released in 1966), when, at a close get-together at Mehboob Khan's place, Mukherjee Sahab said: 'Yousuf, this young girl is crazy to work with you.' I smiled, and trying to deter her from this idea, I ran my hand through my salt-and-pepper hair and said to Saira: 'Have you seen this grey hair? I am so much elder to you, and I eat like a pig!' To which, I still remember, she laughed and said: 'I think grey hair looks very distinguished on you! Very handsome.'

After her maiden venture, *Junglee*, there was no looking back for Saira and, curiously enough, *Gunga Jumna* and *Junglee* were released simultaneously in 1961! Both were stupendous hits! She became the most sought-after leading lady in the industry and she was paired with all the successful leading men of the time – such as Raj Kapoor, Dev Anand, Sunil Dutt, Shammi Kapoor, Rajendra Kumar, Joy Mukherjee and Manoj Kumar – except Dilip Kumar. There was a huge demand in the film market for a film starring her opposite me and talks were on, amongst many, for *Habba Khatoon* with Mehboob Sahab, for which the illustrious film maker required huge chunks of uninterrupted shooting dates (as the film was set in Kashmir and had to be shot there). Therefore she had to forgo doing Vijay Anand's *Guide* with Dev Anand, S. U. Sunny's *Palki* (also director of my 1960 film *Kohinoor*) and, of course, *Leader* for Filmalaya's S. Mukherjee Sahab, for which they were also considering newcomer Priya Rajvansh, who had come to Bombay from The Royal Academy of Dramatic Arts, London. Waheeda Rehman was chosen as the heroine for both *Guide* (1965) and *Palki* (1967). Priya Rajvansh later went on to team up with producer-director-actor Chetan Anand, and worked with him in films such as *Haqeeqat* (1964), *Heer Ranjha* (1970) and *Hanste Zakhm* (1973).

Meanwhile, from Saira herself I would get frequent and insistent messages and requests through the popular producers whom she was already working with to pair us in their forthcoming movies!

Unfortunately, I had to withdraw from *Habba Khatoon*, as I could not foresee myself doing Yousuf Chak's (Habba Khatoon's husband) character, which had some slants of negativity. Moreover, Mehboob Sahab and I did not seem to be like-minded on this aspect and did not see eye to eye. I also remember telling Naseem Aapa at Filmalaya Studios that Naushad Sahab's story idea of *Palki* had a lot of *jhols*. In other words, the story sagged under its own weight and lacked in content.

Giving the *mahurat* clap for *Saaz Aur Awaz* (released in 1966).

As these projects fizzled out, at the same time, I was much in demand to give the auspicious *mahurat** clap at many of Saira's films. *Saaz Aur Awaz* was one such *mahurat* and *Habba Khatoon* was another. At the *mahurat* of the latter film, I told her, to her dismay, that all contenders for the role of Yousuf Chak were present, whereas I was only the clapper boy! Exasperated, she retorted that she was now grown up and taller too, to work with me, and asked if I would only give *mahurat* claps for her films or one day also work with her?

Unfortunately, I had to keep on refusing producers who wished to cast me opposite her, finding it very difficult to come to terms that this very fair and slim girl whom I had met on many occasions had indeed grown up, and was already doing films with Raj and Dev, who were almost the same age as I. I was working with actresses who matched my age and maturity.

*An opportune time for beginning something new.

I confided in Mukherjee Sahab and Sultan that I wanted to cast her in a specially written subject that I had in mind for her where our pairing would be ideal and perfect. This was a subject based with Kashmir as the backdrop, a script that I had written myself entitled 'Song of the Valley', where she had a wonderfully vivacious, effervescent role that ran the gamut of emotions.

At this long wait, she became very annoyed with me. I sensed that the polite, gracious and well-bred young lady was turning into an angry tigress who wilfully wanted to scorn me and seemed to be deliberately impolite to highlight the fact that she was terribly offended. For instance, in the Filmalaya Studio compound, if I were leaving in my car and spotted Ammaji (Saira's grandmother) and Saira making their way from the stage floor towards their make-up room for a break, I would as always step out of my car and wish them Salaam Alaikum (peace be upon you). Ammaji would respond graciously, whereas Saira would turn away impetuously and strut away like a proud peacock as if she did not know me or hear me! I was amazed at this attitude! What a turn of events! She thought this kind of behaviour would have some effect on me!

In a double role in *Ram Aur Shyam* (1967).

The incredible beauty of life is that we never know what is about to happen next!

As we were to start *Ram Aur Shyam*, B. Nagi Reddy and A. Chakrapani (co-producer of the film) had, at the outset, suggested Saira's name for the heroine opposite Ram, the timid character bullied to nervous shreds by Gajendra, his brother-in-law (played by Pran). Ram runs away from home and finds himself in a village and does not know what to do with the energetic, sprightly girl Shanta, who thinks he is her beau Shyam (a lookalike of Ram), who has mysteriously disappeared from the village for quite some time. Nagi Reddy was all admiration for Saira and her recent performances and was certain that her pairing with me in the comedy situations would be a huge draw since she possessed a wonderful flair for spirited comedy. Since it was my practice to take an active interest in the making of my film, I voiced my opinion that I did not agree with Nagi Reddy on this issue because I felt she was too delicate and innocent in appearance for a character that had to have loads of seductive appeal and a bold, buxom appearance. At the same time, Mehmood Ali, the famous comedian, was persistent that for this role we should cast vivacious Mumtaz, his co-star in many of his and wrestler Dara Singh's movies. He was so sincere in his recommendation of her that he even carried tins of film reels depicting Mumtaz to exhibit how talented she was. Mumtaz eventually bagged that role.

My refusal to work in *Ram Aur Shyam* with her was the proverbial last straw on the camel's back! Hell hath no fury like a woman scorned! Sure enough, I received more than my fair share of brickbats from Saira in various ways!

Ram Aur Shyam was progressing on the floors at a hectic pace and, as usual, I was completely immersed in my work when I received an invitation from Naseem Aapa to join her and her mother Shamshad

With Saira and Mumtaz during the shooting of *Ram Aur Shyam*.

Begum Sahiba in the celebration of Saira's birthday and the house warming of their newly built bungalow, which was a stone's throw from my own bungalow on Pali Hill.

On the evening of 23 August 1966, when I specially flew to Bombay from Madras to attend the party that was being hosted by Naseem Aapa, I had no inkling that the course of my life was all set to change and the evening was destined to remain indelibly imprinted in my memory to this day!

When I alighted from my car and entered the beautiful garden that leads to the house, I can still recall my eyes falling on Saira standing in the foyer of her new house looking breathtakingly beautiful in a brocade sari. I was taken aback, because she was no longer the young girl I had consciously avoided working with because I thought she would look too young to be my heroine. She had indeed grown to full womanhood and was in reality more beautiful than I thought she was.

I simply stepped forward and shook her hand and for us Time stood still. For once, she let go of her annoyance with me and looked straight into my eyes and it did not take more than an instant for me to realize that she was the one Destiny had been knowingly reserving as my real-life partner while I was refusing to pair with her on screen!

We moved from the foyer to the large drawing room, which was fast filling up with friends of Naseem Aapa, who included Mrs Mehboob Khan, Mrs S. Mukherjee, R. K. Nayyar (producer-director), Shankar and Jaikishen (music directors), Fali Mistry (a famous cinematographer), Subodh Mukherjee (the producer and director of *Junglee*), Sanjeev Kumar (then an upcoming actor) and heroes such as Dev Anand, Rajendra Kumar, Sanjay Khan and Manoj Kumar, who were close to me as well. While conversing with Saira, I realized that for someone who had grown up in England and had studied at a privileged English school, I found her to be intrinsically very Indian and rooted to her native culture in the way she spoke respectfully to her mother's friends and conducted herself.

My mind went back to one of my sojourns in Coimbatore (now in Tamil Nadu) where I had shot for *Azaad* (1955). I happened to meet, through S. S. Vasan Sahab, a noted astrologer who was known for the accuracy of his predictions. He made a chart simply by observing my facial features, expressions and the lines on my palm. I remember his narrow eyes, the sacred ash smeared across his brow and his thin arms, chest and neck. He sat before us silently studying the chart he had made and I remember the smile he gave us when he was ready to unveil my future. He spoke glowingly about my career and literally had me spellbound as he proceeded to describe in detail our house in Peshawar, the flowing water by the side, where I spent my childhood, about my parents, my siblings and my grandparents! Then, he paused and said that his forecast was sourced from ancient Bhrigu Sutras and categorically told me that I would marry late when I would be in my forties and my bride would be a girl half my age, as fair and beautiful as the moon and she would keep me on the lids of her eyes and love and worship me unselfishly, unconditionally. He also predicted that she would be from the same profession – to this I categorically commented: 'Never! I will not marry a girl from my profession!' Unfazed, he went on to say that, soon after the marriage, she would take the blow of my 'karmas' with a prolonged and near-fatal illness to absolve me and she would go through it ungrudgingly.

Both Vasan Sahab and I did not expect this categorical prediction about something that was neither on my mind nor on Vasan Sahab's. It shook me up for a moment but, at that point of time, I was neither a believer nor a disbeliever of astral configurations that could make or mar one's life. As mentioned earlier, I had had the childhood experience of my Dadi (paternal grandmother) who took the forecast of a fakir so seriously that she unintentionally disfigured my face with soot all through my school-going years in Peshawar. I was restored my smart, good looks as a school boy only when we moved to Bombay and I began to study at Anjuman Islam.

The whole episode did not mean much at that point of time and, as a busy young man, I gave little importance to it and moved on, forgetting about it in the flurry of day-to-day existence.

Strangely, the memory of that chance meeting surfaced now.

After the birthday celebrations, before taking my flight back to resume my shooting in Madras the next morning, I called up, wanting to thank Naseem Aapa for the wonderful get-together. Saira answered the phone and when I said '*Main* Yousuf *bol raha hoon*' (I am Yousuf speaking), she mischievously replied: 'Who? Yousuf? *Kis se baat karni hai?*' (Whom do you want to talk to?) Knowing fully well who I was, she was hell-bent on pulling my leg! I then said that I wanted to thank her for being an excellent hostess at her party and that I had enjoyed the evening very much, unwinding from all the stress and hectic work that I had been ploughing through recently. I finally told her that I would call from Madras, and I did. I found myself soon calling up again after a couple of days, strangely missing this sprightly, mischievous girl who was a rare mixture of traditional, deep-rooted Indian values and Western culture and education.

I planned to fly down and meet her in the evening soon after her birthday. I had landed in Bombay when I received a call of distress from a colleague who was in a fix with regard to a tax problem and needed the help of my auditor. Saira was then shooting at Mehboob Studios for Lekh Tandon's *Jhuk Gaya Aasmaan* (released in 1968) and I could not contact her as there were no mobile phones those days.

She came out from the sets to Mrs Mistry's (the studio operator) kiosk in the foyer of the studio. She was totally drenched from a rain song they were doing and, when I told her that I may not be able to see her then, well, she suggested that I had better not see her at all! As simple as that! Sensing Saira's disappointment, I suggested that I would attend to the exigency with my auditor friend G. N. Joshi and help my colleague and then asked if I could take her to the Taj Sea Lounge for some time. We did just that, but, unfortunately, at the Sea Lounge also I was paged repeatedly on the phone by a lady friend with whom I had broken off a relationship months ago. This had been a stressful phase of my life. Anyway, as Saira and I were on our way home, I asked the chauffeur to park at the seafront on Cuffe Parade, and there was just silence between us for some time.

As she quietly gazed out at the sea, we listened to the gentle sound of waves that spread a serene calm that descended on us and I looked at her and said: 'Saira, you are not the kind of girl I want to drive around with, or be seen around with ... I would like to marry you ... will you be my wife?'

Still upset with the irritating, disturbing calls that I had received and answered while sitting with her and G. N. Joshi at the Sea Lounge, Saira just turned around sharply to answer me with '... and how many girls have you said this to?' Normally, I would have been enraged with such a line, but instead, enamoured with her straightforwardness and simplicity, I found myself telling her that she was loveable and I wanted her to be my wife. My inner voice, which I have always believed is Amma's voice, had sealed the approval without hesitation and I knew deep within me that I had found the woman with whom I wanted to share my life, my sorrows and my joys. As she smiled and held me in her gaze with the love of a woman who had loved me since she was in her teens, we slowly drove back to Nepean Sea Road to her mother's Sea Belle flat. I said I wanted Naseem Aapa, Ammaji and Sultan and his wife Rahat Beg's approval, that I sought her hand.

I knew that Saira's career had soared to extremely popular heights and also that she was passionate about her work, always praying every night before her sleep: 'Allah, make me a big movie star like my

In *Leader* (1964).

mother, Pari Chehra* Naseem Banu and make me meet and Inshallah soon become Mrs Dilip Kumar.' It would be very hard to relinquish the work that generated such euphoria of popularity.

We found Ammaji and her elder sister, Khursheed Bajijan, at home and I presented my proposal, like a good Pathan, to both the eldest members in the family. Ammaji most happily kissed my forehead, blessing us and was overwhelmed with tears of joy for the two of us: '*Allah har khushi de aap dono ko aur Yousuf mian ka iqbal buland rakhen . . . . Aameen.*'** Ammaji, always after, blessed me with this *dua* on every occasion throughout my life. We then proceeded to meet Naseem Aapa, Sultan and Rahat, at the Pali Hill bungalow, to which they were in the process of shifting. As a youngster, Sultan and the bunch of the Mukherjee boys, Rono, Joy and Debu, had always cycled around Pali Hill for fun and then stood outside my 48 Pali Hill gate like eager, keen children to have a glimpse of me. Later, Sultan, when he came back after schooling in London, joined the team of *Leader* (released in 1964) to watch the making of the film, learning the ropes of becoming a film director.

*Literally meaning 'with a face like a fairy'.
**May Allah give you both every happiness and may the fortunes of Yousuf be on the rise. So be it.

Naseem Aapa received us at her Pali Hill bungalow in ecstatic wonder; she was overwhelmed, joyously embracing us with the love that this graceful lady always showered on us. She and Sultan became my great support system in everyday life, as also my own extended family, ready to love and protect me.

We were first given the auspicious *dahi* (curds) and *meetha* (sweets) on this occasion with Naseem Aapa's hand and then served a sumptuous meal synonymous with her refined and exquisite hospitality. Saira was so excited and must have been raring to eat, but self-consciously just bit on a morsel, chewed so slowly, until I had to tell her: '*Saira aap issey apna hi ghar samajhiye aur khana khaiye!*' (Saira, consider this your own house and have your food!)

Soon after, Saira took permission from Naseem Aapa to go for a short drive and then to drop me home, just a stone's throw away from her own bungalow. Although London schooled and bred, Saira had been very protectively brought up by Ammaji and Naseem Aapa as a young girl, taking the best out of Western education and upbringing but essentially and strictly inculcating Indian values. This was what appealed to me most about her personality. Hers had been a close-knit family of four members (apart from herself) – her grandmother, mother and elder brother, who were the world she grew up to know, love and understand, even as she became an entity on her own: a successful film star.

We drove by Carter Road, past Delphin, a two-storey structure where my dear brother Nasir and his wife, actress Begum Para, lived with their children on the top floor and my friend 'Gobindo' (actor Abhi Bhattacharya) resided on the first floor. I asked my chauffeur to honk loudly until Gobindo came running out to the window, alarmed, thinking that something was wrong. I shouted out to him to hurry and bring down a bottle of drinking water. No sooner than he scurried down, he bent into the car window to speak to me and he practically fainted upon seeing the most unexpected sight: Saira sitting by my side, smiling away at him!

It seemed incredible to Gobindo because he was just recently shooting with Saira on K. Asif's *Sasta Khoon Mehnga Pani* (a film that remained unfinished) at the outdoor locations in the deserts of

Jodhpur, Rajasthan. Gobindo was one of the many emissaries, apart from actor Nazir Hussain Sahab and Sanjeev Kumar, who carried messages of how upset Saira was with me! These artistes were working with me too and I would meet them frequently.

After that, we turned towards the beach at Juhu for a short stroll – the sky was beautiful, laden with layers of dreamy August clouds and we silently walked, hand in hand, enjoying the bracing, placid breeze when suddenly a beautiful, light shower descended upon us as though God himself had blessed this union of two hearts. I immediately took off my jacket to wrap it around Saira's delicate frame and, to this day, amongst a thousand things she has safely kept in her treasure trove, is the same jacket!

As we were returning home, at my gate, I saw Nasir's car parked, indicating that he was there. Nasir commuted between our poultry farm at Nasik and Bombay to keep the family business going. I was so very happy that I wanted him to be the first in my family to know the glad tidings. Nasir was my much-loved, ever-smiling, outgoing and warm-hearted brother. He was therefore my favourite companion, born just after me and so dear to me.

We took the stairs up to the hall and finding Saira very nervous, I held her hand reassuringly. Nasir was alone and looked up with a huge warm smile as he always did, and we sat down. In the next couple of minutes, I said to him: 'Nasir, Saira and I are getting ... married!' To which he replied: 'Oye! *Yaar*! You're pulling my leg! You're joking! How did this happen?' He then laughed and tightly held me in his embrace and exclaimed: '*I can't believe this yaar! Wonderful news!*' My happiness was complete.

During the next week, I flew down every other evening to Bombay from Madras, and dined and spent wonderful time with Saira, her granny and Naseem Aapa at their Nepean Sea Road home where Saira still was living, or at her newly built bungalow at Pali Hill where at times we would be joined by Mrs Akhtar Mehboob, Mukherjee Sahab and my dear friends Pran and Satish Bhalla. (Pran's daughter Pinky later married Satish Bhalla's son.)

Years later. Saira jovially sang to me '*Ik ghar banaya hai, tere ghar ke samne*',* telling me that, in actuality, when she wanted to build her own home, the family set about looking for a suitable plot of land around 48 Pali Hill, holding my house as the landmark, being close to which was the first criterion in their choice!

Events moved at a fast pace thereafter, as the news spread everywhere.

---

*'I have built a house in front of yours.' She was inspired by the title song of the 1963 movie *Tere Ghar Ke Samne*, starring Dev Anand and Nutan.

18

THE BIG DAY

——⊙ ⦂⊙⦂ ⊙——

*Came the day of the marriage: 11 October 1966. What did
I feel? Was there a gush of nervousness? Having remained
a confirmed, eligible bachelor for so long, did I have any
trepidations or any qualms as the hour of the relinquishment
of my bachelordom drew near?*

AT THE OUTSET, I FELT IT VERY NECESSARY TO ACQUAINT MY
future wife, my life partner-to-be, with the scenario at home, with my
family and with my dearest ones who were of paramount importance
to me. Years ago, after losing Aghaji and Amma so early in my life,
I suddenly became the 'parent-brother' to my five brothers and six
sisters, of whom three were elder and the rest younger to me. I had
literally stepped into my parents' shoes, caring for them and taking
time off from my shoots to be with them. I would take great joy in
personally shopping for their every need, even for fabrics for the
younger siblings and give them to our family tailor to be stitched.
When I needed some help in this area, Bhabi Akhtar Mehboob would
give me helpful guidance for the girls.

221

We would spend long holidays at Lonavala (a hill station in Maharashtra, about 100 km from Bombay), in the house I rented every year where the children would romp in the garden happily and never want to go back home soon enough. When they all grew up, whether the boys or the girls, I endeavoured to give them the best areas of study they chose for themselves. When they wished to go abroad for further studies, I encouraged them without any second thoughts. Their happiness became the purpose of my existence.

One day, I sat with Saira on a quiet stretch of beach and told her that I had been such a confirmed eligible bachelor for so long with a family in tow that was very accustomed to being in charge of me, whether we attended functions together, arm in arm, or we reserved a whole row of seats in a popular cinema house for films based on Tennessee Williams' stories (for instance, *A Streetcar Named Desire*, 1951, and *Cat on a Hot Tin Roof*, 1958). I pointed out to her that it

With my sisters. (*L to R*): Sakina Aapa, Saeeda and Taj.

would be difficult, if not impossible, for them to easily reconcile to a new person in my life, as also for her to live together with the family without any problems arising between them. I went on to tell her that it was inevitable that '*Main saatve aasmaan ki hoor bhi laaoonga, to usey* accept *nahin kar paigi meri* family'. (Even if I bring a celestial angel from the seventh heaven, my family will not be able to accept her.) They were so used to my being a loner and were not used to sharing me with anyone.

In such circumstances, I told her that to give our marriage the right beginning and environment, we would have to live separately, on our own. I assured her that I would get suitable alternative accommodation for my unmarried sisters Sakina Aapa and Farida and for my brother Ahsan, who lived with me, as also for all the married 'visiting' sisters such as Taj, Saeeda and Fauzia, who often came to stay.

Saira explained to me that since I knew that she was herself the prime member of her own small, close-knit four-member family, which she dearly loved, hence I should understand that she would never want to separate me from my brothers and sisters, whom I loved very much. Another thing she stated was that just a year ago her elder brother Sultan had married Rahat Beg and they were naturally living in the new bungalow that Saira had built just across the road. By acceding to my decision, she did not want to set a bad precedence for her own family – she insisted that Sultan and Rahat must continue to live with Ammaji and Aapaji, or her elders would be alone in the autumn of their lives. Saira wanted to live in togetherness with my family; that was her firm decision, saying that if she and I moved out to be independent of the family responsibilities it would be wrong on our part.

As noted earlier, I had already told Nasir of our proposed marriage and I proceeded to break the news with mild trepidation to Sakina Aapa. She was totally in charge of the house and the members of the family, particularly the girls, and was loved and feared at the same time. Earlier, Aghaji used to have frequent altercations with her as he did not approve of her high-handedness, which was quite in contrast to Amma's gentle ways.

When Amma had turned very unwell and bedridden with asthma, she had devised this habit of storing a number of clean socks, hankies and other such items, meant for Aghaji and all of us boys, right under her bed. She would draw them out, doling them out to us as needed!

I had my own fears of how she would receive this news from me, knowing fully well that poor Nasir, whenever he met Sakina Aapa, the occasion would never be bereft of the scalding criticism he was subjected to time and again from her about marrying actress Begum Para no matter how many years had gone by! I would always spring to the defence of my dear brother who constantly warded off these attacks with smiles and laughter. He said this was the best way to deal with a tricky situation!

As I faced Sakina Aapa now, I knew what was going on in her mind. Her thoughts were crisscrossing between disappointment at having had no say in the decision and also great surprise at my having chosen a partner who was from the same profession as mine and much younger to me.

I tried to set her mind at rest, by clarifying that it was no doubt a quick decision, but it was, without doubt, a considered one as all my decisions have been. Yes, I had altered my earlier stand that I would not marry a girl from the same field, but I had changed my mind because I had good reason to do so, because I knew Saira's illustrious family lineage. Her grandfather was Khan Bahadur Mohammed Solaiman, OBE, who had been the chief engineer of the Delhi Municipal Corporation and had the distinction of structuring the Viceroy's House (now known as Rashtrapati Bhavan) as also the surrounding Parliament House and the other buildings in that area. Mohammed Ehsan Sahab, her father, educated and brought up in London, had turned into a noted film producer. Her mother was the beautiful Naseem Banu, a first-rate film heroine of her time with a flawless reputation, and her grandmother Shamshad Begum Abdul Waheed Khan, a renowned classical vocalist, who used to sing live over All India Radio Delhi and had recorded for Columbia Records.

Above all, Saira by herself possessed virtues and qualities that I considered essential in the woman I was going to spend the rest of my life with. I did not feel the need to explain more to Sakina Aapa. I concluded by saying that I was convinced that I had taken the right decision and that I was very happy. She heard me out with a vacant expression and did not argue since she knew it was a fait accompli and she had to accept it.

The announcement of our engagement on 2 October 1966 reverberated with sensational and joyous tidings all over the country. It was an indescribable experience.

The media was splashing the news all over and the radio stations kept on announcing the event every couple of hours. There was an air of great festivity in Bombay (and probably elsewhere as well) as all available loudspeakers belted out our favourite film songs!

With Saira and Satish Bhalla among others.

The news of our forthcoming marriage came as a surprise to all those who had thought I was an unrelenting, highly eligible bachelor who would never settle down. My fans and also my friends, such as Satish Bhalla, Raj Kapoor, producer Ved Puri, Hiten Choudhary, Pran and Balraj Kohli, were agog with 'how did this happen'? Saira's career was just five years old; we had never worked together and were never linked romantically. Consequently, there literally was a storm in people's minds, who were eager to see us together and have a glimpse of us together.

As for Saira, Naseem Aapa had told me, in her own dignified manner, that she was beside herself with joy, celebrating the granting of a long-cherished desire of being my wife.

At that point of time, I was to finish the final schedules of *Ram Aur Shyam* in Madras and then travel with producer-director H. S. Rawail to Calcutta to do some scripting work and also to finalize a temple outdoor location there for the film *Sunghursh* (eventually released in July 1968). Saira and Naseem Aapa were also headed for Calcutta to shoot outdoors for director Lekh Tandon's *Jhuk Gaya Aasmaan*.

At the Calcutta airport, there was a tumultuous sea of people such as we had never seen before in our lives – not even at premieres, functions and rallies that I was so familiar with. As the doors of the aircraft were opened for the passengers to disembark, we had to beat a hasty retreat. Heaven knows how, despite security barriers put up by the police, fans had accessed even the tarmac, not just the airport. Eventually, we somehow got to our car, which was surrounded by thousands of fans and, as a gesture of great love, the car was lifted up by them as we sat inside! We could hear just one voice chanting: '*Mubarak! Mubarak!*' (Congratulations! Congratulations!)

Somehow, we managed to drive away from the airport and were rushed inside the Grand Hotel (where we were to stay) through the kitchen entrance and up to our suites on an upper floor. Soon enough, there was a storm of 'knock knock' on all the doors on our floor! Lo and behold! How had the fans got past security and reached outside our suites? The hotel management was flustered and nervous and Naseem Aapa and film producer H. S. Rawail were of the view that it would be impossible to go out and work in these conditions. Sure enough, at seven the next morning, on looking out of our windows we saw the extensive maidan in front of the building strewn with odd pairs of shoes, umbrellas, clothing and other items as though it had been a battlefield the earlier night! Saira's outdoor unit of *Jhuk Gaya Aasmaan* simply had to pack up. There was no way anyone could access the shoot spot because of the happy fans blocking the area in their joyous delirium, hoping to find us there!

All of us conferred and I decided that it was best that to fulfil the yearning of our fans to see us together. I insisted we must at once accelerate our marriage plans from the end of the year to immediately. Now! I suggested to Naseem Aapa, and phoned Sultan who was in Bombay, that we should get back home forthwith. I was clear in my mind that I wanted a simple *nikah* (marriage) with Saira in the next couple of days. At the same time, I lost no time in conveying my decision to Sakina Aapa, my elder brother Noor Sahab and Aquila Bhabi, taking their *ijazat* (permission) for the most important step in my life. Similarly younger brothers Nasir, Ahsan (Aslam had settled in America) and my sisters Taj, Saeeda, Farida and Fauzia were informed. Akhtar was estranged from the family after her alliance with K. Asif. There would be no time for any grand arrangements for the event; nor would there be any finery vis-à-vis wedding clothes and jewellery. In fact, I said that all we needed was a Maulvi Sahab to solemnize our *nikah* and *chuaaras* (dried dates) to distribute as per the ritual. We did not even have time to print cards or prepare a proper list of guests! Close friends were just a phone call away!

So, Saira and I, who had in our professional lives and otherwise, worn the most elegant, custom-made apparel throughout, just wore what Naseem Aapa could quickly muster together in a short while! Naseem Aapa had been the power house of guidance to Saira, in her make-up and wardrobe, the lady who designed and created all of Saira's gorgeous costumes and jewellery at a time when there were no designers as such and her name had become synonymous with great taste. People looked forward to see what Saira would wear in her films, or even at a premiere.

Coverage of our marriage by the media, as the date was hurriedly fixed and announced as 11 October 1966, generated nationwide

The *mehndi* ceremony, with Rahat (Saira's *bhabhi*) and Naseem Banuji.

attention and created headlines in newspapers. We had very little time to ourselves as the attention we continued to get from the media, friends, relatives and close family members just wouldn't stop!

There was a beautiful, but simple, *haldi* (turmeric) and *mehndi* (henna) ceremony, during which the ladies of my family headed by Sakina Aapa and my younger sisters carried *thaals* (plates) of finely ground henna decorated with bright, illuminated candles to Saira and sacredly anointed my emotional, ecstatic bride. This was the first step towards our *nikah*.

Similarly, a whole contingent of glamorous ladies from Saira's family headed by Naseem Aapa and Rahat Bhabhi (Sultan's wife) swooped down to make mirth and mischief with the bridegroom and put some pep into the *haldi* and *mehndi* ceremony at my house!

Saira and I had got so used to spending time together during the whole of September 1966, that when after the announcement of the marriage and the nearing of the rituals began, we were put into individual isolation! Our elders forbade us from seeing each other and we found it heart-wrenching. If I went to her house to discuss formalities with Sultan and Naseem Aapa, I had to remain downstairs and Saira would mischievously try every window of the house to get a glimpse of me!

Came the day of the marriage: 11 October 1966. What did I feel? Was there a gush of nervousness? Having remained a confirmed, eligible bachelor for so long, did I have any trepidations or any qualms as the hour of the relinquishment of my bachelordom drew near?

No. Instead, what I felt was a serene calm and tranquillity, as though having reached a safe Haven of Peace. I always had Amma's inner strength to take on life with grit and draw the best out of it. I had been lucky to attain fame and all that goes with it, but now I had the person who would share my life and would be my very own, to look after me in every way to put in their place my shirts, my socks and my hankies, instead of my things being bundled and pushed any which way into drawers somewhere in the house by my man Friday, Anwar.

19

CELEBRATIONS GALORE

Saira and I began our lives together as husband and wife in the most erudite and culturally wealthy city of India, enjoying peaceful mornings with breakfast served in the garden followed by hectic work on the sets, with breaks for tiffin and coffee and ending with a quiet dinner in the room.

$\mathscr{I}$ HAD THE BENEFIT OF MY SISTERS LIVING IN MY HOUSE, BUT THEY were growing up too, finding their feet in life; some were married off and were away. My food was what I would draw *garam garam* (piping hot) from the *pateela* (cooking vessel), in the kitchen and wrap it up with bread and off I would go for my shooting. A bachelor's domain, free as a bird, but with its disadvantage of no attention being paid to the small, but important, things in life!

To come back to the *shaadi* (marriage), I spent the busy morning in an atmosphere that seemed to be electrified with excitement; my little cabin had the hustle and bustle created by Noor Sahab and Nasir, who as the evening proceeded, ceremoniously placed the Peshawari *kulla* (topee) on my head and tied the gorgeous silken *saafa* (a long piece of cloth) around it with great love and pride, which were visible in their eyes. Their brother Yousuf was a *dulha* (bridegroom) at last!

My own luxurious limousine was gorgeously bedecked with tons of flowers to take me to Saira's house, and bring my bride home with me, but lo and behold! Lalay Noor and Nasir disclosed to me that they and Sakina Aapa wanted me to ride a *ghodi* (a mare) and take the *baraat* (marriage procession) to Saira's home. 'Heavens,' I tried to tell them, 'me on a mare!' I also told them that I would go in my car and pointed out to them that, down the road towards the bride's gate, there was a steep slope. I was apprehensive that the mare would slip and fall and, god forbid, I would too! It would be such a sorry spectacle!

My argument, however, was in vain and as I hesitatingly sat astride my magnificently decorated *'sawari'* I never imagined that the distance of just two minutes to Saira's house from my own home would take an hour. We had thought that about 500 guests would turn up for the marriage, but goodness, the multitude of fans and friends was legion.

As my mare was happily led by Prithvirajji, Shashi Kapoor and Nasir, I could feel the enormous push of the people behind and around us and, to make the proceedings all the more alarming, each step of the way there would be an unceremonious 'thud' on my *kulla*- and *saafa*-bound head from the oriental, *zari-**studded umbrella, which auspiciously 'protected' the bridegroom astride his mare! My head reeled with the impact each time!

To make matters worse, the poor mare, in all its finery and well-manicured hooves and *naal* (horseshoe) kept religiously sliding and slipping on the polished and cemented slope. It was a miracle that I survived the '*dhab, dhab*' on my head and the '*grrrh, grrrh*' of the slippery slope!

---

*Fine gold thread work.

As the gate of the bride's house opened in full splendour to admit me and my entourage, lo and behold! Thousands of people who just could not be held back by any security on earth barged in! I could get a glimpse of dear friend and colleague, producer-director Nasir Hussain, who was dangerously perched on top of a van with his unit, photographing the entire proceedings. It was such a wonderful and loving gesture from a friend. In the rush of the enthusiastic crowd, he and his team were almost thrown to the ground. Thank God that no one was injured.

Our marriage was a surprise to all those who knew me. Naushad Sahab was the only one among my close friends who had the forthrightness to ask me if I wasn't making a mistake. 'How can you think of marrying a girl who is more than twenty years younger to you?' he asked me with the authority he always had as a friend and well-wisher. I had no hesitation in telling him that I had considered the step I was taking with serious introspection and I knew Saira was the girl Amma and Aghaji would have approved had they been alive.

As already noted, Naushad Sahab knew my parents well and he was specially very attentive towards Aghaji when he visited our home in Bandra. Aghaji, too, liked talking to Naushad Sahab and they spent time making easy, casual conversation whenever he dropped in. Aghaji had almost stopped going to Crawford Market due to failing health and he enjoyed the company of friends when they called on him at home. Now that they were no more there, Naushad Sahab was justified in wondering and asking me: 'What about you? Are your sisters and brothers happy about your decision?' I answered that the least I could expect from my family was a warm, good-natured welcome to Saira. There was no pressure on Saira to marry me and there was no pressure on me to marry her. It was the will of God that was bringing us together. Her mother, Naseem Aapa, had told me in her own dignified manner that Saira was beside herself with joy, celebrating the granting of a long-cherished wish by Allah. As for me, I was more than sure that the Coimbatore astrologer's words (mentioned earlier) were coming true and I was being blessed with a loving and adoring wife.

Naushad Sahab did not attend our *nikah*. His absence was compensated by the presence of all my other friends who went all out to make the occasion one of the happiest of my life, whose memories I still cherish.

Raj Kapoor had joked once in a media interview that the day I would marry he would walk into my house on his knees. So, when Raj arrived at 48, Pali Hill, he was promptly reminded of his jovial declaration. He instantly went down on his knees to everybody's surprise. My eldest sister, Sakina Aapa, was in the balcony and she called out to him, bidding him to get up on his feet at once. Raj was as close to me as any of my brothers and Sakina Aapa knew it.

I was overwhelmed by the warmth and the affection I received from all my relatives and friends who thronged the house. As already mentioned, it took an hour for the *baraat* to reach Saira's house. Saira was not overdressed as brides usually are. Her mother, who always had a say in her make-up and fashioned her wardrobe, had kept the finery to the minimum to let her daughter's genetically gifted grace and beauty stand out in the simple elegance of her bridal attire. Both our wedding attires were quickly put together as there was hardly any time.

Eventually, Nasir and Sultan managed to instil some order into the melee and successfully cordoned off the areas meant for the media and the invitees from the gatecrashers who had flooded the garden and the surroundings! Later, I got to know that Sultan and his aides had scattered a dozen men in an attempt to get more food from all the restaurants around so that they could feed even the gatecrashers.

The *nikah* was beautiful – all my loved and dear ones were by my side, General Shahnawaz, Raj Kapoor, Nasir, Sultan, Mukri, Satish Bhalla and everyone whom I held important in my life. Pran had braved a storm in Srinagar and yet flown in to Bombay for my marriage.

The wedding function. (*L to R*): Qazi Murghey, Ahsan, me, Raj Kapoor, Mukri and Nasir.

As required, Saira and I signed the *nikahnama* (marrige document) and individually said '*qubool hai*' (I/we accept the marriage) in reply to the question asked by Qazi Murghey a smiling, saintly, benevolent and holy maulana (a religious scholar). Then Raj escorted me to the bride, who waited to see me first in an *aaina musaf* (mirror) ritual, in which the bride and groom first see each other through a reflection.

After that, Raj asked for a bowl of milk and dipped the wedding rings in it before we exchanged them and became man and wife.

The next evening was the *walima* (marriage feast) at my home, where all our dear family friends gathered, headed by the chief minister of Maharashtra, Vasantrao Naik, for a wonderful celebration.

Saira and I spent the *walima* night in my own little outhouse in the garden. Initially, I felt a little awkward to tell Saira that I wanted us both to stay in this small, segregated part of my bungalow, which had become my frequent domain. It had its own independent entry from the road. Here I needed to be alone at times, to be given my

The day of the marriage. With Naseem Banuji and Saira.

own space when I worked on the scripts of my films, ensuring that the people who came to see me regarding my work did not intrude into the privacy of the women in my family. Much to my relief, Saira showed no dismay; her eyes eloquently expressed her contentment and happiness to do as I had said. In later years, as she shared my life with me, this one quality to happily fall in line with what I said was the essence of the success of our marriage. I will talk of this in detail in later chapters.

Early next morning, we were to leave for Madras. I had to finish the patchwork on *Ram Aur Shyam* and Saira was to spend a day or two with me and proceed to Darjeeling (a hill station in West Bengal) to shoot and finish *Jhuk Gaya Aasmaan*.

Saira was ready and eager to travel with me and we felt we were going to be left alone at last in each other's company away from the ceaseless bustle of Bombay. Madras had become second home for me and I was already making arrangements to purchase a house in a quiet and exclusive locality.

Arriving at the Madras airport for the shooting of *Ram Aur Shyam,*
along with Pran, Baby Farida, Nagi Reddy (behind Farida), Saira,
Nirupa Roy and A. Chakrapani.

When we arrived at the Meenambakkam airport there was a
marvellous surprise awaiting us. There were red rose petals strewn
from the tarmac to the arrival area and there was Nagi Reddy himself
with the cast and crew of the film waiting with garlands and wide
grins to greet us on the tarmac. We were told that huge crowds had
gathered outside the airport and so we would have to leave quietly.

On reaching Nagi Reddy's studio, he told us that there were even
bigger surprises for us. My suite at the Oceanic Hotel was decorated
fabulously and a large, ornate bed had replaced my old single bed.
Tons of fragrant *mogras* (jasmine blossoms) covered every nook
and corner of the room and the bed, too, was decorated with *mogra*
garlands. When the airconditioner was switched on, the heady
fragrance of the milky white blossoms filled the entire room and gave
us the feeling of being in a distant world.

I had once jokingly told Reddy Sahab's son Prasad, who had
become a dear friend, that I liked the incredibly large size of a bed
and its brass knobs and ornate bedsteads that gave it an antique look.

Prasad had jokingly replied that he would gift me the bed when I married. Since at that time there was no bride on the horizon, he had humorously said that his offer of the bed as a gift should be taken as an incentive for me to look around for a suitable bride at the earliest. That was strangely prophetic because, soon enough, I found myself seeking the hand of the beautiful girl I began to love and wanted to marry.

Silken bed linen had taken the place of the cotton sheets that covered my bed earlier. It was as if the room had been readied not for Mr and Mrs Dilip Kumar but for an emperor and empress. Candidly speaking, the surprise was most welcome. What I wanted to offer to Saira in my own house and I couldn't due to shortage of time was here in full splendour before my eyes. In more ways than one, Saira and I began our lives together as husband and wife in the most erudite and culturally wealthy city of India, enjoying peaceful mornings with breakfast served in the garden followed by hectic work on the sets, with breaks for tiffin and coffee and ending with a quiet dinner in the room.

Everything was idyllic and, since we both loved the delicacies served by first-rate South Indian cooks, we hardly missed the food we relished at home in Bombay. In fact, Saira became a permanent fan of *idlis, dosas* and *medhu vadas*.

Whenever I packed up early from the shooting, we used the time we got to drive through the city, taking in the sight of cycle rickshaws jostling with cars and buses fearlessly on busy streets lined with flower stalls that displayed strands of jasmine and multihued flowers ready to be sold to women for the adornment of their long, flowing braids.

I became aware that Saira was not one to make friends with anyone instantly. Even so, I found her amiable and friendly towards my co-stars in *Ram Aur Shyam*. We spent most evenings after the day's work meeting the unit members and having interesting interactions. I noticed that she was shy and a trifle reserved by nature but was making an effort to come out of the shell. I could understand her attitude because I was aware that hers was a close-knit family of four members. For Saira, her mother, grandmother and her elder brother, Sultan, was the world she grew up to know, understand and love. I felt she needed to have friends of her own age and meet more people from all walks of life. In subsequent years, she did just that and her sprightly personality began to emerge.

20

COLLEAGUES AND FRIENDS

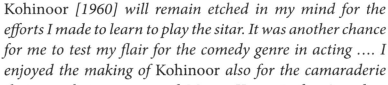

Kohinoor [1960] will remain etched in my mind for the efforts I made to learn to play the sitar. It was another chance for me to test my flair for the comedy genre in acting .... I enjoyed the making of Kohinoor *also for the camaraderie that grew between me and Meena Kumari after* Azaad *as we, who were known for our forte with emotional drama and tragedy, came together for another light-hearted film.*

*R*AM AUR SHYAM WAS COMPLETED AHEAD OF SCHEDULE. ITS work was a jolly experience for all of us. I was working with my friend Pran in *Ram Aur Shyam* and *Aadmi* at the same time. Pran and I were friends in the real sense of the term. We met at the work place and we met informally as often as we could either at his house or mine since we lived in the same locality: Bandra. At work, we were invariably pitted against each other – our characters were always caught in a conflict over something or the other. It used to be very amusing for onlookers to watch the change that would come over him when he faced the camera with me in the frame after all the friendliness and affection they had seen a while ago between us. Well, that's the challenge we actors face all the time. To become what we in reality are not and to assume the character and persona of an unfamiliar chap who has no resemblance whatsoever to our real self is not as easy as it appears.

For Pran one could say it must have not been easy at all when he plunged into those wily, indecent and deceitful characters in the films that made him famous as a first-rate villain. It must have taken quite some effort for him to keep the goodness, gentlemanliness and honesty in his real nature subdued and hidden under the ferocious sneer and fiery looks he adopted for that transient moment before the camera.

We had enjoyed being together during the shooting of Bimal Roy's *Madhumati* (1958) in the forest location where almost everybody else spoke in Bengali while we conversed heartily in Punjabi. He loved the evenings we spent sitting around a bonfire reciting exquisite poetry. We had some wonderful times in Madras when we were shooting for *Ram Aur Shyam* and *Aadmi*. We had just completed *Dil Diya Dard Liya* (1966) and the joke on the sets in Madras was that *Pran aap ka peecha hi nahin chodta* (Pran does not stop pursuing you). It was fine with me and fine with him because we liked each other's company and respected each other as artistes and co-stars.

The most memorable demonstration of his care and affection for me was when he braved a storm in Srinagar, from where he determinedly took a flight to Delhi, when all other passengers had wisely decided not to board the flight, and then a flight to Bombay to reach my house before the *baraat* left for Saira's house. He hugged me again and again without uttering a word.

Pran had made yet another contribution to the solidarity of our friendship when I was shooting for *Azaad* (1955). I was doing full-fledged comedy in that film and it was a step I had taken against the advice of some of my well-wishers and close friends who thought I should not depart from the position I had acquired as a tragedian. After the first schedule, Pran came up to me and told me with utmost sincerity that I was going to give a wonderful surprise to all those who thought I was making a wrong career move. He said the picture would run to full houses and people would want to see me in more films with comedy content. As forecast by Pran, *Azaad* turned out

With Manoj Kumar in *Aadmi* (1968).

to be a blockbuster and its acceptance by the masses proved to my detractors that my fans were ready to accept me in a performance that made them laugh as much as they accepted me in performances that made them shed tears. Pran was very happy that in *Ram Aur Shyam* I would be having some truly funny scenes and it gave him great delight to watch my rehearsals and finally tell me which of my innovations was the best. Once again he and I (in *Ram Aur Shyam*) were pitted against each other. As the timid Ram, I was to cringe before the despotic and cruel Thakur Gajendra and, as the flamboyant Shyam, I was to give him a taste of his own medicine by overpowering him with whip lashes in a scene that is now part of Indian cinema history.

In that scene, Shyam seizes the whip from his cruel brother-in-law's hands and starts whipping him. For a quick rehearsal I took the whip and gently touched Pran's back with its tip. The camera unit was waiting for Pran to give the shocked expression he was supposed to in that situation. Instead of giving the shocked look, Pran started laughing and running away from me. There was surprise and shock because nobody knew why he was running away. I went after Pran with the whip to find out what was happening, unintentionally pointing the whip towards him, and, to my bewilderment, he was laughing uncontrollably. The entire unit was now laughing.

'I have a problem Lalay [as he affectionately addressed me]. *Mujhe gudgudi bahut jaldi hoti hai.* I get tickled very fast.' We had to shoot without a rehearsal and, going by the expressions Pran gave as I 'lashed' him with the whip, I think he made it one of the most gripping scenes in the film.

Ram Aur Shyam also featured another friend who was very dear to me. Mukri was my school mate at Anjuman Islam and he had become an actor before I joined Bombay Talkies. So that gave him the leverage to tell me at times when I ticked him off about something that he was senior to me. At school I hardly knew him and it was during the production of *Pratima* (1945) at Bombay Talkies that I got to know him as an old school mate. By then Mukri had worked in a couple of pictures and he was very friendly with my brother Nasir.

After *Pratima* we found ourselves greeting each other again on the sets of *Anokha Pyar* (1948). This time we spent considerable time together and we became friends despite there being little in common between us. In my view, it is not mandatory that the friends one makes along one's journey in life should be of the same temperament and nature. Mukri was fun loving and happy-go-lucky and he often took liberties with me, which occasionally embarrassed me. I must digress slightly here to narrate an amusing and awkward episode involving Mukri and Nadira during the shooting of Mehboob Khan's *Aan* (1952) at Igatpuri (in Maharashtra).

Mehboob Sahab was a gem of a human being who took good care of his actors and technicians when we shot on locations. He had arranged rooms for everybody in a decent hotel. Mukri, without mentioning it to me, went to the reception desk of the hotel and told the person on duty that he would be sharing my room and so he did not really require a separate room. The hotel's housekeeping staff therefore did not bother to keep the room allotted to him equipped with items such as blankets, towels and bedspreads.

It was late in the night when we packed up on the first day and I retired to my room for a good night's sleep. It was winter and it was pleasantly cold. I had a quick, small meal and slipped under a quilt on my bed and was soon asleep. I had probably not locked the door for, half way through my sleep, I felt someone creep under the quilt. I woke up with a start and, to my great surprise, it was Mukri in his pyjamas and kurta all set to share my bed!

I was naturally very irritated because I am a normal Pathan with normal instincts. I asked him what he was doing in my bed and he went into a lengthy explanation, which was as hilarious as it was crazy.

Apparently, Mukri did not want to sleep in a room that was cold and had no blankets. So he walked down the corridor and, without knocking, entered a room, which he assumed was mine. As he could not see in the dark who was asleep in the room, he crept into the bed and there was Nadira screaming in fright and embarrassment and showering choice abuses on him. He was too scared to move for an instant but he gathered his wits and apologized profusely before she ordered him to leave at once or else …

With nowhere to go, he had taken refuge in my room. He expected me to be kind and understanding but I was in no mood to tolerate his nonsense. I made sure that he went back to his room and did not come back. The episode did not end there. The repercussions were even more serious the next day. While a furious Nadira recounted what had happened the previous night, a suspicious Mrs Mehboob Khan's imagination was running wild and the question that nagged her was: why was Nadira sleeping with her room unlocked? Was the door left open for Mehboob Sahab, who was rumoured to be having a soft spot in his large heart for the pretty, young newcomer?

A showdown was in store between the couple. I sensed it because a tearful Mrs Mehboob Khan expressed her suspicions to me in private. It took all the diplomacy and tact I possessed to erase the doubts from her mind and calm down Mehboob Sahab who was enraged at Mukri's audacity.

From then onwards, I cautioned Mukri against taking rash decisions of his own and gave a standing instruction about two issues. One was that he would not trail behind me in hotel rooms and make-up rooms because I valued my privacy and independence. The other request to my dear friend Mukri was to stay away from alcohol during working hours. I was aware that he slid away quietly between shots at times to gulp down a small dose of what he called an energizer. It was alright as long as it was a small measure but there had been occasions when he went overboard and embarrassed me. So he was told very strictly by me not to touch the stuff during the shooting of S. U. Sunny's *Kohinoor* (released in 1960). I also gave instructions to the unit hands not to oblige him if he asked for a drink during shoots.

One afternoon, while I was wrapped up in a serious discussion with Sunny, I was taken by surprise by a swaying Mukri walking up to me and asking me as to what I thought of myself! He was very angry that the unit boys refused to arrange a drink for him, so he had made his own arrangement and had got hold of a bottle. He repeatedly slurred the question: 'You think I can't help myself? I am Mukri your best friend and you told the boys not to give me a drink!'

In that state, he was not in a position to work and it upset my concentration. I called for pack-up and drove out of the studio leaving Mukri to find his way back. He soon realized I was angry with him and for the right reasons, too. As it always happens between friends we forgot the episode when we met after a few days and he promised me that it would not happen again.

Kohinoor will remain etched in my mind for the efforts I made to learn to play the sitar. It was another chance for me to test my flair for the comedy genre in acting. I was very confident after *Azaad*'s success and I had a fine rapport with S. U. Sunny, who understood me and my tenacity to get as close to perfection as is possible in everything I did. He gave me ample freedom and time to take lessons before I did a scene. I enjoyed the making of *Kohinoor* also for the camaraderie that grew between me and Meena Kumari after *Azaad* as we, who were known for our forte with emotional drama and tragedy, came together for another light-hearted film.

While on *Kohinoor*, I must narrate an interesting and eerie experience while location hunting for that film. Sunny and I decided

With Meena Kumari in *Kohinoor* (1960).

to go by road beyond Nasik (in Maharashtra, about 190 km from Bombay) to find an apt location to shoot some nocturnal outdoor scenes for the picture. I suggested to Sunny that we start in the evening so that we could reach the proposed location after dusk and thus gauge the appeal of the place in the night. Sunny agreed and he went home to pack a few essential things for our travel and was to return by evening to my house.

Sunny's wife always seemed to be a mysterious lady, full of unusual and curious questions. She was greatly interested in the supernatural and kept asking him if she could accompany us for the trip. She was perhaps in no mood to buy Sunny's genuine reasons for setting out in the evening and his sudden decision to go with me. Sunny at once dismissed her request to go along with us and he quickly packed his bag and came to my house much in the adventurous spirit of the Sagitarian in me.

He neither told me about his wife's desire to travel with us nor did he let out the secret that his wife practised witchcraft. We were four men (including the camera assistant and the driver) in a car and there was no room for a woman and Sunny thought it pointless to explain this to his indignant wife.

As we drove a few miles, the sun began to go down and the night was steadily setting in. Quite unexpectedly, the weather changed, taking us completely by surprise with gusts of wind and rain beating on the car's front glass ferociously. We still had quite some distance to go. Sunny and the camera assistant, who was seated in front beside the driver, felt we should stop somewhere and wait for the rain to cease and then proceed on our onward journey. I agreed and we began looking for any sign of habitation along the stretch of barren land on either side of the highway we were cautiously moving on.

Soon, we spotted a remote, dilapidated shed and we stopped the car gingerly. Sunny and I got out and began walking to the ramshackle shed that we could now clearly see. It had a broken thatched roof and there was an open gunny bag tied across with a bit of rope, like a curtain while a goat tied to a shrub was shivering and eyeing us with the forlorn hope of being taken into the shed for shelter.

Inside the shed, there were logs of wood, some debris and a broken bench. I sat on the bench and Sunny strolled over to the goat to see if he could free the poor animal. The gunny bag fluttered in the wind and lightning flashed in the sky. The gale continued unabated. Sunny was walking back to where I was seated when the gunny bag parted and there in front of us was, suddenly, believe it or not, Sunny's wife. She was standing defiantly and staring at us puissantly with a victorious smile on her face as her hand crossed over her face to mysteriously wipe something crimson from her lips. If I remained unshaken by the sight of the woman who was physically miles away from us, it was because of my steely Pathan grit. The camera assistant was trembling and Sunny was rooted to the spot he stood on.

The downpour ceased and we silently resumed our journey in the car. Sunny was speechless with shame or embarrassment and the camera assistant had no words either. The driver was oblivious of the whole episode since he had remained in the car. I tried to ease the chill I could feel by humming a song I knew in Pushtu.

We reached the location, surveyed it and returned to Bombay. Back in the safety of my home, the next afternoon I had just narrated the grisly experienced graphically to my sisters who heard me out spellbound as if they were watching an Alfred Hitchcock movie when we heard the horn of a car that had entered through the gates of our bungalow. The girls ran to look down from the terrace on the first floor as is their wont when a visitor drove into the front yard. To my shock they were shrieking with fear and the younger girls were trembling. The visitors were none other than Sunny and his wife. Was it coincidence or some mumbo jumbo of black magic?

21

TAKING CARE OF SAIRA

—◦◦ ⟡ ◦◦—

Sir Francis Avery-Jones [the doctor treating Saira Banu]
paid a handsome tribute, saying that he had never seen such
loving caretaking of a patient by a husband and a mother.
He went on to say this could only happen with Eastern
people with Eastern values and emotions. Saira recovered
almost miraculously as a result of our collective efforts and
by the grace and benevolence of Allah.

AS MY CAR DROVE IN TO THE LOCATION FOR HER WORK SPOT, SHE
joyously came running down the hill and we left there and then in
a luxurious limousine on a long drive for our honeymoon in nearby
Bhutan. By now she was familiar with my preferences for obscure,
or rather unfrequented, places for outings, rather than the popular,
celebrity-studded areas. Having travelled the world over during her
childhood and teens, first with her mother and then for her shoots,
Saira was very much accustomed to Europe, seven-star comfort
and the hubbub of big towns. Whenever in later years we travelled
to some spot abroad, she had already been there! However, as a
bachelor, I liked the solitude and the quietude of a daak bungalow.
My chauffeur and man Friday used to load my car dicky with eggs,

248

onions, potatoes and all the basic necessities for survival on home cooking. My love of nature and of pristine isolated surroundings with a good book by my side – that was my recipe for good living and a satisfactory holiday.

Bhutan's beautiful landscapes and difficult access through sheer drops of mountainous terrain held great promise of an unusual 'never-before' holiday. It was gorgeous. We had been invited to visit Bhutan by the royal family. There was a beautiful forested area wherein there were wonderfully constructed log houses amidst the greenery all around and we opted to spend our night there. It was very cold and the wind was gushing and strong, indicating the advent of a chilly winter. With no heating as such, except huge charcoal burners (*sigdis*) that warmed up our log cabins, we snuggled into our blankets and dozed off to sleep. Noorjehan, Saira's chief maid-in-waiting, who came as part of the '*dahej*' (dowry), as was jokingly mentioned, was deep in slumber in the next cabin.

All was quiet and well as the breeze outside sang its own song merrily. I suddenly awoke to the feeling that Saira was not by my side. I hurriedly got up, looked everywhere possible and then darted to the bathroom.

What I saw was a nightmare. She was lying unconscious, her body curled and quite still in a white nightgown, her long braid of hair cascading on the floor. By sheer providence, her head had not been injured. She had missed falling on the basin. As I quickly bent and carried her in my arms to the room, all I could utter was 'Ya Allah! Nothing must happen to you, nothing must happen now that I have found you.'

Hurriedly, doctors were called and they pointed out that we had made the terrible mistake of shutting off fresh air by closing all windows and since there was a *sigdi* with burning coal in some part of the cabin, obviously, some of the coal was left unburnt and hence the dangerous presence of carbon monoxide everywhere inside the cabin. It could have been lethal.

My mind darted to the Coimbatore astrologer's predictions, which I had just dismissed nonchalantly.

We quickly returned home to Bombay. Saira had to report for the shooting of one of the films she was committed to.

Since I had been single for so long, I sensed that it was difficult for my sisters and brother Ahsan to share me with Saira, my wife. This was something I had anticipated and was prepared for, but the surprise that awaited me was their resentment of the fact that my wife had her own fame and her own lifestyle. In her own house she lived like a princess, the apple of her family's eye who had everything done for her without asking. Here she was in a joint family, ruled by my elder sister Sakina Aapa, who was not easy to get on with, and apart from that, my married sisters such as Saeeda and Fauzia and the latter's husband also decided to come and stay with us after our wedding. As a working person who reported for her shoots well on time, Saira needed her own space and particular facilities to meet her schedules.

Unfortunately, commonplace amenities, such as the availability of her own washroom for a shower, were not easy to come by, since,

Saira with my sisters and *bhabhi*. (*L to R*): Farida, Saeeda, Taj, Sakina Aapa, Aquila Bhabhi and Fauzia.

for instance, Fauzia would invariably want to use it at the same time. Saira never once complained and she found it easier to simply walk across in a couple of minutes to her own bungalow, bathe and then get ready in her make-up room, before leaving for her shoot.

I could see that it was not the ideal situation for us. Unfortunately, our family's old maid Rabia and my valet Anwar were on a trip of their own, making things difficult for Saira's maid Noorjehan to muster together breakfast for her. It was in a way a very comic strategy, as you see in film situations.

I was silent and quietly observed the happenings till a given time, always being supportive of my sisters, so that they would not feel that I was letting them down. In such situations Saira and I had an understanding and I wondered how this young person had such patience and forbearance to ignore annoying, trivial issues. In all fairness to Saira, who was at the time a very timid and vulnerable girl, I must acknowledge that she tried to cement her relationship with my sisters with a genuine effort to win them over with love and respect.

The stress began to tell on her health. Soon Saira became very ill with ulcerative colitis. It was the result of the emotional stress that had been building up within her in the hostile atmosphere that she was living in and the unfriendliness she was suddenly exposed to after leading a happy, secure and sheltered life in her own home. The physicians treating her made no secret of the medically psychosomatic causative and predisposing factors that had led to such painful intestinal inflammation. Saira and Naseem Aapa gracefully tried to cover it up by blaming it on a bad omelette that she ate. As it was, to cater to Saira's doctor prescribed bland, stipulated diet, Naseem Aapa took it upon herself to send us breakfast and lunch, if we were home, and also dinner if we were not dining out.

The debilitating effect of the intestinal malfunctioning began to show and, for a while, we had to treat this condition at St Elizabeth's Nursing Home in Bombay. This decision was indeed wise and timely and she seemed to recover somewhat. However, physicians advised us that to repair the damage completely it would be recommended to shift her to the London Clinic (one of the largest hospitals in the UK) under the expert supervision of the world-famous gastroenterologist Sir Francis Avery-Jones, one of Queen Elizabeth's doctors.

Ammaji (Saira's grandmother), Sultan and Rahat rallied around to quickly enable me and Naseem Aapa to carry out all the required formalities and immediately send us off to London. Amongst other dear friends, Yash Chopra, Satish Bhalla and Balraj Kohli were always around to help us and came right up to the airport to see us off.

At the London Clinic, I felt completely humbled by my helplessness when I sat by her bedside, her beautiful eyes smiling feebly at me, expressing even in her fear and pain how much she loved me and appreciated my being there all the time. The London Clinic was very strict and would not allow outsiders in the patient's room, but through the sympathetic good offices of Sir Francis Avery-Jones, Naseem Aapa was allowed to sit in a chair all day and night as Saira received the specialized cortisone-based treatment. Sir Francis Avery-Jones knew that Naseem Aapa herself had been debilitated earlier in Bombay with a slipped disc problem and yet she continued to sit in a small chair that was allotted to her by her daughter's bedside. Sir Francis Avery-Jones paid a handsome tribute, saying that he had never seen such loving caretaking of a patient by a husband and a mother. He went on to say this could only happen with Eastern people with Eastern values and emotions. Saira recovered almost miraculously as a result of our collective efforts and by the grace and benevolence of Allah. She rested for about a month in the clinic and resumed her shooting for Manoj Kumar's *Purab Aur Pacchim* in London. (The film was eventually released in 1970.)

Here I must say that Manoj's stand as the producer-director of the film was admirable. He assured me he would wait for Saira to recover fully and only then shoot for *Purab Aur Pacchim* as he had written the script with Saira in mind. If she did not do it, he would shelve the project, he told me. Years later, when Manoj wanted me to consider doing *Kranti* (released in 1981), I must admit this one memorable deed on his part made me take up the project without my customary reading of the complete script. I agreed to work in the film after listening to the subject in a nutshell because I wanted to pay back a debt.

On the other hand, Subodh Mukherjee – with whom Saira had made her debut in *Junglee* (1961) and had worked in three films thereafter for his production house (and who was considered part of her own family) – let her down completely. She had specially acquired a subject from writer Gulshan Nanda (*Sharmeelee*) for Subodh to make with her in the leading role and she had allotted outdoor shooting dates for the picture. However, when she took unwell, she was unceremoniously replaced with another artiste without as much as telling her! So much for courtesy and ethics! *Sharmeelee* was released in 1971, with Raakhee as the heroine (in a double role).

In the early 1970s, we spent some weeks in the fashionable First-World city. (It was here that Saira had spent her childhood and adolescence.) We spent our days just being with each other or going on long drives across the countryside. As is well known to those who have been visiting London frequently, the face of the city has a deceptive constancy about its appearance and it takes a keen eye to observe and recognize the changes. At that time, the skyscrapers had not come up and the grey skyline held out a unique appeal of grandeur combined with simplicity in its famous sights.

Saira and I enjoyed revisiting places we both found interesting and, during one of our drives past Westminster, she mentioned to me how wonderful it would be if we could just drive into Buckingham Palace and meet Queen Elizabeth. As luck would have it, that very week I had received an invitation to attend a tea party to be hosted by the Queen. This was an annual event meant for important citizens and foreign visitors besides members of the diplomatic corps. Wanting to give Saira a surprise, I chose not to tell her about the invitation. I excited her by saying I wished to take her out to a nice place I knew for tea and, as expected, she was delighted and got dressed. She was rather surprised to see me in formal attire but she did not ask why I was so dressed. We got into the car and I could see the sparkle in her eyes as she quizzed me about the place we were heading for. She was quite well by then and the pallor that the illness had caused was gone and she was glowing with her natural healthy fairness and she was indeed looking beautiful and regal.

The chauffeur-driven Rolls Royce took the route to the palace and you could have knocked Saira down with a feather when the car entered the gates of Buckingham Palace, which were thrown open for the invitees. She couldn't believe it when I told her we were going to meet the Queen and have the tea served in her garden.

We walked through the awesome halls and passages of the breathtaking, many-splendoured palace, to the sprawling gardens where Queen Elizabeth, Prince Philip, the Queen Mother, Prince Charles and Princess Anne were meeting guests. As we entered and drew near Her Majesty, lots of Asian officials from our own and various other high commissions and embassies swarmed around us lovingly, seeking autographs and chatting with us, much to Queen Elizabeth's amusement. As she graciously shook hands with us, she smiled and told me: 'You are a very popular man! Delighted! How nice to meet you!

On our return to India, I took the decision to now shift with Saira just across the road to her own bungalow because she needed special caretaking and also a specific diet that was prescribed by Sir Francis Avery-Jones, the essence of the treatment of ulcerative colitis. The cortisone therapy administered at London Clinic had, of course, relieved the alarming condition that she was admitted with, but we sought a complete cure from alternative medical practices. Naseem Aapa, Sultan and I took the added help of the best homoeopaths in the country such as Dr Pathak, Dr Kundert, Dr Sankaran, Dr Anil Bhatia, Dr Naidu of Poona and the cream of hakeems such as Janab Aleemuddin Sahab and Delhi's Harbanslalji. They came and stayed with us, to treat Saira and observe her health graph and to study the reactions to their medicines. All these factors, and the care and attention bestowed by Naseem Aapa, helped Saira in making a quick recovery. Caretaking of this dimension was possible only at her newly built bungalow, which was constructed keeping in view her comforts and requirements.

As the treatment was going on, I had to keep her away from disturbing and volatile situations because they would exacerbate her ailment and would lead to setbacks in the recovery process. In my own place, tempers ran high. That was one reason why I had myself spent more time in my outhouse. Earlier, for instance, after the premiere of *Ram Aur Shyam*, I remember that Manoj Kumar and his wife (Shashi) had come home, specially wanting to speak to me regarding the go-ahead for Saira to do *Purab aur Pacchim*. After some time, Shashi and Saira were to go upstairs from the hall to the washroom, but on the stairs, they were abruptly ticked off and rudely told to be quiet by one of my sisters. Saira, as I have said earlier, had a very happy, child-like disposition and belonged to a small, close-knit family and had been very protectively brought up. She was unbelievably timid. After a spate of unsavoury incidents, which I would not like to mention, I called in Nasir, the brother closest to my heart, and I said to him that I wanted to shift to the Sun-n-Sand Hotel or to Nasir's empty flat (since Nasir and and his wife Para were living in the Nasik farm). Once more, my wife pleaded with me that all these were meaningless incidents and she requested me to let things be. There are so many queries from people down the years on issues regarding my life, that I felt I should take this opportunity to address them.

Being a man, I hardly took any time to bathe and get ready, whereas Saira did everything so minutely that it took a lot of time. Her life pattern was marked by specific appointments and a particular protocol, whereas I was used to my guests just being welcome at any given time – be it a celebrity or a common man – and I had the good health to support this gregarious disposition to just casually meet my friends and visitors.

Soon enough, Saira adapted to my lifestyle and my pace. Naseem Aapa and Ammaji made the necessary arrangements for three huge deep freezes to stock provisions enough for a cricket team, because sure enough, visiting cricket and sports teams as also others would come unannounced and would be welcomed. It was no issue for me to announce at 1.30 p.m. that lunch should be rustled up for them as soon as possible. I must mention here that Saira's staff was wonderful. She still has the same staff of 45 years ago and their successive generations that served Ammaji and Aapa. Starting from Noorjehan and her family, to great cooks, Narmada Gawde and Kavita, there was later a line of them who thought nothing of presenting a full meal to numerous guests at very short notice on the spur of the moment. In fact, believe it or not, they even joined our family and relatives to make formidable sports teams! Saira, Sultan and a retinue of close friends and relatives such as Farida Jalal, her husband Tabrez Barmavar (who also flew kites from a building opposite our house to to take on my own kites), Baby Farida (a child actress), my nephews Amjad and Javed (Noor Sahab's sons who used to spend most of their time with us), Al-Huma (actress Veena's daughter) and dozens of others would form our own little teams to play and revel in good sporting fun – be it cricket or football – all day on the lawns of our house.

I had a travelling '*chakr*' (wheel) in my feet said the old wise men and so did Saira (her name means 'one who travels'). A team of our staff travelled with us with the necessary mirch masalas in trunks and they cooked biriyanis, irrespective of being in far, forsaken locales with no amenities such as in Mercara (now in Karnataka), where we lived surrounded by awesome gigantic moths in a coffee plantation.

A marriage that is for keeps, even with all the good intentions of the couple, is not easy to sustain for either partner. We have had our share of ups and downs, but apart from our outwardly contrasting personalities (to look at us, we seemed different: I would be the quiet, introspective, brooding man given much to silences and Saira the effervescent, carefree, vivacious young woman), we also had much in common. We were both the heads of our respective families, committed to our dearest ones wholeheartedly and, in essence, we shared the joy of living.

Playing a prank on Saira.

Despite my serious demeanour, I was always fond of playing pranks. If we were in a lonely, mysterious locale such as Panhala (a place in southern Maharashtra), where, at that time (in 1967), power supply would time and again go off, I would quietly slip away unnoticed into the compound and pelt the windows with tiny stones. The tick tick, tick of the stones in the eerie wilderness of that place, charged with the fright of an ominous, whistling wind, had Saira and her staff shrieking! We were both addicted to long walks after pack-up even in the most deserted locales. As we strolled, when there would be a lull in the conversation, I would stop mid-track, turn around to her and ask, with my most mysterious expression: 'And the man you are walking with just now, who do you think he is? Your husband? No …' Saira would nearly faint with the impact of this little drama!

At other times, I scared the life out of her old maid Noorjehan. In 1968, from the airport at Bangalore, Saira and I got into our car and drove to our favourite suite at the West End Hotel, had a sumptuous breakfast and waited for Noorjehan to come join us with the luggage. Soon enough, I disappeared. Saira looked helter-skelter but in vain. No sooner did Saira and Noorjehan enter the room and move towards the tall, spacious cupboards to place the suitcases inside than I suddenly pounced on them ferociously with a roar of a lion! Noorjehan was down on the floor and Saira was shaking uncontrollably. After that, back home, Naseem Aapa had to 'samjhao' (explain to) me: 'Yousuf *beta*, Saira is a very timid girl, God forbid, she will have a heart attack like this!'

Soon, however, I toughened her up and then she started playing pranks on me! Just a few weeks ago, we have, by the grace of God, affectionately been given a memento for being the 'Timeless Couple' and people want to know what has gone into the lasting of a 48-year-old relationship. (Amitabh Bachchan came home to hand over the memento as Saira and I could not make it to the event.) I changed myself a lot and Saira changed herself more than I did!

No sooner than we were married, my male friends such as Pran, Satish Bhalla and Balraj (Balli) Kohli would stop by outside my gate at 2 a.m., blow the car horn to its crescendo and expect me to come down and go for a drive. This had been our ritual as of old, and we boys were full of zest and the evening would be of wonderful food at Satish's Bates Hill home (Pali Hill was always an address to be reckoned with). There would be some great poetry recitations and singing sessions as our group was full of joie de vivre. Pran and Satish were well versed with the works of great Urdu poets such as Mirza Ghalib, Mir Taqi Mir and Faiz Ahmed Faiz, but soon enough, our *bhabhi* (Satish's wife Shalu) would draw out a big *Diwaan-e-Ghalib* and, in her heavily accented Urdu read out a *sher* (couplet) as far as she could; for the rest of the couplet she'd finish off with 'something, something'. It was so funny that I copied this in *Ram Aur Shyam*.

For a glamorous young woman to step in line with my five-minute routine of dressing up meant cutting short her time drastically. At the start of the marriage, one evening, she took an hour to get ready. Finally she emerged, looking bedecked and beautiful. She had great love and good taste for jewellery designed and made for her by Naseem Aapa and, on that occasion, she had put on a lot of ornaments. Naturally she asked me: 'How am I looking?' I could only reply with a smile: 'Beautiful! But you have to carry a *tokra* [basket] and put all your jewellery in it, because people must know you have so much!' After that, more often than not, Saira would restrict herself to just a string of pearls and earrings when stepping out with me.

In short, the glamorous girl who took an hour for putting on her makeup and doing up her long hair before a grand function, suddenly, changed totally.

I remember an occasion when we were new to each other and she was just into films, I had unexpectedly visited at her flat at Sea Belle. On ringing the doorbell, Saira had opened the door and, on seeing me, she shrieked so loudly that one could have fainted. Her hair was in well-oiled pigtails and she was wearing a simple cotton salwar kameez. She ran into her room, and did not come out, telling Naseem Aapa: 'Now he has seen me like this, he will never work with me!'

In contrast, soon after our marriage, if she had applied *mehndi* (henna) to her hair to condition her tresses and I called out to her to come with me to a friend's place for a ceremony, she would just cover her head in a turban and think nothing of accompanying me in that state. Once when I was travelling to Hyderabad for attending a marriage, she came to see me off at the airport as usual and got to know there that her shoot for the day had been called off. I suddenly thought: 'Why not ask her to come along and hop on to the flight with me?' She did just that, attended the grand marriage function in the casual salwar kameez she was attired in!

What I got to love and appreciate about Saira down the years that I have lived with her is her innate simplicity and softness of heart. Her other qualities include her quickness to say sorry to rectify a situation and not harbouring any false pride. Any spat or tiff gives her heartache and she never can rest until she has mended fences. As a man, I was used to taking time to cool down after I had been ruffled in family encounters.

I had distanced myself from my most bright and intelligent sister Akhtar on her surprise marriage to K. Asif. I was not seeing her at all.

One day at lunch, Saira got up to take a call. On the other line was a doctor from Bombay's Breach Candy Hospital informing us that Akhtar wanted to see her brother and that she was critically unwell. She had lost Asif by then (he had passed away on 9 March 1971) and was living with her daughters. I told Saira emphatically: 'I will NOT go.' Saira requested me to go and see her, as she was after all my sister and also very unwell. I repeated that I would not see her. She had shamed me and we had distanced ourselves after a life of doting and affection.

In her own gentle way, Saira coaxed me to just see her for now, at her behest, lest, God forbid, anything untoward happened. She took me to Breach Candy and there began a reunion of brother and sister wherein, for the first time, Akhtar (who had been very much against my marriage to Saira), got to know and understand my wife. In later years and even now, Saira is the one Akhtar is the closest to and they are constantly tuned to each other.

By the grace of God our long relationship also endured and benefited because we both had 'no fuss, no bloated ego' personalities. It was painful to see couples go on relentlessly bickering over minute details and for us there was no keeping up with the Joneses either.

Actor Richard Burton once famously proclaimed to the media: 'You have to pity poor Liz [Elizabeth Taylor the celebrated star and his wife]. She is travelling with last year's diamonds.' Saira and I were always content and down to earth, being so very blessed in every way. Our life has always been full of fun and laughter.

If I said to Saira, 'be ready to go to a function with me, wait at home' and I quite forgot about it and went alone to the venue, Saira never picked up a quarrel. Instead, she just laughed at my forgetfulness and was done with it. I must recall here an incident that aptly illustrates this wonderful trait in her. We were invited to a grand evening to felicitate the great Oscar-winning actress Shirley Maclaine. Saira and I, amongst others, were invited to have dinner with her and, understandably, my wife was a great fan of Shirley Maclaine. The hitch was that I was in Delhi on the day of the event. Anyway, I flew back to Bombay in the evening and Saira was at the airport to receive me. She was dressed and ready for the occasion and had thoughtfully carried my necessary dark suit and the needed accessories.

As I sat in the car with her, I gently asked her if she really wanted to be lost in such a crowd of admirers and guests circling around Shirley or would she prefer to spend some quality time between just the two of us, since we had been away from each other for a couple of days. That was it! We had a candlelight dinner, just the two of us, which we never got to do too often.

Another sterling quality she possesses is her ability to forget the past and live in the present. Soon after our *nikah* (marriage), while we were staying in Madras, I received a message from Madhubala that she wished to see me urgently. I confided in Saira as soon as we returned to Bombay about the message. Saira at once insisted that I should meet Madhu since it must be something she was distressed about. When I went to Madhu's home, I was pained to see that she was frail and looked very weak. The pallor on her face not only belied her ill health, but her magnificent, impish smile seemed such an effort. She was happy to see me and said: '*Hamarey shehzade ko unki shehzadi mil gayi hai, main bahut khush hoon!*' (Our prince has got his princess, I am very happy!)

She was worried about some personal matters that she needed my advice on and we discussed them until she was somewhat satisfied that they could be sorted out. She then relaxed. That was the last time I saw her. She passed away on 23 February 1969.

On another occasion, when I was suffering from a heart ailment in 1998, Uma (Kamini Kaushal), after many years, called my office. She had some close lady friends who wanted to meet me and Saira arranged for them to come home. She also made me speak to Uma, who had come to know about my condition and that I was to undergo open heart surgery.

Uma said that she would send some tapes of children's films she had liked. She was writing stories in children's magazines and some of them had been chosen for filming. She thought it would be a good idea for me to watch some entertaining children's films to while away my time post-surgery. She also sent lots of little toys for us to string up in our cars. Saira and I appreciated the gesture and I felt it was very thoughtful of her.

I can never forget our sojourns in Madras, be it for work or for pleasure. As luck would have it, our first film together, *Gopi* (released in 1970), was set to roll, of all places, in Madras.

22

The Husband–Wife Team

*I began to discover the capacity my wife had for hard work
and the pursuit for flawless work. She was receptive to sound
advice and was quick to absorb the guidance I gave her in
the scenes we came together. She co-starred with me in three
films and I saw her tenacity and determination to get the
nuances and emotional curves of the performance right.*

*G*OPI (DIRECTED BY A. BHIM SINGH) WAS A DELIGHTFUL
experience. It was like an extended honeymoon for me and Saira.
We had a secluded house – more like a cottage – at Kodambakkam (a
locality in Madras) in the midst of a lot of greenery with mango trees
all over the backyard and with golden yellow sand covering the entire
compound. For our recreation and exercise, Nagi Reddy had a huge,
high-walled badminton court made for us close by with a thatched
roof of palm leaves.

Saira was very happy not only because we were left alone in the
large house after pack-up from the shooting during the day but also
because she was working with me for the first time. By now she had
shed some of her shyness and the reservations of a conservative
upbringing. On the sets, she enjoyed the jokes between me and Om
Prakashji – a renowned comedian and character actor – and she

responded warmly to the upcoming actress Farida Jalal's attempt to befriend her. In fact, she and Farida Jalal struck up a friendship that continues to this day. Saira's Kathak guru, Roshan Kumari, who was choreographing her song and dance numbers in the film was also a friend, who provided company in Madras. Roshan Kumari and Saira would spend hours in their rehearsal of the choreographed movements for the song picturized on both of us, *Gentleman, Gentleman, Gentleman …*,* which became a craze after the film was released.

On the first day of shooting, after our first shot together as co-stars was canned, a dream Saira had cherished for years, Rajinder Krishan, the poet who was watching the way Saira was following my brief and performing perfectly, took her aside after all the clapping had died down, and told her: '*Beta*, I think you performed brilliantly. However, I must tell you something in your own interest. You should not try to be Dilip Kumar in your enactment. Be yourself, be Saira Banu. This is what all his heroines have been doing. All of them have tried to be Dilip Kumar and failed. It is only natural when you have an actor of his stature in the same frame. Don't do it. Try to be yourself.'

When we were back at our cottage, Saira related to me what Rajinder Krishan had told her. It then struck me that his observation was right. I had always tried to help my co-artistes by enacting their part for them in a scene during the preparation not because I wished to overpower them but simply because I wanted them to be a scale better than I was. It was also something I had imbibed from S. Mukherjee Sahab and Mehboob Sahab who were well known for depicting facial expressions and body movements before actors.

Mukherjee Sahab, for instance, could become a graceful woman giving that glance of loving acceptance to her lover when he enacted it for Vyjayantimala's observation during the shooting of *Leader*

*Sung by Lata Mangeshkar and Mahendra Kapoor, penned by Rajinder Krishan and composed by Kalyanji Anandji.

(1964). Likewise, Mehboob Sahab, with all his avoirdupois, could demonstrate the gait of a slim and agile village maiden when he was directing Nimmi (born as Nawab Banu on 18 February 1933) in *Amar* (1954).

I explained the finer points to Saira by showing her how Mehboob Sahab feigned the shyness and the gait of the village girl with his bulky figure and chubby face undergoing a metamorphosis all of a sudden. Saira went into peals of laughter but she understood how helpful the two great men were and how passionate they were about getting the result they desired in a period of Indian cinema when there was no formal training available to artistes and directors.

As a matter of fact, when my brother Nasir and I were working together in *Gunga Jumna* (1961), Nasir would sit quietly and watch me explain scenes and demonstrate the facial expressions I wanted from the artistes. During lunch one afternoon, I heard him telling Nitin Bose (the director of the film) about a young lady who was smitten by him and how I had read her facial expression, which had betrayed her feelings for Nasir who was hardly aware of the young lady's interest in him.

The truth is that I was fascinated by facial expressions right from my childhood. I found out even as a child that facial expressions could convey what words sometimes failed to. When Aghaji was angry or upset, he always remained aloof and silent. But his eyes and the lines on his brow could never hide his feelings. I observed all the members of our family residing in the large house in Peshawar because I was either trailing behind Amma or sitting by her side when she made free-wheeling conversation with visitors from her side of the family.

I took less interest in what she spoke or they spoke but I paid keen attention to the way in which they expressed their feelings and thoughts. I enjoyed observing their expressions, the use of their hands and the modulation of their voices. Amma sometimes noticed what I was doing and gently told me to leave the room, explaining that children shouldn't be listening to conversations between elders. Though I never sat next to Aghaji when he conversed with his friends, I observed them, too, from a distance. There were men whose hearty

With Saira in *Gopi*.

laughter enlivened the atmosphere and there were men who didn't react at all. The strong silent ones, I guess.

Among my leading ladies, it was Nargis who once jovially asked me how I knew so much about the way women expressed themselves. It amused her no end when I told her about my childhood observations.

To get back to *Gopi*, I began to discover the capacity my wife had for hard work and the pursuit for flawless work. She was receptive to sound advice and was quick to absorb the guidance I gave her in the scenes we came together. She co-starred with me in three films and I saw her tenacity and determination to get the nuances and emotional curves of the performance right. In the two other films we did together, *Sagina* (1970 and 1974)* and *Bairaag* (1976),

*The film was first made in Bengali (as *Sagina Mahato*) in 1970 and in Hindi in 1974. *Sagina* and *Sagina Mahato* have been used interchangeably.

she had to bring to life characters that bore no resemblance to her
real self or anyone she knew. She had to draw from the well of her
own imagination and take the helpful directions given to her by the
directors and writers with a sincere commitment.

We signed *Sagina* while *Gopi* was in the making and it entailed
my going frequently by the time-consuming flights to Calcutta (now
Kolkata) for meetings that director Tapan Sinha arranged. I had met
Tapanda earlier in the company of my friend Hiten Choudhary, but
we did not talk much about films. Tapanda was a man of few words
and he preferred to converse as most highly educated men do. I
understood he was a postgraduate in physics like S. Mukherjee Sahab
and had started his journey in cinema as a sound engineer like the
latter. While Mukherjee Sahab was very eloquent and enjoyed a lively
conversation with people he knew well, Tapanda spoke only when
needed. Ashok Bhaiyya (Ashok Kumar) had spoken highly about
Tapanda after he had worked in the Bengali film *Hate Bazare* (1967)
with that director. I had watched the 1957 Bengali film *Kabuliwala* in
Bimalda's (Bimal Roy's) company. I had liked Tapanda's adaptation
of the story by Nobel Laureate Rabindranath Tagore and I had
complimented the actor Chabi Biswas for his performance in the film.

Tapanda came across as a director who was receptive to suggestions
and observations not only from me but also equally from other actors.
He had long academic discussions with me about the backdrop and
the period of the story and he urged me to read some literature he had
compiled about the pre-independence labour union movements and
about the birth and spread of Naxalism in certain parts of east and
north-east India. Such literature was very helpful to me in understanding
the characters and their vulnerabilities against the backdrop of the
revolutionary political scenario that had surfaced there.

I was fascinated by the character of Sagina – his complete lack
of guile in dealing with critical issues and conniving people, his
perceptions and instinctive abilities, his maverick behaviour at times,
his love for Lalita (to be played by Saira) and, above all, his chequered
destiny. There was depth and realism in the way Tapanda had created
the character of Sagina on paper and he told me that I was free to
improvise if I wished. In fact, he was a director who left much to the

actors to study and understand the demands of the situations in the screenplay and come up with their improvisations. To work with such a director is a genuine pleasure for actors who possess fertile minds and have the will to enhance the appeal of the character by repeated improvements, whereas it becomes a burden for actors who prefer to follow directorial guidelines. The actors in *Sagina Mahato* were, to my delight, eager to participate in improvisations and improvements. As mentioned earlier, the first version was in Bengali and it meant my delivering my lines in that language. I had already a soft corner for the Bengali language in my heart, having been in the constant company of Ashok Bhaiyya, Mukherjee Sahab and so many scholarly Bengali writers and directors in the early years of my career. As such it did not take a Herculean effort on my part to speak the lines in Bengali but the non-Bengali artistes from Bombay (including Saira) had to be given recorded tapes of their Bengali dialogue to hear and rehearse. The reward for all the effort I put in to render my Bengali dialogue with conviction came after the film's release, when the local media wrote glowingly about it. I was more than happy therefore to accept the prestigious Bengal Film Journalists Association's award for my acting in the Bengali original. Four years later, the producers, J. K. Kapur and Hemen Ganguly, encouraged by the success of the Bengali film, went on to remake it in Hindi at considerable expense, reshooting the scenes at the same locations.

The song situations were inserted in the Hindi version after some thinking to provide relief in the original narrative, which was moving at a slow pace that could bore the mass audience in the northern India states. The song, *Tumhre sang to rain bitayi ...,** picturized on me and Saira, was choreographed in the most unconventional manner with our own inputs in the movements. It was a song suggesting the intimacy between Sagina and Lalita the previous night in much the same way that *Dhoondo dhoondo re sajana more kaan ka bala ...***

*Sung by Lata Mangeshkar and Kishore Kumar, written by Majrooh Sultanpuri and set to tune by Sachin Dev Burman.
**Sung by Lata Mangeshkar, written by Shakeel Badayuni and composed by Naushad.

With Saira in *Sagina*.

suggested the consummation of the relationship between Gunga and Dhanno after they were hurriedly wed by a captive *purohit* (priest) in the jungles in *Gunga Jumna*.

If there was one thing that I insisted on while such situations were conceived was that there should be no explicit depiction of physical intimacy. My condition went down well with the majority of directors I worked with, thanks to our like-mindedness on the subject. It was always left to me then to work out the scenes. This did not mean that I was (or am) puritanical or orthodox. I certainly understood the mass audience's expectations but, at the same time, I was acutely aware of the moral responsibility I shouldered as an actor. As the head of a family comprising six girls and five boys, I was innately averse to any display of indecency and the first thought that always crossed my mind was about the embarrassment such scenes could cause to my own sisters if they watched me in, albeit, a make-believe situation in a film. The film I chose to do may be a comedy, a labour-oriented subject, a historical, or a socially relevant theme, but I have generally chosen scripts with a social concern as its core content. One can't get what one wants all the time, but, given the choice, I gave preference to such scripts.

Sagina Mahato, therefore, interested me as a subject for its inherent comment on, and exposure of, the politics that impacted the proletarian labour movements. It was also interesting as an unusual love story woven into a turbulent flow of events. Saira was originally not supposed to be cast in the role of Lalita. She had her own workload to carry and the character was not major enough for her star stature at that point of time. But Saira being Saira, she volunteered to play the part just so that she could be with me at the secluded hilly locations chosen near Kurseong and Gayabari (near Darjeeling in West Bengal) for the film. The character turned out to be quite a fiery one and she took up the challenge 'manfully' and played the part with a courage and vigour that surprised me. The reviews she received for her performance and the compliments she got from her colleagues made her justly proud.

Her work in *Sagina Mahato* convinced me further that it would be unjust to abort her career just to have her by my side as my wife. Within weeks after our marriage, I had watched rushes of *Shagird** and it was the first time I was seeing her on the screen. At the end of the screening, I told her it would be criminal on my part if I stopped her from continuing her career.

The location for *Sagina Mahato* was a treat for the eyes, as beautiful and mountainous as some parts of Peshawar that still linger in my memory. It was bleak and grey on most days, with mist and white clouds descending from the mountains in the distance. Being an outdoors-loving man, I spent much of my free time trekking up the hills or exploring the markets where I would stop to buy white orchids to present to my wife. On one such outing, I was taken to watch a play staged by a local theatre group and there I discovered a promising

*Released in 1967 and directed by Samir Ganguly. The hero was Joy Mukherjee, the son of S. Mukherjee Sahab.

actor named Kader Khan, who met me backstage and expressed his wish to work in Hindi films since he was well acquainted with Urdu. I spoke to Tapanda and cast him in a small part in *Sagina* and later in *Bairaag*. Kader justified my faith in his abilities when he went on to make a mark later on in numerous Hindi films as an actor and writer. I have not seen any of the films that made him famous but I learned he was in great demand.

While shooting for *Sagina*, as always, I had a badminton court made next to our cottage, where I played the game every day with whoever wanted to play with me. In the evenings, when the temperature dipped and the darkness of the night eclipsed the skyline and the landscape, we got together and formed a jolly ring around a bonfire singing and even dancing and miming. It was our way of dispelling our alienation and loneliness at a beautiful but far-away location. One evening Saira's guru, Roshan Kumari, a shy conservative Kathak exponent, who only performed before connoisseurs as per the tradition of the Jaipur *gharana** she belonged to, spontaneously put on her *ghungroos* (anklets) and performed extempore. She came up with variations of *tatkaar* (footwork) while a unit member played the tabla for her. We watched spellbound the difficult pirouettes she effortlessly performed while she danced with abandon.

I must not forget to mention the scene I greatly enjoyed performing in *Sagina Mahato*. It was the sequence where Sagina feels claustrophobic in the office and he gets out to enjoy a breath of the open air he loves and there he sees a speeding train. He takes off in a sprint alongside the running train competitively keeping pace, running faster and faster with the wind beating against his face. When I suggested the scene to Tapanda, he liked the idea very much. He looked at me and asked me in his quiet manner if I could wait for a double to be arranged for the run. He stared at me in disbelief when I told him I would do the sprint myself. I told him about my athletic

Gharana means a specialist school of classical music or dance.

days but he could believe me only when the scene was actually filmed in one take! To this day I receive compliments from avid filmgoers for the bracing impact the scene had on them and the emotional empathy it evoked.

23

A New Role: Taking Up Noble Causes

———◦•◦ ⁝◦⁝ ◦•◦———

I do not know if it is in my genes or if it is something I have assimilated from the environment I was brought up in. It gives me great contentment and joy to espouse a good cause.

Sagina Mahato was described by many critics as a political film. Journalists who met me then were keen to know whether I had any interest in joining a political party and getting actively involved in politics. I had no hesitation in replying that my involvement with politics would be limited to the pre-election campaigns that I would take part in and I would never ever hanker after a seat in either of the houses of Parliament.

The first time I campaigned for a Lok Sabha candidate was in early 1962 when Prime Minister Jawaharlal Nehru (popularly known as Panditji) personally spoke to me on the phone from Delhi asking me if I could take time off to visit the office of the Indian National Congress (INC) in Bombay and meet V. K. Krishna Menon who was contesting from North Bombay. His opponent was none other than Acharya J. B. Kriplani, a former president of the INC who had broken away from the party and founded the Kisan Mazdoor Praja Party, which, in 1952, had merged with the Socialist Party of India to become the Praja Socialist Party.

I obeyed Panditji at once, my love and respect for him being next only to the affection and admiration I had for Aghaji. I visited the office of the INC in Juhu as instructed by Panditji. As Krishna Menon was delayed in arriving at the office, I waited for him. I was eagerly looking forward to my meeting with him, having read so much about him and his brilliant marathon speech in January 1957 – lasting almost eight hours – defending India's stand on Kashmir at the UN Security Council.

With Pandit Jawaharlal Nehru.

As I waited, a well-dressed man hurriedly entered the office and, seeing me seated alone in the room adjacent to the main office, he came up to me and introduced himself saying: 'My name is Rajni. I practise law for a living.' (I later came to know that his full name was Rajni Patel.) I stood up and extended my hand, saying: 'I am Yousuf. I don't do anything for a living.'

He was somewhat taken aback and he held out his hand rather hesitantly. As we shook hands, Krishna Menon walked in, taking brisk, long strides towards us. He greeted me with a familiarity and warmth that brought a look of surprise to Rajni's face. He walked into the main office room, talking to me in his impressive and refined voice about Panditji's phone call to him informing him about my visit to the local office at Juhu.

Rajni and I followed him silently. In the main office, Krishna Menon introduced us properly and Rajni, apologetic about not recognizing me, confessed that he was not a movie buff and he had not been inside a cinema house for ages. There were quite a few attendants in the room and Krishna Menon smiled at all of them and joked that they were all there perhaps to take a good look at me. Krishna Menon had an imposing personality and an air of authority when he spoke, which could have seemed like arrogance to many.

Krishna Menon did not lose time in senseless talk. He came to the point and told me he wanted me to campaign for him in the forthcoming stiff contest for the North Bombay Lok Sabha seat. Panditji had spoken to him about me and he (Krishna Menon) was wondering if I could oblige and also get the support of the film fraternity to join in some rallies to support the Congress party. He emphasized that Panditji had stated that I was fluent in Urdu, Hindi and Marathi and I was very articulate when I took off on a subject I was passionate about. As he spoke, Rajni was listening intently but remained silent. It was as if no one spoke when Krishna Menon did. I wanted to inform Krishna Menon that it was going to be a new experience for me, having had very little to do with public speaking in real life.

I could understand how Panditji had been impressed by my ability to speak effectively. In late 1960, my film *Gunga Jumna* had been refused a certificate by the Film Censor Board. This refusal was most unjust as Raj Kapoor's *Jis Desh Mein Ganga Behti Hai*, which had also been seen by the board in the same week had been cleared with minor cuts. Raj's film too had dacoity and dacoits as the backdrop and also its fair share of depiction of violence.

My appeal to Dr B. V. Keskar, then information and broadcasting (I & B) minister, fell on deaf ears because he had his own ideas about morality, decency and violence and had urged a stringent application of the censorship guidelines to all mainstream films. He would not listen to my reasoning and it became difficult to communicate with him. Desperate, I had sought a meeting with Panditji and had made a strong plea before him not only for my film but also for all the films held back by the Censor Board for flimsy reasons. Convinced by my appeal, Panditji ordered a review of *Gunga Jumna*. The board cleared the film just days before its scheduled release; not just that film, but also all others held up until then.

As I took leave of Krishna Menon, Rajni said we should meet the following day to plan and discuss the campaign strategy and other details. When we shook hands, it was a firm and warm clasp.

Rajni Patel and I became close friends as our meetings became regular and purposeful from then onwards. His intellectual sharpness was complemented by his caring nature and the principles he stood for. The 1962 election for the North Bombay Lok Sabha seat was one of the most dramatic contests in the poll history of the city. I went wherever I was taken by Rajni and it was customary for him to acquaint me with the agenda of each rally that I addressed only at the last minute.

Actually, the very first large political gathering I addressed was at the Cooperage grounds in South Bombay. Rajni and I were travelling by car to the venue and I had no idea that I would be called upon to make a speech. Somewhere near Marine Drive, Rajni informed me that I was among the speakers who would be called to address the large crowd. I got annoyed with him and told him it wasn't funny. I pointed out that I was no politician to take off on a topic and enthral a crowd with extempore verbiage. He merely patted my hand and said: 'Who expects a political speech from you? Leave that for the politicians. You speak to the crowd as Dilip Kumar.' I could not fathom what he was saying. We were at the venue by then and I could sense the excitement of the crowd waiting to see me and hear me. Rajni was avoiding eye contact with me now, having put me in the most challenging situation of my life.

As I was ushered in, I heard people calling out for Dilip Kumar and it became imperative for me to go on the stage, grasp the microphone and speak. The shouting was more audible now that I was face to face with the crowd. I remembered how I recited the poem, 'I have two eyes ...', before a cheering audience in Peshawar and the repeated encores I received. I drew a deep breath and spoke for 10 minutes! The applause was deafening when I concluded. The crowd was reluctant to leave the grounds and Rajni was beaming at me with a look of triumph. It was the start of a new chapter in my life as a public speaker.

I have been complimented so frequently by my relatives and

friends for the many speeches I made during my campaign for Krishna Menon. I had to address not one but several public meetings every day. Everywhere, I was given the microphone and asked to speak. It required some amount of preparation but generally I relied on the knowledge I had gained by reading books on virtually all subjects. I am a book lover and my closest friends and my sisters and brothers knew how happy I was when they brought a good book for me as a gift.

My campaigning for the Congress party became a regular exercise after the splendid success achieved by Krishna Menon, who emerged victorious. My bonding with Rajni became stronger as we discovered our common goals, interests and values. Although Rajni was leading the Congress party in Bombay, he was not a politician in the strict sense of the term. He was more of a barrister and we had many common friends from the legal fraternity. Neither he nor I yearned for power and recognition. One day, while chatting casually, I told Rajni that a cosmopolitan city like Bombay deserved a spacious and grand venue to hold exhibitions and classical dance and music recitals, literary exchanges between eminent writers and a science centre that would give a fillip to the young upcoming scientists of the city. I had immense admiration for the work going on in the field of space technology and I was keenly following the progress and advancements in the field under Professor Vikram Sarabhai. Rajni responded excitedly and, in the early 1970s, he began preparing the first-ever proposal for an art, culture and science centre in Bombay to be presented to Prime Minister Indira Gandhi. Like her father Pandit Jawaharlal Nehru, she too took very little time to decide and she categorically stated that a cultural venue that would also exhibit the progress of science and technology was a requirement in Bombay; she gave the green signal to Rajni to prepare a proposal. Thus the first step towards the creation of the Nehru Centre at Worli was taken.

For Rajni and me, the meaning of politics was to serve the common people. Both Rajni and I could have won elections and been in the fray as active politicians but that thought was far from my mind and his. We were happy and satisfied every time we organized a fund collection drive to swell the government's kitty for flood, famine or earthquake relief work. It took considerable planning and logistics management prowess to organize the processions of stars in vehicles moving slowly through the busiest roads of Bombay. I remember the truck processions we took out in Bombay after every natural calamity to provide relief to the victims.

We had to be very polite to the people who brought clothes, money, medicines, groceries, blankets and other items as their contribution to the relief funds and wanted to shake hands with their favourite stars in return. At the same time, we had to take optimum care of the safety of the actors as well. Not all fans behave with decency and respect when they are allowed to shake hands with the leading ladies. It was up to us, the men, in the trucks to take care of that aspect. On the whole, all of us enjoyed the drives through the main roads of the city and experiencing the adoration of the people we entertain with our acting. At the end of the day our collections made us feel rewarded and proud that, in our own small way, we had done our duty as citizens.

The day chosen for the laying of the foundation stone for the Nehru Centre at Worli by Indira Gandhi – 2 November 1972 – was one of great fulfilment and happiness for Rajni and me. In the evening Rajni decided to add to his happiness by getting married to Bakul, a charming and accomplished colleague in his profession he had long been wanting to propose marriage to. You can read Bakul's account of the surprise midnight event in her own words in the second section of this book.

Rajni had a habit of springing surprises. One morning (sometime in early 1980), he woke me up while I was holidaying at Mahabaleshwar (a hill station in Maharashtra, located about 220 km from Bombay) to announce that he and Sharad Chandra Govindrao Pawar, who was then chief minister of Maharashtra, had decided to appoint me the sheriff of Bombay. For a moment I thought it was a prank. I was about to laugh it off when Rajni explained that there was no going back for me as the news had been officially given to the media and I could myself hear it if I switched on the radio.

Sharad Rao (as I called him) had been introduced to me by Rajni when the former was in the Congress. (He had quit that party in 1978, but rejoined it in 1987.) I had taken time off from my work to campaign for Sharad Rao when he had contested in the Maharashtra Legislative Assembly elections from Baramati (about 250 km from Bombay) in 1967.

The three of us met often at my residence or at Rajni's apartment at Worli. Mention of my becoming the sheriff of Bombay had cropped up a couple of times earlier and I had expressed my inability to accept the position since I had just begun work on Manoj Kumar's *Kranti* (released in February 1981). In my absence, my wonderful friends, Sharad Rao and Rajni, had accepted the position on my behalf. While I was trying to deter them from going ahead, Rajni informed me that there would be a great controversy leading to embarrassment for both of them if I did not accept the position. He assured me my new job was not going to interfere with my work. He clarified that it was an apolitical position and it did not entail my going to an office every day. Now that it was a fait accompli, I had no option but to accept.

The first person to get wind of the news and express his happiness about the appointment was Manoj Kumar who was making perhaps his most ambitious movie, *Kranti*, and it surprised me that he was least concerned about the schedules of his film possibly going haywire during my tenure as sheriff. Instead, he was agog with excitement about the honour being bestowed on me. He wanted me to seek permission from the Raj Bhavan to film the swearing-in ceremony before the governor of Maharashtra, Sadiq Ali.

As expected the news created a stir as it was the first time an actor was being given the position of the city's sheriff. There was no respite for me for an entire year from the day of the swearing in till the last day at the sheriff's office as the number of functions to attend started

Being sworn in as sheriff of Bombay.

as early as 10 a.m. and went on till midnight. It was so hectic that Saira used to keep a suitcase packed with the different suits I would be wearing to the different functions in the dickey of my car and she found places for me to change into the suits if she could.

Everywhere I was expected to 'say a few words', a cliché that annoys me for its silliness. How does one speak only 'a few words', for example, when requested to speak on the ugly state of the municipal hospitals where the poor of this country go for medical treatment and medicines? This and many other concerns had to be addressed by me on different platforms during my tenure as sheriff. I was invited to speak on every possible topic and I was aware that I was under scrutiny by the smart alecs who waited to catch me on the wrong foot when I spoke on a specialized subject.

For some reason, there is a misconception that film personalities by and large have little general knowledge compared to other professionals and are capable of talking only about themselves and their work. I had to prove that assumption wrong. Without sounding boastful, I must say that I addressed large gatherings of professionals from such diverse areas as cardiology and poultry farming, horticulture and pharmaceuticals, and anything you can think of under the sun during the twelve months that Bombay suffered me as its sheriff. Although the shooting schedules of *Kranti* were in disarray due to my numerous social engagements as sheriff, I found time to shoot for the film, which made Amul butter come up with a tongue-in-cheek hoarding: 'Sorry, pardner, the Sheriff's out shootin'!'

My stints as sheriff and much later (from 2000 to 2006) as a Rajya Sabha member from Maharashtra were significant for me only for the opportunity they gave me to do some good social work. As the sheriff I enjoyed my interactions with people from various walks of life and, as a member of the Rajya Sabha, I felt very happy when I was able to make a contribution to deserving causes from the government funds that were at my disposal. I derived immense pleasure from the contributions I made over the years. I contributed to hospitals in the state so that they could acquire essential equipment and ambulances. I provided finances to build primary schools in rural areas of Maharashtra and to schools across the state (including some in Bombay) to purchase computers and other modern learning devices. I allocated money for laying roads in several places such as Bombay, Satara, Nasik and Nanded. I allotted funds to beautify gardens and create new parks in Bombay, especially at Bandra's Bandstand. Above all, I contributed resources to construct clean and modern public washrooms in the slum areas of Bombay.

I am of the firm belief that the well-being of any society has much to do with the health care and basic education that it can offer to its poorer sections. There never was a request I ignored when I was approached for funds to start a school. Unfortunately, not all my good deeds bore the results I desired. I was pressurized by a friend in the political sphere of Maharashtra to give away a prime piece of land I possessed in Bombay near my residence at Bandra for development by the Municipal Corporation into a park. Unfortunately, the sad story is that the same land has remained undeveloped and unattended to this day.

The Amul hoarding.

I have always strongly endorsed the necessity for actors to possess a reasonable degree of social responsibility. The actor who is adored by millions of people owes something to the society, which has given him an elevated and highly respected position. I have considered it a blessing that I have been able to give a helping hand to the National Association of the Blind (NAB), of which I was the chairman for many years. It was something I got involved in at the instance of Vijay Merchant, ace cricketer and a former captain of India, who was a dear friend. I was called upon to play a character who loses his eyesight in Nitin Bose's *Deedar* (1951) and it was rather difficult for me to determine how a blind person would look at the camera or at other characters in the film while enacting his scenes because of his handicap especially since he had had sight in the early portions of the film. I spoke to Mehboob Sahab about this aspect and he advised me to go to Bombay Central Railway Station and find a blind beggar who came there every day and sat outside the station asking passersby to drop a coin in his tin box. Mehboob Sahab said I should sit by his side, observe him, try to talk to him and understand his dark, lonely world.

I did just that and let me tell you it was a revelation. I used to go at a time when it was dark and the people passing by would be hurrying to catch the trains to their destinations and they did not bother to give the man or me seated next to him a second look. One day, I spoke to him and it so happened he had a visitor, who was also blind, sitting by his side. When the visitor heard my voice he asked: 'Who are you? You sound like an actor whose film I have seen recently.' I was stumped. I asked him: 'How did you see the film? You cannot see.' He said, very poignantly: 'You don't have to see a film; you can hear and feel a film if you have a heart to feel. *Hum dekh nahin sakte lekin hum soch sakte, mehsoos kar sakte, hans sakte, ro sakte.*'*

I was deeply touched by his courage and optimism. He blithely told me he had seen the film in which I had acted a few times because he liked the songs and the words. When Vijay Merchant placed the idea of the NAB before me and left it to me to do whatever I could to raise the funds required to champion the cause, it was the beggar's face that came before my eyes and I felt I should not shirk my responsibility for want of time or patience. A voice inside me said that I should go whole hog and make the NAB self-sufficient and resourceful enough to help as many sightless people as possible to lead their lives with dignity and the self-respect that comes with self-reliance.

I was fortunate to get the wholehearted support of a young, vivacious, positive-thinking woman, Veera Rao, who had just emerged from Bombay's Tata Institute of Social Sciences with flying colours, and whose forte was fund raising and fund management. She came up with several ideas and one of them was to run a special train from Bombay to Poona once every year with tickets that people would buy for the sheer pleasure of travelling with Dilip Kumar and talking to him and taking photographs with him. She had persisted in telling the office bearers of the NAB about the train that ran between Bombay and Poona on the Derby days and how the possibility of getting a seat in that train was as remote as getting a seat aboard a spaceship to Mars. Nobody paid heed to what the excited girl was saying and the idea remained in her head till I listened to her and adopted it at once.

---

*We cannot see but we can think, we can feel, we can laugh, we can cry'.

Greeted by a passenger on the festive train.

Despite opposition from the pessimists who always like to jeopardize fruitful ideas, the train started its first journey with a large number of passengers and a lot of media attention. I was told that I would have to walk from the guard's cabin to the very end of the train and I would stop to talk and exchange pleasantries with people along the way. I had no hesitation in doing so and, every year, I made the first announcement of the donation, which was Rs 50, 000. The first trip, in 1960, was a thumping success. So much money was collected from donations alone that we could order the best Braille books in the world market for the blind students.

For ten years, I travelled by the special festive train to Poona. It was an experience I looked forward to because of the enjoyment it gave me and the pleasure I got when I sat down with people who had brought something special in their tiffin boxes for me and I also had food packets to offer them from the NAB. It was like a picnic and the best part of the journey was the opportunity I got to speak to the passengers in different Indian languages. They were simple folks who had seen my films and there was the initial shyness to open up and speak to me and my wife who accompanied me on most occasions. The diffidence dissolved instantaneously when I spoke in their own tongue and they realized that Dilip Kumar was a simple chap with simple tastes and a simple wife who walked two steps behind him and gazed admiringly at him when he talked in Tamil, Telugu, Konkani, Gujarati, Bengali and, of course, Punjabi, English, Hindi and Urdu. On different occasions I invited my friends from the film fraternity to join me and I recall the most popular guest I had on the train was Johnny Walker.

I do not know if it is in my genes or if it is something I have assimilated from the environment I was brought up in. It gives me great contentment and joy to espouse a good cause. Sometime in early 1988, I received a letter from a well-wisher in Peshawar (the city of my birth, now in Pakistan) saying that the city, despite all its material progress, had been without a blood bank for years to provide that vital liquid to those who suffer from thalassaemia and, for the first time, a social service body had come forward to set up a blood donation centre and a blood bank for the treatment of patients afflicted with the serious blood disorder. My well-wisher asked whether I could make it convenient to visit Peshawar and inaugurate the services of the blood bank.

Peshawar was no longer occupying my thoughts, though Raj (Kapoor) and I often recalled our childhood years spent there whenever we met. The invitation to visit Peshawar for a worthy cause was, however, irresistible. I discussed the invitation with Saira and she too was of the opinion that I should lend whatever support I could to the Fatimid Foundation, which was setting up the blood donation centre and the blood bank. I accepted the invitation and was surprised when I was informed that Pakistan President General Muhammad Zia-ul Haq had come to know of my acceptance of the invitation and he had decided to host my visit and invite me as a state guest.

The simple invitation to inaugurate a blood bank had turned from a quiet personal visit into a big event now, with the Pakistan president declaring it a state visit by an Indian dignitary, which somewhat both appalled and humbled me for the simple reason that I have never ever seen myself as anyone but an industrious actor who made it to the top by dint of hard work and some luck. I was no head of state or envoy of the Indian Government to merit the honour. As can be imagined, the preparations for the visit from our side had to be on a much bigger scale since I was going to travel with an entourage of attendants, family members and media persons.

In the midst of the flurry of arrangements for the journey that was being marshalled by Naseem Aapa and Saira, I found myself overwhelmed by the prospect of setting foot once again in Peshawar on the soil that once belonged to India, the country I proudly call my own. When the partition of independent India occurred in August 1947 and Aghaji came to know that his land and his belongings were now in Pakistan, the new country that had taken birth, he was no doubt disturbed. Even so, his first spontaneous reaction to those who urged him to go to Peshawar and hold on to his properties was: 'We will remain in India and die in India.'

A caravan of memories kept passing before my inner eye as I immersed myself in the mental preparation for the visit. The sounds and smells of our house and its surroundings, the faces of friends and family members, the resounding sound of the temple bells that often merged with the deep-throated *azaan* (a call to prayer) resonating from the nearby mosque in the twilight hours, the commanding voice of Dadi, the chill of winter and the heat of summer ... were all back in my consciousness. I felt a pang in my heart that Amma and Aghaji were not with me to share the jubilation of my visit as a state guest, an honour conferred usually on heads of state. Aghaji would certainly have felt proud, as proud as he would have been if I had secured an OBE!

We were due to travel in early April 1988 to Karachi. Ahead of our visit, we learned that the pilots in Pakistan were vying with each other as to who would be flying the Pakistan International Airlines flight carrying me on my first-ever visit to their country. Anyway, the captain's excited voice welcomed me and my entourage with emotion-packed words conveying the pride he and his crew felt to have me on board and be part of what was described by them as a historic visit. Likewise, when he announced the transit of the flight across the Indo–Pak border into Pak territory, his voice was once again full of pride and happiness that PIA had been accorded the privilege and honour of flying me to Pakistan.

It was understandable that mine was a significant visit that gave the inhabitants of Pakistan a sense of jubilation and thrill because Peshawar, my native city, was now in their country. The boy, Yousuf – with the shaven head and disfigured face who had left Peshawar in the mid-1930s for Bombay with Aghaji, Mohammad Sarwar Khan, who had a good social standing in that city as a prosperous fruit merchant – was now returning as Dilip Kumar, the actor who had worked hard and earned a fine reputation for his work. It gave the natives of Peshawar and Pakistan a just sense of pride that was natural and expected in the circumstances. It was appropriate from their point of view, but for me, the emotional import of the visit had more to do with the reliving of a past that had receded from my mind in the perennial bustle of my professional and personal commitments in Bombay, where I had long since grown roots.

On the appointed day, 2 April 1988, Saira, yours truly and a group of close friends and family members besides our attendants and a camera crew, took off for Karachi. We landed to a tumultuous welcome at the Karachi airport and, for every single day thereafter, we moved around in a motorcade that took hours to reach any destination because of the excited crowds breaking the security barricades and making a beeline for the open car that I travelled in. We lived through an unforgettable experience of love and adulation that moved all those who were accompanying me, including my brother Ahsan, to tears.

The trip was hectic and tiring, with ever so many grand state functions hosted by Zia Sahab, plus dinners, lunches, teas and visits to familiar and now-famous places, such as my house in Kissa Khwani Bazaar, besides get-togethers with cousins and their families, umpteen interactions with the electronic and print media and powwows with school friends who were surprised that I had not forgotten their names and their pranks! What gladdened my heart was that I was able to make my visit to Peshawar purposeful with the inauguration of the Fatimid Foundation's blood donation centre and blood bank. What was even more heart warming was the loud and clear affectionate response I got from the crowds when I addressed them and I visualized a day when the two countries could have friendly ties and fruitful and productive trade relations for the mutual betterment of their economies.

No striking changes were visible in Peshawar. Our old house was as it was and so were the other houses in the street. The bazaar bristled with the appetizing flavours and the sizzle of chapli kebabs and the man who was at the tea stall, where the men accompanying me stopped to have the hot, fragrant brew, was as friendly as his predecessors were. The tea served in the tea stalls always had a strong aroma whether it was served with milk or without milk as *kahwah*. The old places I passed by were unchanged except for a new structure here and there but the cityscape at other places certainly confirmed the impact of welcome modern architectural influences.

The drive through the main roads, especially at night, was an unusual experience. The roads were carpeted and, at every hundred feet, there were decorative arches with lights and chandeliers hanging from them. It was as if the city was celebrating a festival of lights. The crowds lining the two sides were too excited to be kept back by the policemen on duty. They were daring enough to defy the police officers and climb on to the bonnet of my car to shake hands with me. The experience was like a dream and it filled me with a feeling of gratitude to the Almighty.

During my visit to Peshawar in 1988.

I returned to Bombay to receive the bad news that my dear friend Raj (Kapoor) was in hospital in Delhi. The news shattered me completely as I had spoken to him when the invitation had come from Peshawar and again before I had left for Karachi. I flew to Delhi to visit him at the Apollo Hospital where he had been admitted. I prayed in vain to Allah not to take him away from us. Raj passed away on 2 June 1988.

My second visit to Pakistan was in the latter half of March 1998 to receive Pakistan's highest civilian award, the Nishan-e-Imtiaz, which translated means Order of Excellence. It is more or less equivalent to the Order of the British Empire and the United States Presidential Medal of Freedom and it is not restricted to Pakistan. The recognition stirred a controversy when the Shiv Sena supremo, Balasaheb Thackeray (known for his anti-Pakistan stance), proclaimed that I should not receive the award. He indirectly cast aspersions on my integrity and patriotism, which were uncalled for and hurt me

Receiving the
Padma Bhushan
(1991) award
from President
R. Venkataraman

Receiving the
Dadasaheb Phalke
Award (1995)
from President
Dr Shankar Dayal
Sharma

Revisiting, with Saira, in 1988, the house in Peshawar where I was born

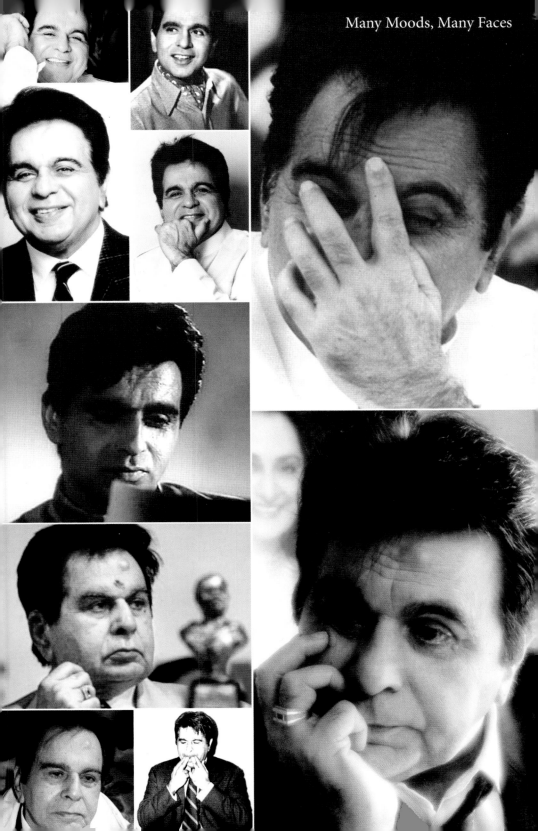

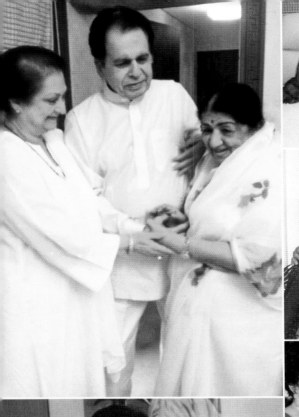

Facing page: In the company of good old friends Ashok Kumar, Raj Kapoor and Sunil Dutt • With Dharmendra, Dara Singh, Shammi Kapoor and Pran • With Sunil Dutt • With Dharmendra, Waheeda Rehman and Nanda, among others

Saira welcomes Lata Mangeshkar at our house (March 2014) • With Mumtaz, my co-star in *Ram Aur Shyam* • With celebrated film makers Yash Chopra and Subhash Ghai • With the actress-cum-danseuse Hema Malini at an event • Flanked by Saira and Vyjayantimala • With Nimmi, my co-star of five films, and Saira

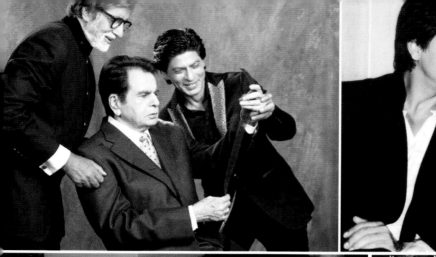

Top to bottom: Shahrukh Khan providing entertainment for Amitabh Bachchan and yours truly • Explaining a point to Shahrukh Khan • With the happy-go-lucky Anil Kapoor • Being greeted by Salman Khan • In the company of Rani Mukherjee and Aamir Khan • With the Bachchans – Amitabh, Jaya and Abhishek • With Javed Akhtar, his wife Shabana Azmi and Saira • In the company of Rishi Kapoor, his son Ranbir Kapoor, Subhash Ghai, and Saira's niece Shaheen

My *shareek-e-hayat* Saira
– a loving wife, a dedicated companion, a faithful friend
and, above all, a beautiful person

deeply. I sought the advice of the then prime minister of India, Atal Bihari Vajpayee, and he declared categorically that I *should* receive the award. As he eloquently put it: 'You are an artiste and as such you are not restrained by political or geographical barriers. You have been chosen for the humanitarian work you have done and your efforts to improve the relations between the two nations is well known.' Had I even considered declining the award, which had no political or communal colour to it at that juncture, it could have only soured relations further and produced bad vibes between India and Pakistan.

The pleasant part of the story, which must be told, is that my dear friend Sunil Dutt (a noted film maker, actor, Member of Parliament and cabinet minister known for his humanitarian work) came to my house and asked me if he could go with me to Pakistan to witness my receiving the award. I was naturally more than delighted and it was agreed that we would all travel together up to a certain point and, after that, Sunil would take off to his birthplace, Chotala (in the Punjab province of Pakistan), while I was visiting Peshawar. During this visit I had also undertaken to inaugurate, in Lahore, Pakistani cricketer Imran Khan's charitable Shaukat Khanum Memorial Trust Hospital, for cancer patients, named after his mother, Shaukat Khanum.

I do not wish to dwell on unsavoury memories. Balasaheb Thackeray is no more (he passed away on 17 November 2012) and we forgot our differences and re-established our relations without much ado since neither he nor I believed in making ourselves and others around us miserable. To his followers and the political world he dominated he was known as 'Tiger'. But I always felt he led more like a lion than a tiger – inspiring trust, loyalty and admiration in his followers. We had been introduced to each other before he became the Shiv Sena chief in June 1966. We respected and liked each other's work – he liked my output as an actor and I admired his sharp, incisive cartoons.

In our long, enduring friendship what remained constant was our respect for each other's professions. When we met at his home in Bombay to iron out differences that arose between us, it did not take more than a second for us to overcome past differences and to put aside everything to renew our respect and affection for each other. He was witty and entertaining when he was in his element. He and his wife Meena Tai were wonderful hosts and it was always a treat to share the simplicity of their life that never changed with the passage of time and the rise of his political career. In her own quiet way, Meena Tai kept him grounded and in touch with reality. She was the one who was in touch with old friends like us, calling us over to their home for simple meals and giving us a feeling of belonging. Meena Tai was a gem of a woman who taught their son Uddhav good manners and the importance of respecting elders.

On one occasion, when Saira and I were invited to a common friend's house where the Thackerays had also been invited, Saira was suffering from a severe backache. Meena Tai noticed her discomfort and she mentioned it to Balasaheb. He stopped all the partying and went into the kitchen, asked for an empty glass bottle, had a vessel of water heated, poured it into the bottle and brought it to Saira to rest her aching back on it. His wife and daughter-in-law told Saira that he would show the same concern for them when they took ill at home.

We saw the sensitive and noble side of Balasaheb during the trying times Sunil Dutt faced when the latter's son Sanjay was in jail.* He responded to Sunil Dutt with patience and understanding, which was exemplary at a time when all the so-called well-wishers Sunil counted upon were discreetly distancing themselves from him.

*Sanjay Dutt was accused of being involved in the 12 March 1993 serial Bombay blasts and in April 1993 he was arrested. He was permitted to be released on bail by the Supreme Court in October 1995 but was rearrested in December 1995.

24

'The Second Innings'

After the completion of Bairaag *[1976], I found myself once more at the crossroads and, this time, I made a firm resolve that I was not going to work for the sake of working as many actors do for want of other pursuits in life …. It was during … this trying phase that Manoj Kumar came to me with the idea of* Kranti *…. By the time* Kranti *was released in 1981, I was once again seized with the urge to bring the curtains down on my acting career and go on a holiday. Destiny, however, would not have it my way. Subhash Ghai came to me with the story of* Vidhaata …

I AM OFTEN ASKED WHY I TOOK A SABBATICAL FROM WORK FOR nearly five years after Asit Sen's *Bairaag* (1976) till I signed Manoj Kumar's *Kranti* (released in 1981), followed by Subhash Ghai's *Vidhaata* (1982). I was fifty-four when *Bairaag* was released and I worked arduously to define the three roles I enacted in it differently and distinctively. I felt I had worked for long and deserved a holiday. As a matter of fact, I had seriously decided to call it a day after the release of *Ram Aur Shyam* (1967) when I was just a little more than forty-four. The decision shocked Saira when I disclosed it to her

With Saira in *Bairaag* (1976).

confidentially. She could not reconcile with my reasoning that I felt I had made an unmistakable mark and I thought I should not be accused of milking the stardom and popularity I had achieved. I explained to Saira that I was more than content with all that I had achieved by ceaseless hard work and I did not wish to continue to tire myself out. *Ram Aur Shyam* was heading for record-breaking collections then and I was happy about it but the mature actor in me was missing the deep sense of satisfaction and achievement that a *Devdas* or a *Naya Daur* or a *Kohinoor* or an *Aan* stirred within when the product reached the audience.

Saira was equally serious in her disagreement and did not give up her persuasion to change my resolve and brushed aside my attempts to tempt her with the vision of both of us going on long holidays to virgin destinations and exploring the flora and fauna of those places. Saira is no wild-life enthusiast and shudders at the thought of living in seclusion and tranquillity with only the roar of a lion to break the silence, whereas I love spending days in wild-life sanctuaries and waking up to the sight and sounds of beautiful birds with exotic plumes, cocking their heads and inspecting us from the lush green tree tops. It was a prospect that stimulated my imagination more than the prospect of perusing scripts of films that held little or no promise.

❦

After the completion of *Bairaag*, I found myself once more at the crossroads and, this time, I made a firm resolve that I was not going to work for the sake of working as many actors do for want of other pursuits in life.

I thanked the Almighty that I was not desperate for work and I had other engrossing interests like reading, music, theatre, studying languages and may be writing my own film scripts. Knowing the situation in Indian cinema, which differed greatly from the situation in Hollywood and Western cinema, where actors who had attained a certain maturity and stature in the profession, got meatier roles to perform as they advanced in age, I felt the time had come for me to write my own scripts and direct movies.

Also, there was an influx of unknown and unseen faces in the production sector and they were mostly from other shady businesses, who wanted to be seen with well-known stars in public. Since they had surplus money which could not be accounted for and had to be squandered away in cash, they approached established actors with abominable scripts and tried to lure them with the promise of unheard-of remunerations. The situation was not unfamiliar to me.

I could not see eye to eye with the strangers who were trying to enter the industry through the dubious back door. It was also the time when a law suit that was slapped on me by a producer – A. R. Kardar – was coming up for repeated hearing and I was determined to fight tooth and nail to prove the falsehood of his charges. The irony was that the confrontation was provoked by an individual for whom I had done all that I could do as a star to redeem him from sinking into abject penury when his wife and children, who were in dire straits, came to my house several times to plead with me to work in the film he wished to produce. I accepted the film, *Dil Diya Dard Liya* (released in 1966), without giving it the serious thought I was known to give to the films I was offered. I worked tirelessly to hone the film and make it memorable so that I could give the man a place among the successful film makers of the country and end his hardships. In return, he perfidiously framed me on the basis of false allegations and accusations.

I am one of those patient men who can withstand immense trouble and pain to fight for justice if the need arose. I was so provoked by the ingratitude of the man that I diligently studied all the complex laws governing taxation in the country with the help of my dear friend, Narendra Kumar Salve (popularly known as N. K. P. Salve), a professional in the field, who went on to become a Union minister in the early 1980s.

Until this vexing situation arose in the mid-1970s, Salve Sahab and I enjoyed our conversations about the splendid future of Indian cricket. Salve was an enthusiastic cricket player during his college days and so was I. We spent our evenings at the picturesque Cricket Club of India (CCI) and the Bombay Gymkhana exchanging recollections of some fine matches we had watched with brilliant players on the field in our youth. By 1982 Salve had become the president of the Board of Control for Cricket in India (BCCI) and he was dreaming of India winning the one-day World Cup as a true patriot and lover of the sport. His dream came true in June 1983.

I was aware that Salve Sahab was a chartered accountant by profession but it never occurred to either of us that we would be putting our heads together to fight a legal battle one day. As a friend and well-wisher, Salve Sahab stood by me and gave me the encouragement and fillip to succeed in convincing the tax tribunal that I was no wilful tax evader or law breaker.

Salve Sahab's able and eminent son, Harish, has given a detailed account of the trauma I was forced to experience for six long years which, like all the unsavoury memories in my professional life, I have long since relegated to oblivion. Those who will read and relish Harish's uninhibited account in the second section of this book will not only get a picture of the mental harassment and ignominy I faced but also realize that good men like Salve Sahab, Purohitji and G. N. Joshi are God's good men sent by Him to help the honest to prove their honesty and redeem their honour.

With Saira and Harish Salve at a party.

The regret apart, the wound I have nursed for years, about the five years of self-imposed absence from the screens across the country and elsewhere, which has mystified those who have followed my career graph avidly, is that I could not focus attention on the scripts I had written for myself and Saira to act as a lead pair in films that I wished to launch. The most engrossing of them, 'Kashmir Valley', was written for Saira to co-star with me before we married. It had a spectacular backdrop and a canvas comparable to that of David Lean's epic creation *Dr Zhivago* (1965). I had thought of producing it after *Bairaag*. The other scripts included 'Kali Sarson', which focused on a dark-skinned girl's saga and was also written with Saira in mind, apart from 'Kala Aadmi' and 'Babajan'. The last mentioned had a riveting, suspense plot centering on a schizophrenic banker's diabolic bid to rob a bank. I had several meetings with Jabbar Patel to whom I wished to entrust the direction of 'Babajan'. I had to shelve all the projects for which financiers were more than willing to loosen their purse strings.

With Shatrughan Singh in *Kranti* (1981).

It was during the fag end of this trying phase that Manoj Kumar came to me with the idea of *Kranti*. I have already explained in an earlier chapter how and why I agreed to work in *Kranti* without reading the full script.

By the time *Kranti* was released in 1981, I was once again seized with the urge to bring the curtains down on my acting career and go on a holiday. Destiny, however, would not have it my way. Subhash Ghai came to me with the story of *Vidhaata*. He met me a few times and he impressed me with his credentials and his sincerity. He was honest that his previous film was not a success and he said he hoped to make that setback the stepping stone to his future success. I liked his optimistic enthusiasm and his passion. The subject was interesting and offered the actor in me the scope to do some good work. What was more, like my role in *Kranti*, the role in *Vidhaata* was of an earthy character, a railway engine driver, who becomes the axis of the screenplay as the protagonist.

By the time we finished work on *Vidhaata*, we were ahead of its completion schedule and Subhash was very triumphant and bubbling with joy like a schoolboy who had received a good report card. The reason was that some of his friends in the industry had told him that

With Amrish Puri in *Vidhaata* (1982).

a film with Dilip Kumar would sap him of all his youth and energy and he would be an old, tottering man when the film would be complete. Just the opposite had happened. His so-called well-wishers had made me out to be an ogre who would destroy him. He disclosed this to me on the last day of the last schedule for the film. I laughed and told him that it should teach him not to believe all that is said about anyone and it was always prudent to judge people by one's own discernment.

Subhash was even more thrilled when the film became the highest grosser of 1982. It was the beginning of an enduring friendship between us that made it possible for me to feel at home and engage myself in two more productions, *Karma* (1986) and *Saudagar* (1991), which he directed.

Curiously, Subhash came to me each time with an apprehension tucked away in his mind. When he approached me for *Karma*, he was afraid that I would ask for an astronomical remuneration since *Vidhaata* had become a blockbuster. After some casual conversation, he came to the point. It naturally irked me because I expect a director to talk about the basic premise of the script he wants the actor to read or a different treatment of the script he was

With Anupam Kher in *Karma* (1986).

planning to employ. Money and money talk should have no place in such a conversation.

Since we had established a rapport by then and Subhash was looking up to me as an elder brother, I took the liberty of telling him he should not be talking the language of a trader in the commodity market and he should be talking like a director. He took my mild reprimand in the right spirit and did not broach the subject thereafter, but he defended himself saying it was just the industry norm that he was following. I certainly agreed with his point, but I told him I was happy not to be a part of the norm. We had a good laugh after that and our bond was strengthened.

When Subhash visited my home to talk to me about *Saudagar* and he briefed me about the interesting plot revolving round two thick friends that he was developing, I could see that he was slightly fidgety and he was waiting for the right moment to say something that was on his mind. Sure enough, he came out with it when he was about to leave. He told me rather nervously that he had the veteran Raaj Kumar in mind to play my friend who turns hostile in the dramatic twist that would surface in the critical juncture of the plot build-up. Apparently, he expected me to react adversely. I eased his mind by telling him it would be a pleasure to work with Raaj and I had quite enjoyed his company whenever he was on the sets of *Paigham* (1959). Instead, I suggested he should ask Raaj if he welcomed the idea of working with me. Smiling naughtily, Subhash said he had already spoken to Raaj, who was looking forward to working with me.

To my delight, Subhash also had a love for shooting outdoors and he found picturesque and eye-filling locations to film not only the song situations but also some demanding dramatic sequences. For *Saudagar* he had selected sylvan locations in Himachal Pradesh's Kulu valley as backdrop for some crucial dramatic sequences, which made the rendering more impactful than it would have been if they had been shot indoors. After a long schedule in the Himachal location, we moved to Mahabaleshwar (a hill station in Maharashtra). It was like a long picnic and it must be said to Subhash's credit that he understands the need to keep his actors in good humour and extends the kind of hospitality few film makers care to.

The media was on the alert during the entire making of *Saudagar* to smell any kind of conflict between me and Raaj, thanks to the

With Raaj Kumar in *Saudagar* (1991).

many silly stories circulating about Raaj's temperament. Come to think of it, in some ways, Raaj was different from most of us actors of his age. During the shooting of *Saudagar*, he insisted on two heavy vehicles following him to the places marked by the art director and cameraman for the shooting. Raaj sat in a car alone, in solitary splendour, without an attendant while the vehicles trailing behind his car carried the entire wardrobe of costumes created for him for the entire film with his browbeaten attendant in charge of the suitcases and trunks filled with items such as clothes, footwear and wigs. It amazed me and the others and led to all kinds of hush-hush talk behind his back. Subhash stoically dismissed it as a quirk and had given standing instructions to his assistants to see that the vehicles were ready each day and the clothes and accessories were transported exactly as Raaj wished.

One evening at Mahabaleshwar, the cameraman, his assistants and all the young spot boys were in a nervous flutter because Raaj was missing at the actual location and they had found him seated on a chair on the perilous edge of a cliff. If he took one step forward from the chair, it would have plunged him into the dark mysterious chasm below. The boys came running to Subhash and the rest of us seated comfortably at the shooting spot to tell us what they had seen. Subhash asked them what they thought he was doing there and they said he was seated on his chair with a faraway expression in his eyes that were fixed on the misty horizon.

Subhash requested me to accompany him to the spot where Raaj was sitting. We went up to him quietly and engaged him in a conversation, which distracted him from the hazy horizon he was staring at. Fortunately, he always responded to me in a friendly manner. So I managed to bring him back to the shooting location without much ado.

Raaj, I could see, was a thinking man. He preferred to be alone at times perhaps to immerse his mind in thoughts. He also read books and discussed the contents with me when he was in the mood to do so. He was known for his idiosyncrasies and eccentricities but I found him always very normal and gentlemanly. He was among the many friends who arrived early at my house on the day of my *nikah*

With Amitabh Bachchan in *Shakti* (1982).

(marriage) with Saira. When Saira and I invited him to our silver wedding anniversary, he came to attend the party with his wife but seeing the large gathering of film personalities, he left quietly without meeting us. He was perhaps not keen to mingle with the others. He left a gift for us, a beautiful silver platter with an inscribed message: 'To Lalay and Lalay ki Jaan, many happy returns!'

All the films I selected at this juncture, be it the period film *Kranti* or *Vidhaata* or *Shakti* (1982) or *Karma* or *Saudagar* or *Mashaal* (1984), were chosen because they offered me the satisfying pivotal role in the script. *Kranti* was set in the period of India's freedom struggle amidst the turbulent upsurge of patriotism in the hearts of even simple, toiling masses whose love for the native land surpassed everything else in their life. But the rest of the films that I picked had themes that celebrated the courage of the central character to stand up to odds. I was drawn to the characters and I felt I could make them inspiring and unforgettable if I applied myself to rendering them with conviction and realism.

I was intrigued by the basic premise of *Shakti*, which evoked thoughts on the wisdom of ordinary individuals practising the moral principles of dharma. The question was raised provocatively in the script through the character of one of the two heroes, a police officer, who places his duty to be honest and gritty above his duty to rescue his young son who is kidnapped by criminals.

The plot had a deceptive simplicity at the surface level, yet its power to move the audience emanated from several forceful sequences that bared the emotional wounds the police officer endured as a consequence of his adherence to his principles of dharma. It was Salim Khan (of the acclaimed Salim-Javed script and dialogue writer duo) who narrated the story to me. (Later, Salim and Javed parted company.)

I learned from Salim that Ramesh Sippy would be the director. I was very close to Ramesh's father, G. P. Sippy, who was my ally when I sought to resolve several issues my colleagues had with the producers' body, Indian Motion Pictures' Producers Association (IMPPA), over which he reigned as president for many years. However, I was frankly unsure initially whether I would be comfortable under Ramesh's direction since I hardly knew him apart from the brief greetings we had exchanged at his father's house. All through my career, I had worked with directors I had close personal ties with.

The lurking doubt made way for immediate confidence when Ramesh met me and had a long chat with me, during which he revealed that he intended to cast Amitabh Bachchan as the parallel hero, the police officer's unforgiving son, who is lured to crime by the very criminals who had manoeuvred the kidnapping. The simmering tension between the father and the son who does everything his father dislikes in order to punish the latter for not rushing to his rescue when the kidnappers threatened to kill him could be brought to the surface on the screen by a younger actor of great calibre. I congratulated Ramesh, I remember, for the appropriate casting as no other actor of the time would have fitted the part and added immense value to the product as Amitabh. Quite understandably, there was huge media attention and speculation when the casting of the film was announced.

The *mahurat* was watched not only by the entire Fourth Estate but also by avid fans who gathered on the beach at Juhu (in Bombay) to get a glimpse of what was going on. I could see the happiness and excitement on Ramesh's face as he prepared to direct the first shot featuring me and Amitabh.

The common element in *Shakti* and *Mashaal*, which I took up a year later, was the integrity and guts the characters enacted by me possessed. Both films had unforgettable sequences that reverberated in public memory and became reference points for directors and actors. In *Shakti* it was the sequence where the officer's wife (played by the talented Raakhee) is slain by the criminals and he talks senselessly standing beside her lifeless body and the ensuing sequence in which he breaks down when his alienated son walks into the house to have the last *darshan* of the mother he loved dearly. In *Mashaal*, there was this sequence shot on a desolate road at night amidst pouring rain, in which the honest and intrepid journalist Vinod Kumar (the character played by me) tries to stop passing vehicles to take his dying wife to a hospital, but in vain. It was a sequence that demanded a convincing rendering as it reflected the unenviable plight of a less privileged citizen with no vehicle of his own on a bandh day in a heartless city like Bombay when an emergency arises in his life.

Both the sequences turned me inwards into the deep recesses of my mind for a trigger to bring forth the emotions I had to simulate. As mentioned in an earlier chapter, the deep pain I saw on Aghaji's face when my brother Ayub Sahab breathed his last and the helpless cry for immediate medical aid from Aghaji once when Amma fainted after a bout of breathlessness, as he held her listless body in his arms, were images that surfaced from my subconscious to spur me. No matter how much an actor may have in his emotional reservoir as personally experienced moments to build his make-believe responses before the cameras, when it actually comes to giving a final take, it takes all that he has and much more to render the scene credibly and powerfully. I think the sequence in *Shakti* turned out the way it did because Amitabh was as intensely tuned in as I was.

I was running a high fever when I arrived for the shooting of the much-written-about sequence of *Mashaal* on the first of the four days it took to film it on a rain-swept street on actual locations at Ballard Estate in Bombay. The director, Yash Chopra, asked me if I was up to it and I told him I would rather go back to the room at the Taj Palace I had occupied to save commuting time from Bandra to the location every day. I needed the rest since I had told Yash I would render the entire scene without an interruption once the cameras rolled on the location. I kept my commitment and completed the scene unhindered on the third day.

When we completed the work, it was pretty late in the night and I could see moist eyes all around me and there was an eerie silence. For a second or two it disturbed me. Yash came up to me and I could see that he was unable to say whatever he wanted to say because he was choked with emotion. After a while, everybody relaxed and the admiration surfaced. There is no greater award for an actor than the genuine appreciation of his colleagues. Yash too could speak now and he disclosed to me that it took three decades for him to approach me with a subject that he felt I would not refuse.

As noted earlier, my friendship with Yash began during the production of *Naya Daur* (1957). He was assisting his brother B. R. Chopra Sahab. He was young and eager to learn direction and as he was much younger than the senior Chopra, he kept a low profile and took instructions obediently from his elder brother. One of the instructions given to him was to look after me. So, the first time he came to see me at my house the instruction was to ask me what time a car should be sent to me to take me to Poona where the first schedule was to start. He told me a limousine would pick me up and he would follow me in a small car so that if I needed anything he would be close enough to attend to me. I asked him if I may travel with him in his car as I did not desire to travel alone in another car.

Yash was visibly taken aback but he agreed. The journey to Poona was wonderful and it marked the beginning of a long and genuine friendship between us. We discovered many common interests, food being one of them.

In the early 1970s, when Yash branched out on his own and began making an impact as an independent producer and director, I often visited him at Rajkamal Studios in Bombay where he had a small,

With Anil Kapoor in *Mashaal* (1984).

cosy office and planned most of his films. The office served as a store room for all sorts of trappings used in the shootings as well as for the large tin cans that contained the reels of the footage shot. He sat amidst all the bric-a-brac behind a small table. He used to open a tiffin carrier and place the food sent from his house on the table and eat quickly straight from the tiffin bowls and wash it all down with a glass of buttermilk ordered from the canteen.

He had his dreams as most young visionaries have, but the exceptional quality in Yash was that he pursued his vision. It was his dream to build a studio like the studios he had visited in Hollywood and in the United Kingdom. It was a great moment of wish fulfilment for Yash when he started working from his own Yash Raj Studios. He invited me to inaugurate the studio and it was such a pleasure for me and Saira to see his enthusiasm as he showed us around.

We met often and whenever he felt like sharing his deepest thoughts, he telephoned me unhesitatingly more like a brother than a friend. It was a pleasant surprise, therefore, when he dropped in casually one evening and gave me the script of *Mashaal*, saying Javed Akhtar had developed the protagonist's character painstakingly, keeping me in mind and, it was after years of waiting for the right subject that he had found something that could be brought to me. 'Please read it, you will like it,' he mumbled before leaving.

When I began to read the script I could see that the character of Vinod Kumar, the firebrand journalist, had some streaks of my character in him especially in his resilience and fearlessness in dealing with unscrupulous social elements. The protagonist was, for a change, a middle-aged character, an upright editor of a daily newspaper who understood the ethics and responsibilities of investigative journalism and had the courage to oppose the mafia. He dealt with attempts by the powerful sections of society to manipulate and stifle the truth, which he exposed through news items published on the front page every day. What appealed to me in the script was the unyielding spirit of the journalist and the sensitivity with which Javed had loaded high-voltage drama into some of the starkly realistic situations.

I am glad I made up for the loss of five years of my professional life by doing the aforementioned films and derived job satisfaction from them.

25

FAMILY MATTERS

… the first goal I set out to achieve when I had attained my own target of securing myself in my profession and gaining a reputation for my work … was to give my brothers and sisters the best education in the fields they chose, be it in India or abroad. There was no doubt that each of them had his or her individual intellectual strengths and flair and they had the potential to become achievers. What they needed, I felt, was motivation and facilities.

$\mathscr{I}$ HAVE ACTUALLY LOST COUNT OF THE NUMBER OF TIMES I HAVE been asked this question not only by the media but also by friends who have walked with me in my long journey. The question is whether there is anything at all that I regret and wish to obliterate from the canvas of my life. I have refrained from answering partly because I believe that, as Yousuf Khan, I am entitled to my privacy and the right to keep certain events in my life away from prying intruders.

As all those who know me well will endorse, I do not revel in talking about my private life. I have often been in the company of men at small intimate social gatherings where they came out with stories of their 'conquests' and the women they have known with great flourish and with an indecent sense of pride. I have squirmed at such exposure and tried to put a stop to it.

Well, the one episode in my life that I would like to forget and which we, Saira and I, have indeed pushed into eternal oblivion is a grave mistake I made under pressure of getting involved with a lady named Asma Rehman whom I had met at a cricket match in Hyderabad (Andhra Pradesh) where she then lived with her husband. She was a mother of three when she was introduced to me as a fan and she seemed like umpteen other admirers, who were introduced to me by my sisters, Fauzia and Saeeda, at public places. She was a friend of my sisters.

My sisters often received requests from ladies to meet me and, maybe, have a light conversation with me. I was used to such introductions and I always took extra pains to be cordial and warm with the men my brothers invited home or the young ladies my sisters brought along.

In this case, however, I was completely unaware of a connivance that was being mischievously perpetuated and a situation being cleverly created by vested interests to draw a commitment from me. Not once, but many times I was surprised by the lady and her husband who popped up from nowhere even when I was in different places out of Bombay to come up to me and greet me and linger on and on. Strangely, they were aware of my travel plans and my itinerary!

In 1982, when the news spread that I had married Asma and Saira read the sensational 'revelation' in a tabloid, it was very painful for me to console her as she trusted me and loved me unconditionally. I was not at home when Saira read the news and, truth be told, neither she nor her mother (Naseem Aapa) believed what they read because of their implicit faith in me and the sincere commitment I had given at the time of my *nikah* with Saira that there was no question of a second marriage and there should be no talk of it.

I can never forget or forgive myself for the hurt I caused to Saira and the shattering of the unshakeable faith she had in me. It needs to be said that even in that situation when a self-respecting woman cannot but hate the man who has humiliated her, my wife Saira stood by me when I admitted the grave mistake and asked her to give me some time to undo the wrong through proper legal processes and restore the sanctity of our marriage of sixteen years. I requested Saira to give me some time to sort it all out.

Saira, despite the hurt caused to her pride and to her intense faith in me, stood solidly by me on the advice of Naseem Aapa and her brother Sultan Ahmed. I immediately reinforced the faith Aapaji and Sultan had reposed in my promise to Saira by signing a letter of commitment long before the legal processes of divorce were initiated and completed vis-à-vis Asma. Some of my close friends signed as witnesses. I must mention the names of Rajni Patel, his wife Bakul Patel, Sharad Pawar and Mama Kapadia as my well-wishers who helped me tide over the crisis with their sound advice and guidance to restore the stability of our marriage and give my wife Saira the emotional and moral support she needed then. From the film fraternity, it was Shuklaji (Pran's wife) and Prakashji (B. R. Chopra's wife) who took a bold stand and unflinchingly stood by Saira because they genuinely loved her and were protective about her. They expressed their displeasure and ticked me off as real *bhabhis* (one's brothers' wives) should and told me either I rectify the situation or lose them forever as people I consider my own.

I would not like to devote more space to the forgotten episode and conclude by saying without the slightest hesitation that, as a human being, I was not infallible and I became a victim of a situation that was set to precipitate a deep crisis in my marriage with Saira. I strongly believe that there is a divine purpose even in the untoward happenings in one's life. The whole episode strengthened our closeness and our emotional dependence on each other.

During the episode it was also wrongly represented that Saira could not bear a child. The truth is that Saira had borne a child, a boy (as we came to know later), in 1972. We lost the baby in the eighth month of pregnancy when Saira developed high blood pressure and the obstetricians attending on her could not perform the surgery in time to save the full-grown foetus, which had been strangulated by the umbilical cord. We took the loss in our stride as the will of God.

The curious question that never goes unasked is whether I am unhappy not having my own children. Well, it would have been great if we had our own kids. But it is not a shortcoming for us. Allah has blessed us with so many lovely children in our family. All our youthful days were spent with the children of my sisters and brothers who came visiting us and stayed with us when they had school and college holidays. We loved their presence in the house, the resonance of their laughter and the girls' giggles as we played the games they invited us to play with them. They were enough to make us feel like parents. As infants they were brought to me and it was mandatory for the babies to sleep soundly on my large chest as if they were on a foam mattress. As they grew up, they came home to play interesting games with 'Mamu' as all of them addressed me.

Years ago, my elder brother Noor Sahab's sons Amjad and Javed were in Bombay for a long training programme at a corporate office and I made it mandatory for them to visit me every day at 8 p.m. come what may. The young fellows had come from Nasik and I felt I should keep them away from possible bad company. It made good reason for me and Saira to gather all the other young nephews and nieces who could make it for some fun in the house ending with an invigorating game of badminton in the garden.

It is Saira who always went all out to get the family together and still goes all out to be the grandaunt to the grandchildren in the family. It is wonderful to love and be loved by them and be there solidly when they need us and vice versa. Today, at times, both of us feel their absence from our lives since practically all my nephews and nieces are busy with their own lives or their families. Though we meet less often, I enjoy every moment I spend with them when they visit me. Perhaps if we had our own sons or daughters, they too would have gone to places far away to pursue their dreams and we would have got to see them once or twice a year!

The truth is that I became a parent to my brothers and sisters when I was in my late twenties. It gives me both pleasure and pain to narrate about my brothers and sisters. I have contemplated over this subject, asking myself whether I should write at all about my six sisters and five brothers who mean everything to me because I am a Pathan who zealously takes pride in and guards his family, especially the women, from public exposure.

I am talking about them largely because the story of my life will not be complete if I don't devote space to them who are the world to me and for whom I had dreams that I did not even remotely have for myself.

We grew up amidst abundant love and emotional security. The parental grooming and discipline we received lacked in no way. It was fated perhaps that I would become more of a parent than a brother to my younger siblings at an age when most young men are envisaging the goals they wish to achieve. Circumstances had propelled me to forget about pursuing a university education and attaining the OBE my father saw in his dreams for me. True, he had no regrets because he lived to see my success in the profession Allah had ordained for me. I never found out but I think he was happy and secure in the thought that I had achieved a social and economic status that gave me the capacity to provide the best facilities for my younger sisters and brothers to make a mark in their own chosen fields.

Indeed, the first goal I set out to achieve when I had attained my own target of securing myself in my profession and gaining a reputation for my work by dint of sheer hard work and patience was to give my brothers and sisters the best education in the fields they chose, be it in India or abroad. There was no doubt that each of them had his or her individual intellectual strengths and flair and they had the potential to become achievers. What they needed, I felt, was motivation and facilities.

I left no stone unturned to give each of them the impetus to scale the heights of success that I visualized in my dreams for them. I wished to see them surpass me in fame and fortune and attain enviable stations in life that well-educated professionals do. I hoped that one day Dilip Kumar would be known as their brother and not the other way round. Amidst all the hard toil that I was putting into my work, I found time to ensure that they interacted with me and expressed their desires.

The pleasure of narrating this piece is that it gave me great happiness that I was able to fulfil their wishes and send them out to places where they wanted to pursue their interests. The pain of writing this piece arises from the disillusionment. My dreams remained just dreams. Today, I cannot but wonder what went wrong and where the lacuna was when all of us came from the same stock.

Was it Destiny that laid out the road for whatever I went on to achieve with only a college education and limited resources and no training in the profession I found myself in? Yes, it was Destiny and Allah's will, but it was also loads of painstaking work and relentless pursuit of my goal, which has always been to deliver work that made the producers of my films feel proud and commercially rewarded. Did my brothers and sisters lack that drive and propensity for hard work to fulfil the hopes I had pinned on them? Did I expect too much in my love for them and my brotherly pride about their native intelligence and talents? These are questions that I have asked myself time and again.

There was nothing I could do to change anything in my eldest sister Sakina Aapa's circumstances; nor could I change the way my elder brother Noor Sahab wished to conduct his life. So the mission I took up was to weave dreams about the younger ones who grew up in front of my eyes.

My sister Taj was always the homemaker, a first-class cook who could serve a splendid meal at short notice all by herself. I think she was domesticated like Amma, cool and collected and ever willing to feed us with goodies. Akhtar was the academically bright one from her school days and her flair for language studies and poetry made her the second intellectual in the family after Ayub Sahab. She was the one who had the capacity to become either a professor or a littérateur. She desired to study abroad and I was more than glad to give her the opportunity and fulfil her wish. When she returned from the USA, I was shooting for *Mughal-e-Azam* (released in 1960) and K. Asif (the director of the film) was a frequent visitor at our house. I was not aware that love was blossoming between Akhtar and Asif and that they had decided to marry without my consent, knowing full well that I would not approve of my most accomplished sister marrying a twice-married man who was much older and had contrasting views and thoughts and a totally different lifestyle. Akhtar had a weakness for Urdu poetry and Asif had evidently drawn her to him with his fluency and knowledge of the Urdu language. Akhtar disappointed and disillusioned me and I distanced myself from her and Asif for some years (as mentioned in an earlier chapter).

Saeeda resembled Amma and it was wonderful to look at her petite figure move around the house treading softly like Amma used to. She not only acquired Amma's sweet, delicate looks but also her gentle way of speaking to people. She too chose to marry and not opt for a career. Farida was always the tomboy of the family who wanted to be economically independent and create a niche for herself in journalism. I nicknamed her 'sunshine' because she was always full of brightness and buzzing around like a bee in the house. She took up a job as a journalist in The Times of India Group's *Femina* magazine. I remember Farida being forever late to leave for her job and requesting me to spare the car to take all the way from Bandra to Bori Bunder (about 16 km), where her office was located. She too could have made a mark in her field.

Fauzia married a young man she met and settled down after her graduation. Her husband, Dilip Surve, had a good job in one of the establishments of the Mahindra Group.

My younger brothers Ahsan and Aslam were sent to Bombay Scottish School and later they preferred to study at St Xavier's College, Bombay. Both wanted to go for higher education to the US. It was with great expectations that I had sent Ahsan and Aslam abroad for their advanced studies. I don't remember ever expressing my dismay when they did not live up to my hopes. Among the many truths I have learned from the ups and downs of life is that it is all right to be ambitious and desirous of success but it is not in everybody's destiny to achieve what he or she desires to achieve.

Nasir was two years younger to me. He was always the centre of feminine attention because of his handsome looks and his gallant ways. Around Pali Mala where we lived, he was the heartthrob of young women who stole surreptitious looks at him when he walked out of our house looking elegant and dapper in his well-ironed trousers and long-sleeved shirts bought from the best clothiers. It was no wonder that he became a popular actor when he debuted with Filmistan's *Mazdoor* in 1945. He starred in some interesting films teaming him with talented actresses like Nargis, Meena Kumari and Nutan. He was attracted to Begum Para, also an actress. She was a woman of fine manners and taste coming from a good family background and he married her at a time when a strange deficiency in his body was robbing him of his hair on his scalp and skin. He then wanted to produce a film and act in it. Since financiers were ready to back me I told him I would produce a film that would give him a platform to bounce back and receive the acclaim he deserved as a sensitive actor. I produced *Gunga Jumna* (released in 1961) and he received overwhelming praise for his work, which made me feel very proud. The illness, however, could not be contained by the medicines and medical attention we got for him then. Willy-nilly he had to close shop.

I am often asked how I came to terms with the passing away of my brothers Ayub Sahab, Noor Sahab and Nasir and my sisters Sakina Aapa and Taj. I can only say each death was painful and it took all the courage I possessed to believe their non-existence in my life.

I can still recall the phone call from Abrar Alvi (a well-known writer and director) very early one morning in 1972, which was picked up by Naqi Ahmed, Saira's relative staying with us. The call was for me and it conveyed the bad news that Nasir had passed away in Dalhousie (now in Himachal Pradesh) where he was scouting for locations for *Zid*, the film he was producing. *Zid* had Saira and Sanjay Khan in the lead roles and its shooting was slightly delayed because Saira had been ordered bed rest by her doctors as she was being taken off the cortisone drugs that necessarily had to be tapered in their dosage under strict medical supervision. Meanwhile, Nasir had thought of using the time at his disposal to search for picturesque locations in Punjab for the film.

I was numb with shock and devastated. I had to keep the news away from Saira as the doctors treating her had told us it would be dangerous to subject her to any kind of emotional distress as she had just recovered from ulcerative colitis and a relapse could be fatal. How could I manage to keep the news from her? Saira and Nasir shared a bond of mutual regard and admiration. He was the only member of my family who gave her the respect and love she deserved besides understanding the alienation she was subjected to by my sisters and by Ahsan. Nasir himself was not in the good books of Sakina Aapa because he had married an actress. When Nasir was unhappy he turned to Saira for solace.

It was imperative for me to pretend before Saira that nothing serious had happened and I had to tell her that Nasir was in hospital with a mild heart attack. Naseem Aapa knew about it and she assured me that she would take care of Saira while I was away to attend to the sad and painful formalities connected with Nasir's funeral. I must confess it took all my capabilities to behave normally before Saira while my heart ached and my soul wept silently.

When I returned from the *kabristan* (burial ground) late in the evening, I found Saira waiting to know from me how Nasir was. She was insistent that I should take her to the hospital to meet him. It was difficult to maintain the façade and I broke down in front of her uncontrollably.

As adults, we have the wisdom to accept the stark reality of death but how did one tell Nasir's children that their father would not be coming home ever again?

As I reflect on the absence of my brothers Noor Sahab, Ayub Sahab, Nasir and my sisters Sakina Aapa and Taj, I cannot but sorely miss some of the wonderful men who were with me in my journey, including Raj Kapoor, Ashok Kumar, S. Mukherjee Sahab, Mehboob Sahab, Nitinda (Nitin Bose), Bimalda (Bimal Roy), Tapanda (Tapan Sinha), B. R. Chopra Sahab, Dev Anand, Pran, Yash Chopra and producer Yash Johar. I miss them as much as I miss my own brothers who are no more.

When was that moment when I felt proud and had that lump in the throat, which made expression of thoughts difficult for a fleeting

With B. R. Chopra.

moment? I can pinpoint the occasion and moment when Lata Mangeshkar rendered the *shraddhanjali* (homage) to the martyrs of the 1962 India–China war on Republic Day (26 January) 1963 at a function in Delhi. Prime Minister Jawaharlal Nehru, who was present there, wept and so did all of us who had gathered at the venue.

The night before, at the Ashoka Hotel, where Lata was staying, I had met her briefly and she was her shy, unassuming self. After I retired to my room in the hotel after a long day of meetings, I phoned Lata and asked her if she could sing one of my favourite devotional songs *Allah tero naam** for me and she gladly obliged. I went to sleep with her peerless voice soothing my tired mind. Little did I know that Lata would outshine herself the next day with her soulful rendering of *Ae mere watan ke logon ...***

*From the 1961 film *Hum Dono*, penned by Sahir Ludhianvi and composed by Jaidev.
**Penned by Pradeep (real name: Ramchandra Narayanji Dwivedi) and composed by C. Ramchandra.

With 'younger sister' Lata Mangeshkar.

In March 2014, Lata visited me at home and we revived memories of the many times we met at Bombay Talkies over *batata wada* (a highly popular savoury dish) and tea in the canteen and at Mehboob Studios where she recorded her songs. She was a chit of a girl when composer Anil Biswas had introduced her to me in 1947. She met me with the same smile when she called on me despite the passage of time. There were tears of joy that she tried to hold back as she leaned her head on my chest and I remembered how petite she was when she stood on the impressive stage of London's Royal Albert Hall in 1974 and how she blushed when I introduced her to the awestruck audience as my *chhoti bahen* (younger sister).

She surprised me with her visit and she stayed on and left only when I let her leave like an obedient little sister. It is always a pleasure to meet old colleagues, especially the ones who refuse to change despite achieving tremendous fame and glory.

FILMOGRAPHY AND AWARDS

1944: *Jwar Bhata*

P: Bombay Talkies

D: Amiya Chakraborthy

M: Anil Biswas

C: Dilip Kumar, Mridula, Shamim, Agha Jan, K. N. Singh, Pithawala, Arun Kumar, Khalil, Bikram Kapoor and Mumtaz Ali

1945: *Pratima*

P: Bombay Talkies

D: P. Jairaj

M: Arun Kumar

C: Dilip Kumar, Swarnalata, Jyoti, Mumtaz Ali, Pithawala, Mukri, Zebu and Shah Nawaz

1946: *Milan*

P: Bombay Talkies

D: Nitin Bose

M: Anil Biswas

C: Dilip Kumar, Meera Mishra, Ranjana, Pahari Sanyal and Moni Chatterji

1947: *Jugnu*

P: Shaukat Art Productions

D: Syed Shaukat Hussein Rizvi

M: Feroz Nizami

C: Noor Jehan, Dilip Kumar, Ghulam Mohammed, Sulochana Sr. (Ruby Myers), Latika, Zia, Jilloo, Agha, Shashikala and Mohammed Rafi

Here, P stands for producer, D for director, M for music director and C for cast.

1948: *Anokha Pyar*

P: Ambika Films

D: M. I. Dharamsey

M: Anil Biswas

C: Dilip Kumar, Nargis, Nalini Jaywant, Sankatha Prasad, Mukri, Ved, Kesarbai, Uma Dutt, Habib and Sheikh

1948: *Ghar Ki Izzat*

P: Murli Movietone

D: Ram Daryani

M: Gobindram

C: Dilip Kumar, Mumtaz Shanti, Jeevan, Manorama, Dixit, Suleman, Gulab and Gope

1948: *Mela*

P: Wadia Films Ltd.

D: S. U. Sunny

M: Naushad

C: Dilip Kumar, Nargis, Jeevan, Amar, Roop Kamal, Alauddin, Abbas, Noor Jehan, Chandabai, Rehman, Khalil and Baby Zubeida

1948: *Nadiya Ke Paar*

P: Filmistan

D: Kishore Sahu

M: C. Ramchandra

C: Dilip Kumar, Kamini Kaushal, Maya Banerji, David, S. L. Puri, Hari Shivdasani, Samson, Tiwari, Kanta Kumari and Ranibala

1948: *Shaheed*

P: Filmistan

D: Ramesh Saigal

M: Ghulam Haider

C: Dilip Kumar, Kamini Kaushal, Chandramohan, Leela Chitnis, V H. Desai and Shashi Kapoor

1949: *Andaz*

P: Mehboob Productions

D: Mehboob Khan

M: Naushad

C: Dilip Kumar, Raj Kapoor, Nargis, V. H. Desai, Cuckoo, Murad, Anwari Bai, Amir Banu, Jamshedji, Abbas and Wasker

1949: *Shabnam*

P: Filmistan

D: Bibhuti Mitra

M: S. D. Burman

C: Dilip Kumar, Kamini Kaushal, Jeevan, Paro, Mubarak, Haroon, Rajender Singh, Shyama and Cuckoo

1950: *Arzoo*

P: Indian National Pictures

D: Shahid Latif

M: Anil Biswas

G   Dilip Kumar, Kamini Kaushal, Gope, Cuckoo, Arif, Prem Dhawan, Shashikala, Sita Bose, Neelam, Khan, Ganju and Chandabai

1950: *Babul*

P: Sunny Art Productions

D: S. U. Sunny

M: Naushad

C: Dilip Kumar, Nargis, Munnawar Sultana, Amar, A. Shah and Jankidas

1950: *Jogan*

P: Ranjit Movietone

D: Kidar Sharma

M: Bulo C. Rani

C: Dilip Kumar, Nargis, Manju, Pratima Devi, Pesi Patel, Purnima, Baby Tabassum, Anwari, Ramesh Thakur, Darpan and Rajendra Kumar

1951: *Deedar*

P: Filmkar Ltd.

D: Nitin Bose

M: Naushad

C: Ashok Kumar, Nargis, Dilip Kumar, Nimmi, Yakub and Baby Tabassum

1951: *Hulchul*

P: K. Asif Productions

D: S. K. Ojha

M: Mohd. Shafi and Sajjad Husein

C: Dilip Kumar, Nargis, Balraj Sahni, Yakub, Jeevan, Sitara Devi, K. N. Singh, Geeta Nizami Faizee and Cuckoo

1951: *Tarana*

P: Krishin Movietone

D: Ram Daryani

M: Anil Biswas

C: Dilip Kumar, Madhubala, Shyama, Kumar, Jeevan, Gope, Gulab, Devaskar and Bikram Kapoor

1952: *Aan*

P: Mehboob Productions

D: Mehboob Khan

M: Naushad

C: Dilip Kumar, Nimmi, Premnath, Mukri, Sheela Naik, Murad, Cuckoo, Nilam Bai, Amir Banu and introducing Nadira

1952: *Daag*

P: Mars & Movies/Amiya Chakraborthy

D: Amiya Chakraborthy

M: Shankar Jaikishen

C: Dilip Kumar, Usha Kiron, Nimmi, Lalita Pawar, Kanhaiyalal, Jawahar Kaul, Leela Mishra, Chandrashekhar and Krishnakant

1952: *Sangdil*

P: Talwar Films Ltd.

D: R. C. Talwar

M: Sajjad Husein

C: Dilip Kumar, Madhubala, Leela Chitnis, Pratima Devi
and Shammi

1953: *Footpath*

P: Ranjit Movietone

D: Zia Sarhadi

M: Khayyam

C: Dilip Kumar, Meena Kumari, Kuldip Kaur, Anwar Husain,
Ramesh Thapar, Achla Sachdev, Ramesh Thakur, Akhtar,
P. Kailash, Jankidas, Maruti and Sumati Lajmi

1953: *Shikast*

P: Asha Deep

D: Ramesh Saigal

M: Shankar Jaikishen

C: Dilip Kumar, Nalini Jaywant, Master Kapoor, Om
Prakash, Durga Khote, K. N. Singh, Leela Mishra, Shamlal
and Hemavati

1954: *Amar*

P: Mehboob Productions

D: Mehboob Khan

M: Naushad

C: Dilip Kumar, Madhubala, Nimmi, Jayant, Ullhas, Mukri,
Amar, Husnbanu, Murad and Shakil Nomani

1955: *Azaad*

P: Pakshiraja Studios

D: S. M. S. Naidu

M: C. Ramchandra

C: Dilip Kumar, Meena Kumari, Pran, Om Prakash, S. Nazir,
Badri Prasad, Raj Mehra, Randhir, Achla Sachdev, Murad,
Deepa Sai, Subbalaxmi and Shammi

1955: *Insaniyat*

P: Gemini Pictures

D: S. S. Vasan

M: C. Ramchandra

C: Dilip Kumar, Dev Anand, Bina Rai, Vijayalaxmi, Jairaj, Jayant, Shobhana Samarth, Agha, Kumar, Badri Prasad, Mohana, Ishwarlal and Zippy, the chimpanzee

1955: *Uran Khatola*

P: Sunny Art Productions

D: S. U. Sunny

M: Naushad

C: Dilip Kumar, Nimmi, Surya Kumari, Jeevan, Agha, Nawab, Roopmala, Amar and Tuntun

1955: *Devdas*

P: Bimal Roy Productions

D: Bimal Roy

M: S. D. Burman

C: Dilip Kumar, Suchitra Sen, Vyjayantimala, Motilal, Johnny Walker, Nazir Hussain and Pran

1957: *Naya Daur*

P: B. R. Films

D: B. R. Chopra

M: O. P. Nayyar

C: Dilip Kumar, Vyjayantimala, Ajit, Chand Usmani, Jeevan, Manmohan Krishna, Nazir Hussain, Leela Chitnis, Radhakrishan, S. Nazir, Pratima Devi, Daisy Irani, S. N. Banerji and Johnny Walker

1957: *Musafir*

P: Film Group

D: Hrishikesh Mukherjee

M: Salil Chaudhury

C: Dilip Kumar, Usha Kiron, Kishore Kumar, Suchitra

Sen, Nirupa Roy, Shekhar, Durga Khote, David, Daisy Irani,
Bipin Gupta, Rashid Khan, Nazir Hussain, Raj Laxmi, Mohan
Choti, Keshto Mukherjee, Paul Mahendra and Heera Sawant

1958: *Madhumati*
P: Bimal Roy Productions
D: Bimal Roy
M: Salil Chaudhury
C: Dilip Kumar, Vyjayantimala, Pran, Johnny Walker, Jayant,
     Tarun Bose, Tiwari, Misra, Baij Sharma and Bhudo Advani

1958: *Yahudi*
P: Bombay Films
D: Bimal Roy
M: Shankar Jaikishen
C: Dilip Kumar, Sohrab Modi, Meena Kumari, Nigar
     Sultana, Nazir Hussain, Murad, Anwar, Minoo
     Mumtaz, Tiwari, Baby Naaz, Bikram Kapoor, Romi,
     Cuckoo, Kamla Laxman and Helen

1959: *Paigham*
P: Gemini Pictures
D: S. S. Vasan
M: C. Ramchandra
C: Dilip Kumar, Vyjayantimala, Raaj Kumar, B. Saroja Devi,
     Motilal, Pandari Bai, Johnny Walker, Minoo Mumtaz,
     Vasundhara, David, Pratima Devi, Banerji, Shivraj, Ishwarlal
     and Amar

1960: *Kohinoor*
P: Republic Film Corporation
D: S. U. Sunny
M: Naushad
C: Dilip Kumar, Meena Kumari, Jeevan, Kumkum, Mukri,
     Kumar, Leela Chitnis, S. Nazir, Wasi Khan, Azim, Master
     Nisar, Tuntun and Rajen Kapoor

1960: *Mughal-e-Azam*

P: Sterling Investment Corporation

D: K. Asif

M: Naushad

C: Prithviraj Kapoor, Dilip Kumar, Madhubala, Durga
Khote, Nigar Sultana, Ajit, Kumar, Murad, Sheila Dalaya,
Jalal Agha, Vijayalaxmi, S. Nazir, Paul Sharma, Surendra,
Johnny Walker and Tabassum

1960: *Kala Bazaar*

P: Navketan

D: Vijay Anand

M: S. D. Burman

C: Dev Anand, Waheeda Rehman, Nanda, Vijay Anand, Chetan
Anand, Leela Chitnis, Rashid Khan, Kishore Sahu and *Dilip
Kumar (in a fleeting guest appearance)*

1961: *Gunga Jumna*

P: Citizen Films

D: Nitin Bose

M: Naushad

C: Dilip Kumar, Vyjayantimala, Nasir Khan, Azra,
Kanhaiyalal, Anwar, Nazir Hussain, S. Nazir,
Leela Chitnis, Praveen Paul,
Helen, Akashdeep, Baby Aruna and Baby Naaz

1964: *Leader*

P: Mukherjee Film Syndicate

D: Ram Mukherjee

M: Naushad

C: Dilip Kumar, Vyjayantimala, Motilal, Jayant, Nazir
Hussain, Sapru, Hiralal, Amar, Jankidas, P. Kailash,
Jagdish Sethi, Leela Mishra, Merlyn and Madhumati

1966: *Dil Diya Dard Liya*

P: Kay Productions

D: A. R. Kardar

M: Naushad

C: Dilip Kumar, Waheeda Rehman, Pran, Rehman, Shyama, Rani, Sajjan, Sapru, Shah Agha, Murad and Johnny Walker

1967: *Ram Aur Shyam* (first double role)

P: Vijaya International

D: Tapi Chanakya

M: Naushad

C: Dilip Kumar, Waheeda Rehman, Mumtaz, Pran, Nirupa Roy, Kanhaiyalal, Nazir Hussain, Sajjan, Mukri, Amar, Leela Mishra, Zebunissa and Baby Farida

1967: *Paari* (Bengali)

P: Pronoti Ghosh

D: Jagannath Chattopadhyaya

M: Salil Chaudhury

C: Dharmendra, Dilip Kumar, Abhi Bhattacharya, Dilip Roy, Keshto Mukherjee and Pronoti Ghosh

1968: *Aadmi*

P: PSV Films

D: A. Bhim Singh

M: Naushad

C: Dilip Kumar, Waheeda Rehman, Manoj Kumar, Simi Garewal, Pran, Sulochana, Ullhas, Padma Chavan, Mohan Choti, Shivraj and Agha

1968: *Sunghursh*

P: Rahul Theatres

D: H. S. Rawail

M: Naushad

C   Dilip Kumar, Vyjayantimala, Balraj Sahni,
     Sanjeev Kumar, Jayant, Durga Khote, Sulochana,
     Sunder, Ullhas, Iftekhar, Sapru, Mumtaz Begum,
     Padma, Lata Sinha, Anju Mahendru,
     Ranu and Deven Varma

1968: *Sadhu Aur Shaitan*

P: Bhim Singh–Mehmood Productions

D: A. Bhim Singh

M: Laxmikant Pyarelal

C: Mehmood, Bharati, Kishore Kumar, Om Prakash, Pran,
     Baby Farida, Mukri, Manju, Raj Kishore, Keshto
     Mukherjee, Tuntun, Jankidas and *Dilip Kumar (in a
     guest appearance)*

1970: *Gopi*

P: Prosperity Pictures/T. S. Muthuswamy and
     S. S. Palaniappan

D: A. Bhim Singh

M: Kalyanji Anandji

C: Dilip Kumar, Saira Banu, Om Prakash, Pran, Johnny
     Walker, Lalita Pawar, Nirupa Roy, Farida Jalal,
     Sudesh Kumar, Durga Khote, Mukri, Tiwari, Shyamlal
     and Aruna Irani

1970: *Sagina Mahato* (Bengali)

P: Hemen Ganguly and J. K. Kapur

D: Tapan Sinha

M: Tapan Sinha

C: Dilip Kumar, Saira Banu and Aparna Sen

1972: *Anokha Milan*

P: R. J. Vazirani/Vazirani Movies

D: Jagannath Chattopadhyaya

M: Salil Chaudhury

C: Dharmendra, *Dilip Kumar (in a guest appearance),*
      Pronoti Ghosh, Abhi Bhattacharya, Dilip Roy and
      Keshto Mukherjee

1972: *Dastaan* (second double role)

P: B. R. Films

D: B. R. Chopra

M: Laxmikant Pyarelal

C: Dilip Kumar, Sharmila Tagore, Prem Chopra, Bindu,
      I. S. Johar, Padma Khanna, Madan Puri, Jayshree T., Nana
      Palsikar, Manmohan Krishna, Iftekhar, Badri Prasad and
      Keshav Rana

1974: *Phir Kab Milogi*

P: Hari Mehra/Shivalay Films

D: Hrishikesh Mukherjee

M: R. D. Burman

C: Mala Sinha, Biswajeet, Deven Varma, Bipin Gupta, David
      and *Dilip Kumar (in a guest appearance)*

1974: *Sagina* (Hindi)

P: J. K. Kapur/Rupasree International

D: Tapan Sinha

M: S. D. Burman

C: Dilip Kumar, Saira Banu, Om Prakash, Aparna Sen, Anil
      Chatterji, Swaroop Dutt, Rajni Gupta, K. N. Singh and
      Kader Khan

1976: *Bairaag* (first triple role)

P: Mushir Alam and Mohd. Riaz/M. R. Productions

D: Asit Sen

M: Kalyanji Anandji

C: Dilip Kumar, Saira Banu, Leena Chandavarkar, Prem
     Chopra, Nasir Khan, Helen, Nazir Hussain, Jairaj, Madan
     Puri, Sujit Kumar, Purnima, Asit Sen, Leela Mishra, Mukri,
     Kader Khan, V. Gopal, Naaz, Paintal, Jankidas, Praveen
     Paul, Mohan Choti and Sachin

1981: *Kranti*

P: VIP Films

D: Manoj Kumar

M: Laxmikant Pyarelal

C: Dilip Kumar, Manoj Kumar, Hema Malini, Shashi Kapoor,
     Parveen Babi, Shatrughan Sinha, Nirupa Roy, Shashikala,
     Sarika, Prem Chopra, Pradeep Kumar, Madan Puri, Master
     Aditya and Master Kunal

1982: *Shakti*

P: Mushir Alam and Mohd. Riaz/M. R. Productions

D: Ramesh Sippy

M: R. D. Burman

C: Dilip Kumar, Amitabh Bachchan, Raakhee, Smita Patil,
     Kulbhushan Kharbanda and Amrish Puri

1982: *Vidhaata*

P: Gulshan Rai/Trimurti Films Pvt. Ltd.

D: Subhash Ghai

M: Kalyanji Anandji

C: Dilip Kumar, Sanjeev Kumar, Shammi Kapoor, Sanjay
     Dutt, Padmini Kolhapure, Sarika, Amrish Puri,
     Dr Shreeram Lagu, Suresh Oberoi and Madan Puri

1983: *Mazdoor*

P: B. R. Chopra/B. R. Films

D: Ravi Chopra

M: R. D. Burman

C: Dilip Kumar, Nanda, Raj Babbar, Padmini Kolhapure, Rati Agnihotri, Raj Kiran and Suresh Oberoi

1984: *Duniya*

P: Yash Johar/Dharma Productions Pvt. Ltd.

D: Ramesh Talwar

M: R. D. Burman

C: Ashok Kumar, Dilip Kumar, Saira Banu, Rishi Kapoor, Amrita Singh, Prem Chopra, Amrish Puri and Pran

1984: *Mashaal*

P: Yash Chopra/Yash Raj Films

D: Yash Chopra

M: Hridaynath Mangeshkar

C.   Dilip Kumar, Waheeda Rehman, Rati Agnihotri, Anil Kapoor, Nilu Phule, Madan Puri, Mohan Agashe, Saeed Jaffrey, Amrish Puri and Iftekhar

1986: *Dharam Adhikari*

P: U. V. Suryanarayan Rao

D: K. Raghavendra Rao

M: Bappi Lahiri

C: Dilip Kumar, Jeetendra, Sridevi, Anuradha Patel, Pran, Kader Khan, Shakti Kapoor, Asrani, Rakesh Bedi, Sujit Kumar, Mayur, Rohini Hattangadi, Preeti Sapru and Geeta Siddharth

1986: *Karma*

P: Subhash Ghai/Mukta Arts Pvt. Ltd.

D: Subhash Ghai

M: Laxmikant Pyarelal

C: Dilip Kumar, Nutan, Jackie Shroff, Anil Kapoor,
     Naseeruddin Shah, Sridevi, Poonam Dhillon, Anupam
     Kher, Shakti Kapoor, Dara Singh, Satyanarayan and Bindu

1989: *Kanoon Apna Apna*

P: A. S. R. Anjaneyulu/Madhavi Productions

D: B. Gopal

M: Bappi Lahiri

C: Dilip Kumar, Nutan, Sunjay Dutt, Madhuri Dixit, Kader
     Khan, Anupam Kher, Gulshan Grover, Tej Sapru, Satyen
     Kappu, Mayur, Jayashree Gadkar, Meethy,
     Pinky, Abhilasha, Vijayalakshmi and Disco Shanti

1990: *Izzatdaar*

P: Sudhakar Bokade

D: K. Bapaiah

M: Laxmikant Pyarelal

C: Dilip Kumar, Bharati, Govinda, Madhuri Dixit, Asrani,
     Tina Ghai, Rakesh Bedi, Dilip Dhavan and Shafi Inamdar

1991: *Saudagar*

P: Subhash Ghai/Mukta Arts Pvt. Ltd.

D: Subhash Ghai

M: Laxmikant Pyarelal

C: Dilip Kumar, Raaj Kumar, Jackie Shroff, Manisha Koirala,
     Vivek Mushran, Deepti Naval, Anupam Kher, Amrish
     Puri, Gulshan Grover, Dalip Tahil, Mukesh Khanna, Dina
     Pathak, Anand Balraj, Akash Khurana,
     Abhinav Chaturvedi, Archana Puran Singh, Malvika
     Tiwari, Sucheta Vajpai and Shubha Khote

1998: *Qila* (third double role)

P: Eagle Films

D: Umesh Mehra

M: Anand Raj Anand

C: Dilip Kumar, Rekha, Mukul Dev and Mamta Kulkarni

A LIST OF SOME OF DILIP KUMAR'S SHELVED/ INCOMPLETE/UNRELEASED FILMS

Bank Manager (shelved)

P: R. C. Talwar

D: R. C. Talwar

M: Madan Mohan

C: Dilip Kumar, Meena Kumari

Taj Mahal and *Aakhri Mughal* (planned/shelved)

P: K. Asif

D: K. Asif

C: Dilip Kumar

Chanakya Chandragupt (shelved after extensive preparation)

P: Kishore Sharma

D: B. R. Chopra

M: Naushad

C: Dilip Kumar, Dharamendra, Hema Malini, Parveen Babi, Helen and Vijayendra

Haar Singaar **(1950)** (shelved after a few reels)

P: Allied Art Productions Ltd.

D: Mahesh Kaul

M: Anil Biswas

C: Dilip Kumar, Madhubala, Kuldeep, Baby Zubeida, Bikram Kapoor and Moni Chatterji

Janwar (shelved after a few reels)
P: K. Asif
D: K. Asif
C: Dilip Kumar and Suraiya

Shikwa (launched in early 1950s – shelved after a few reels)
P: Rajendra Jain
C: Dilip Kumar and Nutan

Mera Watan (shelved)

Samandar (shelved)

Kala Aadmi (after much research, shelved)
P: Ramesh Saigal
D: Ramesh Saigal and Dilip Kumar
C: Dilip Kumar

Untitled venture (shelved after *mahurat*)
P: Nasir Hussain
C: Dilip Kumar and Asha Parekh

Kalinga **(1995)** (incomplete)
P: Divya Citizen Combines
D: Dilip Kumar
C.   Dilip Kumar, Raj Babbar, Amjad Khan and Meenakshi Seshadri

Aag Ka Dariya (completed and censored in 1995 but unreleased)
P: Premalaya/R. Venkataraman
D: S. V. Rajendra Singh Babu
C: Dilip Kumar, Rekha, Rajiv Kapoor and Padmini Kolhapure

Asar **(2001)** (shelved after *mahurat* and some shooting)
P: Dinesh Patel
D: Kuku Kohli
M: Nadeem Shravan
C: Dilip Kumar, Ajay Devgan and Priyanka Chopra

SOME OF DILIP KUMAR'S LEADING LADIES
(WHO WORKED IN MORE THAN ONE FILM WITH HIM)

1. Nalini Jaywant
    1948 *Anokha Pyar*
    1953 *Shikast*

2. Kamini Kaushal
    1948 *Nadiya Ke Paar*
    1948 *Shaheed*
    1949 *Shabnam*
    1950 *Arzoo*

3. Madhubala
    1951 *Tarana*
    1952 *Sangdil*
    1954 *Amar*
    1960 *Mughal-e-Azam*

4. Meena Kumari
    1953 *Footpath*
    1955 *Azaad*
    1958 *Yahudi*
    1960 *Kohinoor*

5. Nimmi
    1951 *Deedar*
    1952 *Aan*
    1952 *Daag*
    1954 *Amar*
    1955 *Uran Khatola*

6. Nargis
    1948 *Mela*
    1949 *Andaz*
    1950 *Babul*
    1950 *Jogan*
    1951 *Deedar*
    1951 *Hulchul*

7.	Nutan	1986	*Karma*
		1989	*Kanoon Apna Apna*
8.	Rekha	1995	*Aag Ka Dariya* (unreleased)
		1998	*Qila*
9.	Vyjayantimala	1955	*Devdas*
		1957	*Naya Daur*
		1958	*Madhumati*
		1959	*Paigham*
		1961	*Gunga Jumna*
		1964	*Leader*
		1968	*Sunghursh*
10.	Waheeda Rehman	1966	*Dil Diya Dard Liya*
		1967	*Ram Aur Shyam*
		1968	*Aadmi*
		1984	*Mashaal*
11.	Saira Banu	1970	*Gopi*
		1970	*Sagina Mahato*
		1974	*Sagina*
		1976	*Bairaag*
		1984	*Duniya*

LIST OF AWARDS

1. 1953   *Filmfare* (Best Actor): *Daag*
2. 1955   *Filmfare* (Best Actor): *Azaad*
3. 1956   *Filmfare* (Best Actor): *Devdas*
4. 1957   *Filmfare* (Best Actor): *Naya Daur*
5. 1960   *Filmfare* (Best Actor): *Kohinoor*
6. 1964   *Filmfare* (Best Actor): *Leader*
7. 1967   *Filmfare* (Best Actor): *Ram Aur Shyam*
8. 1982   *Filmfare* (Best Actor): *Shakti*
9. 1991   Padma Bhushan (awarded by the Government of India)
10. 1993   *Filmfare*–Raj Kapoor Lifetime Achievement Award
11. 1995   Dadasaheb Phalke Award
12. 1997   Nishan-e-Imtiaz: The highest civilian award of
            Pakistan (presented on 23 March 1998)
13. 1997   N. T. Rama Rao Award
14. 1998   Ramnath Goenka Award
15. 1998   Lux Zee Cine Awards (presented on 14 March 1998)
16. 2000   Rajiv Gandhi Sadhbhavna Award (presented on 20 August
            2000)

And many more, far too numerous to list here.

ACKNOWLEDGEMENTS

ORDS CANNOT ADEQUATELY EXPRESS GRATITUDE. YET, THE MOST urgent of all duties when a dream task is completed with a sense of pride is to express thanks to all those who contributed to the fulfilment of the dream.

First and foremost, I must thank Saira's only brother Sultan Ahmed (Sultan Bhai for all her friends) for finding time to read the chapters objectively and giving valuable suggestions in his own gentlemanly manner.

My thanks also to my dear colleagues in the media, Satya Swaroop (managing editor) and Dev Varam (group editor), who have been leading the New Media group for many years now. I owe my gratitude to them for sincerely egging me on to take up the challenge and go full steam into the assignment and offering all help from the creative team at New Media, especially from Santosh Nawar, the art director.

I am grateful to Farida Dadi (famous child star Baby Farida now sought after by television channels) for sparing time from her busy work schedules to segregate relevant photographs from Saira's unlimited collection for use in the book. Thanks also must go to her assistant Anil Rawate for helping to make the photographs and the audio and video tapes available at short notice.

My thanks to Murshid Ali Khan, Dilip Sahab and Saira's secretary, for assisting me with the documenting of the manuscript at various stages and coordination with the publisher.

I am indebted to Hygino D'Costa and Bashir Colombowala, secretary and manager respectively, in Dilip Sahab's secretariat for their legal advice under Sultan Bhai's competent guidance.

My thanks to Dilip Sahab's ardent fan, Himanshu Kumar, for his encouraging words through many phone calls from Kolkata.

My gratitude to Bhupendra Valji Sachade and Vijay Bhupendra Sachade, of Mulund, Mumbai, who gladly offered to share the blurbs, photographs, newspaper and magazine write-ups they have collected over decades out of their deep admiration and love for Dilip Sahab.

A final word of thanks to Naqi Ahmed for simplifying the chaste Urdu that Dilip Sahab spoke at times. Like any admiring listener, I sat wonderstruck by his absolute command over the pristine language and did not dare to butt in and spoil Sahab's mood. It was very kind of Naqi to listen to the audio tapes and educate me later on.

– Udayatara Nayar

REMINISCENCES

RAIHAN AHMED*

$\mathscr{D}$ILIP KUMAR. THE VERY SOUND OF THIS NAME RAISES EYEBROWS and [quickens] heartbeats in respect. Very few privileged people know that this name is not just a name of a legend but a magical name. I for one have been privileged to experience this. Being his nephew is the greatest gift God gave me. My Yousuf Uncle as I call him is a person of so many talents that words cannot describe and a book cannot contain. To write my experiences with him will require several volumes. To pen my memories of this great man is difficult as I cannot hold back tears, as every memory has his love, care and a child-like innocence attached to it.

Travelling with Yousuf Uncle is guaranteed fun and adventure. Rain or shine we never had a dull moment with him. He would pass the wittiest comments keeping a straight face leaving us laughing till our cheeks hurt. Road trips were the best as he would make us try all kinds of street food, while my aunt would try her subtle best to stop him, but to no avail.

He insisted we eat *idlis* [a typical South Indian breakfast dish] every morning in Kashmir, which was in total contrast to the [cuisine] of that geographic location. He would have a mischievous grin and tell us: '*Idlis* taste better in the North than in the South', something our young brains couldn't fathom but took his word for it.

He would constantly play pranks on us, keeping us wondering what would he pull off next. He has the ability of blending in with any age group, keeping us intrigued by [accounts of] his camping trips in his youth.

Kite flying with Yousuf Uncle is an experience only a few lucky people can mention. He has a huge trunk filled to the brim with custom-made kites, specially made for him by kite masters. Selecting a kite as children was the greatest honour of the day. He would let us choose the kite and fly it for us. He would cut most of the kites engaging him that day, making him

*Saira's brother Sultan's son.

341

the master of the sky as well. He would accept defeat with such humility that the winner would bow down to him.

He is a sportsman to the core, be it soccer, badminton, cricket, hockey, golf or chess, he mastered it all. Few people know that he is a great magician and has a box full of tricks which, he would pull out and keep us wondering how he did them.

I can go on and on and about my life spent with Yousuf Uncle and every experience is better than the last one. He has been there for us in every walk of life, supporting us and protecting us, guiding us and educating us with his great wisdom.

I owe everything to him. I thank Allah for Yousuf Uncle and letting me grow in his shadow. I wish I could be a fraction of him, but I realize no one comes close even to his shadow. Allah made just one DILIP KUMAR and I am fortunate to be one of his loved ones. LOVE YOU YOUSUF UNCLE ALWAYS.

SHABANA AZMI

Hamare yahaan yeh maana jaata hai ke apne se badon ki tareef karna bhi badtehzeebi hoti hai … hum kaun hotey hain tareef karne wale? Hum to bas sar jhukakar apne ehtraam ka izhaar kar sakte hain …[*]

I FEEL HUMBLED AND DEEPLY HONOURED TO BE joining the ranks of those writing about Dilip Sahab. My inclusion in this book is not because of any merit on my part but because I have been such an admirer of his persona and his craft.

He has inspired generations of actors in the Indian film industry – some have survived by directly imitating him; others have drawn succour

---

[*]In our place, it is considered uncultured if one praises one's elders … who are we to praise them? We can just bow our heads and express our respect to them …

from his incredible body of work. Unknown to him, I have been an Eklavya to his Dronacharya. I've watched him from afar and learnt from him that an actor's resource base must be life itself; that an actor must be interested in poetry and politics; and that an actor must have a strong social conscience.

Acting is not a horse race in which the one who runs the fastest past the post is the winner. An actor can play a definitive Hamlet but be a disastrous Othello. How then is he to be judged? Surely, versatility is the true hallmark of an actor. And Dilip Kumar stands tall when it comes to that yardstick. Who can forget the intensity of Devdas, the insouciance of Gunga, the irreverence of Shyam, the depth of romance as Salim in *Mughal-e-Azam*? Each performance finely calibrated. He plays the sophisticate and the rustic with equal felicity. Drama, comedy, romance – he is a master of them all. He has become a reference point for actors working within the paradigms of mainstream cinema, yet being able to find truth in the larger-than-life context. I remember my director Vinay Shukla tell me during the making of *Godmother* (1999) 'bring to the character of Rambhiben the truth of Dilip Kumar's Gunga – a constructed reality but one that is entirely credible'.

Dilip Sahab has changed the course of acting in Hindi cinema, which largely survived on 'representative' acting in broad strokes – laugh when happy, cry when sad, raise your eyebrows when surprised – much as it happens in dance, in *nritya*. Dilip Kumar showed us how the subtext can be revealed, how to play against the emotion, how less is more and how simulated spontaneity can be as effective as the real thing.

Paeans have been sung in praise of the actor Dilip Kumar. But there are other aspects of his behavioural conduct that are exemplary as well.

The first image that comes to mind when you think of Dilip Kumar is dignity. He arouses awe and respect. He walks into a room and people automatically stand up because such is his aura and his commanding presence. He has always been a cut above the rest because he has never succumbed to anything crass in the name of popular appeal. He has entertained without ever having to resort to crudity. Lessons that we will do well to learn.

The long and the short of it is simply this: if you desire legitimacy as an actor and as a human being, simply follow in the footsteps of Dilip Kumar. There is no other like him!

V. BABASAHEB*

I KNEW IT WOULD BE A GREAT ACHIEVEMENT IN MY TRACK RECORD if a sequence came alive on the screen the way Dilip Sahab had visualized. But I was at a loss as to how we would do it. I was thinking about it even in my sleep and I was seeing dreams of utter failure.

When the day arrived to shoot that particular scene for *Gunga Jumna*, I confessed to Sahab that it was not possible. That was when he showed me what he had worked out on paper. He had calculated the speed of the train and the galloping of the horses precisely and he asked me and the fight master, Azim Bhai, only one question: Were we afraid of taking risks?

We were standing in front of Sahab and his intense eyes were fixed on us, demanding an honest reply. Unanimously, we replied that we were not afraid. Sahab then explained to me how he wanted the camera to be tied beneath the door of the compartment to capture the hooves of the galloping horses raising dust as they advanced parallel to the running train. He had me strapped to the floor of the doorway of the compartment in such a manner that I could operate it from that position and get the shots.

There was a bridge under which the train had to pass and there was some worry about how we would synchronize the movements of the horses as the track narrowed before the train reached the bridge. Azim Bhai had to execute the action involving Sahab in a split second at a particular point and he did not know what to do as Sahab was not in favour of using a double.

We managed to complete the shooting exactly the way Sahab wanted only because he had done the arithmetic of speed and action so precisely in his preparation for the scene, which went on quietly for days in advance. It became the most talked about sequence in Indian cinema and a technical wonder even for the technicians of Technicolor laboratory at Pinewood Studios in London.

There was another superb scene in *Gunga Jumna* where Gunga flees from the village and runs as fast as he can to avoid the pursuing crowd. Sahab wanted the camera to be mounted on a lorry to capture the fast movement of Gunga's legs as he runs through the wilderness between trees that have no leaves left on them to give shade and cover to a fugitive. Once again we

---

*A cinematographer by profession.

achieved the impossible only because Sahab's calculation was precise. Azim Bhai was in the lorry with me and he just couldn't believe that Sahab could run as fast as he did. Later, Sahab told him he had been an athlete in his college days and covered 100 metres and 200 metres in record time.

Gunga Jumna gave me the opportunity to learn something new every day from Dilip Sahab. Why me, the make-up man, Sarosh Modi, learnt how to work on an artiste's face according to the situation, the camera's exposure, the intensity of the scenes and the texture of the artiste's skin. He went on to become the most sought-after make-up artist in the industry after *Gunga Jumna* and *Leader*.

The scene that I can never forget is Gunga's death scene. Sahab once again gave me an opportunity to know his genius. He briefed me that I should place the camera a few steps from the entrance of the set of Govindi's* house erected at Mehboob Studio where we had done most of the indoor work. He told me I would get a signal when he would be at the entrance and the camera should run. He was going to take several rounds of the studio on foot, jogging, running, etc., in order to be out of breath when he entered the house and gave the climax shot. There could not be a retake because he would be so exhausted by then.

We were ready and I prayed and set up the camera at the point he had marked. I received the signal and I was ready when he reached the entrance. I saw him and the stunning expression on his face, but I think I missed the timing, so awesome was the moment! The entire unit was wonder-struck when he staggered in and moved to the position to collapse with the words, 'Hey, Ram'. There was a lump in every throat and the silence was chilling. When Sahab recovered from the shot and I found the courage to go up to him, I told him that there was a possibility that I missed the initial timing. He was silent. I knew he was angry but he complied with my request for a retake. He went through the whole gamut again and with more intensity the second time and we canned the shot.

---

*The character played by Leela Chitnis, the mother of Gunga and Jumna.

AMITABH BACHCHAN

*B*EFORE I STEPPED INTO THE FILM industry, I had come to Bombay (now Mumbai) for a holiday and a friend took me to a restaurant for a treat. To my great surprise and joy, Dilip Sahab was with one of his friends at the restaurant. I wanted to get his autograph and so I rushed to a nearby stationery shop to get a proper autograph book. When I returned Sahab was busy talking to the many admirers who had surrounded him. I felt it would be improper to intrude and interrupt the conversations. So, somewhat crestfallen, I returned to my table.

After I entered the profession I briefly met Dilip Sahab at a get-together I was invited to. On both occasions I yearned for the day when I would be worthy of being in his presence in front of a camera – a dream that seemed like an impossibility then because Sahab chose the scripts he liked, the director he liked, the banner he preferred and the actors he found suitable to work with very carefully. I did not reckon then that an eventful day would come when I would be cast with Sahab in a film!

By the time Ramesh Sippy's *Shakti* [released in 1982]was conceived as a film starring Dilip Sahab as the upright, unrelenting, duty-conscious police commissioner and Salim-Javed, the writers, told me I would be cast as the commissioner's rebellious son, I had gained considerable experience in acting. For the film industry, and for cinema lovers, it was a momentous casting triggering unprecedented curiosity. It couldn't have been otherwise since it was a healthy test of competence for any actor to match the class of Sahab's work.

I, however, was scared on two counts. I feared how I would stand in the presence of the actor I had been idolizing for years and appear unmindful of his awesome personality. Secondly, the character of the son nurtured a strong resentment and hostility towards the father. Even though it was all make-believe, I winced at the thought of confronting the man I respected, admired and loved so much.

To go back in time, I had always admired the actor in Dilip Sahab much before I came across *Gunga Jumna*. But the film became special to me after seeing Dilip Sahab's versatility as the villager from UP possessing the perfection of the dialect and its delivery. It was impossible for me to imagine at that time, being from UP, how someone not connected to the state, could deliver a flawless performance, nuances and all, for the character. To me that has been his ultimate performance, one that I have, and shall always, cherish.

Now, as a member of the same fraternity I can understand the effort and the dedication it must have taken from him to perfect the routine. His performances have all been flawless, and the main reason for this has been two very elementary, yet most important, aspects – the perfection in speech and the ability to listen. A correct diction takes care of almost all that you perform. And the power to listen to what the other character in front of you is saying endorses the genuineness of the moment in cinema. Dilip Sahab possessed both qualities in abundance, which was why I appreciated his greatness.

I learnt from him the need to work relentlessly till perfection was achieved. I also imbibed from him the importance of respecting one's co-artistes and their work. I recall an afternoon when we were shooting my death scene for *Shakti*. For all of us actors the most difficult scene in a film is a death scene. That's because we have to die in different ways in different films and we have to prepare ourselves mentally for the scene to be performed the way the director has perceived it. As the scene had to be rehearsed at least once, Dilip Sahab and I got moving to go through the rehearsal on the airstrip at Juhu where it was to be shot. There were several members of the crew and the unit at the location and as is always the scenario at a shooting, there was a lot of talking and yelling going on between the lightmen and others. Dilip Sahab noticed that, as is my wont, I had come mentally and emotionally prepared for the scene. As we readied ourselves for the rehearsal he saw that the crew was least bothered about our rehearsal and were causing a lot of commotion. He asked me to wait and summoned them all for a minute. He spoke to them kindly but firmly explaining how an artiste prepares for his work throwing his entire being into the acting and the least he expected from his colleagues on the sets was silence and respect for the work he was doing. 'Learn to respect artistes,' he told them and packed them off to do their work. I was moved by the incident and so were the crew members. It was significant because it was my scene all the way and he wanted me to give it my best.

Dilip Sahab is an exceptionally good human being. He is always playing the father-figure in real life to anybody who seeks his guidance. Perhaps it comes from him being the father-figure at home to his siblings. I remember one late night when the writer duo Salim-Javed egged me on to go with them to Sahab's house without a prior appointment. I was both embarrassed and reluctant as it has never been my habit to take such liberties, especially with elders. They said it was all right. We drove over to Dilip Sahab's bungalow; on reaching we learnt from the watchman that Sahab had retired for the day and was in his bedroom. I told Salim-Javed that we should leave but they told the watchman to inform Sahab that some friends were at the gate to see him.

The next thing we knew was that lights were switched on in the living room and his personal valet was ushering us inside. Sahab came down from his bedroom all smiles and genuinely happy to see us. He was so hospitable and warm even at that unearthly hour. He regaled us with anecdotes from the past and it was only around four or so in the morning that we reluctantly took leave of him. Such is his care and warmth.

No art in the entire universe can ever exist, flourish, or even take birth without an 'unconscious assimilation' of influence that eventually propels it to its creation. Writers, poets, painters, artists of any category need stimulation from what they may have encountered during the process of their creativity. If you attribute my source of influence to be Mr Dilip Kumar, then that would be the biggest compliment you could pay me, because I believe that he is what was and is, correct, right and the best.

The history of Indian cinema shall in my reckoning be 'before Dilip Sahab' and 'after Dilip Sahab', because of his impeccable presence. When you measure a journey you never change the milestone. Dilip Sahab to me is that milestone in our film industry. That landmark is permanent, whether you wish to count the miles before, or after, it!

One can only thank the graciousness of the Almighty when you find that your idol and object of great admiration has such kind thoughts and words to express about you. Dilip Sahab has more than once spoken kindly about my work publicly and personally to me. To me Dilip Sahab has not just been the mammoth performing talent that he is, but also one that has enveloped this great capability of his with supreme eloquence, considerate co-starring and collaborativeness, and a personality that demands immediate respect!

He graced the premiere of my film *Black* [2005] and after the film was over he waited outside the theatre till I emerged. Then Sahab walked up to me and took both my hands in his and looked into my eyes for what seemed like an eternity. He did not speak a word but I can tell you those were the most eloquent words that anybody ever spoke to me. Thank you so much Dilip Sahab and thank you for that wonderful letter that you wrote to me after seeing the film. It is a letter that I have framed and put up in my office and it shall remain with me forever.

JAYA BACHCHAN

*I*F THERE IS ONE REGRET I HAVE IN MY professional life, it is that I did not get a chance to work with Dilip Sahab. I regard it as a loss because he is the only actor in Indian cinema whose iconic performances in film after film throughout the 1950s and early 1960s inspired me.

I began watching his films even before I joined the Film and Television Institute of India, Pune, as a student of cinema. As a youngster, I used to watch his films with my father, Tarun Kumar Bhaduri, who was a great admirer of Dilip Sahab. Much later, after I acted in Satyajit Ray's *Mahanagar* (1963; in Bengali), when serious interest in the medium seized me, I watched all Dilip Sahab's starrers and each was a revelation.

I intently observed his body language that conveyed what a torrent of words could not do for other actors, the pain he expressed through his eyes, the way he modulated his voice and never shouted in the dramatic scenes and the simple and natural stance he took in the commanding scenes. As for comedy, he has remained unparalleled from *Kohinoor* (1960) onwards. He played the anti-hero way back in the 1950s and set the trend for others to follow. His sense of timing was completely different and unique. He never acted. In a scene he listened to his co-star and responded with a mere glance …. Amazing!

That he conveyed so much without speaking was what inspired me the most. May be, unconsciously, I conveyed the same in my performances.

In fact, when my son Abhishek took the decision to become a film actor, I told him to watch all of Dilip Sahab's classics and learn some essential lessons from them without trying to copy him. For instance, how many actors of our cinema know how to use silence to enhance the import of a dramatic or emotional moment? Dilip Sahab has expertly used the eloquence of silence in some of his iconic performances in a way no actor before him had. I am happy that only one Dilip Kumar classic has been remade. [Dilip Kumar's 1955 *Devdas* was remade in 2002 with Shahrukh Khan in the lead role.]

The Padma Bhushan is too minor a recognition for him. The Dadasaheb Phalke Award too was given very late to him. It is his graciousness that made him accept both without resentment. What he deserves is the Bharat

Ratna (India's highest civilian award) and it should have been given a long time ago. All of us know that such honours matter little to him. An artiste of his stature is certainly beyond the lure of glory that such recognitions give. Yet, it is the duty of those who bestow the recognition to have taken note and made us all proud by honouring him.

On a personal level, I have always found him ever so humble and charming. I joked with him once that I was so smitten by his personal charm that I could surprise him one day with some pure and harmless flirting. He laughed because he has always seen me as a spirited young girl, an ardent fan. The unique thing about Dilip Sahab is that his peers and two generations of actors, film makers and technicians within the industry unanimously love him and admire him. It is easy to win the admiration of filmgoers with your work but it is not easy to win the unconditional love, respect and admiration of the film industry. It goes without saying that future generations too will admire him because he is timeless.

He is a playful person with people he feels at home with. Once I was shooting at Rajkamal Studios in Mumbai for a film and Dilip Sahab also happened to be shooting on one of the other floors. I went over to meet him and I said something silly on purpose and he chased me all over the premises in mock indignation. There were no snoopy cameras those days. If it were to happen today, you can imagine the inferences that would be drawn and the breaking news it would have made!

The one compliment I treasure came from Salim Khan and Javed Akhtar. They said quite spontaneously that I possessed the same sense of timing in my acting as Dilip Sahab. Dilip Sahab's acting of course is timeless and so modern that coming generations of actors must necessarily watch all his works and learn from them because I feel no school of acting can teach what a student can learn from his performances. He is a national treasure, an institution to be preserved and revered for generations to come.

MOIN BEG*

I HAVE HAD THE OPPORTUNITY OF SPENDING SOME WONDERFUL DAYS travelling with Yousuf Bhai especially during elections, first for Indira Gandhi and then for her son, Rajiv. Those were days of hectic campaigning all over the country, spent travelling far and wide and by almost every mode of transportation. There were many hilarious moments in spite of the situation we were in. It was during these times that I got to know the real 'Dilip Kumar' – his real and humorous side. He would always be very caring and thoughtful of the smallest of details with the fun element intact. We were to travel to Jaipur for campaigning, flying first to Delhi and then onwards. We were put up in the splendid Rambagh Palace in Jaipur in their most lavish suite. From there we headed to Sikar in the Shekhawati region [of Rajasthan] by car to address a huge rally. After a point we were shifted onto a truck as the crowds were impossible to control. This was in the peak of the summer and [it] was as hot as hell! We reached the venue of the rally with thousands calling out 'Daleep Kumar! Daleep Kumar!' to which laughingly Yousuf Bhai repeated 'Daleeeeep Kumar!' We climbed on to the dais where instead of chairs were these mattresses with huge bolsters! We sat down and the minister for whom we were campaigning took the mic and began his speech. Now, the most hilarious part was that we were seated behind the minister at his bum level. And as luck would have it, his itch was not just restricted to his speech, for before we knew it he started scratching his bum in right earnest. The minister was facing the public, which was oblivious to where exactly his itch was but Yousuf Bhai and me were literally facing it! We both tried to keep a very straight face till Yousuf Bhai leaned over to me and said: 'He's giving himself a good time!' I could have died laughing but instead had to sit poker faced. That day I got my very first lesson in acting, and is an experience I will never forget. No one really knows the mischievous side of Yousuf Bhai. He is such fun to be with. At that moment I didn't know it but there was more in store for me! Yousuf Bhai spoke at length to a thunderous applause and the crowd's reaction was unbelievable.

It had been an exhausting day under the sun and we were ready to hit the bed. Ah! At last so I thought! The one thing not many people know about

*Sultan's brother-in-law.

Yousuf Bhai is that neither can he sleep alone in a room nor can he sleep with the lights switched off. This was something I hadn't known till the time I was with him in the hotel. Bone tired, I got into bed covering my face with the bedsheet to keep out the light as I tried sleeping next to him. I was almost dozing off when I was slapped awake by him. There was this large trophy up on the wall in front of the bed with bulging eyes and huge horns! 'That fellow is looking at me and I cannot sleep,' said Yousuf Bhai adding, 'come on, let's find something to cover its face.' Aghast I asked, 'How on earth do we do that?' He went into the other room and pulled out the bedsheet from the bed there. Below the trophy head was a console with two tall chairs on either side. Yousuf Bhai climbed on to one chair, gave me one end of the bedsheet and told me to climb on to the other chair. 'Now all we have to do is throw the bedsheet over the horns and the face is covered … simple.'

So while we were attempting this extraordinary feat in walked the minister with his entourage. Thanks to our extreme fatigue we had forgotten to latch the door. Our plight can only be imagined! Perched on chairs with a bedsheet stretched between us was funny, but the look on the minister's face was priceless! But this was not all. Yousuf Bhai, in a matter-of-fact way, let go of the bedsheet, and then hopping off the chair with a straight face said, 'Dekho, yeh Munoo kya kya karata hai!' (See what all Munoo makes me do!) Dying of embarrassment, there I stood on the damn chair with this huge bedsheet feeling very much like Draupadi with the unending saree. Later when they had all left both Yousuf Bhai and I were rolling on the floor with laughter. Such times only the fortunate experience.

At another rally the impossible happened. We were to campaign for a Congress candidate in Pilibhit [in Uttar Pradesh] against whom Maneka Gandhi [of the Bharatiya Janata Party or BJP] was pitted. Both parties had organized rallies at the same spot on either side of the road. Huge pandals, blaring speakers and throngs of people going wild. Seeing Dilip Kumar the crowds surged forward breaking the cordons and before we realized we were wrongly ushered on to the dais from where Maneka Gandhi was to speak. But Yousuf Bhai being as gracious as he is handled the situation deftly. He spoke saying that Maneka was the daughter-in-law of the greatest family and said he knew her parents too. He then walked off across the road to the dais we were supposed to be and gave a speech to a thunderous applause! I don't know of anyone else who could have handled such a tricky situation with such dignity and grace except Yousuf Bhai. No offence to anyone and rightly handled.

MAHESH BHATT

*H*OW DOES ONE BEGIN TO TELL THE story of a legend?

Do I begin with the first memory of him in *Devdas*, which I saw as a child when I was six years old, where he essayed the role of the tragic lover, who spirals into the abyss of doom? This tale of unrequited love is the greatest tragedy that came out of the golden era of Indian cinema. Dilip Kumar gave the character of Devdas, a man falling apart, a dignity that no one till date has been able to match.

Or should I begin with that chilly September night of 2004, in Bradford, UK, where at the close of the Bite the Mango film festival, I was given the privilege of interviewing him in front of an eclectic audience of Asian origin, from India, Pakistan and Bangladesh?

'Mr Yousuf Khan, how does it feel to be masquerading as THE Dilip Kumar, who has paved his way into the hearts of millions all over the world?' I remember asking him. 'Tell me something about this journey of yours.'

Dilip Sahab was sitting in his classic Dilip Kumar pose with his hand covering his face. He took a moment to think, and then spoke. 'It has been enchanting, excruciating and baffling,' he said candidly, and then turned to look at a giant cut-out of his from *Devdas*, which was towering behind us. 'When I look at this person called Dilip Kumar, I don't know who he is,' he said. 'Nothing seems to have added up in my life to deserve this. I don't know why all of you want to deify me to this extent.' 'Perhaps because deifying you is profitable Sir?' I ventured. 'Let me explain. Yesterday I took the early morning train to London from Bradford. The attendant on the train was Bangladeshi. Recognizing me, he came forward shyly and asked me if would like something to eat. I asked him for a sandwich. He then asked me who, according to me 'is the best Indian film actor of all time'. Without a moment's hesitation, I said: 'Dilip Kumar, Dilip Kumar and only Dilip Kumar.' He smiled a broad smile. A few seconds later, I asked him how much I owed him for the sandwich. 'Nothing at all,' he said. 'We share the same love. Even I love Dilip Kumar. Your sandwich is free.'

The hall erupted in laughter and thunderous applause. But what was uncanny about that moment was the way in which Dilip Saab had been listening to the story. It was as if I was talking about someone else totally and he was a mere spectator. He too smiled warmly and clapped, but his delight was more about the way I had narrated the story and less about the fact that he was the hero in it.

Unlike most people who are party to their own myth making, Dilip Kumar looked at it as if from a distance, with as much wonderment as perhaps bewilderment at the legend that was apparently him.

They say the word is not the thing. The Dilip Kumar that enchants me is not only the one who has acted in fifty-seven movies, got countless awards, was once the sheriff of Bombay, the Dadasaheb Phalke Award winner, or the Rajya Sabha member, or the man who won the Nishan-e-Imtiaz from the Government of Pakistan. He is so much more than these glittery adornments.

The Dilip Sahab who enchants me is also a man who is a hero in real life. The plural heritage, which is the bedrock of this nation, radiates from his entire being, not only on the screen but in real life as well.

The way Yousuf Khan alias Dilip Kumar utters the words 'Hey Ram' in *Gunga Jumna* reveals that his heart is rooted in the ideas of the Mahatma.

But unlike most screen icons who embrace the politics of silence when it comes to contentious issues, Dilip Kumar actually fought for the values for which he stood in his day-to-day life.

In 1998, Dilip Sahab persuaded Javed Akhtar and me to join him to approach the Supreme Court of India with a public interest litigation [PIL] on the protests against the film *Fire* [directed by Deepa Mehta], which was pulled out of the theatres by the right wingers. This had created such a furore in the Rajya Sabha, that the business of the House was adjourned because the thespian was called 'a Pakistani' by a member of the right wing party.

'The freedom of speech is the very breath of the artists' community. We are film makers, actors, writers. How can we remain silent and pretend to be blind when that ideal is being strangulated?' he said to us that wintry night when we were being advised by some apprehensive film folks not to take on the establishment. But, after all, democracy thrives through dissent, and. through dissent, one has to be open to face discomfort: that is the lesson I learnt from my screen idol that night.

Five years ago, on Dilip Sahab's eighty-seventh birthday, like every year, I went to his Pali Hill abode to wish him. He greeted me with his charismatic smile and held my hand like only someone who considers you to be his own would. And through that touch, he perhaps communicated to me that which words could never have. It meant simply, I am with you, I stand with you.

Those were troubled days for me. I was going through a firestorm. The alleged connection between the infamous David Headley, the architect of the Mumbai carnage of 26/11 [26 November 2008], with my son Rahul Bhatt, had turned our lives into a mini hell overnight. The right wing political parties, whose politics I had always questioned, were now using this as grist for their mills to grind against me. I was busy fighting on behalf of my son, to make sure he was not victimized by the vested interests around us. Since Dilip Sahab had been in this space before himself, he could empathize with me.

Just then, a lawyer of great repute appeared from nowhere and, with great gusto, wished Dilip Sahab a happy birthday, adding that everyone was praying for his long life and protection. Dilip Saab, pointing towards me, cut him short. 'Miyan, pray for his protection not mine. He is fighting a lone battle and paying the price today for sticking his neck out for all of us. He needs to be protected, not me!' His words touched the very core of my being. It was not what he said, but how he said it. I suddenly felt validated and not all alone anymore.

I looked into his eyes and smilingly said: 'No Dilip Sahab, how can I be alone when I have you holding my hand. I have inherited this courage from you. You have walked this path before all alone. It's my turn to walk it now.' My words reached him and he gave me a smile that I will never forget until my dying day. My memories of Dilip Sahab are my prized treasures, which I will cherish all my life. In fact, they have helped me to define to myself who I really am. Thank you Sir. You have touched my life in ways you cannot imagine.

CHANDRASHEKHAR

*T*HE WORLD MAY KNOW DILIP KUMAR AS THE greatest actor of India; I consider him the finest human being. I am a year younger than Dilip Sahab and, though I was a leading man in the early years of my career, I cannot claim to be anywhere close to the stature he attained, yet the respect and position he gave me each time we worked together to support causes, including those of the film industry workers and artistes, warms my heart even today.

I used to visit Bombay Talkies like so many aspiring heroes of that period and I would see him there. He was handsome and lean, spoke very politely in impeccable English and Urdu. Ashok Kumar, fondly called Dadamoni by the entire industry, too, would sometimes be shooting there. He would look towards Dilip Kumar and quietly tell us: '*Usko dekho, khoya khoya sa rehta hai aur chup rehta hai. Ek din sab se bada star hoga aur uska naam puri duniya mein phael jayega.*' [Look at him. He appears to be lost in thought and remains silent. But there will come a day when he will become the biggest star and attain fame and recognition the world over.]

Dilip Sahab's approach to whatever he did remained the same even after he attained huge stardom. He would sit quietly watching the actors, directors and technicians working on the sets of films that were being shot in the studio. He put his heart and soul into everything he did. Some rallies we organized to raise funds for national causes involved considerable management of human resources and motivation; the whole exercise used to be taken over by Dilip Sahab not because he wanted to be in the limelight but because he genuinely cared.

Whether it was the Bihar famine or the droughts in Maharashtra and West Bengal in the 1960s and 1970s, he wasted no time in getting the industry together to collect funds. He inspired us all. His best friend, Raj Kapoor, was always there to help him but the nitty-gritties were invariably left to Dilip Sahab to organize. I remember an occasion when actors Jairaj, David and myself spent days assisting Dilip Sahab to organize a benefit cricket match to aid the devastated victims of the Koyna earthquake [in Maharashtra in 1967]. We managed to collect lakhs of rupees for rehabilitating the homeless victims.

He would be equally concerned to raise funds for needy artistes and workers; the first cheque always came from him. The Film Industry Welfare Trust and superannuation schemes for old, retired artistes were his initiatives. He was the first from the film industry to propose to the Government of Maharashtra for the Dadasaheb Phalke Chitranagari (Film City), which came into existence in 1978. The Nehru Centre [at Bombay] also was Dilip Sahab's idea. He had big dreams for the Indian film industry and he worked selflessly for it. In contrast to today's actors who lust for Hollywood, Dilip Sahab turned down David Lean's offer to cast him in *Lawrence of Arabia* [released in 1962]. He was proud to be an Indian actor.

YASH CHOPRA

MY ELDER BROTHER B. R. CHOPRA SAHAB was very keen on making a film with Dilip Kumar in the lead. B. R. Sahab had arrived on the scene as a director with the Ashok Kumar starrer superhit *Afsana* [1951] and he wanted Dilip Sahab to star in the production house's first offering.

Dilip Sahab remained genuinely unaffected by the extraordinary success that was coming to him with his every new film. He was choosy about the subject, the director and the production house. He was also known to work in only one or two films at a time and remained uninterested in cashing in on his huge mass appeal.

Chopra Sahab had the story of *Naya Daur* [released in 1957] and was confident that Dilip Sahab would like it. It had a social intent and a timely message for the country, which was on the threshold of changes in the rural economic scenario. He approached Dilip Sahab who had recently swept film-lovers off their feet with his moving portrayal of Devdas in the eponymous film [released in 1955]. His character, who takes heavily to alcohol as an escape from his desolate and lovelorn life, had had the most incredible impact on the youth; the message was clear – resorting to alcohol wasn't a means to escape reality. I don't think any other actor could have achieved that.

It was a day of great excitement when Dilip Sahab decided to visit our office near Lido Cinema [in Bombay], to listen to the narration. We were instructed to be well-dressed as Dilip Sahab was noted for his impeccable sartorial sense – white trousers and full-sleeved crisply ironed white shirts. When he alighted from his car, he smiled at me as I rushed to open the door; he then spotted Chopra Sahab who had come out to receive him, and shaking his hand warmly, turned around to greet every staff member. After the narration, Dilip Sahab admitted that he liked the story idea but unfortunately he was committed to do a film for Gyan Mukherjee with whom he had an old association from his Bombay Talkies days. He would surely consider the project after completing Mukherjee's film. As noted earlier, he acted in only two films at a time and a third would not be accommodated no matter how interesting the offer. He was very particular about that.

My brother was visibly disturbed for some days. He had discussed the subject of *Naya Daur* with two men he respected very much: The first was Ashok Kumar who categorically told him it would be foolish to cast anyone but Dilip Sahab in the lead because the role fit him to the T; he also spoke to Mehboob Khan whose counterpoint was that the story had little dramatic potential and Dilip Kumar would be wasted in the lead role.

And then an unfortunate incident changed everything. Mukherjee passed away and the project was dropped. So there was room now for one more movie in Dilip Sahab's work plan for the year. Talks resumed with him and I was witness to the exuberance in the B. R. Chopra unit, as it was an honour to be associated with a Dilip Kumar starrer.

I was third assistant to my brother at that time, having arrived in Bombay just five years ago. Within the unit I was receiving training in direction, production management, editing, cinematography and so on. As B. R. Chopra's brother, I had access to all the departments of film making but as a unit hand I was on par with the others.

To my excitement and nervousness, I was put in charge of Dilip Kumar, who suggested that his shack in Juhu be used for the story sittings, and it was my responsibility to accompany him. Dilip Sahab spent an entire month with the writer, Akhtar Mirza, and Chopra Sahab. He took up each scene with the dialogue and enacted it bringing in drama, sentiment, humour, pathos and deep emotion that would dazzle us all and render us speechless. He would show us variations in the enactment that would enthral us. He not only dwelt on the moulding of his character but also on the character to be played by Ajit. He was unselfish to the core and made sure that Ajit's part was equally strong and sensitively written. The same measure of sincerity went into the delineation of the heroine's role.

That one month was an education I cherished all my life. For a student of the medium, it was like going to an institution and learning the craft of acting, direction, writing and visualization. Dilip Kumar became my guru in the real sense during the making of *Naya Daur*.

The climax of the film was a big challenge for Akhtar Mirza. How was he to convince the audience that a horse-driven tonga could beat a motor vehicle in a race? Well, it was Dilip Sahab who gave Mirza the idea of the tonga taking a short-cut route to touch the finishing point – something that was logical and convincing.

Naya Daur was to bring together the charismatic Dilip Kumar–Madhubala pair. However, Madhubala's father, Ataullah Khan created a problem after a schedule in Poona (now Pune). He simply stated that his daughter would not work in a film that was to be shot outdoors. Chopra Sahab was livid! It was an unreasonable demand as it was well understood by the actress and her father that a large chunk of the shooting would be outdoors when the script was presented to them. Evidently, Ataullah Khan had his own axe to grind, but Chopra Sahab was adamant about taking the daughter–father duo to court.

It was no secret that Dilip Sahab and Madhubala were in love. But when the law suit was slapped on Madhubala, Dilip Sahab supported Chopra Sahab.

There was a day's shooting in a timber shop near Andheri railway station [in Bombay] before the last hearing. Dilip Sahab came to the shoot looking rather disturbed. After the shooting he said to me: 'Yash, I am relieved that it is all over. Let us not have any bitterness on either side.' He also told Chopra Sahab who won the case: 'You have proved to the world that they let you down. Now forgive them and let them be.' Chopra Sahab did just that.

It was like a blessing in disguise for Chopra Sahab when Vyjayantimala walked into the project. Dilip Sahab calmly went along, firmly of the opinion that the producer had the prerogative to choose the cast and technicians. Vyjayantimala and Dilip Sahab made a superb pair.

Dilip Sahab is not a method actor as many cineastes think. He is a spontaneous actor who draws from his inner emotional reserves when he performs those marvellous dramatic scenes. I am saying this after watching him closely for fifty years or more. This alone was the reason why he had to seek the help of a psychiatrist to purge himself of the melancholy that had set in after all the tragic films he did in a row at the start of his stardom. In his personal life he was a loner till he married Saira. His evenings were spent with friends whose intellects could hardly match his. His siblings were different from him. He spent a lot of time reading and writing and working on the interpretation of the roles and screenplays that he selected.

I recall that as the shooting for *Naya Daur* was about to commence, it was my responsibility to escort Dilip Sahab from his bungalow to the shoot in Poona. I was given a small car, which was to follow the limousine arranged for him. When he came out, ready to leave he looked at both the cars. He understood that the limousine was meant for him and the small one for me. He walked to the small car, opened the door and sat in the backseat, asking me to sit beside him. I was worried as I knew I would be pulled up by my brother if I let him travel by the small car. However, when we sat in the car he gave me a warm smile and assured me that he would handle things.

Our journey to Poona was most memorable for me. Dilip Sahab put me completely at ease and regaled me with various episodes from his life, including how he earned his first big income with his enterprise at the Army Club in Poona. He described the sandwiches he sold at the stall he had set up there while engaging me in a lively Punjabi conversation.

The privilege of spending long hours with him during rehearsals and when he gave his final shots is unmatched. He was extremely serious about his work; emotions just surfaced naturally when he was before the camera. In the final take, therefore he invariably did what he felt was best.

In Bhopal we shot in a village called Boudini. We travelled by train and had a new building meant for a hospital entirely at our disposal. Both the outdoors had a contingent of 250 junior artistes and a hundred other unit members, including technicians and their assistants. Not even once through the entire course of the shooting in both Poona and Bhopal did I see or hear Dilip Sahab asking for preferential treatment. If the assistants brought outdoor umbrellas, he would ask for them to be given to the ladies in the unit or to the older junior artistes. He would sit with everybody and eat the food cooked for the unit. In the evenings, after pack-up, he took the initiative to create entertainment. He played football, badminton, carom, table tennis, sang, joked, patiently listened to personal anecdotes and shared genuine camaraderie.

I thank god for giving me the opportunity to befriend a man who was exceptional in every respect.

FARIDA DADI

*M*Y FIRST CASTING ITSELF WAS IN A FILM STARRING DILIP SAHAB. It was Filmalaya's *Charity Master*, produced by S. Mukherjee Sahab, sometime before his next production *Leader* (released in 1964). *Charity Master* was never made for some reason. After that, I was selected to play a child character in *Dil Diya Dard Liya* (released in 1966). By then, I was quite aware of what film shooting was all about. Although A. R. Kardar was billed as the film's director, it was Dilip Sahab who was directing the film in actuality.

I watched him in awe as he arranged everything in minute detail for the shots and, at the same time, took care of everybody on the sets. He was ever so respectful towards the elders on the sets and my mother was completely floored by the genuine respect he gave her and took care of her comforts. It was not every day that we come across such a celebrity who spoke with humility and put us at ease without being condescending.

On the first day of my shoot at Kardar Studios in Bombay for *DDDL*, I could not reach on time as I was held up in Madras. Dilip Sahab cancelled the shooting saying: '*Agar ek bada artiste nahin aa sakta to shoot cancel hota hai to Farida ke liye bhi cancel ho sakta hai.*'* That was a great gesture.

The outdoor shooting of *DDDL* took place in the fortified city of Mandu in Madhya Pradesh. While we moved from one location to another in Mandu, picturizng scenes against rocky landscapes and performing our scenes on the rugged plateaus, I saw the selfless and tireless devotion with which Dilip Sahab was doing not only his own work but also egging on other artistes to do theirs.

I think I must have done my scenes in *DDDL* to Dilip Sahab's satisfaction. When the casting for *Ram Aur Shyam* (released in 1967) began, he asked the production manager to bring me and my mother to his bungalow to brief me about my character and the dresses that had to be stitched for me. It was an achievement for me to be chosen by Dilip Kumar.

He told my mother about the shooting that will go on in Madras and he assured her that my studies would go on and he would speak to the school authorities to give me leave of absence. I was even more thrilled when I heard that the character required a much younger girl to be cast but Dilip Sahab had insisted on casting me.

The entire production of *Ram Aur Shyam* in Madras was memorable. All the artistes were accommodated in the Oceanic Hotel and once again it was Dilip Sahab who was marshalling the manpower and organizing everything from the covers of the properties on the sets to the curtains to the artistes' wardrobes and jewellery. I trailed behind him everywhere and I saw how he synchronized the colours of the curtains and sofa covers

---

*If a big artiste cannot come, then the shoot is cancelled. For Farida too the shoot can be cancelled.

with the paint on the walls much to the amazement of the art director and never took the credit for it; instead he always let the compliments go to the art department. It was an education for me just observing him. It gave me some knowledge of how a film was made and I also learned valuable lessons of polite behaviour and speech.

All our evenings were spent in the open badminton court where Dilip Sahab played badminton with whoever wished to partner him. He was also busy editing *Aadmi* (released in 1968) during spare time and I think he refreshed himself by playing in the evenings. For me it was mandatory to open my books and study after one game. He was very particular about that. Dilip Sahab always had lunch with the entire unit and saw to it that everyone was comfortable.

One experience I cannot forget on the sets of *Ram Aur Shyam* relates to the scene in which Pran Sahab (who plays my father in the film) flings the birthday cake and shouts at me. I was supposed to cry spontaneously when the cake is thrown away. When the time for the take came, somehow the tears would not come. I tried a few times and I could see that Sahab was getting impatient. I went up to him and told him quietly that when he wanted the tears in the final take he had to just come to me and whisper in my ears and I would bring out the tears. I requested him not to shout at me in front of the crew. He agreed and, as I had requested, he came and whispered in my ear that all was set. He called for action and try as I might there were no tears coming from me. He got really angry and yelled at me and told the entire gathering how I had requested him not to shout. There it started! A cascade of tears began to flow from eyes and the final take was at once canned. Whenever I watch the film with my grandchildren I tell them to observe that memorable scene carefully and it amuses them no end.

I remember an evening when I set out with Dilip Sahab to the room where *Aadmi* was being edited. I had forgotten to inform my mother. When I returned, my mother was waiting for me with a stick. She whacked me but Dilip Sahab did not intervene. He let me have it because he felt my mother was right: I should have asked her permission before going out.

During the shooting of *Ram Aur Shyam*, Dilip Sahab married Saira Banu. It was like a royal marriage and the reception planned by the producer Nagi Reddy Sahab and the entire unit at the Meenambakkam airport (in Madras) when Dilip Sahab came back with his beautiful bride to resume the shooting was also like a royal welcome. All the artistes and Nagi Reddy Sahab waited at the airport with large garlands to welcome them on the tarmac itself. Rose petals were strewn for them to walk on and I could not take my eyes off Saira's beautiful face. For days after that *mogras* (jasmine) were regularly arranged in their room. I had heard that Saira was snooty, so I kept away from her, little knowing that it was really not true. She was reserved by nature and nothing more! Hardly did I know then that she and I were destined to become fast friends over a period of time.

With Saira's arrival, the atmosphere on the sets became more lively and festive as Dilip Sahab was in a really great mood most times and it was wonderful to see the camaraderie between Pran Sahab and Dilip Sahab.

As time passed, I became a frequent visitor at Saira's bungalow in Bombay. Dilip Sahab was like an elder brother and Saira became, more than a friend, a sister. As time passed, they taught me to respect and love my mother and father and perhaps unconsciously their feelings for elders in their family began rubbing off on me. Whether it was a marriage or a sad occasion in my house they have always been by my side. I think I was born lucky or else I would not have met them in this life.

DHARMENDRA

*S*OMETIME IN 1952 WHEN I WAS IN THE second year of college I travelled to Bombay from the small town of Ludhiana, in Punjab, where we lived. I had no definite plans of becoming an actor back then but I definitely wanted to meet Dilip Kumar whose acting in *Shaheed* had touched a deep emotional chord within me. For some inexplicable reason I began to fancy that Dilip Kumar and I were siblings.

The very next day after I reached Bombay I boldly went to his house in Bandra's Pali Mala locality to meet him. I wasn't stopped at the gate by anybody, and so I walked right into the house through the main door. There was a wooden staircase leading to a bedroom upstairs. Again, nobody stopped me, so I climbed up the stairs and stood at the entrance to one of the rooms. A fair, slim, handsome youth was asleep on a couch. He must have sensed someone's presence and suddenly woke up somewhat startled. I stood still not knowing what to do. He sat up on the couch and stared at me, quite taken aback to see a total stranger standing gingerly at his bedroom door gazing admiringly at him. As for me, I couldn't believe my eyes: It was Dilip Kumar, my idol, in front of me. He called out to a servant loudly. Now scared, I ran down the staircase and bolted out of the house looking behind to see if I was being followed.

When I reached a cafeteria I went inside and asked for a cold lassi. As I sat in the cafeteria and thought back to what I had done, I realized how reckless I had been by intruding into the privacy of a star. So what if there was no watchman at the gate and no family member in the house to stop me? In the villages of Punjab the houses were always open to anybody who cared to drop in. There was a strong bond amongst the people with no barriers and you could just walk into a house without any formalities and be welcome at any time of the day or night. I was very happy to see my idol living just the way we lived in Punjab. But then, I had blundered by taking it for granted that I did not need an introduction. This was Bombay, the big city, and the house belonged to the star Dilip Kumar!

Six years later, I returned to Bombay to take part in the United Producers' and *Filmfare* Talent Contest. I was truly keen on becoming an actor now and I had convinced my father who had yielded to let me join films. I was declared a winner and, following that, I was asked to report at the *Filmfare* office for a photo shoot. I did not know how to apply make-up and the photographer was impressed by my face but he wanted a little touch up. A fair, slender girl came to me with a make-up kit and she began to touch up my face. The then editor of *Filmfare*, L. P. Rao, asked me softly whether I knew who the girl was. On saying I didn't, he told me she was Farida, Dilip Sahab's sister, who was working with *Femina*. I saw her leaving and I ran after her requesting her to [arrange to] meet Dilip Sahab. I told her I firmly believed that he was my brother too. She was amused but she agreed to call L. P. Rao if her brother agreed.

The next day she called me over to their bungalow, 48 Pali Hill at 8.30 p.m. Time stood still for me when Dilip Sahab came out and welcomed me and gave me a chair to sit beside him on the lawns. He talked to me like an elder brother, full of love and concern and narrated how he became an actor and how difficult it was for him in the beginning to understand the demands of the profession since he came from a non-filmi background. I just listened to him spellbound as he spoke in English, Punjabi and Urdu in his soft, refined voice. I just could not believe that I was actually sitting next to him and he was talking to me. When I was leaving, he took me upstairs to his room and gave me a sweater from his cupboard because it was a bit chilly and he had noticed I was wearing just a thin cotton shirt. He hugged me and saw me off at the gate. I can still feel the warmth of that hug because it was genuine.

I met him on many occasions thereafter and it was always he who came towards me and held my hand because I never took the liberty of going up to him as an equal. I remember when I was signed by Bimal Roy for *Bandini* [released in 1963] I was called to Mehboob Studios for a discussion by Bimalda. I waited outside the studio floor for Bimalda who was having lunch with Dilip Sahab. A little later, both came out and it did not take an instant for Dilip Sahab to see me and greet me warmly and tell Bimalda that I was his younger brother. The introduction boosted my confidence and I can never forget his generosity and goodness.

Without exaggeration I can say that every actor who came into the business after him and who are continuing to seek employment in the industry has emulated him. I did not try that or even mimic him simply because I didn't dare to. I evolved my own style of acting. But I have attempted to copy his goodness, his humility, his kindness, his warmth, his sincerity and his concern for the producer who sinks his money into a film project. He became the beacon in my life when stardom and success came to me and I did not know how to handle it. He warned me to keep sycophants away. He said the real test of your own family's love for you will be when you do what you want to do for your happiness and not what they want you to do for their happiness.

I may not meet him for months but I think of him every day because his photograph is the only photograph I have kept in my house beside the photographs of my parents and of my sons. When I was working with Saira I used to tell her jovially that I am in competition with her for the love of Yousuf Sahab.

I learnt from my parents that if you are intrinsically good, god bestows his choicest blessings on you. For all his goodness, Yousuf Sahab has been blessed by Allah with a wife who loves him madly and serves him unselfishly

24/7. I missed attending their marriage because I was shooting somewhere and my producer could not let me go.

I was very close to Dilip Sahab's family. He used to put us all, including his siblings, in his cars and take us for ice-cream to Badshah's at Mohammad Ali Road [in Bombay] during Ramzaan after breaking the fast. I felt on top of the world at every opportunity I got to be with him. I observed his exemplary behaviour and his natural humility when he interacted with his admirers. From the most exalted admirer, Pandit Jawaharlal Nehru, to the lowest paid studio worker who waited to say [sic] salaams to him, his warm extension of his hands in greeting was the same. He never faked anything, be it his appreciation for another actor's good work or his concern for a colleague who was in distress.

I never got a chance to work with him but he made a special appearance in a film I starred in. The film was *Paari* [1967] , produced by [actor] Abhi Bhattacharya's wife Pronoti Ghosh. Abhi Bhattacharya was his dear friend. That, for me, was a feather in my cap.

——•◦ ;◦; ◦•——

Sitara Devi

 *I* saw Dilip Bhai for the first time when my husband K. Asif invited him over to our house to consider him for the role of Salim in *Anarkali*, the film he was planning to make at that time. It must have been around 1945 as the war [the Second World War] had just ended and the need for entertainment in a depressed society was very strong. A financier had come forward to finance Asif and he was all for making a historical subject with spectacle and emotions.

Asif had heard about this handsome new actor and so he said: 'Let me take a look at him.' He had Sapru [who later became a character actor] in mind but was happy considering a new actor if he was good.

When Dilip Bhai came over and he walked into our living room I was speechless for a moment. I had expected a young man of reasonable good looks and personality but right in front of me was a young man who was not just handsome but was radiant, sophisticated and regal in bearing and manner. One could tell in an instant that he was someone special, someone who had Allah's blessing.

Asif and Dilip Bhai talked for a while and then he left. Asif was no doubt impressed but he felt Dilip Bhai was too lean. He felt Salim had to be played by an actor with the physique of a Mughal prince. What he then said proved indeed prophetic. 'May be ten years from now if I rewrite a screenplay of the love story of Anarkali and Salim, he will be the actor I'd choose for Salim because he is born with princely qualities but is not ready yet for the role.'

Our friendship began from that visit. Dilip Bhai went on to attain stardom and Asif cast Sapru in the role. But the film never got completed. The role was destined to be played by Dilip Bhai many years later and create its own magic.* A healthy friendship blossomed between Asif and Dilip Bhai. As everybody knows Dilip Bhai was equally proficient, both in English and Urdu. Asif's flair for Urdu prose and poetry perhaps brought the two close. Other than that there was nothing in common between them. Dilip Bhai was soft spoken, refined, polite, shy and very elegant in his attire and manners. He was a star but was bereft of any pretensions. In fact, those were times when the industry worked more like a family and personal relations counted more than any material consideration when a team got together to make a film.

Dilip Bhai was known as a star who worked diligently and fully co-operated with the producer once he signed a film. He was known to be choosy, of course. He chose his producer and director with care and so it made big news and gave the producer reason to celebrate when Dilip Kumar agreed to work with him. We – Asif, Dilip Bhai and I – went out often to visit common friends. When people began to gossip about our threesome going out to dine and so on, I tied him a Raakhee,** something I have kept up to this day. I go to his house each year on Raksha Bandhan, and my sweet bhabhi Saira, who is actually like a daughter to me since her mother Naseem and I were contemporaries, makes each occasion very special for me.

Dilip Bhai was, and still is, a shy man. The only time I felt he was drawn to a co-star was when he worked with Kamini Kaushal. I feel she was his first love. She was educated and well spoken like him and could engage him in intelligent conversation. Her real name was Uma [Kashyap] and she had

*The film is the epic *Mughal-e-Azam* (1960).
**A sacred thread that a sister ties on her brother's wrist.

married her sister's husband when her sister died and had become mother to her kids. So there was no way Dilip Bhai could have married her. When people started talking about them – the Dilip–Kamini pair had become a hit with *Shaheed*, *Shabnam* – I ventured to ask him one day if there was any truth in the gossip. He remained silent and changed the subject. A couple of months later he dropped in unexpectedly. Asif and I noticed that he was sad and hurt and he would break down. He was only in his mid-twenties then and I guessed it was the pain of breaking up with his love. Uma (Kamini) had been served a warning by her brother and she had informed Dilip Bhai that she wouldn't be working with him or seeing him any more. As he spoke to us, I saw tears welling up in his sad eyes.

In my view the heart-breaking moment in Dilip Bhai's life was not the break-up with Uma but the time he learnt that Asif and Dilip Bhai's sister Akhtar had eloped and married. By then I was out of Asif's life as the wicked man had wooed and married my friend Nigar Sultana. When he had cast Nigar in *Mughal-e-Azam* he had made it seem as if he was doing it to please me as Nigar and I were good friends. But when he told me one fine day that he was going to marry Nigar, I couldn't figure out who was the bigger fool – I or Nigar? I accepted his marriage to Nigar and also embraced the children born of the marriage because the kids would keep coming to me with all their innocent love. But his back stabbing Dilip Bhai was unacceptable to me. So I cursed him and told him he'd die for the sin he had committed by cheating Dilip Bhai who trusted him implicitly and had let him mingle with his sisters. I swore I wouldn't see Asif's face and severed all relations with him.

Dilip Bhai was shattered because he had great hopes for Akhtar. All the six sisters were lucky to have a brother like him. He did everything possible to give them education and a good life. Only his eldest sister Sakina Aapa missed formal education and she remained a spinster. I knew Akhtar had had her college education in the USA and Dilip Bhai was very proud of her. Naturally then, it hurt him when she chose to marry a much-married man, twice her age.

The only reason why Dilip Bhai did not attend the premiere of *Mughal-e-Azam* and even refused to see the movie at trial shows was because Asif had betrayed his trust.

I still remember the day I received the news of Asif's death [9 March 1971]. I had wound up a dance programme at Shanmukhananda Hall [in Bombay]

and returned home. A phone call at two in the morning from Gopi Krishna [a famous classical dancer] sent a chill down my spine. I somehow sensed the news wasn't good. Asif had called me two days ago and I had promised to meet him after the dance recital at Shanmukhananda Hall when I returned home. Gopi gave me the news and offered to go with me to see Asif's face for the last time. I could hear my own voice ringing in my ears for I had told him he'd die a premature death for betraying Dilip Bhai.

M. ASIF FAROOQUI*

$\mathcal{D}$URING THE LOK SABHA ELECTION (2014), I was a little listless, not being able to summon all my energies to campaign. One day, Roshan Baig (a Congress leader and a cabinet minister in Kartnataka) called me and inquired about my well-being and my political activity considering the impassioned state of the elections this summer. I honestly told him that I was unusually low this time. He reprimanded me gently saying: 'You must get your act together Asif. I want to see the Asif of the previous elections.' 'I know', I acknowledged and, as if on an impulse, added: 'Dilip Sahab is not active politically and without him guiding me, politics doesn't seem the same.' Roshan Baig sighed in agreement: 'You are right Asif, you are right. Without Dilip Sahab by our side, things are just not what they used to be.'

Dilip Sahab is my guiding light not just in politics, but also in life. When I first expressed an inclination to join politics, he advised me to get associated with social causes – those that involved the uplift of the downtrodden. For him politics was about humanity. It was not about becoming popular. And that is one of the most important lessons that I learnt from him.

To this date, he enjoys the patronage of the eminent statesmen. When the late Sunil Dutt Sahab (who passed away on 25 May 2005) wanted to resign from his parliamentary seat in early 1996 due to a moral stand he

*A family friend and a member of the Congress party.

had taken, it was Dilip Sahab who stood behind him. This gave Sunil Dutt Sahab the strength to run the risk of earning the displeasure of the then prime minister, P. V. Narasimha Rao. I was a witness to this entire episode. Sunil Dutt Sahab, in a very agitated state of mind, kept calling Dilip Sahab, who was out travelling with me, at his residence. In 1996, mobile phones were a rarity. I had just bought one and Dutt Sahab finally traced Dilip Sahab, whom he called from my phone. All along Dilip Sahab kept saying: 'Don't worry, I'm there with you.' And he did stand behind Dutt Sahab during those testing times. And always he did so.

The world knows and describes Dilip Kumar using epithets such as THE LEGEND and THE SUPERSTAR. However, I know him as a true symbol of the Ganga-Jamuni culture that defines the spirit of India, a true gentleman, an honourable and compassionate human being and an unobtrusive leader of leaders.

I have had the honour of being associated with him for almost 30 years – since my teens – and now as I sit back and try to understand the dynamics of this most unlikely companionship between an icon like him and an unknown person like me, I rummage through the crevices of my memory.

'*Beta, tumhaare liye kisi Yousuf Khan ka phone aaya tha*,'* my mother informed me as soon as I reached home on evening, sometime in 1984. '*Kaun* [who] *Yousuf Khan?*' I asked. My mother replied: '*Pata nahin, par unki awaaz badi bhaari thi*.'** Could it have been Dilip Kumar? I asked myself, that evening.

A friend of mine, one Dr Zuber, happened to know Dilip Sahab and he wanted me to go along with him to meet him. I was reluctant. 'Why should I meet Dilip Kumar?' I asked him. I was not particularly interested in the film world as I come from a family in which religion, tradition and austerity came above all else and films were taboo. Even if one wanted to enjoy a movie, it had to be done surreptitiously. Nevertheless, I agreed to meet Dilip Sahab after much prodding from my friend.

Any outsider always views the cinema world with a lot of prejudice. I ambled along to his house, expecting nothing. But the *mulaaqaat†* was nothing short of an eye-opener, a blind-remover which resulted in an association of almost three decades. My first impression of Dilip Sahab was

---

*Son, there were a call for you from some Yousuf Khan.
**I don't know, but his voice was very heavy.
†*Mulaaqaat* means 'meeting'. However, meeting does not convey the informality of *mulaaqaat* and hence the usage of the Urdu word seems most apt here.

that he was extremely warm and gracious as a host. He enquired about us and I still wonder what made him take down my house phone number. And that's when he called.

I went over and the Dilip Kumar I met during the first visit was as gracious and warm. He wanted to know my whereabouts and what I was up to. It was a magnanimous gesture from a man whom everyone wanted to be familiar with. But I was impressionable, too young to understand that human relationships are forged in the simplest of ways and do not recognize the walls created by prejudices of perception.

As my interactions with him increased, I started becoming acutely aware of the difference between Dilip Kumar and Yousuf Khan. While Dilip Kumar was the icon that the masses loved and idolized, Yousuf Khan was the man who remained unscathed by the ways of the world. Once he told me: 'Yousuf Khan is scared of Dilip Kumar.' I asked him what he meant by this. With an ambiguous glint in his eye, he would exclaim: 'Only Allah knows who Dilip Kumar is and what all he can do!'

I have seen him read the Quran like a true scholar. What is remarkable is the way he tries to understand the message of the Quran. He has minutely read each sentence and made notes on the pages in red, green and blue ink. Whenever he needs clarifications, he seeks the advice of Islamic scholars.

He is basically very simple and down to earth. As Yousuf Khan, he can interact with, say, a chauffeur, a riskshawallah or a domestic help, and they would feel that he is one of them. Dilip Kumar, on the other hand, is the one who effortlessly mingles with the dignitaries and leaders from all over the world. The dividing line between the two is extremely thin and is a matter of perspective.

I knew him for barely a few years prior to my marriage in 1991. We didn't even have the time to print cards for my wedding. I verbally invited him to be a part of the occasion and, quite unexpectedly, he turned up. He could have thought: 'I am THE Dilip Kumar and this boy has not even sent me an official invitation. So, why should I go?' But he did not do so. He has always been above such petty things. Commitment has always been his priority. Once he asked me to attend a wedding with him somewhere in Santa Cruz (east) in Mumbai. I thought it was of a VIP. It turned out to be the wedding of a poor man's relative whom he did not know personally and since the former had invited Dilip Sahab, he felt it was necessary to attend.

That his popularity is legendary, I do not have to overemphasize. However, let me recount an episode. In 1998, we were in Kuwait, when Dilip Sahab was invited for tea by the CEO of Kuwait Airways. The Indian ambassador, who was also invited, asked Dilip Sahab if this was his first visit to Kuwait. He said that he had come here many years ago and tried to recollect the year. The CEO excitedly blurted out: 'In 1963, sir.' We all looked at him in surprise. The CEO continued: 'I was in school at that time and we had a holiday. The buzz was that an extremely popular Indian actor was visiting Kuwait. Imagine my good fortune that I am with you today, thirty-five years later.'

He is part of people's consciousness. I have seen people of all walks of life and belonging to different countries eager to meet him not only in India but also in places such as UAE, the UK and the USA. I was with him in 2013 when he did the *tawaaf* (circumambulation) around the holy Kaaba in Mecca and the amount of attention he got was to be seen to be believed.

They say you know a man only when you travel with him. Over all these years of travelling with him, I have realized that Dilip Sahab, though an extremely renowned person across the world, never asks anything for himself. His heart beats for the underprivileged. I have had the good fortune of being with him at various meetings at the topmost level. One such was with Prime Minister Narasimha Rao, when Dilip Sahab had gone to New Delhi to plead the case of those who were displaced during the 1992-93 Mumbai riots. There have been several such instances where he sough help for others. Never for himself.

Dilip Sahab has often recounted to me his fond memories of Pandit Jawaharlal Nehru, who had influenced him ideologically and he had had the privilege of meeting several times. I think his political idealism was modelled on that of Pandit Nehru. He has told me many times about how Pandit Nehru used to 'encourage us youngsters to indulge in debate about the nation and nation building.' As I mentioned earlier, he has always channelized my political ambitions into social causes. Aspire to work for society and the underprivileged is what I have learnt from him.

Another thing that I have learned is the importance of family. Coincidentally, both Dilip Sahab and I have five brothers each. He loved the fact that there is so much unity among us brothers, since he himself is very close to his family. 'The family is your pillar, Asif. Lean on it and give it your shoulder. Always be together.' This advice has always benefited us.

●◦ ⟨⊙⟩ ◦●

SUBHASH GHAI

*L*IKE ALL SERIOUS YOUNG FILM MAKERS who believe in making great movies I also had a dream of making a film that would be remembered and talked about. And how does one do that? By making a film with the great Dilip Kumar, of course.

I had a subject centring on a grandfather and grandson and a strong desire to cast Dilip Kumar in the role of the grandfather. The year was 1980 and I was trying to zero in on someone who could introduce me to Dilip Sahab as a serious film maker when the well-known film distributor, R. N. Mandre, who lived in Bangalore (now Bengaluru), said he would do the honours. I flew to Bangalore for the meeting; more nervous than excited as I had just made a flop film and was sure Dilip Sahab had read about it. Also, I had a story to tell but no bound script. Many of my acquaintances had said Dilip Sahab did not entertain anybody who came without a bound script.

When I came face to face with him he was warm and cordial. The three of us, Dilip Sahab, Mandre Sahab and myself talked about everything happening in the country except my story. I was hoping he would ask me why I was there and I would tell him. But he did not ask. So I mustered up the courage and told him I had a story for his consideration. He told me to go ahead with the narration. After hearing me out, he said nothing except that he would meet me the next day.

We met the next day, the next and the next, but he didn't bring up the subject. On the fourth day I finally asked him what he thought of my story. Then, he smiled and told me the story had potential and he would consider working in it. That truly was the moment of my life!

I returned to Bombay, triumphant, and informed Gulshan Rai, the producer, that Dilip Sahab had liked the subject and was willing to work in the film. Naturally, he too was thrilled.

Days passed and Gulshanji kept asking me when he could announce the film and splash Dilip Kumar's name. Meanwhile, people started asking me if what they had heard was true and proudly I would say, 'yes,' but the look on their faces would convey: 'This is the end of your career.' Some went to the extent of saying: 'You know how he is. He will make you sit somewhere outside the set and direct the film himself. What's more, at the end of it all you will wonder what happened to your story because he will change everything. And by the time the movie is completed you will have aged because he takes years to complete a film.'

All this was worrying. When we met at his bungalow I was somewhat fidgety and he sensed something was going on in my mind. I told him I was worried for two reasons. First, I needed a confirmation from him because Gulshan Rai was still doubting me and secondly … I took a deep breath… who will direct the film – him or me?

Dilip Sahab smiled gently, pointed his finger at me and said: 'You.'

Gulshanji was very happy but he gave me the responsibility of talking money with Dilip Sahab. I took an appointment with him and went over one evening where a lavish tea was laid out as was customary in Dilip Sahab's house. Both Sairaji and he have this wonderful way of entertaining guests. He serves the guest himself with utmost delight, and will keep you enthralled with his conversation.

I then bravely broached the subject of money. He shot a look at me and asked: 'Is that what you have come to see me for?' I froze and left without talking money. I understood in due course as the shooting began that god had thrown me in the company of a man for whom money, stardom, all visible material trappings and symbols of social status, which mattered to others in the profession, had little meaning. He worked in a film if he liked the subject and more importantly, if he liked the director and the whole set-up. Money was the least of his concerns.

All through the making of *Vidhaata* [released in 1982], Dilip Sahab paid great attention to my visualization of shots and cooperated to such an extent that the film was completed a month ahead of schedule. All the artistes were inspired by his dedication and he was like an elixir when we worked.

The picture was a superhit and it established me in the industry. But I gained far more. Keeping Dilip Sahab's company I changed completely; I became refined, began to speak and conduct myself with confidence, learnt to seize every opportunity to gain more knowledge, developed humility so precious when one achieves success and the world is at one's feet and never be condescending to those who come to you for help.

We kept in touch and we became close, with him treating me like his brother – a privilege I have earned perhaps from my karmas in a past life. When I wrote the story of *Karma* [released in 1986], I went to Dilip Sahab again, but with much more confidence now. This time I told him I had to prepare a budget and it would be ideal if I could get an idea of the remuneration he expected. He gave me that look again and said: 'I think it will be good if you don't behave like a Baniya.'* I feel proud that I made three films** with Dilip Sahab in the central role.

Dr Shrikant Gokhale

I HAVE HAD THE PRIVILEGE OF BEING NOT ONLY THE PERSONAL PHYSICIAN but also a friend of Dilip Sahab for four decades. I first met him when I was establishing myself as a general practitioner in Bandra, Mumbai.

Dilip Sahab's trusted valet Anwar used to come to my clinic for treatment of minor ailments and he always had a hundred rupee note rolled up in his shirt sleeve. Those days we charged ten rupees for examining and prescribing the medication. Every time he gave me a hundred rupee note, it was a problem for me to return ninety rupees as it meant exhausting all the change I had. I only knew him as Anwar and I used to wonder who the flamboyant guy was but I never asked him any questions. It is not in my nature to talk unnecessarily. He used to wear white trousers and white shirts and always walked with a swagger.

One day, he appeared suddenly and looked hassled. He said: 'You must come with me right away. Dilip Kumar wants you to see his sister as she is running a high temperature.'

I was taken aback. How did he know Dilip Kumar, who was the biggest star of Indian cinema at that time? I asked him for the first time who he was and how he was associated with Dilip Kumar. Then, somewhat sheepishly, he told me he was Dilip Sahab's valet.

That explained the white trousers and shirt and the showing off. The eternal truth is that while Dilip Sahab himself has remained extremely humble and untouched by the huge stardom he has always enjoyed, the men around him, including his brothers, never hesitated to pretend they were the star Dilip Kumar. In my long association with Dilip Sahab, I have come across numerous men who wore white trousers and long-sleeved shirts,

*Baniya is a trader community.
**The third film is *Saudagar* (1991).

tousled their hair and tried to be Dilip Kumar. I understand it is natural to be influenced by the idol a person looks up to. At the same time, the fan seldom realizes that there is more to Dilip Kumar than the handsome looks.

That Dilip Sahab is gifted with unparalleled talents is something we all know. The unique thing is that he is also gifted with unparalleled human qualities like honesty, compassion and respectfulness towards all. Even the lowliest admirer who comes to his car or his door is greeted affectionately by him.

When I visited him the first time at the bungalow to treat his elder sister Sakina Aapa, he was staying in the outhouse of his large bungalow, having given the entire bungalow to his sisters and brothers to live in comfort and freedom. He was in the verandah, waiting for me. I was shy because he was a huge star and I did not know how to deal with a celebrity. He noticed my shyness and he began talking to me in Marathi (my mother tongue). In an instant, my hesitation melted and it was as if I was meeting an old friend from my hometown, not a superstar. I prescribed some medicines and I could sense his concern as he repeatedly felt her febrile brow and assured her she would be well soon.

He saw me off and I went home wondering whether it was really Dilip Kumar, the superstar that I met. Thereafter, I was called to treat any of his brothers and sisters if they took ill. By and by I got to know him better and we became friends.

It did not take long for me to realize what a wonderful human being he is. After some months of knowing each other and after several visits to his bungalow to give medications to his sisters for which he always paid me well, I mentioned to him during a visit that I was going on a holiday with my wife and so I would not be available for a week or so. He was happy to hear that and said it would be a good idea to go to some tranquil place and enjoy the change of environment. We shook hands and I left for my clinic. In the evening the same day, I received an envelope from him and it contained a note and a cheque signed by him. The note said: 'This is to make your holiday more special.' I was really touched.

I have travelled with him to places as a friend and physician and it was such a pleasure. He remained completely unaffected by the tumultuous attention he got everywhere and took very good care of all those who accompanied him. I have seen top politicians, ministers and industrialists clamouring to meet him and there was never an air of self-importance when he faced such situations. He met everybody with equal grace and dignity.

Once, in winter, we travelled by train from Bombay to Ratlam (in

Madhya Pradesh) en route to attend a temple consecration ceremony in Ujjain (also in Madhya Pradesh; about 110 km from Ratlam). After all the mobbing and mass hysteria he encountered calmly in Ujjain, we boarded a train to return to Bombay. It was December and very cold. When we reached Bombay Central station, he wanted to have some hot tea. I told him we could stop on our way home at an Irani restaurant in a locality called Mahim, which I knew opened very early. He liked the idea and we headed straight for the restaurant. The waiters were still not fully awake as they moved around. So at first they did not realize who had walked into the restaurant. Then they saw Dilip Sahab and ran to fetch their owner, who came and stood by our table unable to believe what he was seeing. Dilip Sahab greeted him as if he were a regular visitor and ordered chai (tea) and omelette with bun *maska* (butter). Dilip Sahab spoke to him like a true Irani and the man was grinning from ear to ear.

By then, the news had spread and a small crowd had collected outside. It took a while for the dishes to be ready and, in that much time, the crowd had swelled. A police van too arrived. People were shouting 'Dilip Kumar, Dilip Kumar' and clamouring to see Dilip Sahab. The owner was getting scared now because the crowd could go wild. Dilip Sahab was ready to go out and meet his admirers who were now singing songs from his films. It was only 7 a.m. The police now came inside and requested Dilip Sahab to leave by the back door but he was reluctant to do so. Instead, he went to the entrance and spoke to the crowd, which was cordoned off by the police. The people gathered there soon calmed down and I could see how happy they were that their idol had not run away through the back door.

I have always seen the respect he gives to the admirers who come to meet him and to the countless fans who used to gather at venues when he addressed election rallies. He is a deeply patriotic Indian and makes no distinction between religions, regions, communities and languages. His heart goes out to the elderly and the aged and he loves children. When we have driven through the city, he has often asked me: 'Shrikant, how can we change their [the impoverished children] lives and give them decent homes, water to bathe every day, go to school and have a normal childhood?' It pains him when he sees street urchins and little girls who come and press their smiling faces against the car window at traffic signals, recognizing him and hoping to get some coins from him. He gives generously and they know it but they don't know he is concerned and disturbed about their hapless condition.

I have been his friend and constant companion during travel for forty-odd years. His care and love for his sisters and brothers cannot be described in words. Likewise, his love and respect for Sairaji and her parents and grandmother are no less. He has given them and received the care and love of a son, not a son-in-law.

KAMAL HAASAN

I HAVE ALWAYS SAID THAT THERE ARE TWO actors who have been my primers: Sivaji Ganesan and Dilip Kumar Sahab. A slight regret I have is that I discovered the incredible beauty of Dilip Kumar Sahab's acting a bit late thanks to the linguistic politics in the state [Tamil Nadu] because of which one did not get to see Hindi films. It was during a conversation with Ramesh Sippy before I started work in his *Saagar* [released in 1985] that he asked me whether I had seen *Gunga Jumna*. I told him I had seen most of Dilip Sahab's early classics but I had not watched *Gunga Jumna*. He said: 'What are you saying; watch the film before you begin work in *Saagar*, it will help you.' He maintained that every actor should compulsorily watch *Gunga Jumna* for a study of screen histrionics. I did not delay watching *Gunga Jumna* after that chat and what a revelation it was!

I must say that it was after watching Dilip Kumar Sahab in films such as *Gunga Jumna*, *Mughal-e-Azam*, *Devdas*, *Kohinoor* and many other unforgettable classics that I began to understand the meaning of subtlety. I was able to appreciate the Western actors and the refinement of their acting also after I watched his films. It began to crystallize in my understanding of the eloquence of the medium that a mere look or sheer silence can convey so much and so powerfully. I agree it is not easy for every actor to achieve the brilliance he achieved with such seemingly effortless gestures but it is what every actor should try to emulate. My performances would not have been what they are if I had not studied Dilip Sahab's works. He changed much in the way actors performed in his time and he also changed a lot many actors' lives in later times, too, and I confess I am one of them.

I have some of the scenes in *Gunga Jumna,* for example, eternally embedded in my psyche. I am and always will be amazed by the layers of emotion he evoked in the viewer when he, as Prince Salim [in *Mughal-e-Azam*] simply sat in the royal darbar, saying nothing and doing nothing as Anarkali performed the provocative *Pyar kiya to darna kya* number. As an actor I know how difficult it is to create an impact in a sequence like that where you have nothing to do and you have to maintain the composure of the character of Prince Salim. I can go on like this about umpteen sequences in other films. As a student I have learned from them, too. He is the only actor who can hold a frame grippingly and it can be seen in *Shakti.* Rameshji told me he brought together two actors [the other being Amitabh Bachchan] who possessed the ability to hold a frame in many of the scenes of *Shakti,* which were talked about. From Dilip Sahab one learns that there can be immense power in stillness that still waters truly run deep.

I will confess unabashedly that some of the bricks of my house are Sivaji Sir's and Dilip Sahab's. Every time I have met Dilip Sahab I have found his humility and warmth unchanged. I remember Dilip Sahab attending the silver jubilee function of *Ek Duje Ke Liye.** I also recall his presence at the distribution of the trophies on the silver jubilee run of *Thevar Magan.*** I went up to him and told him: 'Sir, what an awesome film.' He was surprised and did not know which film I was referring to. Then, I told him I was referring to *Gunga Jumna.*

He remembers everything about you and is ever so glad to spend time with you every time you visit him. I visited him two years ago and he was so warm and loving that it was difficult to take leave of him and go my way. In the past, he had described some events from his childhood in Peshawar. They were terrific descriptions and they stayed on in my memory. I tried to bring the ambience he described alive on the screen in my *Vishwaroopam* [2013]. His knowledge of the arts and literature is amazing.

I am so happy to be a part of the book you are writing. I cannot wait to lay my hands on it.

———•◦ ⟡⊙⟡ ◦•———

*Released in 1981, in which Kamal Haasan is the hero.
**A 1992 Tamil film produced and written by Kamal Haasan, in which he also acts along with his idol Sivaji Ganesan.

FARIDA JALAL

*A*S A FAMILY WE, MY BROTHER KHALID, MY MOM and I, have been great fans of Dilip Sahab from the time we began to watch films. Khalid and I discussed Dilip Sahab's acting with such ardour that we sometimes even forgot to have our meals. Just talking about him and recalling scenes from his films was enough to fill our tummies. I am giving this background so that you can imagine the impact of a phone call I received one fine morning when I was shooting in Kashmir with my co-stars Rajesh Khanna and Sharmila Tagore in the late 1960s. The call was from Khalid who had heard from a reliable source that Dilip Sahab was considering me for his sister's role in *Gopi* (released in 1970). I first thought that Khalid was pulling a fast one on me. Then, when Khalid insisted he had heard the news from a friend who was not one to pass on frivolous information, I could not contain my joy. The whole day passed with me in a dream-like state and now, when I look back, I don't know how I conducted myself in the scenes I did that day.

The news was correct. As soon as I reached Bombay, I was asked to meet Dilip Sahab at his bungalow. I set out, along with my mother, with excitement and nervousness in my heart. It did not take more than a minute for me to feel completely relaxed when he came to meet us and began talking to me and my mother. He was so down to earth and so polite to my mother that it was an unbelievable experience for a rank newcomer like me.

He explained the role to me and then the most wonderful thing happened. Sairaji's mother, Naseem Banuji, the celebrated beauty and star, came into the room and I was introduced to her. She said that she would design the rustic costume my character would be wearing in the film. I could not believe that it was all happening to me.

Gopi was a learning experience for me not only from the work point of view but also on a personal level. Whatever ego I carried with me about my ability to perform confidently before the camera was dismantled when I witnessed the utter humility with which Dilip Sahab interacted with everybody in the unit and the pains he took to achieve perfection in his work. I was surprised at times when I had to do scenes with him and he asked for retakes. I used to think how come such a great actor was going for so many retakes. I mentioned it to an assistant of Dilip Sahab and he laughed and told me that all the retakes were for me. He wanted my responses to improve and attain the level he desired. That is his greatness and I learned from him that a sequence or scene cannot reach the level of excellence till all the artistes in the sequence or scene gave their best. Most heroes are primarily concerned with the quality of their work and are least bothered about the quality of the work of other artistes in the shot.

I asked Dilip Sahab if I could address him as Bhaijaan (brother) and he said: 'Yes, of course.' That is the way I have been addressing him since then. I used to visit the bungalow where Bhaijaan and Sairabi* stayed in Madras and I was always warmly welcomed. By and by, Sairabi and I became friends. I could see that she was choosy and did not make friends easily. They made such a charming couple.

Following my inclusion in the cast of *Gopi*, I signed several films. Once, for the shooting of *Gopi* at Kolhapur [in Maharashtra], I reached late and Bhaijaan was upset. He said: 'Remember success is the most demanding thing in an actor's life. The more success you achieve, the more you have to work and be more responsible, committed and humble. Don't let it go to your head; it can lead to your downfall even before you know it.'

In Bombay I used to stay in an apartment close to Sairabi's bungalow. I used to be free to call on them informally because Sairabi and I continued our friendship. There was so much laughter and happiness in the house and all the nieces and nephews of Bhaijaan would be there, sometimes playing badminton with him in the garden or, at other times, playing chess in the living room with him. There used to be all sorts of tasty snacks coming from the kitchen for everybody and Bhaijaan always filled our plates before he put anything on his plate. He is a man who likes to give more than receive – something he has done all his life not only for his family but also for whoever has had the privilege of knowing him.

---

*The prefix '*bi*' is used a term of respect for a woman.

ANIL KAPOOR

$\mathscr{I}$ WOULD NOT BE WRITING THIS PIECE IF I had not worked in three precious films with Dilip Kumar. Subhash Ghai and I are the only two people in the industry who can boast of this distinction!

Dilip Sahab's contribution to my acting career is so valuable I will go to the extent of saying that if I am in the industry still working with unabated commitment and dedication it is only because of what I learnt from him indirectly, and what he taught me right from my first lead role in the film, *Mashaal* [1984].

I always speak about *Shakti* [1982] as my debut film for the special attention it gave me as a newcomer. I have a distinct memory of the day the scene was to be shot. I was extremely excited and nervous. I had lines to speak and my fear was that I would be tongue-tied in the presence of Dilip Sahab. At the same time I wished to impress him and cherish that moment forever in my life. So you can imagine how I summoned up the courage to stand before him for the shot.

Amitabh Bachchan was not required for the shooting but for some reason Ramesh Sippy had asked him to come to the set. So it was like a double whammy for me – with Dilip Sahab in front of me, fully prepared for the shot as he always is, and Amitabh looking on with his serious look from a distance. I have no memory of how I delivered my lines. All I could hear was my heart going 'thud-thud', when suddenly I heard applause from the unit hands and all the people gathered on the sets. I realized that I had given my first shot.

Dilip Sahab was very encouraging because he knew my father, Surinder Kapoor, who was an assistant to K. Asif in the making of *Mughal-e-Azam*, well. I remember, as a little boy, not one evening passed in our house without my father talking about the work Dilip Sahab was doing. We listened enthralled to the wonderful descriptions that dad gave us about the scenes shot for the film, how Dilip Sahab prepared for the shots and how impeccable his work was. Dad told us about Sahab's humility, patience, dedication and commitment. The Sheesh Mahal [glass palace] set, he told us, took six months to erect and when the shooting started there were further delays because the director was unable to get what he wanted from the camera crew he had called from abroad. Not once did Dilip Sahab complain or lose his patience.

From my impressionable years, therefore, I was literally breathing Dilip Kumar and my sole aspiration was to grow up and find an opportunity to observe him at work. And that opportunity came with *Mashaal*. Initially I was not chosen to play the lead among the boys. I was to play one of them. Then, one day Yashji [Yash Chopra] called me and informed that I had to go to Bangalore with him. He did not tell me he was going to meet Dilip Sahab and he wanted his approval to cast me in the lead. Dilip Sahab was at the Jindal health resort going through a strict weight loss regime; he instantly recognized me and gave his approval.

I was so happy that I lay awake for nights experiencing a mix of elation and nervousness as the first schedule of *Mashaal* drew close. During the schedule there was a scene to be filmed in a canteen where I would be seated with my rowdy buddies and Dilip Sahab would come looking for me. We had to pretend we were indifferent knowing fully well that he would be in a rage as we had stoned the window panes of his house and rebuffed his wife.

In the rehearsal shot Dilip Sahab walked sturdily into the canteen and began on his dialogue. I kept ignoring him and suddenly I heard him shout: 'Cut, cut, cut!' I walked up to him and he said: 'Why are you not facing me when I am talking to you?'

I said: 'Sir, my character is one that is impudent and ill-mannered, so I thought I should not be looking straight at you while you are addressing me.'

Dilip Sahab immediately turned to Yashji and said: 'Okay, let's do the scene this way. I walk into the canteen, walk straight to Anil, pull him up by the scruff of his shirt collar, make him turn to me and then start talking to him.' Both Yashji and I thought that was just right. He requested Yashji if we could go straight for the take. The entire unit was told that it would be a take and not a rehearsal and there was pin-drop silence. Dilip Sahab walked in briskly, pulled me up by my collar with his strong Pathani hand and I was choking and trembling as I looked into his piercing eyes. The take was okayed! There was wild applause because it was a superb shot and my expression could not have been more real. But I was sweating and still choking. Sahab noticed my predicament and he took me to a quiet corner and said he was sorry but sometimes it helped if the action got slightly real. He said: 'When you see the shot on the screen and you get kudos for it you will know what I mean.' And sure enough he was right!

All through the making of *Mashaal*, I had the privilege to observe the dedication and painstaking preparation he put into his work. He became my institute, my textbook, my encyclopaedia. I can never forget the shooting at night for the most unforgettable scene on a deserted street of Bombay when he begs for help from passing vehicles to take his dying wife to a hospital. Dilip Sahab stayed that night at the Taj Hotel and when he reported for the shooting at midnight we noticed that he was his usual self – cool, warm and affectionate. What followed when the cameras rolled and he became the helpless man desperately trying to save the life of his wife and is pushed mercilessly by a motorist on the rain-drenched street was bone-chilling. We were speechless, amazed and in tears. Only Dilip Kumar could have done that.

Shooting for *Karma* was hugely enjoyable and there are many memorable moments I recall. I saw the fun-loving, sprightly side of Dilip Sahab during the breaks when he regaled us with funny stories from his adolescence and youth. My father visited the sets and it was wonderful to see their bonding while recalling their old association. One thing my father always told me about Dilip Sahab was that he never forgot his old colleagues and associates and it gave him great pleasure to meet them no matter what their status in life may have become in the intervening years. My dad had become an independent, successful producer by then but there were others who had been around when he was rising to stardom and who had not made it big.

My father also told me that Dilip Sahab never wasted his time in frivolous gossip and *gupshup*. He spent his time with writers and intellectually advanced people with whom he could make intelligent conversation and exchange meaningful thoughts, and that I should learn from him. In fact, dad told us that Dilip Sahab had more friends outside the industry than within because he disliked talking shop and never encouraged hangers-on.

Today I tell my children what I have learnt from Dilip Sahab, the way my father told us about him when my brother, Boney, and I were young. I have always personally gone to invite Dilip Sahab and Sairaji to the premieres of my films as his blessings mean the world to me. I remember I returned home after the special trial of *Pukar* [2000] we had arranged for Dilip Sahab. When the show ended there were so many people surrounding him that I could not reach out to him. I was sitting in my study wondering what he would have had to say about my work when I was told Dilip Sahab was calling. He spoke to me for an hour firing from all the barrels of a gun appraising my work and giving me some of the most valuable advice an actor could ask for. He liked my work and he did not mince words to tell me so. I received the National Award months later for my work in the film, but for me the greatest award had come that night when Dilip Sahab appreciated my performance. That conversation rings in my ears even today when I gear up to face the cameras on any set in whichever part of the world I might be shooting in.

RISHI KAPOOR

I HAVE NEITHER BEEN RISHI NOR CHINTU for Yousuf Uncle. I am his 'Sunny Boy'. The childhood memory of Yousuf Uncle that lingers in my mind is of him coming to our home in Chembur [in Bombay], often on the second Sunday of the month, when film workers took a break from film shootings and the stars, too, had to willy-nilly stay at home. He would invariably pass by me in the front yard where I would be playing with my friends. He would stop and ruffle my hair and say, 'Sunny Boy, how do you do?'

I knew he was the superstar Dilip Kumar and also that he and papa were equals in the profession. My friends would look at him and he would smile warmly at them. I would hear papa coming out to welcome him, yelling: 'Lalay, *tune der kar di.** I have been waiting since morning ....' They would hug and get lost in each other's company the whole afternoon.

Yousuf Uncle and papa shared an eternal fraternal relationship, which nobody could fathom or believe. They were in competition with each other as stars and yet they loved each other as though they were born to the same parents. At home it was like a celebration when papa and Yousuf Uncle got together. Since both loved food, my mother would be scurrying around from morning telling the cook what to prepare for lunch and then tea. Papa would be waiting all fresh and scrubbed and ready in his Pathan attire like an excited child. I guess for both of them it was a reliving of their childhood

---

*You have come late.

days in Peshawar, the native city they grew up in or the days they studied at Khalsa College in Bombay or the days they spent at Bombay Talkies, where they worked in their formative years.

I think Raj Kapoor loved him in the same measure as he loved his brothers, Shammi and Shashi. Perhaps he shared thoughts and emotions and secret aspirations more with Yousuf Uncle than he did with anybody in the family.

They sure had their professional rivalry. It would have been abnormal if they did not compete as professionals. The beauty of their rivalry was that they hated to see each other fail or fall from their respective positions as superstars. They were proud of each other and I have vivid memories of their watching rushes of my debut film *Bobby* [1973] in the RK mini theatre as also *Mera Naam Joker* [1970] while these were being made. Papa respected Yousuf Uncle's opinion immensely. I also remember the way they would sit in papa's office and plan fund-raising drives and charity shows to raise money for the government when a national disaster occurred. With them spearheading the whole activity it was natural that the participation from the industry was hundred per cent. Who indeed could say no to either of them?

I have three distinct memories from my adult years that I can share without reservations. First, the memory which haunts me even to this day. It goes back to the last time papa was admitted in hospital and almost every known person in the industry had dropped in to give us emotional support. Papa was in coma and we knew the end was near. Yousuf Uncle was in Pakistan to attend a felicitation by the president when papa was shifted to Apollo hospital in Delhi where he had suffered a cardiac stroke. The day Yousuf Uncle returned to Mumbai he took a flight to Delhi and rushed to the hospital. I remember very clearly how he walked into the room where papa was lying unconscious and drew a chair close to the bed on which he sat holding papa's hand. He began telling papa, 'Raj, *aaj bhi main der se aaya. Maaf kar de mujhe* [I am sorry I came late even today; forgive me] I know you like to be in the limelight and have all the attention on you. Enough is enough. Get up and sit and listen to me. I have just come back from Peshawar and I have brought back the aroma of chapli kebabs to tempt you. You and I will go together and we will walk through the bazaar like we used to and enjoy the kebabs and rotis. Raj, wake up and stop acting. I know you are a great actor. Raj, *mainu le jana hai tusi Peshawar de ghar de*

aangan wich.' [You have to take me with you to the courtyard of the house in Peshawar.] His voice was now choking and tears were brimming over from his eyes as he spoke.

Randhir [Rishi Kapoor's elder brother] and I stood still and mute. I can never erase the memory of Yousuf Uncle's plaintive appeal and the way he left the room reluctantly, turning back at the door to take one last look at his dearest friend lying unconscious on the bed.

The other memory is from a day in our studio [RK or Raj Kapoor Studio] when we were filming *Prem Rog* [released in 1982]. I had to bring the intense expression of a despondent lover, and as hard as I was trying, Raj Kapoor, the director, was not getting the look he wanted, which was irritating him. Then he shouted at me in the presence of the entire unit, '*Mujhe Yousuf chahiye.* I want you to give me the look Yousuf would have given in the situation. I want the look in his eyes when he expresses love, his intensity, his realism.'

The unit was silent. Nobody could believe that he was talking about his professional rival Dilip Kumar. I think it was the ultimate acknowledgement of the actor–director Raj Kapoor for Yousuf Uncle's unmatched ability to portray love with all its agony and ecstasy. It was possible only because they had that kind of genuine respect and love for each other. Would you hear Shahrukh [Khan] say that about Salman [Khan] or vice versa today?

Another incident that showed how much they were in each others' heart was when Yousuf Uncle was facing the brunt of Balasaheb Thackeray's [the Shiv Sena chief] politically motivated objection to his receiving the Nishan-e-Imtiaz from the Pakistan Government [in 1998]. There were ugly demonstrations outside his bungalow and, true to the callous nature of our industry, nobody came forward from the fraternity to put the Shiv Sena in its place. At that juncture Yousuf Uncle gave an interview in which he said, 'I miss my friend Raj today more than on any occasion. He would not have let this agitation against me or any other artiste go unanswered. He would not have let this happen to me.' [Raj Kapoor passed away on 2 June 1988.]

Papa was no more then but it made us feel so proud that someone as intellectually superior as Yousuf Uncle was remembering our father and giving him the credit for being a fearless man who stood up for his fraternity and all artistes in all testing times.

We have kept in touch with Yousuf Uncle and Saira Aunty through phone calls and meeting on festive occasions. Randhir and I had gone, I recall, to invite them for my younger brother Chimpu's [Rajiv Kapoor] marriage. Yousuf uncle was so happy to see us and we sat down for a long chat over cups of hot tea and delicious snacks served by Saira Aunty. It is always such an education to listen to Yousuf Uncle's talk. After the lovely meeting we went to Dev Anand's penthouse at Anand Studio. It was an altogether different experience. He was as usual on his feet, striding across the room and talking excitedly '... Hey man, Chintu, tell me what's happening and you Daboo [Randhir Kapoor's nick name], what's new with you ...' He was all excitement and was so delighted to see us. It made me think how different they were – the three real legends of Indian cinema and the three real big superstars.

I have been fortunate to have worked with Yousuf Uncle in *Duniya* [1984] also starring Ashok Kumar and Pran. A funny thing happened one day while we were all geared up for a dramatic scene between Yousuf Uncle and myself. He was playing my father and in one particular scene had to show his anger and ask me to leave the house. Everything was set and Yousuf Uncle had worked himself up and was ready with his lines. There was pin-drop silence as Yousuf Uncle wanted to go straight for a take. The clapper board was sounded and the director, Ramesh Talwar, called for 'action'. Just when Yousuf Uncle was about to deliver his lines, Ashok Kumar shouted out to him, 'Yousuf, *maine suna tu ne doosri shadi karli. Arre bhai, aadmi ek biwi ko mushkil se sambhalta hai aur tum to do do biwiyon ko sambhalne nikley. Arre Wah!*' [I believe you have remarried. A man can hardly handle one wife and you will handle two of them!] The entire unit was tense as Yousuf Uncle turned his gaze in the direction where Ashok Kumar was seated looking absolutely relaxed. Yousuf Uncle smiled and politely shouted back, 'Ashok Bhaiyya, can we discuss the critical issue you are referring to after I finish the scene? I agree it is a debatable issue but I am sure it can wait!'

There was a wave of laughter and we could hear both Pran and Ashok Kumar having a hearty laugh. That is Yousuf Uncle – a man with a great sense of humour and a man who has great respect for fellow artistes. The camaraderie among Ashok Kumar, Yousuf Uncle and Pran was something to watch all through the making of *Duniya*. It was a wonderful education for me.

I must admit with all sincerity that all of us sons and daughters of Raj Kapoor address him as Yousuf Uncle but he is no less than a father figure to all of us, now and forever.

AAMIR KHAN

*I*BEGAN OBSERVING YOUSUF SAHAB'S WORK on screen as a little boy. I would keep listening to praises about his consummate artistry in conversations that went on in the house between my father, Tahir Hussain, and my uncle, Nasir Hussain Sahab, besides the numerous visitors from the industry who called on them. I was not old enough to notice the finer points of his acting but I definitely saw that he was not like the other actors who 'acted' and strained themselves to become the characters they portrayed. Dilip Kumar was always the character he portrayed for the millions who viewed his films with eager involvement and the great wonder for me was that he did not seem to be acting at all. That was when I was about ten.

When I grew older and my sensibilities and understanding of the medium developed, I began to watch his work with the keenness of one who was going to make a career as an actor. It was then that I realized what a tremendous contribution he has made to histrionics in Indian cinema. I will explain what I mean.

By the time I entered the profession Indian cinema was seventy-five years old. I have been around for twenty-five years now. So when Yousuf Sahab entered the profession Indian cinema was perhaps twenty-five years old; the medium was still evolving and actors were still following the theatrical and loud styles of expressing the characters' feelings.

Yousuf Sahab came from a family that had no connection with either the visual or performing arts and the only references he had were the actors that preceded him. I think he had Ashok Kumar, Motilal and may be K. L. Saigal to observe. Even the technical supports of the motion picture medium like advanced cameras, sound, lights, music and so on were being experimented with and were just as good as they could be in the circumstances. It was in this scenario that he emerged as an admirable actor who brought to the screen a polish and refinement in histrionics that audiences found refreshingly different and pleasantly close to reality. And he did not model himself on any actor from Western cinema, or for that matter, Indian cinema. He was original and his style was novel and unadulterated.

Raj Kapoor was following Charlie Chaplin. Dev Anand was following Gregory Peck but Yousuf Sahab was following his own instincts and, for all of us who have followed his body of work, the amazing thing was the deep belief that went into the portrayal of the characters he played. I understood later, as I faced the cameras for my early films, it was not as simple or as effortless as it seemed. I realized that it takes a lot of self-convincing and emotional courage for an actor to believe that he is not himself but another individual going through the throes of fictitious experiences that are entirely different from whatever he has experienced in his own life.

I found myself watching his films with exhilaration, making mental notes of the authenticity he gave to his rendering of such varied and difficult characters as Devdas, Gunga (in *Gunga Jumna*), Prince Salim (in *Mughal-e-Azam*), just to give a few examples, and I could see how strong was his belief that he became the character he was bringing to life on the screen. I can attribute it to: a) his immense and untiring hard work and preparation for the performance; b) his unmatched mental and emotional strength; and c) the God-given gift of talent and competence.

How difficult it must have been for him to play the historical character of Prince Salim and that too with the formidable presence of Prithviraj Kapoor throughout as Emperor Akbar! Any other actor in the role would have resorted to high pitch dramatic acting to match Prithvirajji's resonant dialogue delivery and his style of acting. But Yousuf Sahab chose to strike a contrasting note, emoting more with his eyes and his impeccable dialogue delivery in his soft, refined voice. If you carefully observe his smile and his walk and the look he gives in the dramatic moments, it all seems so natural that you begin to believe that he is truly the romantic prince who was not ready to sacrifice his love for the throne of Hindustan.

How difficult it must have been also for him to play Gunga and speak the dialect he spoke. I believe both *Mughal-e-Azam* and *Gunga Jumna* were being filmed simultaneously and it would have been so tough on him. I can cite my own plight as I was recently shooting for two diverse films simultaneously – *Dhoom 3* and *PeeKay*. I speak a Bhojpuri dialect in *PeeKay* and on a couple of occasions while rehearsing my lines for *Dhoom 3*, I was unwittingly lapsing into Bhojpuri much to the amusement and surprise of Sanjay Gadhvi, the director of *Dhoom 3*. So I really wonder how Yousuf Sahab, who is known for his complete dedication to his work and concentrates on one film at a time, managed the two diverse commitments – a rustic fugitive from the law in one and a Mughal prince in the other!

I have a distinct memory of the scene in *Gunga Jumna* where he runs and runs, fleeing from the village and he is cornered by the villagers who have come to get him. He feels despondent and helpless till he seizes a gun and he pulls the trigger accidentally and sees the impact it has on the villagers who now start to flee from him and he is surprised and elated at once. Then Vyjayantimala comes running from the opposite side and he breaks down in her arms and tells her how the villagers had chased him like a dog. I don't foresee any actor anywhere in the world creating the tremendous impact he created in that scene with his subdued acting for a long time to come.

He was way ahead of his times as an actor and I still feel all of us actors who are striving to attain world standards are way behind him. He showed tremendous courage in picking scripts and roles that were in complete contrast. He switched from tragedy to comedy as a leading man and set the trend for lead actors to integrate comedy into their roles as he did in *Ram Aur Shyam*. Every choice of film he made was done carefully and on his own terms. He took conscious risks with his screen image breaking all the unwritten rules for lead role actors at that time. It takes guts and a sense of great self belief to do so. He dived each time into an unknown ocean and emerged with a pearl.

I think he could do all that he did because money was not his sole criterion. Also, he did not succumb to the pressure most actors face when huge stardom comes to them. The pressure is to take on all the offers that come at that juncture for fear of losing out on the opportunity to stay ahead in the race and the insecurity of being left in the cold if the success does not sustain [itself] for long. He has never been insecure as an actor and it has not mattered to him how big a star he is and for how long. What mattered to him, I can see, is the work at hand and how much he can give to it with utter sincerity and passion. In later years when he began to play older characters, too, he made his choices carefully. We may disagree with some of the choices but the point to be admired is that he did those films because he wanted to do them and not for the money or any other bait. And in all of them he was brilliant. Be it *Mashaal, Saudagar, Shakti* or any film of that phase, he was the pivot and the hero of the subject. People lined up to see him on the screen though there were [other] popular actors in the cast. So I would not categorize that phase as secondary to his earlier phase or call it character acting.

I have certainly learnt from my observation of his work and the way he conducted himself off screen, doing everything with a quiet dignity and self-assurance. He has remained the biggest superstar of India and I doubt if any of us today can equal him with all the good work we may do in the future.

Ayub Khan*

HERE ARE MY MEMORIES OF MOMENTS SPENT WITH YOUSUF UNCLE ...

Before that, I would have to give you a bit of an insight into my growing up years so as to give you an idea of my relationship with my uncle, my father's elder brother and the greatest actor the Hindi film industry has ever known till now, the thespian, the enigmatic Dilip Kumar, and to me, Yousuf Uncle.

The one instance that stands out the most and has had a huge impact on me was that of the passing away of my father [Nasir Khan] when I was barely five years old.

The memory of Yousuf Uncle comforting me as a child is so vivid. I remember that one day while trying to somehow comfort me about the absence of my father, Yousuf Uncle playfully made me look up towards the bright blue sky, which was filled with beautiful white puffy clouds and directed me to look at the largest, whitest cloud in the sky. He told me that my Abba was right behind that beautiful white cloud, and that he had put up all the clouds in the sky for me. He comforted me by telling me my Abba was busy decorating the sky each day for me.

It left me so tongue-tied. I couldn't get to tell my dear uncle, who was going to such great lengths to comfort me with this beautiful tale, that I was painfully aware of the reality. What was incredibly comforting was that the heart of the one person whom the nation completely idolized had the highest regard for my beloved father. It's such an incredible knowledge to be aware of and to know that, people of this nation were also aware of the love and great bond between Abba and Yousuf Uncle. Whenever they spoke

*Dilip Kumar's nephew; Nasir Khan's son.

of one, the other was never forgotten. Throughout time, wherever I went, people spoke of the great bond between the two.

There were no barriers in the company of Yousuf Uncle. He always made his surrounding very relaxed and kept a child-like approach when around us children but because of experiencing an emotionally charged childhood, I was always weary of displaying my inner emotions. Everywhere we went, awestruck people, within the film industry and outside, sat in front of even a child like me, waiting to hear utterance of insights of shared moments spent with my very enigmatic uncle.

The stamp of his relationship to the family was blindingly strong, and played a huge factor as far as having a status within the film industry or outside it. People almost treated us like royalty because of all the hard work of Yousuf Uncle that had brought about his greatness.

Yousuf Uncle and Saira Aunty made sure that, whenever they met us, they helped us form an easy, natural relationship based on our interaction with them and not by any preconceived notions built in our minds because of his popularity or his position. And even though the interactions were mostly fleeting (and at times at very significant moments) they left vivid memories.

Flashes of images that run through my mind, when I try and recall the earliest memories, are just like in movie scenes (at the cost of sounding melodramatic). The first images that comes to mind, is that of me as a very young child, walking up to Saira Aunty's bungalow terrace with my father and seeing Yousuf Uncle flying a large kite. Kite flying was a big thing and my father and uncle indulged in it. The quintessential heartthrob of the nation was right in front of me flying this large kite. The feeling that remained with me was that of wanting to watch my great uncle display superhuman abilities even while indulging in this act of recreation. And he did not disappoint! His kite was streaking across the skies winning numerous battles with other kite fliers, and every time he won, I would hear his unmistakable laugh, which filled the terrace, leaving me all the more spellbound.

I remember all of us cousins as children, while being treated at one of the open-air restaurants in Bandra's Bandstand, standing around while Yousuf Uncle and Aslam Uncle having a whistling competition (using the fingers while trying to whistle). I clearly remember Yousuf Uncle outwhistling the competition.

I remember vividly when he took all of us cousins to see a magic show. P. C. Sorcar was performing in an auditorium on Marine Drive. We children were given front-row seats and were privileged to come up on stage to participate in some of the acts of the coveted magician: one of the innumerable perks of being related to the thespian. The feeling of being his nephew amongst all those present that day filled my heart with pride as Yousuf Uncle looked over the flock of us children there.

I must mention that Abba was considered very, very dear by Yousuf Uncle and Saira Aunty. In the pile of movies put forth in front of me, my eye caught *Gunga Jumna*. This is an epic film that was partnered by my father and Yousuf Uncle and was an attempt by the latter to cement my father's career. I suggested I'd like to watch the film. Boy! What a moment, I thought, watching my father and my uncle in a movie together, while I sat beside my great uncle. However, the vision of Abba and his beloved brother Yousuf together was too much for my young heart. I burst into tears.

Eid celebrations used to have us cousins flocking to Yousuf Uncle and Saira Aunty's house. Plans of extorting large sums of Eidee [money given as a gift to children] were followed by us kids running around in the gardens of the bungalow, chasing one another as we played cops and robbers. The feeling that filled my heart was that there was no better place then here at the bungalow for Eid.

We cousins as children would get together to have musical parties at the bungalow, where some of us kids would set up the sitting room as an auditorium for Yousuf Uncle. On his arrival he would be promptly be dragged into the room and then made to sit on the 'chair of honour.' After that promptly one by one, each of us would jump out from behind a curtain near the window and enact songs or *qawwaalis* to impress Yousuf Uncle. Of course the motive was always to help Yousuf Uncle lighten his wallet and this was done in the form of tickets for a show, which he had to buy. The catch here was that he had to buy tickets for each and every member in the house, domestic help included. If we had had our way, the whole locality would have been on the list.

I signed my first film and then went to let my uncle know of my decision of becoming an actor.

I remember taking my producer and director to Saira Aunty's house to meet Yousuf Uncle. There were butterflies in my stomach as I waited for Yousuf Uncle and Saira Aunty to descend from their room upstairs to the sitting room on the ground floor.

I remember as I waited in the room, looking out towards the window facing the garden, I heard the shuffling of feet, which were those of my producer and director standing up because of the arrival of Yousuf Uncle in the room. After all the pleasantries, we all sat down and my team promptly began updating my uncle about all that was being planned: the story, the shooting schedules, the ad campaign and so on. What caught my attention was Yousuf Uncle's constant gaze towards me. His eyes spoke so clearly to me. I could feel the room reverberate with the thoughts in his head that were directed towards me.

Without a word being said, it clearly became evident that I was going to be representing a legacy from here on in the film industry. And in my heart of hearts, it was very clear that no one could ever match the greatness of my uncle, let alone me, but I had to at least be able to imbibe the principles of Yousuf Uncle's great work so as to be worthy, if ever my name would be taken in the same breath along with his by the industry.

Very soon the *mahurat* was planned and Yousuf Uncle sounded the clap. It was all a haze. So much was happening. With my proud mother and friends, family members and others looking on the happenings of that day unfolded. What remained with me was Yousuf Uncle's gaze on me. I wonder whether he was being able to foresee the coming hurdles or strengths that were going to take me through this path I had chosen for myself.

My life took many twist and turns. I moved on and made fleeting contact with my uncle. The one point that stood out was during my first marriage. Saira Aunty and Yousuf Uncle held functions at their bungalow for me. Never imposing their desire or trying to dictate anything during these celebrations. I was just stepping into the world of responsibilities and had very limited resources. What gave me great courage was the respect my aunt and uncle bestowed on me during this very eventful time in my life. With such ease they stood by me and my mother's side and gave us so much support that nothing will ever match up to it.

Saira Aunty has always been supportive of my relationship with my uncle. She has always made sure that I was a part of events and celebrations. Even during the time when Yousuf Uncle was hospitalized recently for a heart ailment, Saira Aunty made sure that I spent the evenings with him (when I got back from work), always making sure that nothing interrupted our interaction.

Truly, Saira Aunty has made sure that Yousuf Uncle has remained connected with his side of his family, for which I will always be grateful to her.

SALIM KHAN

I ALWAYS THOUGHT THAT WRITING ABOUT
a great man would be an easy job, especially
about Dilip Sahab since so much material is
available on events, incidents and anecdotes
right from his birth till the present. But when
I sat down to write this piece, I didn't know
where to start. I am, anyway, going to make a sincere effort! I have been
asked to condense an epic into a sonnet!

Dilip Sahab's father, Mohammad Sarwar Khan Sahab, an erstwhile
neighbour and a friend of the formidable actor, Prithviraj Kapoor,
disapproved of films and therefore dragged him to Bombay Central Railway
Station, at the request of Maulana Adul Kalam Azad, an eminent scholar,
a freedom fighter and independent India's first education minister. Azad
gave a patient hearing to Sarwar Khan Sahab and then said to Dilip Sahab:
'Young man whatever you do, do it honestly and sincerely as if you are
offering namaaz [prayer].' Dilip Sahab did so. He brought divine spirituality
to acting, converted his profession into *ibadat* (worship).

Dilip Sahab honed his acting skills gradually by sheer hard work and
immense dedication. He pursued perfection in his profession like a person
possessed. For example, he had to play the sitar for a song sequence in
Kohinoor. He engaged the services of an ustad and practised for months.
In the process of honing his skills, he learnt many languages. He can speak
fluently in English, Hindi, Urdu, Bengali, Marathi and Pushtu. To describe
his acting, I would like to quote Raj Kapoor, his contemporary, childhood
friend and fierce competitor, who after watching Ramesh Sippy's *Shakti*
(1982) rang up from Bangalore and told him: '*Lalay, aaj faisla ho gaya* [today
it has been decided]: you are the greatest actor of all time.' Incidentally,
we (Javed Akhtar and myself) wrote *Shakti* starring Dilip Sahab, Amitabh
Bachchan, Raakhee and Smita Patil. When we had narrated the script
earlier to Dilip Sahab, he revealed that as God had endowed him with
acting talent, he never wanted to write but some scripts and dialogues were
so bad that he had to do so. He added that we had done a perfect job. We
later also wrote *Kranti* (1981), in which he had a pivotal role.

When Devika Rani, the 'queen' of Bombay Talkies, selected Dilip Sahab
to act in *Jwar Bhata* (1944), everyone in the huge studio was shocked because

he was not considered 'handsome' as per the then existing standards, but he soon went on to achieve tremendous success.

When Dilip Sahab joined films in 1944, he observed that actors in films were loud and dramatic, thanks to the influence of the Parsi theatre. He was among the first to underplay a role and bring finer nuances to a performance: for example, his use of long pauses and deliberate silence created a very unusual impact on audiences. I believe that he had heard the speeches of Jawaharlal Nehru, who used to think in English but speak in Hindustani; so the fraction of a second needed for translation created pauses. Nehru's national popularity was well matched by Dilip Sahab's deep impact on cinema audience. In later years, both developed mutual respect and admiration for each other. The young Dilip Kumar was 'disturbingly impressed' with Emily Brontë's 1847 novel *Wuthering Heights*. Years later, he acted in A. R. Kardar's *Dil Diya Dard Liya* (released in 1966), based upon that novel.

Dilip Sahab has always been an extremely sensitive person and introspection is not something he has done periodically; it's a constant process with him. Intensity has been his inborn characteristic, which was constantly reflected in his work. His power-packed performance, marked by unbridled anger, in the 1961 *Gunga Jumna* shall remain unmatched forever. A large number of self-proclaimed stars have projected anger, but, compared to Dilip Sahab, they look like paper tigers.

Dilip Sahab had acquired the status of a one-man institution. Many of his contemporaries and actors from later generation actors tried to imitate him but none could scale the heights he did. In the process of copying him, a number of people attained stardom. Is it not surprising that Dilip Sahab did less than sixty films in a career spanning six decades? Today, youngsters do sixty films in six years. Dilip Sahab rejected more films than he acted in, but he regretted not doing only three movies: *Baiju Bawra* (1952), *Pyaasa* (1957) and our (Salim-Javed's) *Zanjeer* (1973). Many actors sign a large number of films because of their insecurity and fear. Once he remarked that talent and honesty alone can remove fear and all insecurities.

I have been in the industry for six decades and interacted with various people but I have never met anyone like Dilip Sahab. He is a deeply cultured, well-read person of tremendous integrity. His personal relationships are based on emotions such as love, loyalty and faith. I am proud of the fact that I have not only known him but worked with him and he has always considered me to be his younger brother.

Yousuf Khan bin Mohammad Sarwar Khan, alias Dilip Sahab, struck an emotional rapport with audiences many decades ago and broke the barriers of caste, country, religion, language and region. This phenomenal connect with the masses made him a superstar for about sixty years. Film audiences have been secular and truly Indian. Dilip Sahab's phenomenal popularity symbolizes secularism, which has been the inner strength of India.

Let me state the obvious here: Dilip Sahab is the greatest actor ever. Dilip Sahab has given his fans and admirers, including me, so much happiness with his presence and his performances that we are indebted to him and I pray to God that he gives a small part of each of his fans' and admirers' lives to him so as to prolong his life and that he shall be with us for a long long time.

MANOJ KUMAR

 *E*VERYBODY KNOWS MANOJ KUMAR IS a disciple of Dilip Kumar. I have spoken about Dilip Sahab as my inspiration and guru in umpteen interviews. What I wish to bring forth in this piece that will go into the history of our cinema is the simple personal attributes of Dilip Sahab that I have observed over the years and which make him the most loved and respected legend of Indian cinema.

First of all, I must say from the bottom of my heart that if there is anyone other than my parents and my immediate family who has given me love and a sense of emotional security it is Dilip Sahab. From the very first time I met him in a dark cinema hall to this day, he has given me the same measure of affection and fraternal protection.

My first meeting itself is memorable and indelibly etched in my mind. I was a struggler in Bombay those days. I used to go around wearing the few bush shirts I had and I wore chappals because shoes meant a lot of upkeep. A film show was organized by a group of media persons and the then *Filmfare* editor, L. P. Rao, who was very good to newcomers in the industry, invited me to the show. I reached the theatre late and I was looking for a seat in the auditorium when a hand was extended towards me, which drew me to an empty seat. I gratefully occupied the seat and when I turned to see who I was seated next to I could not believe my eyes. It was Dilip Kumar! He was smiling at me and even in the darkness. I could see the natural benevolence shining through his eyes. In a few seconds his sister Farida came rushing to occupy the seat she had vacated perhaps to go to the ladies' room. She frowned, seeing a stranger seated next to her famous brother. Dilip Sahab leaned over to her and told her gently to find herself a seat in a row behind and she obeyed instantly.

As the picture – *The Story on Page One* [1959], starring Rita Hayworth – unfolded Dilip Sahab kept talking to me as if we had known each other for years. When the film ended and the lights came on, he invited me to breakfast at his bungalow the next morning! I felt I had achieved everything I ever wanted in life. Imagine the biggest superstar of the time inviting a rank newcomer to his house for breakfast! I went over to his bungalow the next morning and I saw how simply he lived with his large family and he was ever so cordial and warm with me. It was unbelievable. He asked about my background, my parents and so on; he said he would be happy to meet my father when I told him about my birth in the North West Frontier Province in undivided India. He told me he was busy with the production of *Gunga Jumna* and he said I could call on him whenever I wished. A morning I can never forget.

My next visit to Dilip Sahab's house was when I went to invite him to the premiere of *Kanch Ki Gudiya* [1961], in which I got my break as a hero. Naturally, I was excited. Dilip Sahab was with some important visitors who had come to finalize a programme for the next day and there I was, with my invitation for the premiere the next evening. I felt dejected thinking he would not accept my invitation as he had already finalized everything for the next day.

I could see that he was indeed very much occupied with the release of *Gunga Jumna*. When he saw me he greeted me with affection and asked me if all was well with me. I rather gawkily told him I had come to request him to attend the premiere of my film. I told him H. S. Rawail, the director of the film, had been trying to reach him and I had mustered the courage to come to him at the last minute because I wanted him very much to grace the show. He said: 'Bhai, you just heard us finalize tomorrow evening's programme.' My heart sank.

Then, seeing the disappointment on my face, he said: 'Give me a minute, let me just go upstairs.' He returned in a minute and he called his younger brother Ahsan and told him to cancel the next day's programme. 'I will be with you,' he said and thumped me on my back. Needless to say, he was the star attraction at the premiere. A gesture I can never forget.

It was only after almost a decade of knowing him that I got the chance to work with him as a co-actor in *Aadmi* [1968]. Though Bhim Singh was the director, it was Dilip Sahab who was actually shaping the film. We were shooting in Coimbatore (now in Tamil Nadu) when Dilip Sahab had to go to Bangalore for some personal work. He called me over to his side at the location and told me there were some scenes to be shot the next day and he had to leave for Bangalore. He had written the scenes roughly and he wanted me to can those scenes. He left the same evening and I shot the scenes the next day. That is the kind of trust he had in me. After *Aadmi*, I often addressed him as Raja Sahab, the name of the character he played in the film.

The greatest quality Dilip Sahab possesses is his ungrudging admiration for the achievements of others in the profession. When we were shooting some scenes on a ship for *Kranti* [released in 1981], a journalist had come to interview Dilip Sahab. I heard Dilip Sahab giving the journalist not his own example but that of Raj Kapoor as the inspiration for generations of film aspirants to look up to. In our fiercely competitive profession, such magnanimous praise and respect for a colleague's achievements are rare. Only a good soul like Dilip Sahab can do that.

I must narrate how unaffected he was when he was appointed sheriff of Bombay [in 1980]. When the news spread in Bombay and all his colleagues in the industry were trying to call him, he was on the terrace of his house flying a kite and enjoying himself. Dilip Sahab is like that – not swept off his feet by any honour, any award or any recognition.

I approached him with the story of *Kranti* after taking an appointment with him. It wasn't the right time to meet him because his brother Noor Sahab had been admitted in a hospital that day and he was in a hurry to go to the hospital. He said: 'I am afraid I won't be able to spare three hours today to listen to the story.' I told him: '*Jo kahani teen ghante leti hai sunane mein, woh kahani kahani nahin hoti hai. Main sirf pandrah minute loonga.*'* He sat down and listened for fifteen minutes. Then he rose from his chair, smiled and said: 'The land is very fertile.' I understood that he liked the

---

*A story that takes three hours to be told is not a story at all. I will take just fifteen minutes.

essence of the story. I then said: '*Agar hal achcha chalayenge to fasal bhi achchi ho sakti hai.*'* He gave me the green signal.

All through the making of *Kranti*, he inspired the entire cast with his dedication and commitment and never changed a word in the dialogue or anything in the script. It was again a demonstration of his trust in my capabilities.

He and my father shared a great bond. My father loved him and enjoyed sharing memories of their native land. Once when my father was in hospital, Dilip Sahab visited him and spent quite some time talking to him. It was like an elixir. My father was feeling so much better by the time Dilip Sahab took leave of him.

The nicest memory I have of Dilip Sahab is of the days he sat by Saira's bedside in a London hospital when she was ailing with ulcerative colitis. I had announced *Purab Aur Pacchim* [released in 1970] with her in the lead role at that time. I could read the anxiety and concern on Dilip Sahab's face and I gathered from the hospital's doctors that he did not sleep a wink in the initial weeks when her condition was precarious. She is looking after him now with as much devotion if not more. He is God's gift to her and she is God's gift to him. They make an ideal couple, taking care of each other and giving strength to each other in difficult times.

HEMA MALINI

A JEWEL IN THE CROWN OF INDIAN cinema, a phenomenon so rare and, as he is always called, an *institution in acting*.

My association with Dilip Sahab has been lesser in films and more personally. A magnanimous personality, he packs a whole lot of wisdom, charm and compassion in one

---

*If the ploughing is done well, the harvest could be good.

persona. I had just one opportunity to act with him in the 1981 film *Kranti* (though not opposite him) and his presence at the shoot was electrifying. He also directed me in his home production, a TV serial, and I noticed how much depth he had. It was an experience working with him, something that I would treasure for a lifetime.

He has always been graceful and encouraging to me in every step of my life. I cannot forget my first press meet in Madras in 1968 for the film *Sapnon Ka Saudagar** hosted by B. Ananthaswami, the producer, which Dilip Sahab and Sairaji attended. Years ago, I remember that Dilip Sahab went out of his way to warmly look after me when I performed at his friend Raj Kapoor's daughter Rita's marriage with Rajan Nanda. I was relatively new and there was a bustling, huge crowd of people.

In the late 1990s, when we met at his home to discuss the format and content of the script to be filmed for his home production, an interview-based TV serial *Is Duniya Ke Sitare*, he suggested we make classical dance the base and go ahead with the programme. That was something so close to my heart and we filmed it likewise, showing me practising Bharat Natyam at my residence and then proceeding to the interview. It turned out to be a success. During editing, he intercut the interview with flashes of my classical dance from the film *Mrigtrishna* (1975), which is one of my outstanding performnaces on celluloid. During the shooting of the serial at my home, my mother, Jaya Chakravarti, who was a great fan of Dilip Sahab's movies, was so excited to know that he was coming that she specially ordered the kitchen staff to make him North Indian dishes, with a distinct Punjabi cuisine.

The gentleman that he is, he greatly relished each item, but little did we all know that, having lived in Madras and with a liking for everything South Indian, he would have instead preferred *rawa masala dosa* and the classic *sambhar* and *chutney*!

We have constantly run into each other at various film functions and my happiness knew no bounds when he said he liked my performance in the 1986 film *Ek Chaadar Maili Si* (based on Rajinder Singh Bedi's much acclaimed novel). We also kept running into each other in Lucknow while campaigning during elections. Sahab was all for Congress, of course, while I supported the Bharatiya Janata Party (BJP).

---

*Hema Malini's first Hindi film, released in 1968, in which Raj Kapoor played the hero.

Being a Bharat Natyam artiste, when, for the first time I incorporated Kathak dance portions in my new ballet *Draupadi*, I invited Dilip Sahab and Sairaji (who is a disciple of Kathak queen Padmashri Roshan Kumari) to witness the premiere performance. They sat through the entire ballet and appreciated it.

Dharamji,* who dotes on Dilip Sahab like a brother, and I were touched to the core when he and Sairaji, despite intense traffic jams and huge crowds, attended our daughter Esha's marriage with Bharat Takhtani in June 2012. It meant so much to us to have Dilip Sahab's and Sairaji's blessings for our child.

I am indeed happy to know that Dilip Sahab will be giving the world a rare look into his remarkable life with this book.

Here's wishing him and the lovely Sairaji the very best in life.

MUMTAZ

I OWE MY RISE IN BOLLYWOOD AS A star and an as actress of consequence to Dilip Sahab. At the time when comedian Mehmood suggested my name to Dilip Sahab for a role in *Ram Aur Shyam* (released in 1967), I was mostly working in films starring the famous wrestler Dara Singh, apart from Mehmood himself. The Dara Singh films came under the 'C' category in commercial terminology. As a result some heroes who were nowhere near Dilip Sahab in stature were refusing to work with me. To mention some names, Jeetendra, Dharmendra and Shashi Kapoor, plainly told directors who wished to cast me to come up with the name of some other leading lady. If I secured *Boond Jo Ban Gayi Moti* (released in 1967) with Jeetendra, it was only because the veteran

---

*Dharmendra, Hema Malini's husband.

producer-director, V. Shantaramji, told Jeetendra that he would cast another hero in the film if Jeetu had a problem working with me.

It was in such a scenario that Mehmood took tins of reels of a film starring me with him to Madras to show Dilip Sahab who was looking for a heroine to play the rustic character opposite the character Ram. It was very good of Mehmood to take the trouble because he and I were a good successful team and, in normal circumstances, no actor would like to break a successful team and go all out to recommend his heroine to a superstar and pave the way for her rise.

I was very very lucky because Dilip Sahab liked my work in the film he was shown and he felt I was ideal for the role of Ram's buxom and vivacious sweetheart in *Ram Aur Shyam*. Just imagine the scenario. An actress who has faced the humiliation of being rejected by a few A-list lead actors is picked by the legendary thespian Dilip Kumar to star opposite him. It made sensational news.

I remain eternally indebted to Dilip Sahab for changing the course of my career. Overnight, after the announcement of the casting appeared in the media, I was in great demand. I had the maturity and wisdom to remain level-headed and patient, knowing that God sends opportunities to take the deserving to their goals. The truth is that I was always confident that my day would come if I focused on my work and toiled sincerely. The reward came with a deluge of offers following the casting in *Ram Aur Shyam*.

Dilip Sahab did not pause to see with which hero I was working when he decided to include me in the cast of *Ram Aur Shyam*. He was solely concerned with the suitability of my looks and acting abilities for bringing alive the village girl Ram loves. It was a role that had to contrast with the sophistication of the character of the rich, city-bred girl Shyam meets (played by Waheeda Rehman) when he lands up in the city.

The shooting of *Ram Aur Shyam* passed off like a dream for me. During outdoor shooting at Panhala (in south-western Maharashtra), Dilip Sahab and Saira were newly married and we all got the opportunity to spend quality time together. I remember the whole unit came to their bungalow where they were staying, to celebrate Dilip Sahab's birthday on 11 December 1966 and the ragging was on because both of them took their own time come down from their upstairs room! Saira and I developed a friendship and we began confiding in each other. In between the outdoor shots, there were interesting tête-à-têtes between us, with comedian Mukri regaling the entire unit with funny anecdotes. Later, when I married Mayur Madhwani in 1974, I was so happy and touched that, despite the bed rest she was prescribed by the doctors at the time, Saira and Dilip Sahab had still graced my wedding reception. Just a few days ago, I visited them again after long and we spent a very happy evening together.

Dilip Sahab's greatness lies in his extreme humility and the trouble he takes to groom artistes who work with him. I benefited not only in the positioning I got after the casting of *Ram Aur Shyam* but also in the respect I gained with seasoned directors who eagerly cast me in their films after that.

Eventually, I was sought after by the very individuals who rejected me and I couldn't but thank the Almighty for giving me that thrill and pleasure. Producer-director L. V. Prasadji chose me over many other names suggested to him for *Khilona* (1970), for which I won the *Filmfare* Best Actress Award. Shashi Kapoor eagerly signed N. N. Sippy's 1974 blockbuster *Chor Machaye Shor* with me and Dharamji gladly signed *Loafer*, among the top grossers of 1973.

All this taught me that self-belief and faith can indeed move mountains. I got married to Mayur Madhwani at the peak of my stardom and quit the industry. I have been away from the arclights for around forty years now. I battled against the spread of a killer disease and once again God stood by me. Life does not stop teaching you how to live and be grateful for the bounties granted to you.

LATA MANGESHKAR

I WAS INTRODUCED TO YOUSUF BHAI BY the noted composer Anil Biswas in a local train sometime in 1947. Anilda was taking me to Bombay Talkies and, when we boarded the train, Yousuf Bhai was already there in the compartment. Anilda knew him well, so they greeted each other warmly. I had heard about Yousuf Bhai but he did not know anything about me. So Anilda introduced me to him saying: '*Yeh*

Lata hai, bahut achcha gaati hai.' (This is Lata, she sings very well.) Yousuf Bhai said: '*Achcha, kahan ki hai?*' (OK. Where is she from?) Then Anilda gave him my full name, Lata Mangeshkar.

The remark that Yousuf Bhai made when he found out that I am a Maharashtrian is something that I cherish because it made me seek the perfection I then lacked in my Hindi and Urdu diction. He said very truthfully that singers who were not conversant with the Urdu language invariably tripped in the pronunciation of words derived from the language and that jarred and spoiled the listening pleasure for those who enjoyed the lyric as much as the melody. At first, it saddened me that he thought I had a flaw in my rendering. Then, I thought over the remark and I realized he was right and he had said it with the intention of improving my diction if it needed the improvement.

I went home and sent for a family friend who was an Urdu expert to come over urgently as I wished to take lessons in Urdu immediately. A learned maulana* was arranged by Shafi Imam, our family friend who was like an elder brother to me. As I continued my Urdu lessons, I found myself being appreciated and admired more and more. So, in the first meeting itself, Yousuf Bhai gave a gift unknowingly and unhesitatingly.

We did not meet too often those days. However, whenever there was a recording of a song at Mehboob Studios and Yousuf Bhai was shooting there, I never missed the opportunity to call on him. He was a superstar and I was rising on the horizon as a playback singer, but, when we met, he held me close to his heart like an elder brother and gave me the love and respect that only someone as pure as he could.

Another talented composer, Salil Chaudhury, gave me an opportunity to sing a duet with Yousuf Bhai for *Musafir* (1957),** and it was a memorable experience to observe the pains he took to sing faultlessly. His eldest sister Sakina Aapa was very fond of me and I visited her often. Yousuf Bhai would be around sometimes and one could see how much he loved his family and went to any length to make his sisters feel secure and happy. He had the same measure of affection for me and I always felt he was as protective about me as he was about his sisters. I remember, for instance, an evening at Kalyanji bhai's house where, after the snacks were served, a plate of paan (betel leaves) arrived. (Composer Kalyanji, along with his younger brother

*An Islamic scholar known for his religious learning.
**The opening line of the song, written by Shailendra, is: *Laagi naahi chhoote Rama.*

Anandji, formed a musical duo.) When I took the liberty of telling Yousuf Bhai to have a paan, his expression changed to a frown. He said: 'It is not proper for you to do this. Never do it in future.'

I was taken aback because, at that time, I had no idea that it was not appropriate for a decent lady to offer a paan to a man. I also remember the evening before my concert at the Royal Albert Hall in London in 1974. Yousuf Bhai asked me to give him the list of songs I had selected. I had done so carefully since it was my first concert outside India. The first song on the list was *Inhi logon ne le leena dupatta mera** from *Pakeezah* (1972). Again, I noticed that there were lines on his forehead as he asked: 'Why do you want to sing this song?' referring to the *Pakeezah* number. I told him it was a popular song and the Asian audience would love to hear it live. He was silent for a minute and then he quickly went on to discuss something else. I could sense his objection to my singing the song because the lyric alluded to something he did not want to hear from his sister.

Yousuf bhai's speech at the Royal Albert Hall was a masterpiece. Many speakers have since tried to repeat the same words and phrases in their speeches but no one could match his eloquence and charisma and the dignity he exuded that evening. He graciously introduced me as his *chhoti bahen* (younger sister) and, as is his wont, every word he spoke was carefully chosen.

What makes Yousuf Bhai different from other stars is his unaffected humility and the sense of belonging he gives to each individual in his own way. The *apnapan* [sense of belonging] he radiates is so genuine and from the bottom of his heart. The courtesy, etiquette, *tehzeeb* [culture] and warmth you see in him are hard to find in anyone these days and even in the times gone by. I remember greeting him at the wedding reception hosted by [actress] Padmini Kolhapure's parents at a five-star hotel (I cannot recall when exactly). He returned my *namashkar* [greetings with folded hands] warmly and he recognized my niece Rachna** who was with me, asked her about her brother and chatted with us for a while. It is difficult for most people who meet him to believe that a great personality like him with a worldwide fan following can be so simple and unassuming.

*It is these people who have taken away my *dupatta*, the garment used to cover a woman's head and chest. The *dupatta* is considered a symbol of a woman's modesty.
**Rachna is the daughter of Meena Mangeshkar, Lata Mangeshkar's sister.

He once phoned me after listening to a ghazal album I had cut and told me how much he enjoyed listening to it. A few months later, another album of ghazals I had rendered caught his attention and he listened to it. He did not like what he heard. He phoned me to express his disappointment. Yousuf Bhai is like that: child-like, honest, simple and pure at heart.

Finally, what makes me extremely happy is that he is married to a woman who is not his better half, but his best half. They are made for each other.

RAM MUKHERJEE

$\mathscr{I}$ SURELY MUST HAVE BLESSED WHEN SHASHADHAR MUKHERJEE SAHAB decided to entrust *Leader* [released in 1964] to me as it was every director's dream to direct Dilip Kumar.

Dilip Sahab was very dear to Mukherjee Sahab. They consulted each other on most personal and professional matters and it was obvious that they had discussed and liked my work as a director in *Hum Hindustani* [1960].

Mukherjee Sahab's first instruction to me was to spend as much time as possible with Dilip Sahab. He said: 'Stay with him if you must; spend your waking hours with him and develop the script and screenplay along with him. He is a genius when he crafts a screenplay and it is your good fortune that you are getting to work with him.'

I started visiting Dilip Sahab's Pali Hill bungalow every day. Some days I accompanied him wherever he went, visiting someone or just driving through Mohammad Ali Road, stopping the car at his favourite café to pack some succulent meat kebabs, which he would share heartily with me. People would gather around his car and he would talk unaffectedly and unassumingly with all of them. I could see the pleasure and genuine joy in the eyes of all those simple awestruck people who approached with apprehension that they might be shooed away or insulted for crowding around his car.

Dilip Sahab's love for his fans is something no star of his time or later could emulate. He once told me: 'You know, Ramu, when an unfamiliar hand clasps mine and I feel the warmth of genuine adulation in that clasp I feel a deep sense of reward for all the hard work I put in for a performance which no award can give me. It is all right to be called on to the stage and presented with an award and a thousand hands are clapping in assertion of the acclaim you have won with your dedication. But when compared to a poor man who comes to me, his eyes moist and conveying so much, I feel truly rewarded!'

Dilip Sahab worked on the script and screenplay with untiring zeal, writing, rewriting, reviewing the scenes with me; discussing the sets, costumes, make-up, backdrops, outdoors and indoors in detail. There were nights when I stayed up with him at his house when he would be writing continuously. When he would fall asleep in the wee hours, I would drive back home and catch up with my sleep. It was then I understood why Mukherjee Sahab had instructed me to be with him all the time; it was to be my education – exposure to the dedication and passion of a man who worked relentlessly to achieve perfection in his work.

On arriving at Filmalaya Studios for the first day of shooting [for] *Leader*, I discovered the special make-up room reserved for Dilip Sahab had been given to another popular star also shooting there. The studio manager was in a spot. I was extremely nervous thinking I would have to call off the shooting. Meanwhile, Dilip Sahab arrived and as is his habit he walked into Mukherjee Sahab's office. Now there was no question of my going inside and telling them what had transpired.

Dilip Sahab somehow learnt of the situation; he quietly came out from the office and walked towards me. I could feel beads of sweat erupting on my forehead because, all things considered, it was my responsibility to ensure that the make-up room was not allotted to anyone else. Quietly pointing out to a banyan tree in the compound he said: 'Put a chair and small table for me there. If I do my make-up there, will you have a problem?' he asked.

I was at a loss for words. My first thought was how Mukherjee Sahab would react if he came to know that the biggest star of the industry did not have a make-up room in his studio for his own production. Sensing my confused thoughts, Dilip Sahab smiled and said: 'Leave the matter to me. Just arrange for the table and chair and some clean water.'

The first day's shooting was really one of its kind. Dilip Sahab's cheer was infectious, and we worked like a unit on a picnic.

At all the outdoor and indoor shootings Dilip Sahab's co-operation made my work easy and pleasurable. He had solutions for every problem that cropped up. However, he distanced himself when we had problems with

Vyjayantimala who began to arrive late for our shooting because she was shooting for Raj Kapoor's *Sangam* [also released in 1964] at the same time. He left it to Mukherjee Sahab as the producer to deal with the issue since he was very close to Raj Kapoor and he did not want any misunderstandings.

Dilip Sahab was as much a producer's delight as he was a director's dream. He never let down the producer and respected his authority. He saved expenses for the producer and seldom asked for preferential treatment. When we were shooting at a location in Udaipur, there was a huge crowd outside the palace where we were shooting. He was concerned about the security of the entire unit and especially Vyjayantimala. He would tell me: 'We Pathans always make sure that women and children are safe and secure. It is a rule I was brought up on.'

As we packed up the shooting we heard that the crowd was getting unruly and the local police was having a tough time controlling them. They wanted to see Dilip Sahab. I felt it was not safe for him to go out and greet the crowd but he said it was their right to seek a look at the film stars. He greeted the crowd and addressed them on a public address system. The crowd dispersed when he politely asked. Two cars had been arranged for the stars. Dilip Sahab was with me in one car and Vyjayanti and her grandmother in the other car. As his car drove out a young man on a cycle threw himself in front of Sahab's car with the intention of getting a close look at him or even touch him. Fortunately, the driver braked in time; at first Dilip Sahab was very angry with the youth but he stopped the police from handling him. While Dilip Sahab was helping the young man to his feet, all he could do was stare and shake his head with disbelief.

Wherever we shot for *Leader*, be it at Agra or Jaipur, the fans somehow got a whiff of Dilip Sahab's presence and they thronged the locations. We shot an action scene in which Dilip Sahab climbed up to the turret of a structure without a double while the unit and the spectators watched breathlessly. He wrote most of his pithy dialogue in crucial scenes on the spur of the moment. His erudition and political awareness came to the fore when he wrote lines that perhaps no one could have written for him.

If you watch *Leader* today you will find some of the lines spoken by Dilip Sahab so relevant to the present political climate. It just goes to prove how far-sighted he was as an intellectual.

NANDA

I CAN NEVER FORGET THE FIRST TIME I met Dilip Sahab. I was at a party, which was hosted by Bharat Bhooshanji,* before the release of *Sakshi Gopal* [1957] and suddenly Dilip Sahab walked in. When Dilip Kumar entered a room everybody's attention naturally riveted on him. It was like a dream come true for me to see him in flesh and blood but I was a shy person and I knew I would never be able to go up to him and introduce myself as a fan, leave alone as a newcomer who had just made an impact with *Toofan Aur Diya* [1956]. I requested Bhooshanji to introduce me and he agreed, saying I should wait till the people swarming around him left him alone. I knew that it was not going to happen because people never left him alone. He was a huge star and a man who liked mingling with common folk.

As I stood at a corner of the room feeling dismayed, I could not believe my eyes as Dilip Kumar was actually walking towards me with a smile of recognition. He came up to me and asked: 'Aren't you Master Vinayak's daughter?'

I could hear my heart thumping away as I said: 'Yes!'

He smiled and repeated a dialogue from one of my father's films in Marathi – *'Dhonda asel tar mazya dokyavar maar'*.** I was overwhelmed and speechless. He spoke so disarmingly and with such simplicity that I found my voice and told him I was his fan and my family only watched his films and so on ….

Dilip Sahab was always very protective about me because of his deep respect for my father. Every time he asked me to join a fund collection drive of the industry or any other benefit event, which he organized from time to time to assist the government in providing relief to the victims of natural calamities, he sent his secretary Premji to fetch me and ensure that I was looked after. I think his respect for the ladies and for the seniors in the industry had a lot to do with his family background and upbringing. He was the father figure to his brothers and sisters and he would certainly have had a parental upbringing that taught him to be humble and respectful.

---

*An actor known for playing historical characters such as *Baiju Bawra* (1952).
**If that is so, hit my head with a stone.

My sister Meena was married to C. V. K. Shastry, who was a production adviser to B. R. Chopra. Dilip Sahab knew Shastryji well as he often consulted him on various matters related to production when he produced *Gunga Jumna*. So the ties between my family and Dilip Sahab and Saira grew stronger. As time passed Saira, though she was much younger, became a friend and my visits to their residence became frequent. In fact, Dilip Sahab stood like a family member at the religious solemnization of Meena and Shastryji's wedding ceremony.

In my own way I had established myself in the industry as an actress and I had teamed up with every top actor in the business. The only star with whom I never got a chance to work was Dilip Kumar and that I felt was quite unfortunate. It just did not happen. How I wished for an assignment opposite him because it was the ultimate stamp of success for a star to be cast opposite Dilip Kumar!

When I voluntarily retired from films in 1974 I recall Dilip Sahab asking me why I had stopped working. I told him I felt I should bid goodbye while 'the sun is shining'. He smiled and did not say anything. He had obliged my family by doing the formal inauguration of a road named after our father Master Vinayak near my Perry Cross Road residence in Bandra. My brother Jayprakash had gone to him and requested him to do the honours and he had instantly agreed. He was most approachable and accessible even at the peak of his stardom. All those who copy his acting have failed to borrow from him his intrinsic humility and goodness.

I returned to face the cameras in Raj Kapoor's *Prem Rog*. At that time B. R. Chopra Sahab was penning the script of *Mazdoor*. He asked me whether I would do a small role opposite Dilip Sahab. I jumped at the opportunity. I told Chopra Sahab I would do it even if it was only one scene in the entire film with Dilip Sahab. I worked with Dilip Kumar in *Mazdoor* [released in 1983] and I said to myself: 'Now your track record is complete, Nanda!'

NIMMI

 I HAVE A FUNNY RECOLLECTION of the first time I saw Yousuf Sahab. I was on the sets of *Andaz* [1949] where Mehboob Khan was picturizing a dramatic scene between Raj Kapoor and Dilip Kumar. I had settled down somewhat in Bombay after shifting from Abbottabad, the small town in Uttar Pradesh where I grew up under the care of my grandmother after my mother's sudden death. I was nurturing a desire to get into the acting profession and my aunt Jyothi, who was an actress, had got permission from Mehboob Khan to be a quiet visitor on the sets of *Andaz*, which was being shot at Central Studio at Tardeo in Bombay.

This was post-independence and there was a lot happening in Delhi and UP where there were communal disturbances following Mahatma Gandhi's assassination [on 30 January 1948]. In Bombay, too, there was curfew and restricted movements. Both Dilip Kumar and Raj Kapoor were very popular stars at that time and I was very thrilled to see them in flesh and blood on the sets of *Andaz*.

I was therefore all attention when Raj Kapoor was being briefed by Mehboob Sahab. Dilip Kumar, however, wasn't being briefed and not acting at all! His body movements, his expressions and his soft modulated voice did not show any visible signs of acting! Both my grandmother and I wondered how Mehboob Sahab had chosen an actor who did not know how to act.

When the film was released, we watched it on the first day itself. And I realized what a fool I was! I found myself watching Dilip Kumar not only with admiration for the way he brought the character alive on the screen but with a sense of awe because he was holding the audience attention in every scene, without showing the strain of acting. I realized how silly I was and how little I knew about acting and the medium of cinema itself.

It was during my visit to the sets of *Andaz* that Raj Kapoor noticed me and offered me the second lead in *Barsaat* [also released in 1949] for which he was looking for a girl who possessed the simplicity and naiveté of a village girl. I was among the four girls he screen-tested and he zeroed in on me because I fit the role exactly.

Now I was required to act and I decided not to act, thinking I could be Dilip Kumar. It was a disaster. Raj Kapoor came to my house with a vermillion string that is used in *poojas* [prayers] and he asked me to tie it round his wrist. I asked him what it meant and he told me, 'You are my sister from today. For heaven's sake act and do not ruin your brother's film.' That did it. I understood it was not easy to be Dilip Kumar. Dilip Kumar was a special creation of the Almighty and he was blessed with a gift and ability that was rare. Lesser mortals like me had better act.

I performed as directed by Raj Kapoor. The audience and the industry welcomed me and I began to get leading role offers. Now I was yearning to work with Dilip Kumar. And lo and behold, my second film was with him! It was *Aan*, India's first Technicolor film. My real learning as an actress and a woman started with *Aan* [1952] as I witnessed the greatness of Dilip Kumar as an actor and as a fine, unselfish and caring human being.

At the start of the casting itself he suggested to Mehboob Khan to cast Premnath [he was Raj Kapoor's wife's brother] as the villain. At that time Premnath was a popular lead actor and he naturally turned down the offer. But Yousuf Sahab was keen to have him cast and so took the trouble of going to Premnath's house and convincing him to take the plunge as a villain. He promised him that the script was so good that his negative role and performance would be the talk of the industry. That's how Premnath joined the cast of the film and I remember him publicly thanking Yousuf Sahab at the Ceylon [now Sri Lanka] premiere of *Aan* for persuading him to take the assignment.

What I wish to point out is that Yousuf Sahab is perhaps the only actor in the world who always saw to it that actors of calibre were pitted against him. In usual circumstances, actors make sure that other roles in the script are given to less competent actors so that the spotlight is completely turned on them.

All of us got tremendous mileage from *Aan* from the day it mounted the sets. Mehboob Khan wanted to film the movie in Technicolor and he was wondering how to accomplish the feat. There were no proper cameras and the processing had to be done in London, which meant an enormous expense and it seemed like an impossibility. Yousuf Sahab had a series of meetings with the brilliant Faredoon A. Irani and he convinced the ace cameraman that with his kind of expertise he could shoot the entire film in 16 mm and have it blown up to 35 mm. Faredoon Irani accepted the challenge.

When *Aan* went to the Technicolor lab in London the chief technician in the lab expressed a keenness to meet Faredoon Irani to congratulate him for the skill with which he had filmed the movie using an obsolete camera. When it was blown to 35 mm nobody could find out that it was filmed on 16 mm. All his life Irani kept telling everybody how he would never have had the courage if Yousuf Sahab hadn't encouraged him.

That's the wonderful quality of Yousuf Sahab. He is a great motivator. He will do everything possible to make the actors and technicians working with him achieve the impossible and the unattainable. *Aan* was a worldwide success. At the London premiere British actors and directors were so impressed by Yousuf Sahab that they were inviting him to settle down in the UK and work in English films. I too was asked if I would like to work in English films but the idea of kissing on screen and love scenes put me off completely.

The premiere of *Aan* in Ceylon was one of the biggest in terms of the massive crowds that lined the streets from the airport to the hotel where we were put up. They were all Dilip Kumar fans. Such was the mass hysteria that the crowds broke all cordons at the airport and breached security at the hotel to see him. I have never seen anything so maddening.

The enormous success of *Aan* was a slap in the face of critics who made sarcastic remarks at the start of the film's shooting, saying 'Mehboob Khan *pagal ho gaya.* Tragedy King Dilip Kumar *ke haath mein talwar de di'.* (Mehboob Khan has lost his mind, placing a sword in the hands of an actor who has only performed tragic roles.) In *Aan* Yousuf Sahab played a poor villager who was deft with the sword and was an expert at fencing. I remember the London distributor of the film (titled *Savage Princess*), Sir Alexander Korda, asking Yousuf Sahab how he performed the fencing scenes so perfectly. He was so impressed that he came to India soon after and Mehboob Sahab invited him to sound the clapper board for the first shot of *Amar.*

I worked in five films with Yousuf Sahab: *Aan, Amar* [1954], *Daag* [1952], *Uran Khatola* [1955] and *Deedar* [1951]. The gossip newspapers and magazines used to be ceaselessly speculating about the heroines repeatedly working with him. He was a handsome, educated and extremely charming bachelor and the biggest superstar of the time. He had the bearing of a prince and spoke both English and Urdu with ease and sophistication. It was only natural that not only his countless female fans but also the actresses who co-starred with him nurtured a secret desire to get married to him.

I was often asked then and even now whether I was also one of those who lost sleep wishing to be the one to be chosen by him for marriage.

The fact is that I knew I stood no chance what with Madhubala already in his mind and heart. I preferred instead to be a good family friend and a co-star who pleased him by working with dedication. Yousuf Sahab always expected equal measure of dedication from his co-stars. Appreciation for my work coming from him was like graduation from a college for me.

His break-up with Madhubala was imminent by the time we completed the shooting of *Amar*. I think he came to know about Premnath and Madhubala being more than just friendly co-stars. Yousuf Sahab never revealed his feelings and being a man of few words he seldom spoke about matters other than the work we were doing.

I was close to his sisters especially his elder sister Sakina Aapa. I know how much he loved his siblings. I was the only heroine at his wedding procession, while all the others were obviously shedding tears of disappointment. I was invited on behalf of both Saira and Yousuf Bhai as Saira's mother Naseem Banu was a dear friend. She had extended a warm invitation to me but I walked with the procession from 48 Pali Hill to 34 Pali Hill.

Saira looked so beautiful and innocent with her beautiful eyes sparkling with the happiness of getting married to the man she was in love with from the age of twelve. I think now when I see her and her exceptional love and the devotion with which she looks after him that Allah made him make the right choice and he must have done some *neki* (good work) for which Allah has given him Saira as a reward.

BAKUL PATEL

*M*Y HUSBAND RAJNI PATEL AND DILIP Kumar met for the first time when Rajni was in charge of the Congress party's election campaign of V. K. Krishna Menon, who was contesting as a candidate from the North Bombay constituency in the 1962 Lok Sabha elections. It was one of the most talked about and most written about contests in India's political history because the race was between Congress stalwarts Krishna Menon and Acharya Kripalani, a former Congress president, who had quit that party to form his own outfit.

It was then that the enduring friendship between Rajni and Dilip Bhai began. Rajni thereafter could not think of doing anything without Dilip Bhai. Being a staunch Congress supporter Dilip Bhai was ever willing to stand by Rajni in taking forward any movement or any initiative for the Congress party. Dilip Bhai enjoyed the trust and love of Jawaharlal Nehru and, later, Indira Gandhi saw that he was unselfish to the core, often taking the time to rally round the Congress party when it called for the support of the people in providing relief to victims of natural calamities.

The bonding between Rajni and Dilip Bhai was based on a shared ideology as admirers of Nehru. Both of them rejected all aspirations for political authority by not settling for elective politics. They could have won landslide victories and got voted into Parliament; instead, Dilip Bhai opted to back candidates like Krishna Menon in elections to give the Congress party its triumph in more than one general election. Their common goal was to serve the common man and empower people through education.

Very few people know that the Nehru Centre at Worli is Rajni's and Dilip Bhai's brainchild. They developed the concept and sought the support of the Central Government (Indira Gandhi was in power then during her first tenure in 1966–77). The Nehru Centre was conceived as a tribute to Jawaharlal Nehru and his vision of modern India. The architect was their common friend, I. M. Kadri.

Dilip Bhai has never confined himself to films and his profession as an actor. He is a voracious reader and takes a keen interest in Indian and Western performing arts and fine arts, with friends from all walks of life. And it was during these interactions that he realized the need for a multifaceted cultural centre. He had talks with all his friends from the world of classical music, dance and drama, friends who taught history, science, geography and modern literature, friends who were engaged in research projects and so on for their inputs. Since Rajni and Dilip Bhai had both read Nehru's *Discovery of India* with keen interest, they were enthusiastic about having an entire section called Discovery of India.

On the day the foundation stone was laid for the Nehru Centre by Indira Gandhi in November 1972, there was a party at Rajni's house, which was attended by a couple of close associates of Rajni and of course Dilip Bhai. It was my birthday and Rajni told me he was going to celebrate my birthday. I was there at the party as a colleague and friend of Rajni – I was practising law then – and it was there that he disclosed his desire of marrying me to Dilip Bhai, who told him to go right ahead! And so Rajni proposed to me, adding that the marriage had to take place that night itself. I was naturally astounded and no amount of reasoning could make him change his mind. It was nearing midnight and I had to call my bewildered parents to come over while the real challenge was to find a pandit to solemnize the marriage. Dilip Bhai told somebody in the group to go get a pandit from somewhere. At that unearthly hour they woke up a pandit living near the Babulnath Temple (in Bombay)! They brought the bleary eyed chap and woke up shopkeepers they knew to get the stuff required for the ceremony. The marriage was solemnized with Dilip Bhai showering his blessings on both of us as my elder brother.

PYARELAL*

SAHAB'S CLOTHES HAD TO BE LAUNDERED WITH CARE AS HE ONLY WORE white and he liked his cotton shirts to be starched just right and his collar absolutely crease-free.

In the vicinity of Sahab's Pali Mala residence lived Abdul Bhai who gave Sahab his periodic hair cut. Abdul Bhai used to wonder aloud how Sahab's hair grew so fast after every hair cut. And no matter how hard he tried to give a neat cut the hair got tousled over the forehead. He got irked when young men came to him at his saloon saying: '*Hum ko* Dilip Kumar *ka* style *do*' (style our hair like Dilip Kumar's). And they never believed him when he told them that he didn't create that style – it just got done on its own as if by some magic.

Sahab spoke to me with a warm concern whenever he met me, asking about my family. He was a superstar and I remember his films running for a whole year at Bandra Talkies and how eagerly we awaited the release of his movies because he made only one film in a year. His fans would throng the road to his residence at Pali Mala and later at 48 Pali Hill. He never got irritated when they stopped his car at the gate of his house. He let them gaze at him and sometimes even talked to them for a few minutes.

*Personal *dhobi*.

I have been with Sahab and Sairaji for five decades. Sahab told me recently: '*Hum ko kabhi chod ke nahin jana. Mere bhai jaise ho tum.*' (Don't ever leave me; you are like my brother.) I was so overwhelmed I couldn't sleep that night.

VEERA RAO

I WAS A SHY YOUNG WOMAN WITH A POSTGRADUATE DEGREE FROM THE esteemed Tata Institute of Social Sciences in Bombay wanting to make a mark in the field of social work and social reform when Dilip Sahab took charge as the chairman of the National Association of the Blind. He was a superstar and everybody asked: what will an actor do for an organization like the NAB? At the most, they said, he will make an appearance once in a year and pretend to be concerned. They were all talking from general experience and certainly did not know how different Dilip Kumar was from other stars.

When Dilip Sahab took over as the chairman of NAB, the great challenge was to generate funds for the work we had on our agenda to improve the lot of the visually challenged and provide facilities for the specialized education they required. He had a meeting with all of us office bearers on NAB and I spoke about an idea that I had put forth to people in the management earlier and had got the cold shoulder.

The idea was to run a train once a year during the Derby races in Poona with double the charges of the normal train and call it 'the NAB train for charity'. The idea took birth in my mind when I had gone to Poona once during the Derby days and I was almost stranded there as I could neither get a bus nor a taxi nor a seat in a train to return to Bombay.

I had to come back the same day because I had left my small baby behind in my mother's care. Eventually the local station master helped me get a seat in a crowded train.

I had read about a train that ran during the Christmas season in London, which carried passengers who did last-minute shopping for Xmas and the train's collections were used for charity. I presented this idea to Dilip Sahab and very timidly suggested that it would be a good idea to make it the NAB train in which people could travel with Dilip Kumar. It did not take Dilip Sahab more than a minute to welcome the idea and he asked me to start working on it.

The very first year itself the train was a huge success. Dilip Sahab boarded it at Victoria Terminus station and set it on its journey by waving a green flag. He announced the first donation of Rs 50,000 and he walked from one end of the train to the other talking to excited passengers who had purchased tickets only to travel with Dilip Sahab. The word spread and every year people waited to be in the special NAB train to Poona. Dilip Sahab was such an attraction not only because he was a huge star but also because he was so down to earth and he mixed freely with all the passengers. He was so committed that he did not ignore a single passenger who wished to chat with him. In fact, if a passenger came once and made it again the next year, he would recognize him or her and pick up the threads of the conversation he had the previous year.

For ten years we ran the train and Dilip Sahab never let us down. The ample funds collected were used for many useful equipment and books that were bought. Dilip Sahab came up with many more ideas to encourage education of the blind and along with the ace cricketer Vijay Merchant initiated the social movement to provide job opportunities and absorb the visually challenged into the mainstream of life.

Whenever we approached Dilip Sahab with an idea for a good cause, he obliged at once. There was no dilly-dallying or finding excuses. He came out with the first donation always from his pocket. At one large event for school children at the Brabourne Stadium in Bombay, we had invited Dilip Sahab and a couple of new stars to distribute prizes. I noticed that everybody was wearing dark glasses since it was afternoon. Dilip Sahab alone was not without sun glasses. I realized that Dilip Sahab never ever wore dark glasses. I asked him why he never shielded his eyes from the sun and he said: 'I like to talk to people without hiding my eyes.'

I have been in the social service field for decades now. I have yet to come across someone as genuine and unselfish as Dilip Sahab.

WAHEEDA REHMAN

*M*Y FIRST FILM WITH DILIP KUMAR SAHAB was *Dil Diya Dard Liya*. I remember it took me a while to get adjusted to his style of working. I had been working with Guru Dutt and Dev Anand who were celebrated for the kind of work they were doing. With Dilip Sahab the difference was that he prepared a lot and he involved himself and others in the discussions about the scenes to be shot, taking care of the minutest of details and only then would he be ready for the shot. I was basically a spontaneous actor and I did not do much preparation. By and by, I got accustomed to his way of working and it was smooth sailing.

A piece of advice from my father stood me in good stead when I faced the cameras with Dilip Sahab for the first time. He said to me when I was very young that an artiste should never get awed by the presence of any dignitary or celebrity before whom she or he may be performing. He gave me the advice when I was to give a dance recital in the august presence of C. Rajagopalachari, the governor general of India. I was nervous, but he advised me to concentrate on my performance and not be conscious of the governor general's presence. I did just that.

I got accustomed to Dilip Sahab's painstaking preparation to bring realism to his acting but I continued to work the way I always worked, getting into the role and scene when the lights were switched on and 'action' was called. It was customary when we were shooting for *Aadmi* [released in 1968] to have the scenes and dialogue handed over to us a day in advance so that we could be fully prepared for the work. Even though the director was Bhim Singh it was Dilip Sahab who was at the helm. So, when I did not get my scene and dialogue one day when pack-up was announced, I asked Dilip Sahab why nothing was given to me. Was I not required the next day, I wanted to know. He said: 'You are required but in the shot you are not going to act, instead you are going to react exactly the way you react in real life flapping and waving your hands and speaking through your eyes to convey your excitement.'

I was puzzled. The next day, when I arrived on the sets for the shot, he reminded me that I would have to react exactly as I would if I were in the same situation in real life. He said: 'You have this habit of gesticulating and giving facial expressions when you are talking. That's what I want in this shot.'

It was a new experience for me and it was not only wonderful while I did what was told to me but it turned out to be a scene that got me compliments from my peers and seniors. I think this was the '*tin ka dabba hatao*' [remove this tin box – referring to Dilip Kumar's car] scene in *Aadmi* where Dilip Sahab strolls onto his property and I tick him off, thinking he is an intruder.

It was a mystery to me why Dilip Sahab did not give his name as director in the film credits when all the hard work behind the camera was being done by him, motivating both the technicians and artistes to give their best. If the artistes working with him are seen to be performing way better than they usually perform, it is because he challenges them with his own level of performance and the unrelenting effort he puts into his work.

In our time, we did not go to gyms and so on, but being the excellent sportsman that he is, Dilip Sahab never missed his game of badminton when we were outdoors or in a city away from home. He always asked what sport we enjoyed, making us take part not just to give us physical exercise but also to generate camaraderie in the unit. We were in Madras (now Chennai) for long stretches of time, sometimes for two months at a stretch shooting for *Ram Aur Shyam* and *Aadmi* simultaneously and we were all staying at the same place, which meant that we were bumping into each other after work also. Like a leader he took the initiative to see that none of us had any complaints and we shared good vibes and respected each other. There was a democratic atmosphere on the sets of all his starrers. He used to sit with us for meals and then suddenly get up and go to the table laid out for the technicians and others who were assistants in different departments to see what they were having.

Once, while we were in Ooty [a hill station now in Tamil Nadu] the weather suddenly turned bad and we could not continue with our outdoor work for an entire week. There was no option but to stay indoors with nothing to do. Dilip Sahab disappeared for half a day and nobody knew where he had gone. His friend, Pran Sahab, got very worried. Then, late in the afternoon he returned with a pile of books. He decided to gift us all with books that we could engross ourselves with. There was fiction for those who loved fiction, crossword compilations for those who liked to solve word puzzles, joke collections for those who enjoyed humour ...

There have been two regrets in my mind about Dilip Sahab's splendid career. When I was working in Satyajit Ray's *Abhijan* [1962], Mr Ray asked me if I could speak to Dilip Sahab about a film he had in mind, an idea he believed was perfect for Dilip Sahab. I spoke to Dilip Sahab but he did not give any reply. He just looked thoughtful. So I told Mr Ray to speak to him. I gathered later that Dilip Sahab did not agree to do the film because it required him to appear bare bodied. The other regret is that Dilip Kumar and Guru Dutt did not come together in *Pyaasa* [released in 1957]. It would have become a bigger world classic than it is today.

Harish Salve

W<small>HEN</small> S<small>AIRAJI</small> <small>ASKED</small> <small>ME</small> <small>TO</small> <small>WRITE</small> <small>AN</small> account on the traumatic experiences of Dilip Sahab leading up to the events of the summer of 1975, it brought forth memories etched deeply in my mind – some of shared joys and mirth, some of shared anger, sorrow and disappointment.

I met Dilip Sahab (my sister called him Dilip Uncle – I have always reverentially addressed him as Sir) in 1970. On a warm morning in May, my sister woke me up from a vacation-induced slumber to meet the legend who was there in person. I cannot forget meeting him for the first time. A study in sophistication, he was just as I had thought he would be – and more.

The conversation that ensued gradually disclosed the reasons why there was a visible agitation permeating his calm exterior.

His troubles began when the Income Tax Department decided to assess him on allegations of having earned *black money* – something for which Bollywood was, in public perception, notorious. The assessment would not only result in a large demand for escaped tax, but also penalties equal to the escaped income, and possible prosecution for evasion of tax.

The aforementioned deparment is not reputed for its fairness, but Indian businessmen have learned to take such tribulations as an inevitable cost of doing business in India. A sensitive artiste looks at life differently.

Having grown up in the household of one of India's leading tax accountants, the sight of clients at the wrong end of the tax barrel was nothing new. Seeing Dilip Sahab in the years that followed has imbued me with a sensitivity to the feelings of those who reel at the idea of the ignominy of such allegations.

I kept track of what transpired in the years that followed – the stormy seventies leading up to the events of June 1975.

Having signed up for my articleship for chartered accountancy and having becoming a student of tax law, I came to understand the nuances of the problem. A raid conducted upon the disgruntled producer of a movie called *Dil Diya Dard Liya** (clearly stage managed by him) supposedly yielded evidence by way of secret accounts maintained by him in which there was an entry against *DK* of a sum of Rs 10 lakh. There was no corroborative evidence to show that anything was paid by him or received by Dilip Sahab; nor indeed was there any material to suggest that the producer had a sum of Rs 10 lakh (a king's ransom at that time) to pay in cash. Yet an allegation was made that Dilip Sahab possessed concealed income; penalties were imposed and there was a threat of a potential prosecution.

When the assessment proceedings were initiated, Dilip Sahab reached out to those in Delhi who professed friendship, protesting his innocence, pointing out the malice underlying the allegation and asking for being spared the harassment.

I saw him in Delhi often – at times hopeful, at times dejected, at times stoic, at times angry! It was a learning experience – one thing I learned at that young age was that there are no friends in the capital!

The assessment was made. He wisely pursued legal remedies, and there was some respite when an appeal against this perverse assessment was allowed.

The powers that be in Delhi had, in the meantime, promised Dilip Sahab that the system would be fair and would drop the matter if the first appeal went in his favour. It proved to be a ruse!

The year 1974 saw a spate of preventive detentions of those alleged to have committed economic offences (however tenuous the allegations) and personal liberties became a hostage to a shrill campaign to trample underfoot the rights of those alleged to be economic offenders in the march towards socialism.

In such a surcharged atmosphere, the promises of a sensible and humane resolution vanished as fast as the morning dew in summer.

By 1975, I remember my father, N. K. P. Salve (who later became a Union minister), angrily telling Dilip Sahab that he should now brace himself for a fight and contest the appeal in the Income Tax Tribunal.

---

*A 1966 film whose producer and director was A. R. Kardar.

I finished my graduation in May 1975, and my father decided to allow me to appear with him in the tribunal (carrying his files) until such time as I qualified as a chartered accountant. And my first case was *Income Tax Officer* vs *Dilip Kumar* alias Yousuf Khan, to be heard by the tribunal on a day-to-day basis in June 1975.

The hearing was set for the second week of June 1975. In the two weeks that preceded the hearing, we would sit in a suite in the Oberoi Hotel at Nariman Point, Bombay, and prepare the case. The team was headed by my father, and included his trusted lieutenant – Ajay Thakore, a tax accountant par excellence.

Then there was G. N. Joshi – Dilip Sahab's trusted accountant.

One person I fondly remember was Purohitji – a wise old man who was in the movie finance business, but whose affection for Dilip Sahab was almost paternal.

Our meetings would start around 11 a.m. and end much after the sun had set in the Arabian Sea. Dilip Sahab would sit all day, attentive to the discussions among the team members. And when the accountants found themselves in any difficulty, he suggested a solution – at times in mellifluous Urdu and other times in English that would have been the envy of Richard Burton, a famous British actor known for his flawless diction! His clarity of thought was only matched by the magnificence of expression.

The hearing began and the department's representative – a senior and experienced officer – tried tirelessly to put across the department's case to the tribunal – only to increasing chagrin of the members whose tentative comments were carping to the point of being cynical as to what this case was all about.

And then all hell broke loose.

Just about this time, the Allahabad High Court (on 12 June 1975) set aside Prime Minister Indira Gandhi's election in 1971 to the Lok Sabha, and the Supreme Court vacation judge, Justice Krishna Iyer, true to his mettle, declined an absolute stay. On 25 June the infamous Emergency was declared.

My father had to seek a short adjournment as (being a Congress MP) he had to fly to Delhi for a day or two.

My youthful anger at the injustice heaped upon this iconic Indian, increased exponentially at what I considered dishonest suspension of democracy under the power of numbers and rhetoric – a view I still maintain.

It was in this surcharged atmosphere that the hearing went on for about three weeks.

Realizing the potential of his client's skills in vocal mesmerization, my father obviously decided to unleash him upon the unsuspecting members of the tribunal at some time (although he did not, as a foxy interlocutor, disclose his intentions to us).

The opportunity presented itself in a moment when the tribunal members asked my father about how a movie was produced. My father asked for leave to ask his client to explain the process – this brought the roof down on the department's case!

What chance did those poor mortals – of an age when they possibly swooned over *Suhaana Safar** in their youth – have against the scene that had just unfolded.

By the end of that day, the fate of the case was sealed even if the arguments carried on. Dilip Sahab spoke for over 40 minutes explaining not just how movies are made but how he had been pilloried. This was followed by a two-minute silence – almost as though to mourn the death of the department's case.

Dilip Sahab decided to host a celebratory dinner – even though one last day of hearing remained. It was an unbridled joy to see him in good cheer – I realized the worth of hard work to vindicate the honour of a client.

The evening was magical. Purohitji produced another surprise – he brought along his two sons who were fantastic ghazal singers.

Sairaji was as always – at her best. A gracious host, charming the guests equally by turn of phrase as by her magical smile.

And on a personal note – I met one of Dilip Sahab's dearest friends - the late Satish Bhalla. Little did I know in the summer of 1975, that I would fall madly in love with – and marry – his niece Meenakshi – in 1981.

I joined the bar in 1980 – and the first case I appeared in the Supreme Court was the petition for leave to appeal by the Income Tax Department against the tribunal judgment in favour of Dilip Sahab. To my immense joy, it lasted for all of two minutes before the judges threw it out!

A friendship made in trying times endures forever. Dilip Sahab – the consummate Pathan – was one of my father's closest friends. My mother – an astute judge of the human character and a person difficult to please –

*A hauntingly melodious song picturized on Dilip Kumar in the 1958 film *Madhumati*, sung by Mukesh, written by Shailendra and set to tune by Salil Chaudhury.

was always very happy to meet Sairaji and Dilip Sahab.

My father moved to Aurangzeb Road in New Delhi after he became a minister in 1983 in Indira Gandhi's cabinet. Memories abound of evenings of music, poetry and mirth spent in my father's home with Sairaji and Dilip Sahab.

Over the years, we met often, and our relationship became more special after I married Meenakshi! Sairaji and Meenakshi are very close spiritually.

Dilip Sahab is a tall human being – an icon, and yet a friend – a timeless phenomenon, which the almighty exhibits only infrequently to show the faithful his benevolence and to rekindle their faith in him. And of these memories – it was truly said

> God gave His children memory
> That in life's garden there might be
> June roses in December ...

SAYESHA*
WALTZING WITH THE LEGEND ... *PHUPHONANA*

DANCING TO ME COMES AS NATURALLY AS breathing and I was the typical dancing diva at home! All of five years of age, I was giving my most spontaneous performance to an enraptured audience of my granduncle, my grandaunt and my mother! Little did I know that the man who asked for an encore, clapping enthusiastically along with his shrill whistle that made me cover my ears, and whom I called and revered as my granduncle, was the greatest actor in the Indian film fraternity! How many girls in the world can say they waltzed in real life, not on celluloid, with the great Dilip Kumar? None! Only me. That makes me feel really special!

*Sultan's granddaughter.

He is the most loving, child-friendly grandparent and often took me for drives in his burgundy Mercedes, with the police jeep escorting the car, sometimes using the siren to clear the way. My child-like imagination ran riot at such times, and I believed that the paraphernalia was all for me! I definitely felt like royalty! When he walked at Joggers Park [in Bandra], I held his hand and skipped to keep pace with him. I always noticed that my grandaunt would gracefully slide away so that I could hold his hand. I have never seen devotion to a husband that parallels *phuponani*'s. There is not one day that I remember the two apart from each other. That makes their relationship incomparable.

I entered hand-in-hand with him and my grandaunt to the premiere of the coloured version of his movie *Mughal-e-Azam* [in 2004], which was when I experienced the hysteria that surrounded him, and the immense respect that he effortlessly commanded. His humble demeanour despite his legendary status kept me spellbound. He became a revelation that instant and I realized that *phuphonana* was beyond just my granduncle!

As I grew, I learnt some beautiful Urdu words from him. My best efforts would receive an encouraging '*Umda*' (superb)! The most cherished movie song for me will always be *Koi sagar dil ko behlata nahin* from his movie *Dil Diya Dard Liya** as I have sung this song with him innumerable times. His voice always matched beautifully with the expression in his eyes and he never sang a note out of tune!

Recently I saw his movie *Mashaal*, and the very famous scene in which he is trying to stop a car to take his dying wife to hospital. Then I saw *Gunga Jumna* and his death scene wrenched my heart. My soft and loving granduncle, metamorphosed into a dynamic, powerhouse performer within seconds. With no references for him, just self-study, he is unbelievable! Although he is admired for being the ultimate tragedy king on screen, in reality, *phuphonana* is fun loving, child-like and always ready for a new adventure. He has a wicked sense of humour, which he displays in the most unexpected circumstances that too without ever being caught.

I remember him advising me to speak slowly and keep a pleasant expression at all times. He never liked seeing me frown and would pull me up immediately. Such intricate observations and suggestions from him will remain etched in my memory forever.

*Sung by Mohammed Rafi, written by Shakeel Badayuni and set to tune by Naushad.

I cannot thank god enough to be as fortunate as to be born, during the time where I could witness the presence of the thespian, the legend, and the genius of … my most loving granduncle, my *phuphonana*, Dilip Kumar!

I love you!

– Sayesha

SHAHEEN*
YOUSUF UNCLE AND ME …

$\mathcal{D}$ILIP KUMAR: THE LEGEND, THE ENIGMA, the thespian, the tragedy king; so many words describing him! However, I never even realized that I was living with such an iconic figure in the same home, till I was probably twelve. For me, he is the uncle who married my paternal aunt, Saira, and became a father-figure. Yousuf Uncle is one of a kind! My relationship with him is unique, as I have grown up with him witnessing my life. I have shared all my secrets with him, from my tantrums, to my crushes and he has been my confidant throughout my teenage adventures.

My first memory of him is blurry, but they say little children sometimes remember strange things and so I distinctly recollect him, carrying me in his palm, much above his head, swinging me to and fro, with me gurgling in delight and my aunt shrieking in horror: '*Woh gir jayegi, woh gir jayegi!* (She'll fall down!) My aunt is quite gentle, having been one of two children, and he is definitely boisterous, coming from a family of more people than one can count!

Switzerland for many of us is synonymous with Yash Chopra's movies. But for me, it's the place I spent my school holidays with my family. The

*Sultan's daughter and Sayesha's mother.

boat ride on Lake Geneva with Yousuf Uncle, the fact that he never carried enough money for anything really and had it not been for my aunt checking his wallet religiously, he would probably be stuck everywhere, as he does not remember numbers and of course we are talking about the days when no one had even heard of mobile phones!

I remember an instance when he insisted that his French could be rivalled by all of France, and he took me with him for a drive in Geneva. As luck would have it, a woman who did not know a word of English drove our taxi. Of course, Yousuf Uncle's French was far from smattering, and soon we were miles away from a drive in the mountains that we requested, heading at top speed to an alien destination! At this time, I was fifteen, although, I probably looked older, and the taxi driver mistook me to be a young woman on a romantic excursion with him! Hungry, tired and a trifle frustrated, we asked for a restaurant to have some lunch. It was only after a few bites of the lovely sole fish on a waterfront café, when we realized to our horror that the driver had deposited us on a topless beach. All of Yousuf Uncle's bravado suddenly vanished and he asked me to run with him towards the taxi, completely flummoxed at being in this situation with his niece! His expression was definitely a Kodak moment!

He is exactly the way I would have wanted my son to be. Yousuf Uncle is the typical man, and truly exuberates macho; yet has the most vulnerable look in eyes that can make anyone's heart melt. He loves sports, and would never miss a cricket match or a football game. My childhood was spent holding his *firkee* while he flew the kite. I learnt to fly a kite thanks to him, but was never successful in defeating him although I made several failed attempts in our impromptu matches. But like all other things, he is just an absolute pro at kite flying! He spruces up omelettes that can give the best chef a run for his money; he has his own list of special ingredients that give a dish that extra edge: like ginger in an omelette accompanied by a dash of black pepper! He can buy saris for a woman like no one else. Also like a typical man, he never remembered birthdays or anniversaries. It would only be the arrival of all the other bouquets from friends that would ring a bell in his mind that perhaps it was an occasion that he needed to jog his memory about! On realizing the yearly faux pas, he would pack me off to the nearest florist at Bandstand saying, 'Shaheen, *main toh bhool gaya, aisa karo, zara jaldi jao, aur kuch phool banva lo, phir mujhe bula lena!*' [Shaheen, I have forgotten; so get a bouquet made, then call me.] Endless instructions would follow and I had to organize a huge display of flowers, mostly orchids that were rare in those days. I would spend hours having this arrangement made, with the whole florist [shop] at my service. Then I would ring him up from a landline, and he would sneak out of the house and come to inspect the bouquet. The next hour or two would be spent under the guidance of Mr Dilip Kumar, who at that moment, behaved like he was straight out of Ikebana classes! Now with the bouquet in tow, we would reach home and would then dramatically present my aunt the flowers, as if it was meant to be a surprise, and the occasion was never out of his memory at all. My aunt, a complete sucker for his affection, lapped it up effortlessly year after year gushing about 'Sahab' being so thoughtful!

Children fascinate him. When my daughter, Sayesha, was born, he told me several times that he always wondered what she was thinking as she slept in her cot, wishing he could get a glimpse of her dream! 'What makes her smile as she sleeps,' he would say! It is this curious nature, one of eternal wonderment that wants to learn or read all the time that probably makes him what he is.

One thing that all of us in the family got used to is his habit of rearranging the furniture to his own specifications every time there was a party! Yousuf Uncle always came home with a battalion of guests, who would obviously stay for dinner. The menu had to be simple but elaborate. There was no question of ordering from a hotel.

My sixteenth birthday will remain my most cherished one, as there was a family dinner organized, and he came home having bought around a hundred *mogra gajras* [jasmine strands] for me from the signal on the street in Bandra! That was his love. Bangalore is another fond memory! My aunt and uncle were dutifully being good parents, and took me to an ice-cream parlour on M. G. [Mahatma Gandhi] Road. These were the days when he ruled the industry. He was huge. Needless to say as we went into the ice-cream parlour, a massive crowd gathered outside! We had to rush out, only to find that our chauffeur had vanished to relieve himself! Now never short of ideas, Yousuf Uncle hailed a cab, jumped into the driver's seat and sped away much to the amusement of the public! It was my best taxi ride ever!

I can go on but I don't want to share it all right away. Suffice it to say that he is like no other. He has the prayers of millions and God blesses him. We are blessed because we have him in our lives.

Yousuf Uncle, I will always love you.

SALIM SHARIFEE*

I CAN'T DESCRIBE MY RELATIONSHIP WITH DILIP SAHAB AS ANYTHING but a bounty of destiny. I was a fan of Sahab from boyhood and it was my dream to meet him in person. I spoke about my wish to a family friend who knew Sahab quite well. He said he would try to arrange a meeting when he would be in Bombay. He must have spoken to Sahab about my ardent admiration and desire to meet him. And then the most unforgettable thing happened in my life one day when I was in Bombay for an important official meeting and was staying at the Taj in south Bombay. My diary had Sahab's phone number; I dialled and the voice that answered at the other end was Sahab's. I introduced myself and he recognized me at once as the young banker from Dubai. He said he was meeting somebody in south Bombay that afternoon and he asked me if he could drop by. I was speechless and couldn't say a word! Then I told him I would be honoured and privileged and he must have sensed the thrill and nervousness in my voice. In his gentle voice he simply said: 'I'll be there as soon as I am free from my meeting.'

As I waited for Sahab in my room I couldn't contain my excitement. I couldn't believe it was all happening to me. As promised Sahab arrived and when I opened the door and actually saw him before me in his white high-collared shirt and white trousers you could have knocked me down with a feather.

We spent an hour chatting and all the time I was asking myself – is this really happening to me?

What swept me off my feet was Sahab's unaffected warmth and humility. When I saw him to his car he said: 'We must keep in touch and meet again.' I couldn't believe my ears.

Sahab is like an elder brother to me. He and I were simply destined to meet and bond in this life, I feel. I don't remember a single special occasion when I have not been present at the bungalow and having the privilege of being seated by Sahab's side along with Sahab's brothers. When occasionally he gives us the privilege of having him and Sairaji as our guests at our humble home in Dubai, it was such a pleasure because he puts us at complete ease with his ability to become one of us. My children look forward to his visit with more delight than the visit of their grandfather, i.e., my father.

*A family friend and an ardent admirer of Dilip Kumar.

Sahab loves holidays in unusual places. He spoke to me from a government guest house in Jaisalmer [in Rajasthan] once and he was sounding so happy and excited like a child. He found the location very attractive and he was enjoying himself thoroughly. Another time I received an invitation from him to join him and Sairaji at Mercara, a forest location in Coorg [in Karnataka]. He was charmed by the raw beauty of the place and was very amused by the fact that Sairaji was getting scared of the gigantic butterflies and dragonflies fluttering all over the place.

Even in Mumbai when I go to meet him at Bandra, he's quick to suggest that we go on a long drive and wind up the evening with an early dinner at the Taj. He loves to give his family and close friends surprise treats at any of the restaurants at the Taj, Mumbai. The first time Sahab took me to Rendezvous at the Taj, I was stunned because people sitting at tables and enjoying their conversation and food just stopped eating and heads turned towards us. Subsequently, I have got used to the awe and admiration Sahab commands wherever he goes. Whether it is Dubai or Mumbai, his mere presence at any place changes the aura and ambience of the place completely. He is a man of impeccable manners and royal taste and I shall not hesitate to admit that my own taste for clothes, food and living have changed for the better with my frequent interaction with Sahab.

Not a day passes without my viewing a Dilip Kumar movie. I have a collection of all his starrers. My favourite is *Gunga Jumna*. Irrespective of the umpteen viewings of the film, I get a lump in my throat when I watch the death scene in the climax.

DR R. C. SHARMA

I WAS INTRODUCED TO SAIRAJI BY HER KATHAK GURU, ROSHAN KUMARI, in 1987. I was to treat Sairaji's grandmother Ammaji. When I arrived at Sairaji's bungalow, I was escorted upstairs to Ammaji's room. In the dining room I saw Dilip Kumar Sahab at the table enjoying a well-laid-out lunch with Sairaji and her famous mother, Naseem Banuji. He was so simple in his attire and appearance that in a single moment all the notions I had in my mind about film celebrities just dissolved into thin air. A layperson always imagines that a star would put on airs and here I was standing in front of the country's most revered star and he was talking and joking and eating with his fingers like any of us!

Dilip Sahab met me warmly, excused himself, and went to his room. I examined Ammaji and prescribed medicines for her and left. It was at the next meeting that I really got to know the man he is. Ammaji developed a sudden problem and I was summoned to see her at 10 p.m. When I reached the bungalow the most anxious person in the house was Dilip Sahab. He was by her bedside, stroking her brow and talking to her softly. I prescribed a medicine that unfortunately was not available in any of the chemists' shops nearby. Dilip Sahab held me by my hand and said: 'Doctor, I am coming with you, I know where it is available, let us go.'

We brought the medicine and administered it. Sahab did not rest till Ammaji was breathing and feeling better. That night I saw not Dilip Kumar but a loving man deeply concerned about someone who obviously meant a lot to him.

As the years went by I was slowly getting to know many other facets of the superb actor I had admired during my college days. He was concerned about all the members of his family and Sairaji's family as well as the servants and office staff. He thanked me more than once when I responded to an SOS call at night and rushed to the bungalow. When I told him I was doing my duty he said: 'Doctor, you don't know how reassuring it is to have a doctor at hand when someone develops a serious condition.'

He reads voraciously on all subjects, including medicine. He addressed a medical conference once and all of us from the medical fraternity listened spellbound to his speech, which was replete with information about the latest developments in the field. Nobody could tell that he was an actor and medicine was not his subject.

In 1999 we had to take a decision about which hospital to choose for an open-heart surgery that had to be done on him. All his friends suggested hospitals in the countries such as the USA, the UK and Canada. Dilip Sahab put his foot down and insisted that the surgery be done in India. He said: 'I am an Indian and our doctors and surgeons are the best in the world.' There was a surge of requests from all the hospitals in Mumbai to bring him to them. He chose the Lilavati Hospital (in Bandra) and Dr Ramakant Panda (one the top cardiologists of India) performed the surgery. He went through the procedure cheerfully and joked with all of us about his heart. Indeed, his heart is of gold – pure 24 carat!

I have been going for a walk with him to the Joggers Park (in Bandra) practically every day. We go very late (around 9 p.m.) to avoid the crowds. Even at that hour fans wait to see him. He is a a warm human being who will not turn a deaf ear to anyone who tries to tell him something. At the gate, invariably his purse gets lightened as some distressed man or woman stops to ask for help. When people praise him he becomes more humble.

I was in Jaipur with him once. Sairaji sent me to take care of him as he was slightly unwell. There, I received the bad news that my grandmother had passed away. He at once arranged a car and driver to take me to the Rajasthan village where she had died. He never treated me like a paid family physician, but as a member of his family. He attended all our family functions and knew my close relatives.

He is a man who has walked with Jawaharlal Nehru, received the highest honours and still has the world at his feet almost two decades after he voluntarily stopped accepting films, but has never lost the common touch.

RAMESH SIPPY

AS A YOUNGSTER WHO WANTED TO BE A part of the wondrous world of films, I cherished a desire to direct a film, in which Dilip Kumar would act. Like other aspirants of my generation I grew up watching *Gunga Jumna*, *Devdas*, *Azaad*, *Kohinoor*, etc., and marvelled at the way he performed.

After I had made some films, which got noticed and after the spectacular success of *Sholay* [1975], I thought I was ready to approach Dilip Sahab with a wish to direct him. He and my father (G. P. Sippy) were very good friends and Dilip Sahab used to acknowledge me warmly when he visited our home; he would ask [about] me but he never spoke about my work, so I did not know what he thought of me as a director.

Salim[Khan] and Javed [Akhtar], the writers of *Sholay* had a subject they had based on a Tamil film and they kept telling me that the film (*Shakti*) could be made only if Dilip Kumar agreed to play the father's role. The producers, Mushir and Riaz, were all for the subject and they asked me if I could talk to Dilip Sahab about it.

With some trepidation I approached Sahab and he seemed aware of the story, may be because Salim Khan had told him about it. After some casual talk Sahab agreed to consider the subject and wanted the writers to meet him. I was so happy I went home with a feeling that I had conquered the world not so much because the mission was accomplished but more because Sahab gave me an indication that he was confident about my ability to do justice to the emotional conflicts inherent in the subject.

We told Sahab about the actors we intended to cast in the film and he said he was fine with anybody I thought fit to play the other characters. We mentioned Amitabh Bachchan and he said he was aware that he was a malleable and competent actor.

When you have Dilip Kumar heading the cast you don't really have to tell the other actors much. The admiration and respect for Sahab is such that actors just want to be in the film.

The media hype surrounding the casting of Amitabh Bachchan opposite Dilip Kumar was enormous. I say opposite, because Amitabh was to play the son who grows up with a deep sense of anger and resentment and takes a hostile stand against the father, played by Sahab. The curiosity factor was whether Amitabh Bachchan had the mettle to measure up to the histrionic challenge inherent in the role pitted against the role of the father, which was the pivot of the story.

The first shot of the *mahurat* was taken on the sea front at Juhu with Sahab and Amitabh Bachchan featuring in the scene. There was not only Indian media but also some foreign correspondents who were eager to capture the coming together of the legendary superstar Dilip Kumar and the emerging legend and superstar Amitabh Bachchan together in one frame.

Dilip Sahab was wearing a suit from his own wardrobe and was in the room booked for him in the hotel at Juhu beach. Amitabh Bachchan, full of genuine respect and admiration for Sahab, went to his room and greeted him before going to his room for his make-up. In many of his interviews and chats he has said that he was nervous about facing the camera with the actor he idolized and revered. But certainly he did not seem so when I explained the shot to him amidst so much attention and a crowd watching from the beach. The shot was such that perfect timing and pace were expected from both. In the shot Amitabh had to alight from a chopper and walk towards Dilip Sahab with the strong wind from the sea blowing from behind and slackening the pace of his walk. Sahab had to stand where he was. As we all know from our experience Dilip Sahab does not need the spoken word to act. His mere presence in a frame is kinetic enough to make the scene come alive. All eyes were therefore on Amitabh and he was fully aware of it.

I can tell you that a lesser actor in his place would have found it hard to perform in the glare of so much attention and expectation. To Amitabh's credit it must be said that he performed with splendid confidence and the crowd was going wild when we canned the shot without a retake.

It was the talk of the industry for weeks thereafter. All through the making of the film Amitabh was very respectful and Sahab was very affectionate, and more than once, after an intense shot was canned, Sahab quietly commented to me that he saw immense potential in Amitabh and a day would come when he would rule the industry.

Right from day one Amitabh knew the profile of his character and Dilip Sahab knew the part he had to essay. There was no ambiguity whatsoever. I am saying this because there were speculations that Amitabh Bachchan was not pleased with the way his character developed in the film. He never had any misgivings. It was a media-generated myth. On the contrary, he was extremely elated by the praise he got from knowledgeable critics for his restrained acting and the way he measured up to the histrionic level expected from him in the scenes with Dilip Sahab. Like the scene where the son comes home when he is informed of his mother's death and sees his father inconsolable and shattered by the loss. It was a scene with no dialogue. I remember Sahab telling me after watching the rushes of the scene how interesting it was to observe the way Amitabh acted. Sahab said, 'You know, Ramesh all the years I have spent in the industry I have not come across an actor who intelligently and sensitively performs for the camera. It is a great asset to be able to act for the camera with your subconscious attuned to its swift movements.'

For me personally it was the greatest experience I have had in my career directing Sahab. He was punctual, cooperative, jovial and totally undemanding as a star. There was no fuss about anything. His food exquisitely prepared by the cooks in Sairaji's house came every day and we were all invited to partake of it. He himself had the wonderful habit of going to the table set for the unit and sharing the food on the table and making amusing conversation with the unit hands. They loved him and they waited every day for that moment.

Only once he asked for a change in a scene and when I explained its context with what was to come a few scenes later, he smiled and gave me a pat on my shoulder. He often rehearsed not for his own improvement but for the benefit of the other actors in the scene and he was never tired of retakes that occurred due to someone's unwitting error. There was a scene shot with Raakhee [who plays his wife in the film] on the first day of indoor shooting. It was a scene where she is cooking in the kitchen of the police commisioner's house and he is with her in the kitchen and the phone rings in the drawing room. He then says something and goes to answer the phone. We had to retake the scene thirty times because something kept going wrong with the telephone. As it always happens on the first day of a shoot, it took a while for the technicians and others to get the synchronization right. But Sahab was patient with all of us and he kept making jolly remarks to keep the technicians free from tension.

Shakti was made in the middle of an upheaval in Sahab's personal life. He had got married a second time and it made sensational news. But he remained cool and unaffected on the sets and of course no one dared to ask him anything. He requested me to keep the Fourth Estate out and I did that willingly.

SHARMILA TAGORE

$\mathscr{F}$EW PERSONALITIES ATTAIN A STATURE in their lifetime where they transcend comparisons. Dilip Kumar belongs to this elite club. A great thespian, an icon of icons, an actor's actor, versatile, mercurial, charismatic – Dilip Kumar is all of these and more.

Seven decades after his first film *Jwar Bhata* (1944) and sixteen years after he acted in his last production, he continues to be the final word in screen acting, someone who inspires awe and respect. This is mainly due to Dilip Kumar's appetite for perfection and a strong commitment to his craft. For example, very early in his career, he decided to do only one film at a time, devoting his entire attention to that single project. We must remember the marketing aspect of film making then was not what it is now, and that most of his contemporaries were working in multiple films at the same time, as a form of insurance. Since Dilip Kumar was not a director-producer like Raj Kapoor and Dev Anand, this strategy might have seemed foolish to many, but it speaks volumes of Yousuf Sahab's absolute confidence in himself. He was an actor first and foremost and not a businessman. His quest for perfection is abundantly clear in so many instances – some will remember the way he trained under Ustad Abdul Halim Jaffar Khan so that he could play the sitar in the song *Madhuban mein Radhika** in *Kohinoor* (1960). He could have easily faked it, as a lot of actors have done, but he preferred to learn the sitar before doing the scene. His desire to get things right always added credibility to his performance. His vast and devoted fan following understood this zeal and admired him even more.

Actors like Motilal and Ashok Kumar had already begun weeding out the theatrical elements from film acting by the late 1940s, but it was with Dilip Kumar that it became the norm. He demonstrated that it was not necessary to raise one's voice to be heard. He showed how natural and nuanced body language, and sometimes, even silence, conveyed far more than a thousand theatrical gestures. He introduced novel innovations such as enacting crucial scenes with his back to the camera, using only his voice. To the audience of the era, used to high-voltage melodrama and much gesticulation, this was revolutionary. And if he was unparalleled in the portrayal of tragic emotions – sorrow and heartbreak – in films like *Footpath* (1953) and *Devdas* (1955), he was equally brilliant in bringing comic characters alive in *Azaad* (1955), *Kohinoor* and *Ram Aur Shyam* (1967). He gave film acting a kind of layered edge, which was marked by self-conscious histrionics till that point in time. Many actors have tried to copy his style over the years and rightfully so, as I feel there is much to learn from his school of acting.

Among the friends I made when I first came to Bombay was Ahsan, Yousuf Sahab's younger brother. Later, I got to know his sisters, Farida and Saeeda. I often went to Yousuf Sahab's Pali Hill residence where they all lived. But I hardly ever saw him. And if sometimes I did run into him, I was too shy to talk to him. Years later, when I was better established as an actor, and I

*Composed by Naushad, written by Shakeel Badayuni and sung by Mohammed Rafi.

was shooting in Khandala for the song *Kuchh dil ne kaha** from *Anupama* (1966), Hrishi-da (Hrishikesh Mukherjee, the director of the film) invited Tiger (the ace cricketer and captain of the Indian team, the Nawab of Pataudi, Mansur Ali Khan) to join us at the location. There, in the same hotel as ours were Dilip Kumar and Saira Banu. It was too good an opportunity to miss. Tiger sent him a note requesting a meeting. And Yousuf Sahab promptly said yes. It was a delightful evening with our conversation ranging from cinema and music to poetry, literature and sport. Tiger got slightly fed up as our host had beaten him at chess.

Yousuf Sahab was not just knowledgeable about sports but could actually play some of them quite well. I remember discovering, during the shooting of *Dastaan* (1972, the only film we made together, and not our best either), how good a badminton player he was. B. R. Chopra (the producer and director of *Dastaan*) had an indoor badminton court behind his house (which became a recording studio later) and since quite a few scenes of *Dastaan* were shot in his house, we often played badminton after pack-up.

This talent for badminton turned out to be quite useful for Yousuf Sahab. When his name came up for membership at the Bombay Gymkhana, many questions were asked: Why should Dilip Kumar be allowed membership? How can actors become members of such a venerated institution? Does he play any sport? Bombay Gymkhana was particular about members playing at least one game. Tiger and some of his friends batted strongly for Yousuf Sahab, How could his membership be denied? they argued. For one he was an icon, and two, he played badminton brilliantly.

For me, he also epitomizes a link to a lost era of *tehzeeb* – to a culture, beauty and purity of language. He has always been an exceptional speaker and could charm his audience with his mesmerizing voice and exquisite command of Urdu. In fact, he spoke many languages extremely well – it was utterly delightful to hear him speak in *theth* (pure) Punjabi. There was a tremendous competition between him and Raj Kapoor and yet this never affected the cordiality with which they related to each other. After all they came from the same Peshawar neighbourhood (now in Pakistan) and spoke the same language. Of course, Yousuf Sahab was a private person while Rajji was more gregarious.

*Composed by Hemant Kumar, penned by Kaifi Azmi and sung by Lata Mangeshkar.

After Tiger passed away (on 22 September 2011), Yousuf Sahab was one of the first to send a letter of condolence and took the trouble of even having it hand delivered. Except for the time we worked in *Dastaan*, we hardly ever met, and the only time we really chatted was that evening long ago in Khandala. But I have always thought of him as a well-wisher.

It is sad that after he accepted the Nishan-e-Imtiaz (in March 1998), Pakistan's highest civilian award, he had to go through the turmoil of being branded anti-national by some self-styled nationalists and had to bear the brunt of a controversy. Icons like him are not constrained by geography. They transcend boundaries. They belong to everyone, irrespective of culture, caste and creed.

Dilip Kumar will remain forever immortal as will his unmatched contribution to Indian cinema.

MANI TALATI*

*K*EM CHEY DIKRA'** ARE THE THREE words Dilip Sahab greets me with when he graces every family function at my home with his ever-so-charming wife Saira. His entry starts as a ripple and then resonates into a wave, or much rather like a storm, that electrifies every individual present, young and old. Swarms of admirers try to get a glimpse of this great man, greeting him and often boring him with their old memories. Dilip Sahab has a smile for everybody who greets him. This is what he has been doing for over 60 years.

I remember the funeral prayers for my mom at the Parsi fire temple. As is the practice, no non-Parsi is allowed to enter the fire temple. Dilip Sahab knew it, but, nevertheless, came with Saira and sat quietly outside the temple. For the first time, the compound gates of a Parsi temple were opened for Dilip Sahab. As the word spread that Dilip Sahab had come,

*One of Sairaji's dearest friends.
**How are you kid?

everyone went to greet him, forgetting that he had come for funeral prayers and the head priest's wife herself served tea and potato chips which he and Sairaji lovingly accepted as they kept on reviving fond memories of my mom, perhaps, the best way to bid farewell to a departed soul.

On his eighteenth wedding anniversary, when he came to know that my sister was not well, he tried to find out the right treatment for my sister by referring to his doctor and homoeopathy books, forgetting about his anniversary celebrations. When his beloved wife came into the room to tell him he should be getting dressed, he jokingly sang: '*Saala main to doctor ban gaya*' to her. [This is a variation of the song picturized on him in the 1974 film *Sagina*, which begins with the line: *Saala main to sahab ban gaya.*]

I love to hear him talk in Parsi Gujarati. He has always remained the iconic solution to all my problems. Imagine Dilip Sahab sitting up till 2 a.m. to correct and redraft my yearly self-assessment in office, or visiting my ailing mother to bring a smile on her face, or sending his family doctor to try and cure serious medical problems of my entire family. On Bakhri Eid, he used to send many goodies. For, he is a man who believes in giving and expecting nothing. Even on his birthdays he used to jokingly taunt me about the birthday card that I got for him: 'The best are always for my wife, and the rest is always for me, *Kemre dikra bo beinsafi chey.*'*

He is a true Braveheart, and I use this word for him with a little pun. After the heart operation, when I visited him at the hospital, I was expecting a surgery-weary Dilip Sahab. To my delight when I inquired how he was doing, his reply was: 'Now I am thirty years younger at heart', and that brought a blushing smile on Saira's face.

At every celebration at his iconic 34B, Pali Hill bungalow, in the midst of many celebrities present, he would always care for us, inquire about our well-being in his typical Parsi Gujarati. In these celebrations he used to often state: 'Enjoy life today for these days will never come back.' As I look back, I recall the fun, excitement and happiness of his family and ours being together and I cherish beautiful memories.

There are about one lakh seventy thousand words in an English dictionary with around fifty thousand words that can personify the positivity of a person. I have been given a task of describing the legend of legends in less than 1000 words. There is only one thing I can say that when it comes to describing this legend: even fifty thousand positive words would fall far short in describing the one personality we know of as Dilip Kumar.

*Kid, this is injustice.   ———•◦⋛◦⋚◦•———

Vyjayantimala

*I*n all honesty I would say that until I acted with Dilip Kumar in *Devdas* (1955), I was known for my dances in the earlier films I had acted in. I was not taken seriously as an actress. With *Devdas*, I earned acknowledgement and film makers saw my potential to blossom into a good actress because it was no mean achievement to be selected to co-star with Dilip Kumar, the tragedy king, in an intense drama directed by Bimal Roy. As a matter of fact, when Bimalda came to my house and told me that he wanted me to play Chandramukhi (a dancing girl) in *Devdas* and then, in his quiet manner, he told me that Dilip Kumar would be playing Devdas, I felt both happy and scared. Happy because it was every heroine's wish to co-star with Dilip Kumar in at least one film in her career and scared because he was the most acclaimed actor of the time and enacting dramatic moments with him before the cameras demanded a certain degree of confidence.

I asked Bimalda whether I would be able to measure up to his expectations as Chandramukhi in the critical sequences with an actor of repute like Dilip Kumar. Bimalda simply smiled and replied that he had confidence in me and that was why he had come to me with the offer. That answer made me feel good. The reason was that, till that point of time, I had been reaping praises for my dancing skills and I had not really attempted serious acting. Now, when I look back it is all so amusing because I went on to co-star with Dilip Sahab in seven successful and noted films.

Well, I must describe the first scene I enacted with Dilip Sahab on the sets of *Devdas*. Come D day and I arrived on the sets with butterflies in my stomach but pretending to be confident and assured. The scene had a very simple dialogue for me. The line was: '*Aur mat piyo Devdas*'. (Do not drink any more Devdas.) I had to say the line when Devdas would stagger in completely inebriated. The camera was to capture Devdas and then follow him and turn its focus on me when I spoke that line with an expression of anguish and helplessness. Being a dancer, expressions came to me easily; so I thought it would be easy and I could manage it beautifully. As the technicians announced their readiness to shoot and Bimalda looked at me querulously to know if I was ready, I realized that Dilip Sahab was not on the sets.

'Where is he?' I asked an assistant and he whispered that Dilip Sahab was taking brisk rounds of the studio to get that tired, weary look and he had instructed the cameraman to be ready to start the camera when he would stagger in with beads of real sweat on his brow and a look of exhaustion. When I heard that from the assistant, I began to panic internally. Here was an actor who took so much trouble to endow realism to an act and here was me who had not done any preparation and all set to face the camera with such a tremendous actor. When the camera started and I saw the incredible perfection of Dilip Sahab's performance, all I could do was speak helplessly the line: 'Aur mat piyo Devdas.' The helpless look on my face was what Bimalda wanted and it came quite naturally.

I got compliments from Dilip Sahab and Bimalda but deep within me I knew I had tough tests coming. If I had to raise my acting to the level of Dilip Sahab's acting, I would have to work hard and not leave any loose ends. It was an education for me. I found him working so hard; to bring one particular ras (mood or emotion) to a character he performed with such dedication. I learned from him that the attitude and approach he adopted made all the difference. I took that lesson from him.

I was lucky to work with Dilip Sahab on a variety of subjects. He was a very helpful co-actor who never tired of rehearsals and gave his co-artistes as much time to work up an emotion as was needed in critical situations. In serious dramatic situations and love scenes he went out of the way to create an environment on the sets, which made everybody comfortable. In any case, he consciously saw to it that the love scenes were taken beautifully with looks conveying the emotions rather than any explicit depictions of physical closeness. The famous scene in Paigham (1959) is an instance (see Chapter 14). He wrote the scene himself and he made the situation so funny. Yet, it spoke volumes for the unspoken love the hero and heroine had for each other.

I can give the example of the expressive way he performed the scene in Bimalda's Madhumati (1958), when he hears a voice and he keeps on searching for the source. A girl's face emerges through the fog and he asks: 'Who are you?' She answers: 'Madhumati.' I thought the scene was brilliant in the way it was conceived and the way it was performed. Dilip Sahab always used his voice very effectively, modulating it according to the situation and the best moments in Madhumati showed how well he used the texture of his soft voice to enhance the suspense and mystery.

My best film with Dilip Sahab is *Gunga Jumna* (1961). I play his wife Dhanno in the film. He recorded my dialogue on tape and gave it to me to study. He understood how hard it would be for me to speak the Bhojpuri dialect. So he had me study the dialogue first and then he delivered those lines for me showing me how to articulate each word and how I should give facial expressions at the same time. It was a great help. You know I am a South Indian and getting the inflexions of the dialect wasn't that easy. I could not have done it without his help.

I personally love the scene where he breaks down over his wife Dhanno's death. The pathos that comes through in his performance is amazing. His forte is the painstaking study that goes into characters. The perfection he seeks and achieves in each scene cannot be described in words. His influence on each generation has been such that there is a Dilip Kumar in every successful actor in Indian cinema. Even so, he remains incomparable and unsurpassable. That is because his dedication, honesty and passion cannot be replicated.

The fact is that he is an educated man and has been a voracious reader of literature from various countries. His subconscious, I feel, is a storehouse of characters he has studied from the works of famous authors.

Like all his followers, I have also admired the way he speaks in real life. His choice of words, when he talks even casually, is so good. He has never uttered a cheap word or said anything derogatory or unbecoming about anybody. He is truly special and the real living legend of our times. There can be and will be only one Dilip Kumar.

ZOHA*

*W*RITING A PARAGRAPH OR TWO ABOUT YOUSUF MAMU, TO ME, feels the same as being asked to explain the complexities of the ocean with a glass of water. He used to come over to our home on Mt Mary's Hill (in Bandra) after a shoot or to bring along bread he'd buy from the local bakery that would be still warm from the oven. Every one of those occasions was special, not because he was Dilip Kumar the famous actor, but because he always brought with him a sense of adventure, of possibilities. I felt safe when he was around. He'd smile and raise an eyebrow ... and that would lead to a drive to nowhere in particular, a walk, sharing of a memory or the recitation of poetry ... any one of life's ignored beauties would be acknowledged, explained and explored. Life, while orbiting him, was always kind and pristine, imbued with the warmth of love.

He'd come over to our place and invite us to go for a drive with him. The driver, Abdul, was instructed to drive slowly so that we could enjoy the beauty outside our windows. We'd drive along Bandstand in Bandra, sneak around the church at the end of the road, wind through the neighbourhood of bungalows on our way to Carter Road. We'd catch snatches of the setting sun from between the rows of dried fish strung up by the fishermen, and, if there was a moon, Yousuf Mamu would recite a poem, explaining its intricate shades of meaning in his soft voice, or just hum a classical raga. We'd stop to buy some *ganderi* (a piece of sugarcane) from the man squatting on the side of the road with his tray of chopped up sugarcane illuminated with a Petromax. Mamu always greeted those anonymous hawkers with respect, sometimes remembering their names and inquiring about their families.

The magnificent events that made up the gist of glossy magazines and news articles weren't what endeared Yousuf Mamu to me; rather, it was his ability to enjoy and highlight the ordinary, his awe at the majesty of every day and his skill at communicating that awe to me, a child, that remain in my heart.

*Daughter of Dilip Kumar's younger sister Taj.

INDEX